EUROPEAN COMMUNITY
VISION AND REALITY

EUROPEAN COMMUNITY:
VISION AND REALITY

Edited by
JAMES BARBER and **BRUCE REED**

assisted by
RICHARD GIBBS and **ROBERT MASTERTON**

CROOM HELM LONDON
in association with
THE OPEN UNIVERSITY PRESS

Croom Helm Ltd, 2–10 St. Johns Road, London, SW11

ISBN 0-85664-078-6 HARDBACK
ISBN 0-85664-083-2 PAPERBACK

Printed in Great Britain
by Richard Clay (The Chaucer Press) Ltd
Bungay, Suffolk

Contents

SECTION 7 WORKERS OF EUROPE

SECTION 8 COMMUNITY WELFARE

Editors' Acknowledgements

The editors would like to thank the Librarian and Press Librarian and their staffs of the Royal Institute of International Affairs, Chatham House, and Miss Gail Price, Course Assistant, the Open University, for their assistance in obtaining material on which this Reader has been based; and Mrs. Ann Armstrong, our secretary, for her tolerance in typing the various drafts of the manuscript.

Introduction

HIS MAJESTY THE KING OF THE BELGIANS, THE PRESIDENT OF THE FEDERAL REPUBLIC OF GERMANY, THE PRESIDENT OF THE FRENCH REPUBLIC, THE PRESIDENT OF THE ITALIAN REPUBLIC, HER ROYAL HIGHNESS THE GRAND DUCHESS OF LUXEMBOURG, HER MAJESTY THE QUEEN OF THE NETHERLANDS,

DETERMINED to lay the foundations of an ever closer union among the peoples of Europe,

RESOLVED to ensure the economic and social progress of their countries by common action to eliminate the barriers which divide Europe,

AFFIRMING as the essential objective of their efforts the constant improvement of the living and working conditions of their peoples,

RECOGNISING that the removal of existing obstacles calls for concerted action in order to guarantee steady expansion, balanced trade and fair competition,

ANXIOUS to strengthen the unity of their economies and to ensure their harmonious development by reducing the differences existing between the various regions and the backwardness of the less favoured regions,

DESIRING to contribute, by means of a common commercial policy, to the progressive abolition of restrictions on international trade,

INTENDING to confirm the solidarity which binds Europe and the overseas countries and desiring to ensure the development of their prosperity, in accordance with the principles of the Charter of the United Nations,

RESOLVED by thus pooling their resources to preserve and strengthen peace and liberty, and calling upon the other peoples of Europe who share their ideal to join in their efforts,

HAVE DECIDED to create a European Economic Community . . .

This was the vision in 1958.

We have chosen extracts and articles which measure this vision against the realities of the European Communities. The extracts from newspapers, books, periodicals, learned journals and the British Parliament's *Hansard*—a selection which, we feel, makes for lively and informative reading—help to answer three very broad questions —'How do the communities work?', 'How can we participate in them?' and 'How do they affect us in our everyday lives?'

This introduction is short because we have provided separate commentaries for each section. Some approach these questions directly, while others analyse a particular policy in depth. The historical content of Section 1 sets the whole book in context. It emphasises the dreams of the Continental Europeans and the realities of British politics in the 1950s. The change of attitudes in Britain during the subsequent decade and the messianic communiqué from the October 1972 Summit contrast with Section 2 which analyses the sober realities of the Communities' decision-making process. The process which is set within the framework of the Rome Treaty involves a complex relationship of conflict and co-operation between member States, and between the states and the central institutions. This process is more than a question of nuts and bolts as it will help to determine what will emerge: a 'Europe des patries' or 'Les Etats -Unis d'Europe'.

Even in the realm of participation, the realities of political Europe have not fulfilled the dreams of the 'Europeans'. The Parties at Strasbourg, the trade unions and other pressure groups, the active lobbying in Brussels, are all attempts to take part in the decision-making process. At every turn frustration has met many of these attempts. This is partly due to the complexity of the structure and processes of the Communities, and partly because the European ideal has never captured the passionate commitment of the old nationalisms, resulting in a lack of identification with Europe.

Where the law is concerned, there is an evident impact on our everyday lives. Clear battle lines are drawn between those nationalists opposed to any derogation of sovereignty, and those 'pan-Europeans' who dream of federation. The daily impact is easily overlooked in the semantic jungle.

The aspiration of the founding fathers for faster economic growth to result from closer union is considered in Section 5. Whether Britain will achieve faster economic growth as a member of the Communities is still hotly debated. Furthermore, although growth rates inside the

Communities have been high, the policy of stimulating growth is itself being called into question because of its results.

The Common Agricultural Policy is undoubtedly the best known of Community policies, but has also created the most problems: the actual creation of a common market for agricultural products was a real success in overcoming the complexities of national policies, yet the resultant policy has been accused of creating even greater complexity and even more intractable problems.

The mobility of workers among Community countries has been eased. However, the hope for any worker to move freely throughout the Community is far from fulfilment, especially for professional and skilled workers. Furthermore, the commitment to free mobility has also been called into question because of its potentiality to exacerbate regional imbalance.

Section 8 considers the effect of the Community on social welfare. Here again the Community has not yet achieved the objectives set out in the Treaty of Rome—witness the subject of equal pay for women. It is also likely that the closer integration of Europe will accentuate the demands on the social services, bringing about their transformation and harmonisation.

Paris in October 1972 witnessed a rededication to the fulfilment of the vision:

> The member States of the Community, the driving force of European construction, affirm their intention to transform before the end of the present decade the whole complex of their relations into a European Union.

SECTION 1

Towards a New Europe

1.1 Introduction

This section is concerned with the movement towards Western European unity. A brief chronology is given at the beginning, but there is no attempt to relate the events in detail. The extracts which have been chosen are concerned first with the motives behind the movement towards greater unity, and second, and more particularly, with British attitudes towards it. While it is relatively easy to trace a narrative of events, it is much more difficult to analyse motives, opinions and attitudes or to determine the relationship between attitudes and events. As Kitzinger (pp. 7–22) and the communique from the Heads of Government (pp. 48–50) reveal, the drive towards unity has been a compound of hopes for peace, for economic growth, for a powerful voice in world affairs, and for greater international co-operation and understanding. The particular motives which are stressed vary according to the time, circumstances and the person expressing them.

Those who have led the movement towards greater unity have faced wide opposition. This has ranged from fears about the loss of national sovereignty and identity, to concern for the cost of living and unemployment for some sections of the population. Among the organised political groups, the most persistent opposition has come from opposite political positions—the right-wing concern for national identity combining with the left-wing fear that the European Communities represent a new stronghold of capitalist power. This has sometimes led to odd situations, for example, the Italian Communist Party's strong defence of Italy's national interest in the European Parliament (see Leich, pp. 110–22).

British attitudes towards European unity have been ambivalent. Now that Britain is a member of the Communities there may be a temptation to see an increasingly favourable attitude towards closer European ties as an inevitable process. However, the extracts from speeches by British political leaders (pp. 23–8) show that during the

1

1940s and 1950s there was strong opposition to a primarily European commitment. Britain's absence from the signing of the Treaty of Rome in 1957 amply demonstrated this. Given this determination to see Britain as more than 'an island off the coast of Europe', what explains the change of attitude that led to the British applications for membership of the EEC during the 1960s and her entry into the Communities in 1973? Kitzinger shows that there were both 'negative' and 'positive' reasons. Negative in the sense that ties with two of Churchill's three interlinking circles (the Commonwealth and the Atlantic Alliance) failed to fulfil British expectations so that only the third (Europe) remained. The options had closed. The positive aspect of the change can be seen in the determination to use what choice remained by entering a vast and expanding economic community, and retaining a leading role in international affairs.

The change in Britain's international position has required a substantial revision in British political psychology. Kitzinger looks at this, and so does Patrick O'Donovan in his article 'Who Do We Think We Are?' O'Donovan brings out the uncertainties that have been and continue to be involved in establishing a new sense of identity. While this search continues, now within the Communities, Pierre Drouin's article explains that as a late entrant Britain has to accept what is there. He recognises that the new members (Britain, Denmark, Ireland) will partly reshape the Communities and give them new orientations, but these newcomers cannot roll back the past—there is no *tabula rasa*; they enter a going concern.

The reorientation of British attitudes has not been painless. The question of entry into Europe has divided British society, and during the final stage of 'The Great Debate' it cut so firmly across party lines that at one time the Labour Party appeared in danger of splitting up, while at another the Conservative Government appeared in danger of being defeated in the Commons. The decision was made, but Britain entered Europe with the bulk of the Labour Party, a small section of the Conservative and the majority of public opinion opposed to it. 'The Great Debate' shows how the battle lines were drawn in the Commons. Looking outside Parliament, Kitzinger quotes an opinion poll taken in February 1970 (p. 21)[1] which shows the strength of public opinion against entry at that time. Opposition was particularly strong then, but at no stage in the long negotiations was a majority of the public in favour of entry. Yet, despite this, successive Governments (Macmillan's, Douglas-Home's, Wilson's and Heath's) declared themselves in favour of trying to negotiate membership—a sharp contrast with earlier governmental views.

The change in Government views, and, by the standard of such things, it was a quick and dramatic change, came in 1959 and 1960.[2] From then onwards successive Governments became more and more committed to entry into Europe. The provisions which Macmillan had expressed strongly at the time of the first application—for example, the need for full consultation and understanding from the Commonwealth and EFTA countries—were given less emphasis until finally the drive towards Europe became a major, perhaps *the* major commitment of the Heath Government.

The final piece in this section looks to the future—the preamble to the Charter agreed by the Government leaders of the Communities in Paris in October 1972. It stands with the other pieces because it is concerned with motives and attitudes. It may even provide clues to answer Patrick O'Donovan's question—'Who do we think we are?'

References

1. The opinion poll is not entirely satisfactory as Britain was not a member while the other countries were. It will be interesting in the future to see whether British attitudes after some years of membership will still be so different from the others.
2. See Miriam Camps, *Britain and the European Community 1955–63*, 2nd edition, Oxford University Press, London, 1964.

1.2 Chronology of Events in the Formation of the European Communities

1946

Sept.   Churchill's speech at Zurich urges Franco-German reconciliation within a kind of 'United States of Europe'.

1947

June   General Marshall proposes American aid to stimulate European recovery—European Payments Union (EPU) to distribute this.

Oct.   Creation of Benelux—economic union of Belgium, the Netherlands and Luxembourg.

1948

Mar. Brussels Treaty—Benelux, France and England.

Apr. OEEC (Organisation for European Economic Co-operation) formed from the Committee for European Economic Co-operation, formerly set up by 16 countries to assess their requirements in goods and foreign exchange for 1948–52.

1949

Apr. North Atlantic Treaty Organisation (NATO) formed by 12 states for defence purposes.

May Statute of Council of Europe signed—five Brussels Treaty Powers plus Sweden, Denmark, Eire, Norway and Italy, and soon after, Iceland, Greece, Turkey, W. Germany and Austria. It was to be a forum of opinion for Western European parliamentarians, but could not bring about political unity as hoped. The Governments had given it no real powers, although it had wide terms of reference. Decisions subject to veto.

1950

May Schuman Plan—proposal to place French and German coal and steel under a common authority.
European Defence Community Plan devised and presented by René Pleven, French Defence Minister. The plan was to integrate Germany into the defence of Western Europe. After four years of debate it was rejected by the French National Assembly.

1951

Apr. European Coal and Steel Community (ECSC) Treaty signed by 'The Six'—Benelux, France, Germany and Italy—'to establish, by creating an economic community, the foundation of a wider and deeper community'. To become operational in 1953. Sets up the first common European authority—the ECSC High Authority, subject to democratic control through an Assembly composed of representatives from six national parliaments, and to rule of law through the Court of Justice.

1954

Oct. Western European Union (WEU) formed—the Six plus Britain—the military response to the collapse of the EDC, but did not advance functional and economic integration.

Dec. UK Association agreement with ECSC.

1955

June   Messina Conference of the foreign ministers of the Six, set up a Committee under Paul-Henri Spaak to study ways in which 'a fresh advance towards the building of Europe' could be achieved.

1957

Mar.   Rome Treaties signed, setting up European Economic Community (EEC) and Euratom—the Six.

1958

Jan.   Rome Treaties come into effect.

1959

Nov.   European Free Trade Association (EFTA) formed by Austria, Denmark, Norway, Sweden, Switzerland, Portugal and the UK

1961

July   Association agreement with Greece.

Aug.   Ireland applies for membership.
Denmark and UK request negotiations aimed at membership.

1962

Jan.   Basic features of Common Agricultural Policy (CAP) agreed.

Mar.   UK applies for membership.

Apr.   Norway requests negotiations for membership.

1963

Jan.   Signing of the Franco-German Friendship Treaty.
Negotiations to extend membership broken off after de Gaulle's speech vetoing British entry.

July   Yaoundé Convention signed—Association of 18 African States and Madagascar with the Community for five years.

Sept.   Association Agreements signed with Turkey and Trade Agreement with Iran.

1964

June   Yaoundé Convention comes into force.

1965

July   Council fails to reach agreement on financing CAP. French boycott of Community institutions for seven months in opposition to Commission proposal that all import duties and levies be paid in to the Community budget, and the powers of the European Parliament be increased.

1966

Jan.   Foreign Ministers of the Six reach a compromise and agree to resume full activities of the Community.

July   Association Agreement signed with Nigeria.

Nov.   British Prime Minister Harold Wilson announces plan for 'high level approach' to the Six, with intention of applying for membership.

1967

May   Britain, Ireland and Denmark submit formal applications for membership.

July   Community Executives merged into one 14-man Commission.

Dec.   Council reaches deadlock over enlargement after General de Gaulle objects to UK entry.

1968

July   Customs Union completed—common external tariff operates around the Common Market. The Six adopt basic regulations for a common transport policy.

Arusha Convention—Association Agreement with Kenya, Uganda and Tanzania.

The Six remove remaining restrictions on free movement of workers.

Dec.   The Mansholt Plan for agriculture announced—a radical ten-year reform programme

1969

Apr.   Resignation of General de Gaulle.

July   M. Pompidou elected President of France.

'Yaoundé II' signed—regulates trade and aid relations until 1975.

Sept.   Partial Association Agreements with Morocco and Tunisia.

Dec.   Hague Summit—the Six agree to complete, enlarge and strengthen the Community.

The Council agrees to finance CAP, giving the Community its own resources from 1978 and strengthening the Europe Parliament's budgetary powers.

1970

Feb.   UK White Paper on benefits of EEC membership.

Mar.   Three year non-preferential agreement with Yugoslavia signed.

June   1980 set as target date for Economic and Monetary Union (EMU)

July	Davignon report—advocates twice-yearly ministerial meetings on political co-operation.
	Opening of enlargement negotiations.
Oct.	Trade Agreements with Israel and Spain signed.

1971

Feb.	Common Fisheries Policy takes effect.
Apr.	Association Agreement with Malta operational.
May	Heath-Pompidou Summit paves way to agreement in enlargement negotiations.
June	Agreement reached on Britain's entry to EEC.
Oct.	British House of Commons votes to join EEC on terms secured.

1972

Jan.	Treaty of Accession signed by Denmark, Ireland, Norway and UK.
Sept.	Norwegian referendum shows majority against entry. Norway withdraws.
Oct.	Paris Summit of the Nine prepares a blueprint for the future development of the Community.

1973

| Jan. | Denmark, Ireland and UK join the Community—the Six become the Nine. |

(Compiled by Gail Price.)

1.3 Time-Lags in Political Psychology[1]

UWE KITZINGER

There is one thing you British will never understand: an idea. And there is one thing you are supremely good at grasping: a hard fact. We will have to build Europe without you: but then you will come in and join us.
Jean Monnet

The Mainsprings of the European Movement, 1945–50

The political impetus for the unification of Europe effectively dates from the closing stages of the Second World War. Those were the years when leading statesmen all over the world, following the principles laid down in the Allies' war aims, sought to create a far stronger League of Nations, a United Nations, even a federation of the world. Shocked by the legal and illegal crimes against humanity which they had witnessed in the previous decade, both in the pre-war dictatorships and during the war itself, appalled by the vast problems of hunger and want facing every part of the world at the end of that conflict, the World Federalist movement took as its main aim the abolition of physical force as a method of diplomacy, the abatement or abolition of national sovereignty, and the creation of a body of international law in the full sense of the term, pronounced and sanctioned by a world authority.

The San Francisco Conference of 1944 did not fulfil these hopes. It produced a United Nations which has certainly shown itself stronger than the old League, but is still not even a confederation of states, let alone a world government. Its General Assembly remains an assembly of governments exercising their sovereignty—not one of representatives of the people deliberating in common for the common good. The final contradiction of these dreams of the war years was to be found in the national right of disobedience to any UN majority decision, formally recognised by the right of veto given to the five nations then regarded as big. So hopes for a world government were dashed to the ground.

By 1947 it was clear that more intensive international co-operation was possible only on a less extensive front. A tighter bond could be forged only between a smaller number of nations. Failing progress on a world scale, the countries of Europe (for which the federalists in Europe felt they had the most immediate responsibility) were to set an example to the world. For some idealists at least, European unity was thus not simply a regionalist approach for its own sake but a pilot project for something to come on a wider scale: any abdication of sovereignty, even on a regional basis, seemed better than allowing the nation state to consolidate itself once more after its great moral and material bankruptcy.

It was in Britain in particular that the World Federalist strain was intertwined with the ideal of European federation. The result was not entirely happy. Since federalists were among the most active in post-war relief and in international meetings, Europeans (who could not always tell an English crank from a normal Englishman) over-estimated their strength in Britain. The moral absolutism and salvationist dogma of many of the early post-war federalists stemmed from their belief that federation was a technical prerequisite for translating the Sermon on the Mount into practice in the twentieth century. But because in their preoccupation with ultimate aims many federalists seemed starry-eyed, British observers were tempted to write off the federalists on the Continent as equally cranky and unrepresentative. For a very long time British policy was affected by this image of federalists as outsiders who were not to be taken quite seriously. All the greater was British surprise when they did succeed in pulling off some of their curious plans.

There was indeed a profound difference in outlook and psychology on the two sides of the Channel. In her finest hour Britain had stood alone. She was undefeated, she had escaped occupation, she had not known bitter internal cleavages, she had no feelings of guilt, but came through with greater self-confidence, greater pride in her national virtues and national institutions, than she had known for years. The Continent, on the other hand, had just passed through the worst ordeal of its history. Almost every family had experienced the effects of nationalism run riot, almost every country had been subjected first to national defeat and then to enemy occupation. Their national self-confidence, their national institutions had been shattered. Starting from the ruins, it was imperative to develop new conceptions and more radical ideas that would make any future civil war between European brother nations impossible. In Continental Europe, a federal surrender of sovereignty thus seemed more feasible than in many as yet less disillusioned parts of the globe.

Common opposition to the Hitler régime had brought Resistance fighters and exile governments of different nationalities closer to-gether: against Hitler's new order for a united Europe under Nazi domination, the men from the *maquis* and other underground move-ments set an alternative idea. As activists of nine European Resistance movements expressed it in July 1944: 'Federal Union alone can ensure the preservation of liberty and civilisation on the Continent of Europe, bring about economic recovery, and enable the German people to play a peaceful role in European affairs.'[2] For, if common fear of a third wave of German aggression seemed a bond that could unite many nations for some time, the more far-sighted also knew that it would be impossible to discriminate against Germany for ever. Any such attempt would fail and breed just what it was designed to prevent. If German policy was to be subjected to international controls, and if Germany was to be an equal member in the European family of nations, then there was only one way out of the dilemma—other nations must abdicate to supranational bodies the same measure of sovereignty which they intended Germany never to regain.

Winston Churchill, then Leader of the British Opposition, saw much the same problem: in Zurich in 1946, he called for European unity to be based on 'something that will astonish you . . . a partnership between France and Germany'. But Britain was not included in this concept of 'a kind of United States of Europe' which Churchill advocated: 'France and Germany must take the lead together. Great Britain . . . America, and I trust Soviet Russia . . . must be the friends and sponsors of the new Europe'[3]—its friends, but not part of it. Indeed the notion of a partnership with Germany proved a far more unpopular one for far longer in Britain than it did in Belgium, Holland or France, who were closer to Germany geographically, had been under occupation, in some ways had had to differentiate between Germans on other than purely national criteria, and wanted more quickly to forget experiences which were not always of their proudest. In Britain, on the other hand, emotions about Germans as such had remained less challenged by concrete experience, and were cherished by a whole generation—all the more so as the country increasingly found herself almost needing the memory of a dragon to recall her heroic role as St. George. Not perhaps till the emotionalism had—temporarily—swung almost too far in the other direction at the time of the Queen's visit to Germany in 1965 did this mistrust from the past cease to be an appreciable factor in British attitudes towards building a joint future together with Germany and France.

World federalism in general, and the specific European problem of Germany, thus formed the first two mainsprings of West European integration. Soon, however, the memories of the last enemy became less real than the fear of a new aggressor. Armed Soviet Communism had advanced to the Elbe and beyond, and French and Italian Communism was showing its strength in parliamentary and direct action as far as the Channel and the Pyrenees. The year 1948 saw the Communist *coup* in Prague and the beginning of the Berlin blockade. In the face of this immediate common threat of terrifying proportions, national differences loomed less large, and some important Continental countries hoped to shore up the instabilities in their own political systems by being contained in a broader-based framework. Common defence, a common front in foreign policy, and political solidarity at home seemed the only way for non-Communist Europe to survive the new pressures applied to it from within as well as without.

Here, too, things looked rather different from the other side of the Channel. There was no domestic Communist menace worth mention either under the Labour Government of 1945–51 or thereafter. And the external menace was not one of being overrun in a matter of hours by Soviet land troops, but of air and, in due course, nuclear strikes and longer-term pressures. It was hardly surprising if, given a lesser menace and one which took a somewhat different form, Britain chose, instead of integrating politically with the exposed countries to the south and east of her, to remain turned westwards whence her salvation had come in the two World Wars, and where by the 'forties and early 'fifties the only credible counterpoise and deterrent to Soviet conventional forces were to be found. It was in the special relationship with the United States that she sought protection and a certain guiding influence on the evolution of the balance of world power.

Fourthly, a number of the Continental countries were troubled over the relative position of Europe in the world, not simply *vis-à-vis* Russia (and the United States), but also with regard to the rest of the globe. The rise of the countries of Asia and Africa to a new influence and a new power in world affairs occupied much of federalist thought. Their idealisation of European tradition forced some of the older European federalists of the time to take a gloomy view of mankind's prospects in this imminent shift in the configuration of world power. European political unity would not stem the tide. But some (particularly French) circles hoped it would at least buttress the 'civilising presence' of Europe overseas, while others, faced with the same situation at one remove, felt unity was desperately needed to rehabilitate Europe morally in the eyes of world opinion, and to mark the abandonment of the national concept by the very nations that had served as the model for nationalism overseas. Given the rate of expansion of the Afro-Asian countries, economic unity might produce a margin of economic manœuvre that would allow Europe to provide more aid to those countries and thereby cushion and guide, even as it accelerated, their progress to positions of world power.

Here, too, things looked very different from Westminster. The contrast for Britain seemed not to be between national policies and European ones, but between Europe and the Commonwealth. Both to the Labour Government, which saw the multi-racial Common-

wealth as a potential world-wide bridge between the rich and the
poor, the black, the brown and the white, and to Conservatives, who
valued it in terms of the proven loyalty of the white Dominions in two
World Wars, Europe could be at most a complement, but never a
rival to the Commonwealth concept. Britain, as Winston Churchill
put it in 1950, stood at the intersection of three overlapping circles—
the English-speaking world, the Commonwealth and Europe. It was
by her unique position within all three that she would still, even after
the Second World War, have an opportunity of playing a unique
world role. Therefore none of these three bonds, and certainly not
that with Europe, could afford to be tightened to the extent that they
might damage the other two.

To support the common defence effort, the common political
influence and the joint positive enterprises within Europe for the
future, it seemed essential on the Continent to reconstruct the devastated national economies, not separately, but by co-operation: only
common efforts could make the best use of the scant resources
available. Thus on the Continent economic unity was advocated by
free-trade liberals who wished to diminish the restrictive effects of
political boundaries and the influence of national governments on
economic life. Yet among its foremost champions there were also
those who regarded the national economy as too small an entity for
effective planning, and who strove to set up supranational authorities
to direct production and trade on a vaster international scale.

On the Continent the European Movement thus cut right across
the domestic political disputes in economic affairs. In Britain the
same was true, but in the opposite sense. In the late 'forties and early
'fifties British standards of living, British income per head, and the
strength of the British economy had seemed—indeed, at that time
were—greatly superior to those of most of the Continent (see p. 18
for the 1950 figures). While Britain was prepared to make some
sacrifices in the immediate post-war period (introducing bread
rationing after the war to help feed defeated enemies), there seemed
little to be gained from economic integration with nations suffering
from such economic difficulties—quite apart from their social problems and their political instability. The Labour Government up to
1951 wanted to set up a welfare state, if not actual Socialism, in one
country; after 1951 the Conservative Government wanted to 'set the
people free'. Neither party wanted to load itself with the burden of
open-ended economic commitments to the Continent and of com-

promising their own economic policy with the ideas of the Continentals—interpreted by one side as high capitalism, by the other as dirigist planning. So on this fifth count, too, the same type of reasoning which on the Continent had led to the conclusion that Western Europe must integrate, on the other side of the Channel also led to the corollary that Britain must keep away from any supranational integration that involved a formal surrender of sovereignty, and go no further than co-operation between national Governments —at least unless the United States was equally involved.

It was here that the 'functionalists' (to use the phraseology of the period), who were most strongly represented by the British and Scandinavian Governments, parted company with the 'federalists', who were well represented in the Governments of France, Italy and the Low Countries. It was the hallmark of the 'federalist' that he sought joint action not least as a means for obtaining more effective common political institutions, whereas the 'functionalist' attempted to set up only that minimum of political institutions that was indispensable in order to direct the common action that was most urgently required. While the federalist may be accused of concentrating excessively on legal formalities, the functionalist may have underrated the handicap imposed on effective everyday co-operation by the survival of national vetoes. Federalists and functionalists in the late 'forties failed fully to understand each other, and the federalists—not by accident, but for good historical reasons—were able to sway the policy of six and only six of the countries of Western Europe. What they achieved was something less than a United States of Europe, though Jean Monnet's Action Committee for a United States of Europe retained a more maximalist title. Yet though the terminology, the fervour and the time-scale of objectives changed with the passage of time, this original contrast and even conflict between federalists and functionalists was to mark the whole history of post-war Europe.

But there were divergencies even within the federalist camp. The United States' insistence on European co-operation had been one of the conditions of Marshall Aid. The United States was welcomed as an ally by most of those who sought to unite Europe; yet they were far from agreeing on the policy which Europe was to pursue towards the United States once it had been united. The campaign for European unity as such was thus, in fact, neutral between two sets of correlative political and economic concepts. Political unity was advocated as tending to enhance European freedom of movement—whether towards a more equal partnership within a strong Atlantic alliance or towards a more independent position in the world as a third force. Whichever way that decision might go, only unity, it was argued, could make it effective.

There was a parallel ambivalence or mixture of economic aims. Economic unity, with its advantages of larger markets and greater specialisation of production, was advocated as a means of redressing the balance of dollar payments. But for some the first objective was to form a regional *bloc* embracing only Europe and the countries associated with it overseas, while others saw the discriminatory removal of economic barriers (between the countries of Europe, but not yet against the rest of the world) as a tactical move to strengthen the economies of Europe for full convertibility and non-discriminatory trading relationships with the world as a whole.

Even the historic cleavage of clericals and anticlericals was bridged by the European idea. Certainly three of the men in the van of the movement were devout Catholics born in Lothair's middle kingdom, an area where the liberal conception of the world and its denizens as naturally divisible into neat nation states appears unsophisticated in the extreme: Robert Schuman, a German during the First World War and then Prime Minister of France; Alcide de Gasperi, a Deputy in the Vienna Diet while Austria-Hungary was at war with Italy, and then Prime Minister of Italy; and Konrad Adenauer, the non-combatant anti-Prussian mayor of Cologne who flirted with the idea of separating the Rhineland from Prussia after the First World War. To them, the restoration of Charlemagne's empire of a thousand years before, with the cultural unity it implied, had an emotional appeal. But the stalwarts of the movement came also from the ranks of the anticlerical Left, organised, in the early post-war years, in the Socialist Movement for a United States of Europe. The Socialist Paul-Henri Spaak, a former Belgian Prime Minister, provided the personal driving force in the drafting of the Rome Treaties, and the French Socialist leader Guy Mollet was Prime Minister during the critical phases of the Common Market negotiations and secured the votes of 100 out of the 101 French Socialist deputies in favour of their ratification.

The European idea was thus originally neutral in foreign policy between a third-force concept and the Atlantic alliance, undecided in trade policy between regionalism and multilateralism, ambivalent in its attitude to the problems of emergent nations in Africa and Asia, silent in cultural and educational matters between Catholicism and anti-clericalism, and neutral also in economic policy between *laissez-faire* liberalism and Socialist planning. Approached from very diverse points of view, European unity seemed to make sense to Continental leaders, to small but highly articulate pressure groups, and to many of the war and post-war generation. It would give greater scope to Europe for whatever policy aims were envisaged. A sudden realisation of Continental federation could have produced sharp conflicts over the use to which unity was to be put; as it was, the long common struggle and the course of post-war events softened the contrasts of ultimate aim and produced not merely international but also inter-party understanding. Only the Communists in every parliament of the Six consistently voted against integration.

Britain and the Communities, 1950–70

The story has often been told of how, in 1950, six countries and six only sought to advance beyond the looser and wider organisations of NATO, the Organisation for European Economic Co-operation, and the Council of Europe (in all of which Britain was a member). They set up their Coal and Steel Community as a first step to a general common market and economic community, and they worked out detailed blueprints for a defence community, and for a political community to overarch the rest. Though they failed with the last two, they then succeeded with the EEC and Euratom. Britain's various attempts—through Western European Union, through the Free Trade Area proposals, and by various other arrangements—to get the best of both worlds, as both 'in' and yet not 'of' the emergent Europe, are equally familiar. What is relevant to this theme ... are the reasons for which, by 1961, the British Government had completely changed tack and made its application for negotiations to see if terms could be found on which she could, after all, join the endeavours she had cold-shouldered only five years before.

There were five milestones on that road to Damascus. The first came as early as 1956 with the Suez disaster: even in a traditional sphere of influence, even acting together with an ally, nineteenth-century gunboat tactics had proved humiliatingly self-defeating, and thus the first crack appeared in British post-war self-confidence. With angry young men challenging social smugness and the Campaign for Nuclear Disarmament challenging Britain's image of her place in the world (let alone the forms which military power was assuming in that world), self-questioning became a little more widespread.

Then came the fateful year of 1960, in which the abandonment of Blue Streak on technical and financial grounds represented the abandonment of Britain's claim to any truly independent military deterrent; the collapse of the Paris summit meeting, the last occasion on which a British Prime Minister attempted to play a major role at the top table of world diplomacy; and the first of that series of sterling crises which was to dog the British economy right through the 'sixties, though successive governments of both political parties sacrificed domestic economic growth to the maintenance of the dollar-sterling rate of exchange. Fifthly, there was the demand for faster economic growth at home. Performance indicators on the Continent appeared to be startlingly superior (see the table on p. 18, which shows the comparative dynamism of the Six in almost every one of its sections). Though the Labour Party had in 1959 drawn attention to the 'growth league tables' in which the British economy was shown to have performed substantially worse than most of those on the Continent, the Conservative Government had shrugged them off with the slogan 'You've never had it so good'; it was only in 1960–61 that the Government began to ponder seriously the slow rate of growth in Britain's national product, and turned simultaneously to a form of indicative planning modelled on the French and to the concept of a 'bracing cold shower' of competition through entry into the EEC.

It was much at the same time that there spread among policy-makers in Britain a certain scepticism as to the future of those two other overlapping circles, the Anglo-American special relationship that had been the hub of Churchill's 'English-speaking world', and the Commonwealth. In the 'fifties the Commonwealth had still looked like giving Britain increased economic scope and additional leverage in the world. In the 'sixties it became obvious that the overseas sterling area was the most stagnant sector of British exports (its share of total British exports diminished from 48 per cent in 1950 to 30 per cent in 1960 to roughly 27 per cent in 1970) and that, so far from increasing Britain's political freedom of action, the Commonwealth tended if anything to restrict it. The notion that the Commonwealth would somehow be a means of exporting the Westminster model of par-liamentary democracy and adding to the peace of the world by the sort of internal régimes it would propagate had long been abandoned in the face of experience in Africa. By the 1971 Singapore Conference of Commonwealth Prime Ministers many felt that Britain almost needed liberating from a grouping that stood her in the dock and judged her according to some superior moral standard over Rhodesia—the judges being people whose own racial policies (whether in Biafra, over East African Asians or, not much later, in Bangla Desh) were far more lacking in liberalism and human brotherhood than Britain's own. There remained a general argument about helping the underdeveloped world—a criterion of useful world citizenship in which the Six could claim a recent record by no means inferior to Britain's; there remained also one or two specific economic problems arising out of the Commonwealth sugar agreement or the New Zealand butter trade; but the Commonwealth as an alternative power configuration had virtually disappeared from British policy-makers' minds.

Much the same was true from the early 'sixties as far as the 'special relationship' was concerned. There could be little doubt that, whatever had been true under Dwight Eisenhower's presidency, under the Kennedy administration the relationship between Washington and Bonn was coming to be in some ways at least as 'special' as that between Washington and London. The Kennedy 'grand design' of Atlantic partnership quite explicitly involved a relationship between a United States of America on one side of the Atlantic, and a fast unifying single economic and power complex on the other. Though some were surprised when it became even more obvious in late 1962, the failure of Skybolt was for President Kennedy 'the grand opportunity to terminate the special relationship and force Britain into Europe'.[4] Yet it was largely by reference to that special relationship that President de Gaulle, in early 1963, vetoed Britain's application.

Whatever the realism of looking upon the European Community as a replacement of the other two 'circles' or as a new lever for British political influence, by the end of the 'sixties the arguments had changed. The possibility that the United States might withdraw from Western Europe—a realisation of the old slogan of 'US go home'—raised fears of a void in West European security which only much closer military and logistic collaboration between West European nations could convincingly fill. The spectre of 'collusion' between the United States and the Soviet Union, both of them more concerned with the pressure of China than with the dangers they once seemed to spell for each other, became an argument for diplomatic

		UK	The Six	USA
Population (millions)	1950	50	157	152
	1958	52	165	174
	1970	56	190	205
Gross national product	1950	47	75	290
($ billion)	1958	65	163	455
	1970	121	485	993
GNP per head ($)	1950	940	477	2040
	1958	1258	955	2613
	1970	2170	2557	4760
Industrial production				
(1953 = 100)	1950	94	80	82
(1953 = 100)	1958	114	144	102
(1958 = 100)	1963	119	142	135
(1963 = 100)	1970	125	151	135
Gross fixed asset formation	1958	15·1	20·4	16·9
(% of GNP)	1970	18·0	25·0	17·0
Imports	1950	7·2	11·2	8·7
($ billion)	1958	10·5	22·9	13·3
	1970	21·7	88·4	40·0
Exports	1950	6·3	9·4	10·1
($ billion)	1958	9·3	22·8	17·9
	1970	19·4	88·5	43·2
Exports to (other) EEC countries	1950	0·8	3·0	1·6
($ billion)	1958	1·3	6·9	2·4
	1970	4·2	43·3	8·4
Official reserve assets	1950	3·4	2·9	22·8
($ billion)	1958	3·1	11·8	20·6
	1970	2·8	29·8	14·5
Development aid				
(net official flow $ billion)	1958	0·3	1·3	2·4
	1970	0·4	2·1	3·1

Sources: United Nations Statistical Year Books, OEEC and OECD monthly Statistics, and Development Assistance Committee annual reports.

and political collaboration between Europeans anxious not to have their fate settled over their heads.

In international economics, there was a triple concern: over the comparative lack of autochthonous European technology to set against the USA's lead in research and development; over the 'American challenge' of multi-national but basically American-dominated companies spreading over Europe while remaining largely free of any effective political supervision and control; and finally over the world's monetary problems, exacerbated by the mass of footloose and uncontrolled 'Eurodollars' and the weakness of the United States balance of payments, which threatened to thrust monetary responsibilities on the Community long before it was really equipped to face them.

On Western Europe's internal problems, too, the arguments began to change once more at the very beginning of the 'seventies. In the late 'fifties and early 'sixties, economic growth as reflected in gross national product statistics had been regarded as a cardinal indicator of success; now economic growth (compounded by population increase) was continuing at such a rate that it began on the one hand to be seen more for what it is—a prerequisite for achieving social objectives which have to be politically defined—and on the other hand to be viewed with suspicion for its environmental, social and psychological costs which could not be measured in the economic dimension alone. There might be little hope that the problems of inflation (rampant at different rates in different countries) could be greatly eased at any early stage by Community action. But over as vital a problem as environmental deterioration the Community, it was argued, could act far more effectively than nation states on their own (with the common agricultural policy one possible ingredient in its action). If the original inspiration was the fear that Western Europe might be crushed with a bang, new tasks were now discovered in preventing it from stifling itself with a whimper.

Similarly, within Britain, the argument had also changed. Where in the early 'sixties the Community was still largely a thing of hope and aspiration to be shaped by its participants, with each member and possible member reading into its potential those policies which corresponded to his own needs, by now detailed policies had taken shape on barley prices and on value added tax, on lorry-axle pressure and on food additives. Tailored to suit the six member states, yet for obvious political reasons impossible to nullify and rejig all over again, these policies could not be expected to be optimal for late entrants who had refused to join at the beginning. The combination of an agricultural policy and a fiscal system which taxed imports from outside the Community (on which Britain had hitherto been heavily dependent) for the benefit of farmers (of whom Britain had relatively few) would put a substantial tax burden on Britain; and the combination of high food prices and a value added tax less selective than British consumer taxation was liable to result, unless offset in other ways, in a less progressive tax system within Britain. The consequent additional obstacles to economic growth and difficulties for social policy were potent arguments against entry, at least in the short term.

At the same time, particularly in 1972, the constitutional problems were very clearly displayed. The British Parliament had to take over lock, stock and barrel forty-two volumes of legislation passed by Community institutions—whose legitimacy as democratic representatives even of the citizens of the original Community seemed obscure. Worse still, Parliament entered into an open-ended commitment to incorporate into British law all future Community legislation and make it virtually unamendable by the domestic Parliament. The democratic legitimacy of Community institutions may or may not be a problem that can be solved once Britain is inside the Communities. The relegation of the Westminster Parliament in matters where the Community has competence was not so much an unfortunate accidental disadvantage as inherent in the essence of the Community as such, and thus part and parcel of the aim of entry

We thus touch on the core problem of Community-building: how far the larger unit with which men identified in politically relevant ways remained overwhelmingly the nation state, and how far both smaller subnational and wider supranational units became co-ordinate frames of reference: how far in particular the political use of the word 'we' referred to West Europeans rather than to the British people.

Nothing perhaps illustrates more convincingly the difference between the British public and the population of the Six in their identification with a wider than national group, and their view of the need for wider institutions to take decisions for that group, than the opinion polls commissioned simultaneously in seven countries in early 1970 by the EEC itself. Whereas on the Continent every single question elicited a clear preponderance of 'Europeans', in Britain the 'Europeans' remained on every single question in a minority. While

Continental political leaders could thus count on a fair degree of popular support for their attempts at further integration, the lag between the British public and the Continental public, the British public and the British political leadership, posed serious problems of domestic persuasion, and no doubt also helped make more difficult the problems of foreign diplomacy.

There thus remained profound differences: differences of attitude between the Continent and Britain; acute conflicts in Britain between long-run and short-run, political and economic objectives; divergences of tactics between British policy-makers; and not least a gulf between policy-makers and people.

A Comparative Poll in Seven Countries

Are you in favour of, or against, Britain joining the European Common Market?

	Holland	Luxem-bourg	West Germany	France	Belgium	Italy	EEC	Britain
In favour	79	70	69	66	63	51	64	19
Against	8	6	7	11	8	9	8	63
Don't know	13	24	24	23	29	40	28	18

Assuming that Britain did join, would you be for or against the evolution of the Common Market towards the political formation of a United States of Europe?

	Holland	Luxem-bourg	West Germany	France	Belgium	Italy	EEC	Britain
For	64	75	69	67	60	60	65	30
Against	17	5	9	11	10	7	9	48
Don't know	19	20	22	22	30	33	26	22

Would you be in favour of, or against the election of a European Parliament by direct universal suffrage; that is a parliament elected by all the voters in the member countries?

	Holland	Luxem-bourg	West Germany	France	Belgium	Italy	EEC	Britain
In favour	59	71	66	59	56	55	59	25
Against	21	10	9	15	11	6	11	55
Don't know	20	19	25	26	33	39	30	20

Would you be willing to accept, over and above your own government, a European Government responsible for a common policy in foreign affairs, defence and the economy?

	Holland	Luxem-bourg	West Germany	France	Belgium	Italy	EEC	Britain
Willing	50	47	57	49	51	51	53	22
Not willing	32	35	19	28	19	10	20	60
Don't know	18	18	24	23	30	39	27	18

If a President of a United States of Europe were being elected by popular vote, would you be willing to vote for a candidate not of your own country—if his personality and programme corresponded more closely to your ideas than those of the candidates of your own country?

	Holland	Luxem-bourg	West Germany	France	Belgium	Italy	EEC	Britain
Willing	63	67	69	61	52	45	59	39
Not willing	18	20	20	22	24	19	18	41
Don't know	19	13	19	17	24	36	23	20

References

1. In retelling this story I have naturally drawn on my earlier accounts of the same periods, notably in *The Challenge of the Common Market*, Blackwell, Oxford, 1961, and in the Introduction to A. Moncrieff (ed.), *Britain and the Common Market* 1967, BBC, London, 1967.
2. 'Draft Declaration by the European Resistance Movements, July 1944', reprinted in Kitzinger, *The European Common Market and Community*, Routledge, London, 1967, pp. 29–33.
3. For the bulk of the text of this speech see Kitzinger, op. cit., pp. 33–7.
4. Arthur M. Schlesinger, Jr., *A Thousand Days. John F. Kennedy in the White House*, Deutsch, London, 1965, p. 787.

(Extracted from *Diplomacy and Persuasion: How Britain Joined the E.E.C.*, Thames and Hudson, London, 1973.)

1.4 'With' Them But Not 'Of' Them: Brief Extracts from British Politicians' Views on Britain's Relations with Europe, 1946-61

1. Winston Churchill at Zurich, 19 September 1946

[*Churchill started by speaking of the tragedy of Europe, 'on the whole the fairest and the most cultivated regions on this earth' which had fostered 'most of the culture, arts, philosophy and science both of ancient and modern times' but which had only narrowly avoided being plunged into a new Dark Age. The danger, he said, still remained.*]

'Yet all the while there is a remedy which, if it were generally and spontaneously adopted, would as if by a miracle transform the whole scene, and would in a few years make all Europe, or the greater part of it, as free and as happy as Switzerland is today. What is this sovereign remedy? It is to re-create the European Family, or as much of it as we can, and provide it with a structure under which it can dwell in peace, in safety and in freedom. We must build a kind of United States of Europe. In this way only will hundreds of millions of toilers be able to regain the simple joys and hopes which make life worth living. The process is simple. All that is needed is the resolve of hundreds of millions of men and women to do right instead of wrong and gain as their reward blessing instead of cursing.

'Our constant aim must be to build and fortify the strength of UNO. Under and within that world concept we must re-create the European Family in a regional structure called, it may be, the United States of Europe. The first step is to form a Council of Europe. If at first all the States of Europe are not willing or able to join the Union, we must nevertheless proceed to assemble and combine those who will and those who can. The salvation of the common people of every race and of every land from war or servitude must be established on solid foundations and must be guarded by the readiness of all men and women to die rather than submit to tyranny. In all this urgent work, France and Germany must take the lead together. Great Britain, the British Commonwealth of Nations, mighty America and I trust Soviet Russia—for then indeed all would be well—must be the friends and sponsors of the new Europe and must champion its right to live and shine.'

(Uwe Kitzinger, *The European Common Market and Community*, Routledge and Kegan Paul, London, 1967, pp. 34–7.)

2. Clement Attlee in the House of Commons, 5 May 1948

[*He said that the British Government was anxious to have the closest possible relations with Western Europe.*]
'But there is one condition to such progress which must be absolute, and it is that the Empire is with us in the conception and exercise of that plan at every stage. . . . I was disturbed with the suggestion in the motion that we might somehow get closer to Europe than to our Commonwealth. The Commonwealth nations are our closest friends. While I want to get as close as we can with the other nations, we have to bear in mind that we are not solely a European Power but a member of a great Commonwealth and Empire.'

(*House of Commons Debates*, 5th Ser., Vol. 450, Col. 1314–19.)

3. Anthony Eden at the University of Columbia, 11 January 1952

'Frequent suggestions have been made that the United Kingdom should join a federation on the continent of Europe. This is something we know, in our bones, we cannot do . . . For Britain's story and her interests lie far beyond the Continent of Europe. Our thoughts move across the seas to the many communities in which our people play their part in every corner of the world. That is our life; without it we should be no more than some millions of people living on an island off the coast of Europe.'

(Nicholas Mansergh, *Documents and Speeches on British Commonwealth Affairs*, 1931–52, Vol. 1, Oxford University Press for the Royal Institute of International Affairs, London, 1953, pp. 1156–7.)

4. Winston Churchill in the House of Commons, 11 May 1953

'. . . As I have urged for several years, there is no hope for the safety and freedom of Western Europe except by the laying aside for ever of the ancient feud between the Teuton and the Gaul. It is seven years since, at Zurich, I appealed to France to take Germany by the hand and lead her back into the European family. We have made great progress since then. Some of it has been due no doubt to the spur to resist the enormous military strength of Soviet Russia, but much is also due to the inspiring and unconquerable cause of United Europe. We have Strasbourg and all that it stands for, and it is our duty to fortify its vitality and authority tirelessly as the years roll on . . .

'Where do we [the British] stand? We are not members of the European Defence Community, nor do we intend to be merged in a Federal European system. We feel we have a special relation to both. This can be expressed by prepositions, but the preposition "with" but not "of"—we are with them, but not of them. We have our own Commonwealth and Empire. One of the anxieties of France is lest Germany, even partitioned as she is now, will be so strong that France will be outweighed in United Europe or in the European Defence Community. I am sure they could do a lot, if they chose to make themselves stronger. But, anyhow, I have always believed, as an active friend of France for nearly fifty years, that our fortunes lie together. . . .'

(*House of Commons Debates*, 5th Ser., Vol. 515, Col. 889 ff., 11 May 1953.)

5. Reginald Maudling in the House of Commons, 28 March 1958

'. . . My hon. Friend the Member for Harwich dealt with two very important subjects, agriculture and the Commonwealth, and my hon. Friend the Member of Ashford (Mr. Deedes) also discussed agriculture. I think the position is now fairly clear. The old argument about exclusion or inclusion has, I hope, been finally disposed of. I made a statement in the OEEC last year, which was recorded in *Hansard,* in which I said that it was a misleading question to ask whether agriculture should be included in the Free Trade Area. I went on to say:

"So far as I know, none of the countries represented here, with possibly one or two exceptions, would propose a system whereby their agriculture would be exposed to competition in the way that industrial production will be exposed in the Free Trade Area. We all protect our agriculture in one way or another, and intend to go on doing so." (*Official Report*, 29 October 1957; Vol. 575, c. 27.)

'What we are doing is, simultaneously with the conclusion of, or with the negotiation of, a Free Trade Area agreement, to negotiate an agreement, in the words of the Resolution which contains our terms of reference—

"on methods of further co-operation between all member countries, in agricultural matters, with a view assuring an expansion of trade in agricultural products".

'I think it is generally recognised in Europe that we regard agriculture, as do all other European countries, not only as an industry but also as a way of life, and that the principle of agricultural protection is accepted throughout Europe. We do not consider that we are highly protective. In fact, we think that we are very liberal in our agricultural import policy: we are the biggest importers of agricultural produce from the OEEC countries. We made it perfectly clear that we do not intend to chance our policy in this matter . . .

'. . . The other reason why we must take a different view is because of our special connection with the Commonwealth. As the House is aware we have given a clear undertaking to the Commonwealth countries to maintain their position in our markets for foodstuffs, drink and tobacco. I have found that our friends in Europe well understand our position in that matter. There is less understanding of the true nature of the Commonwealth system. I have been very disappointed to find that, even among some of our closest friends, there is apprehension about the way the Commonwealth and sterling system operates. There seems to be a failure to recognise that it is a balanced system and that, against the preference that we obtain in Commonwealth countries, we give in exchange almost duty-free and quota-free entry to a large range of commodities.

'We also maintain a sterling system very often at considerable cost to our own economy, which is of great benefit not only to the Commonwealth but to the trading areas of Western Europe. It is important to continue to point out to our European friends, when they think about the Commonwealth system, that it is a balanced system and must remain so. It is a system which has contributed not only to our own prosperity of Europe and the whole Western world. If we look at the trade statistics, it is remarkable how trade between the Commonwealth and Western Europe has rapidly expanded in recent years. That is largely because of the existence of the sterling system. . . .

'. . . I repeat what has been said by one or two other hon. Members, including the right hon. Member for Battersea North that it is important for our friends in Europe to understand the nature of the Commonwealth and the fact that it contributes not only to our strength, but also to the strength of Europe. As I have said in public more than once, it would be a sad thing indeed if we were forced to choose between Europe and the Commonwealth. I am quite convinced that there is no necessity for any such choice to be made. It is important for people to realise what a sad day it would be, not only for the Commonwealth, but also for Europe as a whole, if Britain were forced into the position of having to make any such choice. . . .'

(*House of Commons Debates*, 5th Ser., Vol. 585, Col. 792–4, 795, 28 March 1958.)

6. Harold Macmillan in the House of Commons, 31 July 1961

'With permission, I wish to make a statement on the policy of Her Majesty's Government towards the European Economic Community.

'The future relations between the European Economic Community, the United Kingdom, the Commonwealth and the rest of Europe are clearly matters of capital importance in the life of our country and, indeed, of all the countries of the free world.

'This is a political as well as an economic issue. Although the Treaty of Rome is concerned with economic matters it has an important political objective, namely, to promote unity and stability in Europe which is so essential a factor in the struggle for freedom and progress throughout the world. In this modern world the tendency towards larger groups of nations acting together in the common interest leads to greater unity and thus adds to our strength.

'I believe that it is both our duty and our interest to contribute towards that strength by securing the closest possible unity within Europe. At the same time, if a closer relationship between the United Kingdom and the countries of the European Economic Community were to disrupt the long-standing and historic ties between the United Kingdom and the other nations of the Commonwealth the loss would be greater than the gain. The Commonwealth is a great source of stability and strength both to Western Europe and to the world as a whole, and I am sure that its value is fully appreciated by the member Governments of the European Economic Community. I do not think that Britain's contribution to the Commonwealth will be reduced if Europe unites. On the contrary, I think that its value will be enhanced.

'On the economic side, a community comprising, as members or in association, the countries of free Europe, could have a very rapidly expanding economy supplying, as eventually it would, a single market of approaching 300 million people. This rapidly expanding economy could, in turn, lead to an increased demand for products from other parts of the world and so help to expand world trade and improve the prospects of the less developed areas of the world.

'No British Government could join the European Economic Community without prior negotiation with a view to meeting the needs of the Commonwealth countries, of our European Free Trade Association partners, and of British agriculture consistently with the broad principles and purposes which have inspired the concept of European unity and which are embodied in the Rome Treaty. . . .'

[*He went on to say that these consultations had taken place.*]

'. . . Therefore, after long and earnest consideration, Her Majesty's Government have come to the conclusion that it would be right for Britain to make a formal application under Article 237 of the Treaty for negotiations with a view to joining the Community if satisfactory arrangements can be made to meet the special needs of the United Kingdom, of the Commonwealth and of the European Free Trade Association.

'If, as I earnestly hope, our offer to enter into negotiations with the European Economic Community is accepted, we shall spare no efforts to reach a satisfactory agreement. These negotiations must inevitably be of a detailed and technical character, covering a very large number of the most delicate and difficult matters. They may, therefore be protracted and there can, of course, be no guarantee of success. When any negotiations are brought to a conclusion then it will be the duty of the Government to recommend to the House what course we should pursue. . . .'

(*House of Commons Debates*, 5th Ser., Vol. 645, Col. 928 ff., 31 July 1961.)

1.5 The Great Debate: Extracts from the Commons Debate on Entry of October 1971

European Communities

The Secretary of State for Foreign and Commonwealth Affairs (Sir Alec Douglas-Home): I beg to move,

That this House approves Her Majesty's Government's decision of principle to join the European Communities on the basis of the arrangements which have been negotiated.

This debate has been heralded for so long as 'the great debate' that all of us are conscious of the danger of anti-climax. That which has been rehearsed so often in anticipation may seem stale. The issue is just as momentous, but the dictionary does not expand. . . .

I wish to remind the House, in the context of the European Community, of other recent parliamentary occasions which, in the immediate flurry of argument today, are often overlooked. Twice, once in 1961 and again in 1967, this House, after sober, calculated debate, instructed, first, a Conservative Government and, second, a Socialist Government to negotiate terms of entry into the Community.

Unless—it is an unworthy thought which I reject—hon. Members are relying on time to provide them with an alibi, the assumption must be that the votes then given were recorded with the conviction that, in principle, Britain should enter the European partnership. [HON. MEMBERS: 'No.'] I see no other interpretation which can be put on the majority view on these solemn parliamentary occasions and manifestations.

Again, at the General Election in 1970 no elector could possibly have been in any doubt that, had the Socialist Party been elected, it would have resumed the negotiations with the European Community where it had left off. . . .

Added to the fact that, obviously, a Socialist Government would have renewed negotiation, and added to the fact that it was widely understood that a Conservative Government, if they secured the right terms, would recommend entry, we have now, after a year of negotiations, actually got the terms which we think we can recommend to the House.

After all these deliberate parliamentary processes, if we were now to reject the opportunity and the invitation to join the European Economic Community we must pause and ask ourselves in this House how our reputation as a nation for reliable dealing would be looked upon, either in Europe or in the world. With what authority thereafter would British Ministers of any Government negotiate overseas? . . .

Nor do I find valid the claim that while our respective Governments were negotiating we did not know what agreement would involve, such as accepting the agricultural policies of the Community and the rules which the Community had already adopted. Time after our entry might bring change, but for the purposes of entry there were conditions which were broadly understood as inescapable.

If there are subsequent doubts among right hon. and hon. Members who were then prepared, and up to the General Election were prepared, to see their Government negotiate, it seems to me that they must centre upon the terms achieved by my right hon. and learned Friend the Chancellor of the Duchy of Lancaster. . . . some years ago I feared that the Community would be protectionist and exclusive.

An Hon. Member: The right hon. Gentleman was proved right.

Sir Alec Douglas-Home: Perhaps the right hon. Gentleman will listen for a moment. As a Community, the nations concerned negotiated the Kennedy Round of tariff reductions. The external tariff of the Community is on average lower than our own. The Community has sought and is seeking trade arrangements with a large number of countries, including those of Eastern Europe, and it is already the world's largest importer.

In the context of trade, many hon. Members have had anxieties for the well-being of the Commonwealth. But what is the situation now? With the exception of Gibraltar and Hong Kong, all our dependent territories—some 30 of them—are to enjoy associate status with the Community. For Gibraltar, arrangements have been made under Article 227 of the Treaty of Rome, and Hong Kong has been included in the Community's generalised preference scheme. Most of the independent developing countries are to have the option of three types of association: a Yaoundé-type agreement, some looser form of association, or individually-negotiated trade agreements.

For New Zealand's milk products, continuing arrangements have been made on the basis of which the New Zealand Dairy Board has expressed complete confidence in the future of the industry, and the Government have expressed satisfaction. So, too, for the sugar producers of the developing Commonwealth, whose Governments have unanimously accepted the arrangements that have been negotiated.

Naturally, many contacts with Commonwealth leaders have been made. I have had many contacts with them during recent years, and I believe that they have come through a period of anxiety to the belief that it is right, in their own interests, for Britain to enter the Community. Many want it to be soon so that they can get down to business with the enlarged Community and its associate States.

As Secretary of State for the Commonwealth in the 1950s, I, along with other Ministers, negotiated a number of trade and commodity agreements with Commonwealth countries. It was in 1958 that it became really clear to me how quickly and certainly the strong trend to industrialisation and manufacture in practically all the Commonwealth countries would erode the preference system established by the Ottawa Conference and reduce Britain's share of Commonwealth trade.

I recall speaking about this at that time in another place. It has happened. The fall has been dramatic. In the years from 1961 to 1969 our proportion of the Commonwealth countries' imports of manufactured goods fell from 29 per cent to 15 per cent while their contribution fell from 35 per cent to 23 per cent of our total imports.

This trend has become stronger and stronger and is continuing. With the continuing industrialisation and with the interests of Commonwealth countries which since then have grown in regional trading, it is clear that the declining trend will continue. It is no one's fault. It is a fact of life.

There is little doubt that we and they will gain far more if Britain becomes part of a home market of over 250 million consumers than we would under a continuance of the present arrangements if those trends continue, as they almost certainly will.

Sir Harmar Nicholls (Peterborough): Is it not fair to the record to add that, although the percentage has fallen, the volume of trade with the Commonwealth has risen?

Sir Alec Douglas-Home: That has certainly happened, but it is a significant fact that the percentage has fallen so steeply. I do not think that we can ignore it. If the expectation of increased earning power for Britain in the Market is fulfilled, we can invest in the Commonwealth's future in a way which we could not otherwise do.

I have no doubt the balance of advantage to the Commonwealth falls decisively on the side of Britain's entry into Europe.

I turn to the question of the economic base from which any influence and authority which we have overseas must spring. We know that the cost of entry into the Community has been pretty accurately calculated over the transitional period. The argument is used that we cannot risk even paying that subscription because the profit to be earned cannot be foreseen.

What business executive when he embarks upon an exercise can quantify with absolute certainty the profit from year to year? Success can be achieved only by exploiting an opportunity with all the skill available. A market of this size with no tariff restrictions and, which I think is even more important, with the prospect of steadily reducing non-tariff restrictions, because they can be even more dangerous than tariffs, must be an opportunity which British industry can seize and of which it can take advantage.

There is certainly an element of risk. Lord Thorneycroft, speaking in another place in support of entry, put the matter very well by describing forecasting as more a matter of faith than of figure. That is undoubtedly true, but it is noticeable that those who do the country's business are happy to accept this challenge. The Confederation of British Industry certainly looks upon it as a challenge which should be accepted. . . .

I should have thought that recent trends in employment had firmly underlined the need for Britain to gain free and permanent access to its largest and most promising export market. The implications of this in terms of jobs and job security in Britain are surely apparent. We must ask ourselves in our present circumstances, when nobody can say that relative to the rest of the world we are doing well in trade: where do we find the jobs for our people unless we take advantage of an opportunity like this?

Some are afraid of increased competition. In the House of Commons we simply cannot admit that. If we are unable to compete in a free market of ten, what chance have we in the rest of the world with barriers mounted against us? Before the war there was practically no branch of industry and technology in which Britain was not in the lead. That is now no longer so. We have only to see modern Japan to realise the kind of competition to which we have been, and will be, exposed.

Whether or not the world becomes more protectionist—there are ugly signs that it may do so—a home market of this dimension must be invaluable to us. I cannot see how we can afford to be without it.

Another feature of the Common Market which could redound greatly to our advantage is regional policy. My right hon. Friends will speak of this in more detail later. If we go into the Community now we shall be in it before regional policies are far advanced and will have a hand in shaping them. That could be of great importance to Scotland and other areas of Britain where unemployment so stubbornly persists at a high level.

I turn now to the political evolution of a Europe without Britain as a partner. This is another field of activity where, if we enter now, we shall be in at the start and able to influence political development. It is in this constitutional area that fears have been most acute, and for some they still linger.

Some of the advocates of European unity have supported a federal system for Europe. This has caused a good deal of anxiety. . . . Some may still like and pursue the idea.

What has happened within the partnership of the Six? Political change, it is agreed, has to be unanimous. On all important matters they have found that they must proceed by consensus. That is the experience after ten years of practice in the Community.

The reason is clear. Great countries with the history of the European nations cannot be dragooned or coerced into a pattern of political association which one or the other of them does not like. The attempt would be folly. It would break up the Community. Even to try to do such a thing is totally against the spirit of the association.

I remind hon. Members of the wording of the Preamble to the Treaty of Rome, which is so often ignored:

> . . . to ensure by common action the economic and social progress of their countries by eliminating the barriers which divide Europe,
> . . . to strengthen the unity of their economies and to ensure their harmonious development by reducing the differences existing between the various regions and the backwardness of the less favourite regions,
> . . . to strengthen the cause of peace and liberty by thus pooling their resources.

These are the articles not of penalty but of partnership for the common good.

Decisions on the political evolution of the Community are not for now, even for tomorrow, but for the future. Any decision made on political advance must have the unanimous support of all the members of the partnership. But even if on occasion the Commission or some members of the Community tried to introduce something of a lesser nature which was unacceptable to one member or another, why should it be so readily assumed that we should be outsmarted or overruled? I think it is true that in the six years, or perhaps longer, before 1970 we as a nation began to show what the psychologists would call 'withdrawal symptoms'. It is time that we regained some of our confidence and entered into partnership knowing that we are going to pull our full weight. . . .

. . . On all the grounds on which I have spoken, my own conclusion—and each of us can speak only for himself in this debate—is quite clear. It is that such a chance of economic extension, such a base for increased authority, such an opportunity to build security for the future, will not recur for many a day, if it ever comes again. The European Economic Community will be a magnet for EFTA and other countries. It will go on and become more prosperous, and neither Europe nor the world will wait for us any longer.

I trust that when the last speech in this great debate is over the House will give the clearest signal that we should embark on this new adventure in the long story of our nation. I believe that to take advantage of it will give us by far the greatest opportunity that we can have of serving our people and future generations.

Mr. Denis Healey (Leeds, East): This is the end of the beginning of an argument that has lasted for more than fifteen years. . . .

I think nevertheless that there is some common ground in the House. It is that whatever may happen in the future, at present what is called the European Economic Community is not Europe. Even *The Economist* agrees that the Common Market is not much more than a particular commercial set-up covering six out of twenty-four European countries, and even if all the applicants join there will still be fourteen European countries outside it. The Common Market is not Europe, and to oppose entry to the Common Market on the terms which the Government have negotiated is not to be anti-European.

I am very surprised that this afternoon the Foreign Secretary said nothing, or almost nothing, about the argument on which he based his case at his party's Conference only a week ago, namely, that it is vital for Britain to join a regional group or *bloc* so that it can compete on equal terms with the super Powers. But that argument is not relevant today and, as the Foreign Secretary indicated this afternoon, it cannot be relevant unless all the countries in the Community agree to a surrender of sovereignty far beyond what anyone in the United Kingdom today would tolerate.

Even in principle, one must have grave doubts about the value, in the current state of the world, of regional *blocs*. All our biggest problems as a country and as a member of the world community need more than regional solutions. In defence, we need an alliance with Canada and the United States. As we have learned all too dramatically in recent months, in trade and currency matters, we need a worldwide agreement with all the developed countries, including Japan. . . .

But the case for entry, as I think the right hon. Gentleman admitted today, must depend overwhelmingly on economic considerations. It is, after all, an economic community at present and nothing more. If it brought greater growth—if it led Britain to have a growth rate equal to that of every other European country, inside or outside the Common Market, remembering that growth in the other EFTA countries has been as rapid as that inside the Community—then it would be well worth while.

But whether it leads to that sort of growth depends on the price that we must pay for joining, on the state of our economy when we join and on the policies we pursue in the economic and social fields when we are members.

An ice-cold shower of competition might be a bracing tonic for a healthy man, but it can give a sick man a heart attack. . . .

Using the estimates available from Government sources, let us first admit that the United Kingdom must pay certain penalties by joining which none of the original members of the Community had to face. We must give up our Commonwealth and share our EFTA preferences. The Chancellor of the Duchy told the House that the cost of these tariff charges . . . would be between £200 million and £300 million.

If, next, we accept the common agricultural policy, not only do we give the Six access to the largest food market in the world, but we must pay high prices for our food instead of the low prices we pay now for Commonwealth food—[*Interruption.*]—whereas the Six did not face this penalty when they set up the CAP; they have always paid high prices.

. . . If the Common Market were a real community aiming to share benefits and costs alike, I should have thought that the Six would have taken account of the special handicaps we carry by joining when they were considering our contribution to the Budget. They should have been prepared to reduce our subscription accordingly, though in fact the exact opposite has happened.

In the statement presented to the Common Market countries on 16 December last, which was published in Brussels but never in Britain, the Chancellor of the Duchy pointed out that if we made a contribution above 6 per cent of the total contribution of the Common Market Budget, everything above 6 per cent would be a net gain for the rest of the Community.

He based his argument on a paper presented by his delegation to the Community in July, in which the Treasury had given detailed estimates of what, accepting the financial regulations which the Community had agreed, would be involved for Britain.

It pointed out that if we accepted the rules which had been fixed by the Six in our absence, at the end of the day we would be paying 31 per cent of the budget and getting only 6 per cent back; that we would be paying net four times as much as Germany, although Germany's gross national product today is 50 per cent higher than Britain's; and that we would be paying 25 per cent net of the total, when our GNP is only 17 per cent of that of the Community as a whole. That 25 per cent we would be paying would be going to France, Holland and Luxembourg, who would be paying nothing net to the Community budget themselves.

All of them—France, Holland and Luxembourg—have higher living standards than we have and pay nothing whatever to the budget. In import levies alone, according to the Treasury paper, we would be paying more than France, Germany, Italy and Holland put together.

The right hon. Gentleman made a half-hearted attempt in December to bring this scandalously unfair contribution down, but he knuckled under completely in May, after the meeting between the Prime Minister and President Pompidou. He accepted the whole of the proposal in its original form, arguing only about the transitional stages.

The result of that, according to the Government's own estimates which I have been using, is that we would have to carry a foreign exchange burden of £100 million in 1973, £500 million in 1977—and it would go through the roof between 1977 and 1980. . . . Some may say, 'Yes, but after all, the money we are paying to these three countries is in a noble cause. It will help the lame ducks on the soil of their farms.' It is very odd that a Government who are so hostile to helping lame ducks in Britain should be so ready to help them on the Continent.

But the fact is that the overwhelmingly largest proportion of this money will not go to lame ducks. It will go to very wealthy farmers in France, Holland and Luxembourg. Some say, 'Ah, but the number of farmers on the Continent is going down.' That is true. But the cost of the common agricultural policy is rising all the time. As the number of farmers goes down, the amount paid to the common agricultural policy in subsidies and other forms of support has risen from £100 million to £1,100 million in eight years. The tragedy is that Her Majesty's Government should have agreed to give this monstrously unfair subsidy to the common agricultural policy just at the moment when every Government on the Continent, except the French Government, was coming to feel that it would have to be abandoned.

The cost to Britain in foreign exchange hurts us at the most sensitive part of our economy. The additional foreign exchange cost of £100 million in 1973 is equivalent to the whole of the foreign exchange saving through taking our troops out of east of Suez. The £500 million cost in 1977 is twice the current total of our overseas aid to those who are really in need in other parts of the world. The £700 million or more in 1980 is the size of the deficit inherited in 1964 by the Labour Government, the deficit which crippled so many of our hopes.

Mr. John Wilkinson (Bradford, West): Would the right hon. Gentleman acknowledge that he is monstrously misleading the House on the hypothetical figure of the cost from 1977 onwards? If one takes the effect of VAT and of rebate on exports through VAT, and if one takes into account the effect of the extra home production of which British agriculture is capable, the figure he is putting before the House is a fiction.

Mr. Healey: I am sure that the hon. Member will attempt to make this point if he catches your eye, Mr. Deputy Speaker, later in the debate. [HON MEMBERS: 'Answer.'] I am answering. The estimate that the cost of our budgetary contribution will rise after 1977 is agreed by all the pro-Market economists whose opinions I have been able to read . . . there is no evidence whatever that the member countries of the Six grew faster by joining the Common Market; in fact, their overall growth fell . . . the effect of removing the Common Market tariffs. The tariffs between the Six countries in 1958 were very substantial. It could be argued that that really meant new opportunities for all concerned. The effect of removing the current external tariff would be very small. The increase in our export prices in the last 12 months has raised the cost of our goods higher than the average external tariff of the Economic Community at present. But in any case, the most optimistic guess at the growth increase which might follow entry to the Common Market is $\frac{1}{3}$ per cent a year, and on this basis we would break even, costs against benefits, only in 1977. But all this depends on the strength of our economy and on our own economic policies in this country.

Are we now moving towards . . . a situation of steady and sustained growth? The right hon. Gentleman the Chancellor, just after the last debate, gave us his third budget in a year. He told us that it would change the whole of our economic climate in two or three months. Those two or three months are now up and what do we find? Unemployment is still rising. There are 24,000 more men and women wholly unemployed today than there were a month ago. . . . Prices are still rising. OECD and other experts expect prices to rise between 6 per cent and 8 per cent over the next 12 months. But worst of all, and most critical to growth, there is no sign of investment rising. Investment is down. . . .

Where is this surge of investment created by confidence at the thought of entry, which 82 per cent of our people, whether they welcome it or not, do expect to take place? There is no sign of it at all. We look like going into the Common Market in 1973, if the Government have their way, in a state of economic stagnation, with unemployment at a higher level than anybody on either side is prepared to tolerate from either a moral or an economic point of view, and with prices still rising. There is also mounting evidence that those who do plan to increase their investment plan to do it not in this country but on the Continent, closer to the heart of this great new market and where return on investment in profit terms is higher.

Against this background of rising costs, rising unemployment and industrial stagnation, how are we going to meet these foreign exchange burdens which the Government have dumped on us as a result of the Brussels negotiations? There are only two ways. One is deflation, a prolonged period of 'stop'. The other is devaluation. . . .

Devaluation means cuts in welfare, cuts in living standards and soaring prices—prices which will soar even higher than otherwise because of the common agricultural policy. Then, why are the Government so keen on entry? It is because they knew these facts as well as I do—and I have drawn largely on Government statistics for my argument.

The reason is partly, I think, because, as with the last Conservative Government which applied for entry, in 1962, this is the despairing gambler's last throw. The Government have no other answer to our problems. But there is another reason on this occasion which did not apply to Mr. Macmillan's Administration. It is because the present Prime Minister sees the Common Market as a competitive jungle in which 'Selsdon man' can roam at will, in which all lame ducks go to the wall, in which the trade unions are forced to face the facts of life, and in which a few years of misery will produce a Conservative heaven. . . .

Mr. Harold Wilson (Huyton): . . . The right hon. Gentleman the Member for Streatham (Mr. Sandys) asked me about the position of the Labour Party in relation to the Community.

. . . the position of a Labour Government coming into office, after accession to the Community, in, say, 1973 or 1974.

. . . As is well known, one Parliament cannot bind its successor. On the other hand, we recognise what is involved in a treaty signature. What we should do . . . would be immediately to give notice that we could not accept the terms negotiated by the Conservatives, and, in particular, the unacceptable burdens arising out of the CAP, the blows to the Commonwealth, and any threats to our essential regional policies.

If the Community then refused to negotiate, as we should have asked, or if the negotiations were to fail, we would sit down amicably and discuss the situation with them. [*Laughter.*] . . .

We should make clear that our posture, like that of the French after 1958, would be rigidly directed towards the pursuit of British interests and that all other decisions and actions in relation to the Community would be dictated by that determination, until we had secured our terms. They might accept this, or they might decide that we should agree to part; that would depend on them. That is our position.

. . . the Prime Minister must carry the full responsibility for his clear commitments about Europe to the British people before and during the General Election. His claim to a mandate, which he did not seek and did not obtain, is shown to be false by his manifesto: 'Our sole commitment is to negotiate; no more, no less.' A sentence which the Foreign and Commonwealth Secretary forgot to read last week.

Further, the right hon. Gentleman said in May last year: 'It would not be in the interests of the Community that its enlargement should take place except with the full-hearted consent of the Parliaments and peoples of the new member countries. . . .'

On BBC television, on 'Election Forum', he said: '. . . no British Government could possibly take this country into the Common Market against the wish of the British people. . . .' He must tell us tonight whether he believes he has secured the full-hearted consent of the British people. I hope for his sake, because I wish him well, that he will do better than he did on 'Panorama' a week or two ago, when he confirmed that it was still his view that: 'No British Government could possibly take . . . this country into the Common Market against the wish of the British people.' Asked about that, he said that he had had '. . . a lot of letters from official organisations . . . I would have said that the organisations have become more and more strongly in support of our entry into the Community.'

The CBI, no doubt, the Chambers of Commerce, the employers, the merchant banks—oh yes! But not the trade union movement, not the pensioners, not the unemployed, not the housewife.

. . . The right hon. Gentleman holds his office not by the suffrage of the organisations. He has no mandate, for he sought none and obtained none, to take Britain into the Common Market except with the full-hearted consent of the British people. That is not at his command, and no vote of this House can of itself redeem his personal pledge to the British people.

. . . Let him now seek from those people the mandate he spuriously claims by submitting this, and all his policies, to the free vote of a free British people.

The Prime Minister (Mr. Edward Heath): I do not think that any Prime Minister has stood at this Box in time of peace and asked the House to take a positive decision of such importance as I am asking it to take tonight. I am well aware of the responsibility which rests on my shoulders for so doing. After ten years of negotiation, after many years of discussion in this House and after ten years of debate, the moment of decision for Parliament has come. The other House has already taken its vote and expressed its view—[HON. MEMBERS: 'Backwoodsmen!']; 451 frontswoodsmen have voted in favour of the Motion and, for the rest, 58. . . .

Earlier, the world was watching New York. They were waiting to see whether China was going to become a member of the Security Council and of the General Assembly. Tonight, the world is similarly watching Westminster, waiting to see whether we are going to decide that Western Europe should now move along the path to real unity— or whether the British Parliament, now given the choice, not for the first time but probably for the last time for many years to come, will reject the chance of creating a United Europe. . . . Even since we last debated this in the House in July, the situation has been transformed by China showing that, certainly within this century, it will be the third super Power. We could not tell, when this decision was taken in the United Nations, what the consequences of it would be, either for China or for the rest of us in the western world. But we thought that decision right: it is one that British Governments have worked for since 1961.

. . . We as a country are dangerously vulnerable to protectionist pressure if such a satisfactory outcome of a new financial and trading system is not achieved. . . .

In those circumstances, I believe that a Prime Minister who came to this Box and recommended that we should reject the opportunity now before us of taking an active part, a share in these decisions, would be taking a terrible gamble with the livelihood of the British people for many years to come. . . .

As to whether Britain is European, I fail entirely to understand the argument . . . about cutting off our links with the outside world, when the members of the Community itself are the great trading countries of the world; when the Community itself is the greatest trading *bloc* in the world; when, as the Leader of the Liberal Party pointed out this evening, when the enlarged Community is created, it will have arrangements with 80 countries. Twenty-nine of the Commonwealth countries and 19 dependencies will be associated with the Community.

. . . We have confidence that we can benefit as well as contribute, that we can further our own interests and the interests of the Community at one and the same time. After all, the leaders of all three parties in this House accept the principle of entry into the European Community, as the right hon. Gentleman reaffirmed this afternoon.

The Community is not governed by any particular party ideology. How can it be, with a Socialist Government in the Federal Republic, with a Right-wing Government in France, with a coalition in Italy containing Socialists? Of course not. What is more, all the opposition parties in the member countries of the Community support membership of the Community just as much as the governing parties. . . .

. . . the President of France, supported by the Chancellor of Germany, has proposed a summit meeting of heads of Government in the course of next year and probably in the spring. This meeting, will, I believe, settle the European approach to the problems that we have been discussing of monetary arrangements, trading arrangements and future political development.

If by any chance the House rejected this Motion tonight, that meeting would still go on and it would still take its decisions which will affect the greater part of Western Europe and affect us in our daily lives. But we would not be there to take a share in those decisions. That really would not be a sensible way to go about protecting our interests or our influence in Europe and the world. But to be there as a member of the Community, in my view, would be an effective use of our contribution of sovereignty. . . .

Surely we must consider the consequences of staying out. We cannot delude ourselves that an early chance would be given us to take the decision again . . . tonight when this House endorses this Motion many millions of people right across the world will rejoice that we have taken our rightful place in a truly United Europe.

The House divided: Ayes 356, Noes 244.

(Extracted from *House of Commons Debates*, 5th Ser., Vol. 823, Col. 912 ff.)

1.6 Who Do We Think We Are?
PATRICK O'DONOVAN

Like the sound of gunfire on the other side of the hills, the British crisis is a threat that has not yet been realised. You cannot sleep quite easy through the rumble nor ignore the flashes in the night sky. But we cannot ignore the threat with the aid of the old sleeping pills. The prospect of the Common Market compels us to a decision that, in many ways, is more important than deciding to go to war. War, when it comes, is at least made easy by tradition and inflamed emotion. But this is a cold and calculated decision that could change the nature of our being. And what that being is is an essential part of the controversy.

For so great a contest, the manner of disputation is odd and almost irresponsible. It is said that most of the British are against joining and yet believe we shall join in the end. The economics are too contradictory and each citizen can find an expert to back his prejudice. The real dispute goes deeper; it touches our separateness, our sovereignty, our suspicion of foreigners and the fact that one day we may have to defer to them as we do to one another in our polity. There is a suggestion that the Common Market represents a humiliation and a spoiling of the noblest and most gentle political tradition that has existed in Christendom. The Common Market is in name and nature un-English. But what is this Englishry that extends its wings over at least three other equally nervous nations?

In appraising ourselves, all praise is suspect. We could say that our modern history, say since James II threw the Great Seal into the Thames, has been of a comparative serenity: the Gordon riots as against the Paris Commune: the horrors of our industrial revolution against the mass deportations of Russia's modernisation: the tragedy of Ulster against the ferocities in Algeria.

We are not the most beautiful, nor the richest, nor the most polite, nor even the funniest society in the world. It is true that we seldom kill one another except in the desperation of family or sexual extremes. We suspect patriotism and regard nationalism as a disease of State puberty through which less fortunate people have to go to reach that maturity where there is no longer excitement at the waving of a flag.

We allow ourselves to love this country only secretly, but sometimes with that love that an individual can feel for another. The loyalty that the four nations which make up Britain feel both for their separate entities and for the whole is powerful and mainly inexpressible—but according to the opinion polls a majority of us would like to quit these islands and start again almost anywhere else. So what has happened?

It is more than the fact that we have lost an empire and not yet found a role. We are teased, rather than torn, by uncertainties. With all its many imperfections life in Britain is not too bad. But, for the first time in centuries, we do not know quite who we are. We do not know our place in the hierarchy of the world. We do not know if we are a rich nation or poor. We are not even sure if we are happy or not. It is not surprising that protest in Britain is usually peripheral, inconstant and incoherent.

Part of the trouble, I think, is that Britain has been the happy victim of one of the most potent myths in history. The truth or falsity of a myth is not the whole question. Myths are as potent as armies and indeed successful armies are usually animated by them. They are as real in their own way as a battle fleet.

The particular British myth is based on the fact that our history in the last two centuries or so has been singularly fortunate, that a rare national unity has made a series of ancient but constantly evolving political institutions work brilliantly well and that, in consequence, the outstanding characteristic of British life compared with that of other nations has been its success.

This fact has been reinforced by the hazy island syndrome. Because we are separate we must be different. The mainland may know something of pleasure; but real virtue and practically live on our side of the water.

Pure military glory has played only a small part in all this. We have no Valmy. Waterloo is suspect. Our forces have been ordered by gentlemen on a part-time basis and they have not been all that successful in continental adventures. But we have always in recent centuries managed to keep the others out. Our history has, therefore, been seen as one of almost effortless success.

The national myth was firmly enthroned in the nineteenth century through our possession of an empire which, we believed, had been acquired almost accidentally. According to the myth, the motive of duty took precedence over that of greed. But it is a fact that this vast empire was policed with only a handful of troops: vast tracts of Asia and Africa were kept peaceful with a minimum of atrocities and war. We believe that these lands were efficiently administered with a unique brand of selfless integrity. This experience of empire, part fact part myth, was powerful enough to give the British poor a sense of innate superiority and a feeling of great certitude to the largest middle class in the world.

The British myth is still not quite dead. It made the Commonwealth Division in the Korean war different from any other. It produced a possibly unique success in the counter-insurgent operations in Malaya. It is behind the feeling today that Britain has a special responsibility to help in East Pakistan, not because we had sinned there in the past, but because we have an inherited duty in that part of the world.

Now, time and experience have sadly eroded the British myth. Today success appears to elude us. There is little left that is special to us. We are in the painful process of reconstructing ourselves, not out of choice but of necessity. Rather like the Roman Church, Britain is living out a quiet agony, but seldom admits as much.

Meanwhile other people are forming new conceptions of us. Of late we have been flattered by the number of discriminating foreigners, often Americans, who choose to live in this country. We begin to preen ourselves on our Quality of Life. It is almost as if, like St. Francis, the British had chosen to avoid worldly success and concentrate only on what really matters. Of course, no such conscious choice has been made; but it looks as if we are back to Shakespeare's demi-paradise idea. If that is how we are going to view ourselves, it will at least be more fruitful than the lacerating self-contempt of the past few years—which was, no doubt, a necessary part of the process of change. We may even be able publicly to like ourselves again.

Part of the proud old British view of ourselves was that we were insensitive and inartistic. That has completely vanished, to be replaced by its bohemian opposite. We live now, as it were, between myths. So we have an opportunity to appraise ourselves, to discard and to adopt. If we are already in the middle of a process of finding a new identity, the decision to join the Common Market will compel another, deeper revision.

We are a complicated people, both in origin and behaviour. We are more pompous, but less boastful, than most. We pride ourselves on our commonsensical pragmatism, but are probably the most frivolously-minded people in the world. We can be startlingly self-critical and yet, at bottom, approve of ourselves. We appear to have behaved in the past with instinctive wisdom, but now we feel as short-sighted as gamblers in knowing what are our long-term interests. We have a great load of history, even if we wear it lightly. To discover who we have been and what we want to be now is perhaps our most urgent need.

(Extracted from *The Observer*, 20 June 1971.)

1.7 A French View of British Entry
PIERRE DROUIN

What will tomorrow's Europe be like now that the negotiations between Britain and the Six are over and supposing that the House of Commons votes in favour? This is the question that will feed the commentaries for a long time to come. The exercise is fascinating because there are many variables. People's imaginations are greatly excited by this virgin page in the life of the EEC, and the moving forces of economics and politics will be obliged to adopt a new order.

The uncertainties are at least as great in this affair as they were before the signature of the Treaty of Rome. Who would have had the presumption to say, with some scientific solemnity, how the Six would gell and where exactly the operation would lead? Many counted on faith to overthrow the mountain of difficulties. Others described, sometimes apocalyptically, the dangers France was exposing herself to, particularly her industry, by accepting to play the game of the Six.

In this respect nothing has changed. Some see the arrival of the British, Irish, Danes and Norwegians as a new chance for Europe and wager that the enlarged community will find a new equilibrium, a greater autonomy and, at the same time, will enable those who live there to make their voices heard louder in the world. Others already fear breaking up of community constructions, with the wind from the Atlantic blowing through every crack.

Before making forecasts, it is necessary to see clearly in what conditions Britain will enter the Common Market. Not only have the British accepted the fundamental charter of the Six, the Treaty of Rome, but also every decision taken since by the Ministerial Councils whose two achievements are, for the past, the Common Agricultural Policy and, for the future, the building in a decade of an economic and monetary union.

The fundamental character of the EEC is thus preserved. The Six have had to renounce none of their principles, their programmes or their structures to make room for the British.

Thus the British Government has been obliged, despite the cost, to accept the concept of community preference for agricultural produce which implies that food for preference be bought in the

EEC, or that otherwise the famous tax known as 'levies' should be imposed.

To build an economic and monetary union with the other member countries, Britain will have to undress the pound, free it of its status of reserve currency, that is to say progressively liberate it from the famous sterling balances. It is permissible for those who suspect the English of dark designs to say that they are making promises which do not really commit them. In such a perspective London could make the same point about the Six, concerning future arrangements for sugar where the interested countries have not been offered precise guarantees but only the conclusion of a commercial agreement or the status of association.

Everything is possible, even the worst, if the waves of mutual distrust spread out. But sweeping away the accusations on both sides one does not see why the enlarged EEC should not have the same idiosyncracies as the 'little Europe'. When that is said, by the nature of things, the face of Europe of 10 will necessarily not be the same as that of the EEC today.

The centre of gravity of community Europe will shift towards the north-west—and more precisely towards countries with a strong maritime tradition. It is normal that, thanks to this, article 18 of the Treaty of Rome should find a new brightness.

The article states: 'Member states hereby declare their willingness to contribute to the development of international commerce and for the reduction of barriers of trade by entering into reciprocal and mutually advantageous arrangements directed to the reduction of customs duties below the general level, which they could claim as a result of the establishment of a customs union between themselves.'

All those who believe in an opening on the outside world, to the benefit of competition and the great stirring up of men, of ideas and of goods will thus see, in the arrival of the new members of the Common Market, a new chance for its glory. Everything that shrinks into itself leads to decadence. The extension of international solidarity is, on the contrary, a factor of civilisation.

The institutional side of the new community will be much more complicated. The work of the two key organs, the council and the commission, will evidently be burdened—six are more comfortable than ten round a conference table. It will therefore be necessary very quickly to find supply procedures to prevent choking.

But another theme is more important. The cards of a game whose rules were laid down fourteen years ago are to be dealt anew. Will not the chancelleries be tempted in certain circumstances to return to the games of the nineteenth century? Combinations of French and British, German-British or Anglo-German might thus come into being more or less spontaneously following the problems raised perhaps complicated by alliances between 'small countries' against certain 'axes'. If such dance figures were organised, the enterprise would not get far. One must hope that the dangers of completely upsetting the organisation will stop Governments tempted to adopt such methods in time.

Whatever the procedures, the enlargement of the Common Market implies in any case a reinforcement of the collective 'desire to live', that is to say the elaboration at Community level of more and more important decisions hitherto taken at the National level.

(Extracted from *The Times*, 25 June 1971.)

1.8 A Charter for Europe's Future

[*This is the preamble to the Communiqué issued after the Paris Summit meeting in October 1972. The full Communiqué presents in greater detail a set of aims with a timetable leading to a united Europe by 1980.*]

The heads of State or of Government of the countries of the enlarged Community, meeting for the first time on October 19 and 20 in Paris, at the invitation of the President of the French Republic, solemnly declare:

* At the moment when enlargement, decided in accordance with the rules in the Treaties and with respect for what the six original member states have already achieved, is to become a reality and to give a new dimension to the Community;
* At a time when world events are profoundly changing the international situation;
* Now that there is a general desire for détente and co-operation in response to the interest and the wishes of all peoples;

* Now that serious monetary and trade problems require a search for lasting solutions that will favour growth with stability;
* Now that many developing countries see the gap widening between themselves and the industrial nations and claim with justification an increase in aid and a fairer use of wealth;
* Now that the tasks of the Community are growing, and fresh responsibilities are being laid upon it, the time has come for Europe to recognise clearly the unity of its interests, the extent of its capacities and the magnitude of its duties; Europe must be able to make its voice heard in world affairs, and to make an original contribution commensurate with its human, intellectual and material resources. It must affirm its own views in international relations, as befits its mission to be open to the world and for progress, peace and co-operation.

To this end:

(i) The member states reaffirm their determination to base the development of their Community on democracy, freedom of opinion, the free movement of people and of ideas and participation by their peoples through their freely elected representatives.

(ii) The member states are determined to strengthen the Community by establishing an economic and monetary union, the guarantee of stability and growth, the foundation of their solidarity and the indispensable basis for social progress, and by ending disparities between the regions;

(iii) Economic expansion is not an end in itself. Its first aim should be to enable disparities in living conditions to be reduced. It must take place with the participation of all the social partners. It should result in an improvement in the quality of life as well as in standards of living. As befits the genius of Europe, particular attention will be given to intangible values and to protecting the environment so that progress may really be put at the service of mankind;

(iv) The Community is well aware of the problem presented by continuing underdevelopment in the world. It affirms its determination, within the framework of a world-wide policy towards the developing countries, to increase its effort in aid and technical assistance to the least favoured people. It will take particular account of the concerns of those countries towards which, through geography, history and the commitments entered into by the Community, it has specific responsibilities;

(v) The Community reaffirms its determination to encourage the development of international trade. This determination applies to all countries without exception.

The Community is ready to participate as soon as possible, in the open-minded spirit that it has already shown, and according to the procedures laid down by the IMF (International Monetary Fund) and the GATT (General Agreement on Tariffs and Trade) in negotiations based on the principle of reciprocity. These should make it possible to establish, in the monetary and commercial fields, stable and balanced economic relations, in which the interests of the developing countries must be taken fully into account.

(vi) The Member States of the Community, in the interests of good neighbourly relations which should exist among all European countries whatever their régime, reaffirm their determination to pursue their policy of *détente* and of peace with the countries of Eastern Europe, notably on the occasion of the conference on security and co-operation in Europe, and the establishment on a sound basis of a wider economic and human co-operation;

(vii) The construction of Europe will allow it, in conformity with its ultimate political objectives, to affirm its personality while remaining faithful to its traditional friendships and to the alliances of the member states, and to establish its position in world affairs as a distinct entity determined to promote a better international equilibrium, respecting the principles of the Charter of the United Nations. The member states of the Community, the driving force of European construction, affirm their intention to transform before the end of the present decade the whole complex of their relations into a European Union.

(Extracted from Cmnd. 5109, HMSO, London, 1972.)

SECTION 2

The Institutions and the Political Process

2.1 Introduction

After a brief outline of the Communities' institutions this section concentrates on the political process—the way in which policy is shaped and decisions are reached. The political process is complex in any organisation or government. It is especially so in the European Communities. In the first place, policy making and decisions are shared between national Governments and Community institutions. The extract from David Coombes' book (pp. 58–66) shows how a relationship has emerged in which claims to authority and power have been initiated, challenged and counter-challenged. The situation is never fixed. Practices and procedures emerge which are modified in the light of changing circumstances. To understand the process we have to compare formal claims to authority (and these may be in dispute) with the developments that have, in fact, taken place.

While Coombes deals with the political process in general terms, the extract from Stephen Holt's book (pp. 66–74) outlines a particular situation—the classic confrontation in 1965, when de Gaulle's French Government refused to accept proposals put forward by the Commission. This confrontation, which for a time appeared to threaten the whole future of the Communities, was centred upon the key issues of the rights and powers of a particular member in relation to the Community as a whole. The question had been put—'what sort of Europe lay ahead; an association of separate states, or a Community with a common will and identity?' The question could not clearly be answered then or now, but the confrontation left an important mark on the way policies and decisions are reached.

Holt concludes that after 1965, in a 'trial of strength the ultimate power lies not just with the member Governments but with any single Government' (p. 73). But it is not often that there is a situation in which *ultimate power* is being exercised so that normally there is not just one clear answer to the question, 'Who takes the decisions?' A range of factors has to be taken into account—the interests and strength of feeling of the national Government, the personalities

51

involved, the resources required and available, the nature of the decisions, the involvement of pressure groups, the Commissioners' viewpoint, etc. Given that there is this complexity, Lindberg and Scheingold, in the short extract from their book (pp. 78–92) attempt to identify the critical factors required to gain acceptance for a major policy within the Communities. They do this by examining the fate of the agriculture and transport policies. Here they are interested not in the content of the policies but the nature of the process which explains why one was successfully implemented while the other was not. They stress, for example, the importance of the demand for action both inside and outside the institutions of the Communities, the matching of interests between the Commissioners and the member Governments, the activities of pressure groups, and the role of political leadership.

The complexity of the political process plus the technical nature of much of the Communities' business helps to explain why the accusation is often made that the Communities are dominated by bureaucrats. The title of Richard Norton-Taylor's article—'Mountains of Bureaucracy'—strikes a sympathetic chord in many hearts. He mentions, for example, that four years after the announcement of Mansholt's plan to modernise agriculture, a majority of Italian farmers who were questioned had not heard of it. Such examples are legion, but in examining them and the emotive way they are presented, we must beware of journalistic licence and exercise caution. After all, the size of the Communities' bureaucracy is not large in terms of national Governments. In 1972 the EEC in Brussels employed about 5,000 people, or roughly one-third the number of civil servants in the Department of Trade and Industry in London.*

If the Communities have a bureaucratic stamp, it is there not because of the size of the bureaucracy, but because of the nature of the institutions and the political process.

The final piece in this section is concerned with the future. Four Commissioners give their views about the future role of the Commission. Naturally one would anticipate some difference of opinion between them, but perhaps not as much as emerges here. They hold quite diverse views about the future relationships they would like to see emerge. There is controversy not only about *what is* but also about *what should be*.

* Roger Berthoud, 'The Meeting Place of Ideas and Reality', *The Times*, 7 September 1972.

2.2 Community Institutions

The major Community institutions are:

* the thirteen-man executive Commission;
* the Council of Ministers which is composed of ministers from the nine member countries and which meets several times a month;
* the European Parliament, with largely consultative powers, made up of members of national parliaments;
* the Court of Justice to which disputes under the treaty can be referred.

Other Community bodies are:

* the Economic and Social Committee, the General Consultative Committee of Euratom and other specialised committees which are consulted during the policy-making process;
* the European Investment Bank, which helps to finance development projects in less favoured regions of the Community.

The Commission

Composition

* thirteen members, two from each of Britain, France, Germany and Italy, one from each of Belgium, the Netherlands, Luxembourg, Denmark and Ireland;
* Commissioners are appointed by the members for four-year, renewable terms, with the President and Vice-President holding office for two-year, renewable terms;
* each Commissioner is responsible for one or more of the main Community activities; legal affairs, economic and financial policy, external relations, industrial affairs, research and technology, agriculture, development aid, anti-trust policy, atomic energy, social affairs, transport and regional policy;
* administration is divided into departments known as Directorates-General, each responsible to a Commission member. These Directorates-General do the preparatory work on any proposals. The bureaucracy consists of about 6,200 people;
* the members are required by the Treaty to perform their duties with complete independence and may neither seek nor accept

instructions from any Government or from any particular interest. The Commission is a collegiate body and is responsible as a group for all its acts.

Functions

* initiation of policy and drafting of detailed measures for its implementation;
* consultation with national experts and interest groups concerned with issues before it;
* formulation of proposals considered to be in best interests of the Community;
* presentation of proposals to the Council of Ministers and mediation between the members to secure agreement.
* implementation of Community policies;
* watchdog of the Community Treaties by overseeing the application of Community acts and decisions by members;
* issuing of regulations, directives and decisions in certain matters such as the day-to-day working of farm policy or the harmonisation of legislation.

The Council

Composition

* for major decisions of overall policy the foreign ministers usually meet as the 'General Council'; on other occasions specialist ministers attend 'Technical Councils' for particular sectors. For example, it is the minister of transport who represents his country's view at a transport session and so on;
* majority voting is the rule for decisions in the Council—with exceptions, defined in the Treaty, when unanimity is required. In fact, the majority vote is rarely used; member states prefer to find a compromise on which all can agree. Generally, when it is used, the votes are weighted as shown on next page.
   A majority is 41 votes when a vote is taken on the basis of a Commission proposal. If there is no such proposal, the majority is 41 votes from at least 6 countries;
* the ministers present at the Council defend their own country's interests, but seek to arrive at an agreed solution in the Community interest.

Britain	10
France	10
West Germany	10
Italy	10
Belgium	5
Netherlands	5
Denmark	3
Ireland	3
Luxembourg	2
TOTAL	58

Functions

* the decision-making body for practically all major matters covered by the treaties;
* decisions made must be based on proposals from the Commission, except in a few narrowly defined areas;
* to amend a Commission proposal without the consent of the Commission requires a unanimous vote.

The Council can issue:

regulations—(Community laws) are binding on member countries and are directly applicable in the same way as national laws;

directives— are equally binding about what has to be achieved, but leave the national authorities free to decide on the means of carrying them out;

decisions— are binding in every respect on those to whom they are addressed.

recommendations or opinions— which have no binding force.

* As the Council is not in permanent session it has created a new body not allowed for in the original Rome Treaty—the Committee of Permanent Representatives. This consists of the Ambassadors of the nine countries to the Communities. They are advised by committees of national civil servants and are consulted by the Commission at all stages of the policy-making process. The Committee also has the function of preparing for Council sessions, and in practice is often the final level of discussion of Commission proposals. Its existence was formally recognised in

the 1965 Treaty which merged the executives of the three Communities (EEC, ECSC and Euratom).

The European Parliament

Composition

* consists of 198 delegates nominated by and from the national parliaments and not directly elected by the people of the Community:
* Deputies per country:

Britain	36
France	36
West Germany	36
Italy	36
Belgium	14
Netherlands	14
Ireland	10
Denmark	10
Luxembourg	6
TOTAL	198

* members are divided into the following party groupings: Christian Democrats, Socialists, Liberals, Gaullists and the British Conservatives. There are small groups of Italian Communists and Independents.
  These are not national groupings, although the Gaullists and Conservatives may be seen as exceptions.

Functions

* subjects the Community institutions to a degree of democratic control;
* maintains twelve standing committees which discuss the major sectors of Community policy and keep in close contact with the Commission;
* has the power to dismiss the entire Commission by a vote of censure with a two-thirds majority;
* is consulted by and has the power to question the Commission on most major issues. Usually gives its opinions before the Council of Ministers makes a decision. Has no direct veto powers;

* by 1975 the Parliament will have some real say over the flexible part of the annual budget—administrative and information expenses—to add to its present power to propose increases in the budget which must be agreed by the Council.

The Court of Justice

Composition

* consists of nine judges appointed by the member Governments.

Functions

* ensures the observance of law and justice in the application and interpretation of Community rules;
* is the supreme arbiter on all legal questions falling within the scope of the Treaties;
* deals with disputes between members, and between members and Community institutions;
* hears appeals brought by member countries, the Commission, the Council or any individual regarding matters covered by the Treaties;
* binds the member countries, the Community institutions and all individuals by its decisions;
* decides by majority verdict, but dissenting opinions are not publicised;
* has heard cases in most of the main areas of Community policy, between individuals, firms and the Community institutions, and has ruled on the validity of interpretations of Community rules thus establishing a corpus of case law.

Other Bodies

* the Economic and Social Committee meets eight times a year and contains representatives of unions, employers and so-called 'general interest' groups—professions, agriculture, universities, etc. It has a right to be consulted before decisions are made in certain policy areas;
* the Consultative Committee of the European Coal and Steel Community consists of steel producers, trades unionists and a mixed group of coal and steel users and merchants. It meets monthly, and its views have considerable weight;
* the General Consultative Committee of Euratom acts as an

important indicator to the Commission of how far the various member Governments are likely to accept its proposals on research and nuclear affairs;

* there are many other committees, particularly in the fields of economics and finance, the two most important being the Monetary Committee, the only one set up by the Treaty of Rome, and on which the Treaty confers a special advisory role, and the Central Bank Governors Committee.

(Compiled by Robert Masterton.)

2.3 The Political Process
DAVID COOMBES

In a chapter entitled 'The Decision-Making Process' Coombes examines first the powers of the Commission. He states that two essential characteristics of the Commission are:
(a) *that it is 'independent'—i.e. it must treat 'the views of each of the member states with equal respect'; and*
(b) *'European' in that 'it must discern the common interest clearly and accurately and promote it energetically'.*
Then he gives five constitutional powers of the Commission.
   1. To initiate Community legislation.
   2. To implement Community legislation.
   3. To act as a technical and advisory body (e.g. it may help with joint studies and research into common problems).
   4. To act as a diplomatic representative of the Community.
   5. To act as the conscience of the Community ('The Commission can be said to have a general responsibility for "filling out" the provisions of the treaty, for constantly reminding the other parts of the Community of its fundamental objective, and for suggesting new paths for the Community to follow.')

Coombes continues:

From a mere list of these constitutional powers it is now clear that the Commission has a variety of formal duties. It is also clear immediately that they call for different kinds of attitude on the part of the Commission and that they require different degrees of legitimacy for their effective performance. In acting as the conscience of the Community and initiating Community legislation, the Commission seems to be represented in its 'European' guise, as a protagonist of the common interest. As honest broker, on the other hand, it is seen as being strictly 'independent'. Similarly, it demands far less political authority to act as a diplomatic representative of the Community, or as a technical and advisory service, than to act as conscience of the Community. Moreover, implementing Community legislation is quite a different function from initiating it. Although the implementing power gives the Commission some direct executive authority in particular fields of Community activity, this is only within limits prescribed and defined by the Treaties or according to rules laid down by the Council of Ministers: 'Only in a limited sense does the Commission have the margin of decision in changing circumstances that is normally the prerogative of the executive branch of government.'[1]

Yet the fact remains that some of the formal powers bestowed upon the Commission imply a role similar to that of the typical executive branch of government. It is interesting, however, that many other powers normally regarded as vital to the Government of a national state are absent. The Commission (like the Community as a whole), has no powers in fields such as foreign affairs or defence, and has no right to the use of force internally or externally. It has no power to *approve* Community legislation (as this rests with the Council of Ministers). As far as the European Economic Community is concerned, the Commission has as yet no power to raise revenue from an independent source of finance. The Commission cannot appeal for support to any majority in a directly elected Parliament nor to any majority of a general electorate; nor can it hold referenda for the same purpose. Its members are appointed by the Governments of the member States and their term of office is renewable every four years.

The Commission's responsibility to be European would itself seem to demand some degree of legitimate authority which was independent of the member States. The word 'supranational' is used in the Treaty of the Coal and Steel Community to describe the character of the High Authority,[2] but the expression does not reappear in the Treaty of Rome. All the same, in the case of the EEC, the Commission still shares many of the 'supranational' characteristics of the

High Authority—namely the independence of its members as prescribed by the Treaty, and its obligation to pursue the 'common interest'; the fact that it is endowed with formal powers of its own and not simply entrusted with functions by the member States;[3] and, finally, the direct incidence of its powers over the people living in the member countries. On the other hand, its lack of power to make decisions on its own on all the most important questions, and its lack of an independent source or revenue (in theory temporary, but in practice persistent), limit the sense in which the term 'supranational' can be applied to the Commission.[4]

Without getting too involved in these problems at the purely legalistic level, we can conclude with some certainty, as a result of this review of the formal powers of the Commission, that the latter is designed only as a partly executive or 'supranational' body.

It is indeed extremely difficult to come to any satisfactory conclusions in the language of constitutional law regarding this extraordinary and complex institutional framework of decision-making. Reactions vary from claims that it is a refreshing departure from antique methods of Parliamentary government, unsuited as these are to the technical twentieth century,[5] to dismissal of the whole system as a Europe of offices. The supreme legislative decision-making body of the Community is, without doubt, the Council of Ministers, but even the Council refuses to fit ordinary constitutional classifications. Strictly speaking, it is neither a legislative nor an executive body, for it consists simply of ministers representing their respective governments and has no means of implementing Community legislation.[6] The main principle of the system seems to be that the agreement of the Governments must be obtained before any major action is taken. Meanwhile, this is subject to the important qualification that the Governments should reject the conclusions reached by the Commission as to the desirability of such action only for the strongest possible reasons. This is what is implied by the Commission's right to initiate legislation and by the obligation of the Council to amend the Commission's proposals only by a unanimous vote.[7] Thus Community legislation results from a kind of dialogue between the Commission, on the one hand, and the member Governments as represented in the Council on the other.

The member Governments or their representatives are as we shall see also closely involved in the implementation of Community legislation as well as in achieving most of the more general goals of the

Community not so clearly articulated in the Treaty of Rome. The Commission may act alone only when it implements certain technical and rather detailed aspects of the Community laws and, in all the more important of such cases, there exists some provision for the intervention of national representatives. Even where no such special provision has been made, the Permanent Representatives and their staff act as national 'watchdogs', and the Commission often finds it necessary to consult them on its own initiative when it exercises its delegated powers.[8] Thus, the decision-making process of the Community consists essentially of an interaction between the Commission and the representatives of the Governments of the member States.

The Process of 'Engrenage'

The successful way in which the Commission has utilised this interaction to bring about progress towards Community objectives has been celebrated by most authors on Community institutions. In practice a key element is the process called '*engrenage*', a more or less untranslatable word, meaning in this context 'meshing' or 'interlocking'. This process consists in the crudest terms in the Commission engaging national ministers and, particularly, civil servants in the decision-making process of the Community. As one commentator puts it:

'In searching for the main key to the fulfilment of the mission consigned to it, the EEC Commission unhesitatingly singled out above all else the development of relations and collaboration with the national administrations.'[9] Another writer describes the involvement of national representatives as the 'keystone of the Commission's tactics'.[10]

The most significant way in which representatives of the Governments have been involved up to now is in the performance of two major functions entrusted to the Commission, namely, the drawing up of proposals for submission to the Council of Ministers, and the engineering of agreement between member States in the Council. But as we have already pointed out, Government representatives are involved in the exercise of practically all the Commission's tasks. Already by 1962 one of the writers already quoted declared that 'the involvement of government officials in the integration process has been carried to an extent that few could have foreseen', and that 'a vast bureaucratic system is developing involving thousands of national and Community officials in a continuous decision-making process'.[11] The same author estimated that in any one year just under 18,000 officials might participate in all the committees and working groups meeting before and after the Commission submits its proposals to the Council of Ministers. The Committee of Permanent Representatives itself was serving 'more and more as a clearing house for an expanding coterie of specialised committees, reserving for itself only matters of general, or essentially political, importance'.[12] There are now at least twenty or so permanent specialised groups working under this Committee, and numerous *ad hoc* groups are set up from time to time on particular issues. The Committee itself cannot, of course, formally decide any matter other than its own procedure, and cannot take the place of the Council of Ministers in the legislative process. In practice, however, the quantity of decisions to be taken is so great and the proceedings of the Council are so congested that the role of the Committee has had to be greatly expanded. In order to ease congestion at meetings of the Council itself it has been found necessary to adopt a procedure by which a number of technical and detailed matters can be agreed by the Committee of Permanent Representatives, placed on the Council's agenda as 'Points A', and taken as read by the Ministers, unless some member State or the Commission requests a discussion. In 1964, out of thirty-six sessions of the Council, 138 questions were so treated out of a total of 192. The Committee now meets more or less on a regular basis, except during periods when Community business is slight. The Commission has come to approve of this expanded role of the Permanent Representatives and has even encouraged it. Regular weekly meetings are held between the President of the Commission and the Chairman of the Committee 'to exchange information and impressions on important current or future business, to discuss difficulties and possible solutions, and where appropriate to co-ordinate the efforts which the Chairman of the Committee and the Commission will make in their respective fields to bring about any necessary decisions'.[13]

In many ways, however, the growth in importance of the Committee might be regarded as a challenge to the Commission's right of initiative and as a threat to undermine the 'European' element in Community decision-making. The same fear arises with regard to the Commission's consultation of national experts in the preparatory stage of its proposals. The Secretary-General of the Commission has written in this latter respect:

'These experts do not formally commit their governments but, as they are informed of the interests and opinions of the latter, they perform a useful function in guiding the Commission in its search for solutions that are technically accurate and generally acceptable to the six Governments.'[14] How far should the Commission go, however, at such an early stage in the decision-making process in seeking solutions of this kind? At least one author suspects that the consultations must sometimes 'degenerate' into negotiations, because the experts are generally the same people who will later give their advice to their own Governments when the latter come to decide on the Commission's proposals.[15] How far, at a later stage in the process, should the Commission amend its proposals to the Council as a result of what takes place at meetings of the Permanent Representatives and their staff? These are representatives of national Governments, not of the Community, and they are civil servants, not ministers.

On the other hand, the strategy of *engrenage* reflects accurately the 'functionalist' approach which produced the Treaty itself and it satisfies two basic needs of the Commission. In the first place, the Commission feels obliged to draw up proposals which have the greatest possible chance of being accepted in the Council of Ministers. Any failure of the Commission in this regard might seriously retard the development of the Community. At the same time, as we have already seen, it is obliged to act as an honest broker among the interests of the member States. In this respect, the Commission behaves very much like any international secretariat, inventing proposals which are designed to bring about compromise between different national interests. The involvement of national officials at an early stage is partly a way of cutting corners towards such compromise, and co-operation with the Permanent Representatives is seen simply as a means of facilitating progress in the Council of Ministers.

At the same time, the *engrenage* is seen by the Commission as a means of fulfilling another major obligation, that of acting as a champion of the common interest, which it seeks to do in this case by infecting national officials with the European idea. The Permanent Representatives, for example, have a dual role: they act as national envoys to the Community, but also in a certain sense as Community representatives and spokesmen in their own capitals. Most of them have served for quite long periods in Brussels; (anything from five to eight years in some cases). Moreover, the regularity and frequency of formal and informal contact between the staff or the Commission and the Permanent Representatives, as well as with other national officials, is now so great that all commentators attest to the way the latter have come to identify with the Community in spite of their basically national loyalty. In addition, contact between the different national administrations of the Six has been intensified as a result of the Community so that already by 1963 it was no longer 'necessary for contacts . . . to be channelled through the Ministries of Foreign Affairs and the other appropriate Ministries: "We just pick up the phone."'[16] In this respect the Commission acts in a kind of proselytising role, taking responsibility for more than just engineering compromise, and seeking to get the agreement of the Governments to measures involving further integration. In this it behaves less like a normal international secretariat and far more like a promotional group, or even a political party with a firmly rooted ideology. The immediate object is presumably to ensure that proposals which have a strongly European element can be accepted by the Council of Ministers.

The *engrenage* is not, however, confined to national civil servants and ministers. The Commission has also taken positive steps to involve official representatives of socio-economic groups in the decision-making process. In one sense the Commission might be seen as acting rather like a Federal Government seeking to assert the public interest against sectional interests (in this case, the member States), by means of mobilising the support of the general public (in this case, social and economic interests in the member countries). A Federal Government could set about this by appealing to the people by whom it was elected in the States themselves, or by rallying its supporters in the federal Parliament, and thus vaunting its legitimacy. The Commission cannot do this, as it does not derive this kind of support from the people in the member countries. On the other hand, it usually consults Community federations of the main national interest groups even before it consults national civil servants and it has, as we have already seen, sought to pursue an active policy of informing the public and of maintaining direct relations with the press and other mass media.

It also has the European Parliament. The Commission can rely on the Parliament's support at almost all times and, as we have seen, the Parliament has to be asked for its opinion on proposals which the Commission submits to the Council on almost all occasions where such submission is provided for in the Treaty. However, the support of the Parliament is not a very effective sanction since the latter is not directly representative of the people in the member States and is, moreover, widely regarded as having a built-in pro-European composition. The Parliament is usually critical of the Commission only when it feels that the latter has put forward proposals which are insufficiently European. Thus, the main use made of the Parliament by the Commission is as a sounding board for its policies and proposals before the member States or their representatives on the Council have committed themselves. This tactic of canvassing support for its proposals before decision by the Council is regarded as an important guarantee that the European view will not get submerged in negotiations with national officials. . . .

[*Coombes completes the chapter by outlining two different theses which attempt to answer the question 'How far does the process of* engrenage *compromise the Commission's role as a source of European initiative?'*]

References

1. R. Mayne, *The Institutions of the European Community*, PEP, Chatham House, London, 1968, p. 28.
2. Treaty Establishing the European Coal and Steel Community, Article 9.
3. P. Reuter, *La Communauté Européenne du Charbon et de l'Acier*, Paris, Librairie Générale de Droit et de Jurisprudence, 1953, pp. 138–40.
4. R. Lemaignen, *L'Europe au Berceau*, Paris, Plon, 1964, pp. 105–6.
5. Ibid., pp. 100–102.
6. Mayne, op. cit., pp. 29–35.
7. Lemaignen, op. cit., p. 103.
8. For example, in interpreting its powers under Regulation 86 concerning competition between enterprises and in deciding whether violations of the Treaty of Rome have occurred: see L. Lindberg, *The Political Dynamics of European Economic Integration*, Oxford University Press, Oxford, 1963, p. 58.
9. A. Spinelli, *The Eurocrats. Conflict and Crisis in the European Community*, Johns Hopkins Press, Baltimore, USA, 1966, p. 71.

10. Lindberg, op. cit., p. 53.
11. Lindberg, op. cit., p. 62.
12. Ibid., p. 60.
13. E. Noel, 'The Committee of Permanent Representatives', *Journal of Common Market Studies*, Vol. V, no. 3, 1967, pp. 219–51.
14. Ibid.
15. P.-H. J. M. Houben, *Les Conseils de ministres des communautés européennes*, Sithoff, Leyden, 1964, p. 99.
16. Lindberg, op. cit., p. 84.

(*Politics and Bureaucracy in the European Community*, PEP/George Allen and Unwin, London, 1970.)

2.4 Policy-Making in Practice — The 1965 Crisis

STEPHEN HOLT

The Boycott

At the end of June 1965, the alleged irresistible force met the immovable object and the two basically divergent points of view about the directions in which the Common Market should move collided.

The overriding consideration governing the timing of the dispute as far as France was concerned was the uncomfortable proximity of 1 January 1966—the date when, under the Treaty, majority voting in the Council of Ministers was due to enter into force *automatically*.

If France had waited to bring about a crisis until *after* she had actually been outvoted on some issue, she might have been placed in an untenable legal position on the issue in question. Much better, therefore, to get the argument settled on a general level rather than getting involved in a specific and perhaps complicated issue.

Although the details of the dispute are in one sense trivial a number of points of principle were involved and we need therefore to go over them briefly. There is a sense also in which the whole argument was the 'last straw that broke the camel's back'.*

* The following account owes a great deal to the excellent and full description of the crisis by John Lambert in *The Journal of Common Market Studies*, Vol. IV, no. 3, May 1966.

One of the Common Market's signal achievements since 1958 has been its progress in the difficult field of agriculture. The French can justifiably claim credit for having forced the pace considerably and the result has been that free trade in agricultural products will be a reality by 1 July 1968. The consequence of this, however, is that all duties (in agriculture, levies) will have been abolished between Member Countries and levies will only be imposed on goods coming from outside the Six. It would seem unsatisfactory, therefore, that German imports coming through the port of Rotterdam should pay duties to the Netherlands and not to Germany. When there is a common external tariff and no internal barriers for manufactured and agricultural goods, the question of to whom the product of customs duties belongs and who shall dispose thereof cannot be long delayed. It was to this question of 'direct sources of Community revenue' that the Commission turned its attention early in 1965.

After the fixing of Common Cereal prices in December 1964, the accompanying financial regulations had been left over and the Commission had been asked to produce proposals for these prior to the expiry of the old regulations on 30 June 1965. The Common Cereal prices agreed in December 1964, were not actually due to come into force until 1 July 1967, so strictly speaking temporary regulations covering the interim two-year period were all that were required; an extension, in fact, of the previous arrangement whereby the complicated system of financial support for the Community's farmers comes out of a common fund into which all member States make direct, weighted contributions.*

The Commission decided, however, that it would have to cross the bridge of direct Community revenues sooner or later, and that then would be as good a time as any. Accordingly the proposals put forward by the Commission to cover the financial regulations in agriculture after June 1965, were *linked* with proposals for direct sources of Community revenue to enter into force slowly up to 1972.

During previous discussions in Community circles about direct sources of revenue, anxiety had been expressed about the need to subject the disposal of these large sums to adequate democratic control. The new funds would be outside the control of the national Parliaments because they would belong to the Community; on the other hand, an amendment to the Treaty would be needed to give

* The European Agricultural Guidance and Guarantee Fund.

budgetary powers to the European Parliament. If the national Parliaments were to surrender their control over a large proportion of their countries' funds, their express approval would also be needed, and it was in this connection that the Dutch Parliament threw down the gauntlet. On 2 February 1965, the Dutch Second Chamber *unanimously* adopted a motion part of which reads as follows:

> . . . declares that in its opinion there could be no question, on the occasion of the coming revision of the system of financing the European Agricultural Guidance and Guarantee Fund, of replacing the direct financial contributions of the member States by revenues proper to the Community, in accordance with Article 201 of the Treaty, without a primordial role being attributed to the European Parliament in the budgetary procedure of the EEC.

After this ultimatum, the Commission had either to insist that all the parts of its proposals were treated as one, or abandon the idea of tackling the question of direct sources of Community Revenue for a further two years. It chose the former alternative and presented its outline proposals to the European Parliament on 24 March. The Commission, however, got off on the wrong foot with the French from the outset; the member Governments had not been officially informed and M. Couve de Murville, the French Foreign Minister, arrived at Strasbourg on one of his routine visits and learned of the Commission's proposals from a waiting journalist—a most unhappy beginning, about which more was to be heard. De Gaulle himself has spent most of his political life struggling against the French Parliament and against those who believe it should be a strong body; it now appears that the European Parliament must suffer vicariously. Gaullist France has held out against the moves to have the deputies at Strasbourg directly elected, and she has refused to recognise the change of name from 'The Assembly' to the 'European Parliament', decided by the deputies in March 1962. It was to be expected therefore that France would also oppose any extension in the Parliament's powers.

The Commission sent its final proposals to the Council of Ministers on 1 April and made it clear that all three parts were to be treated as one whole—the temporary arrangements for the following two years, arrangements for direct Community revenue after 1 July 1967 (assuming free trade in agricultural produce by that date) and thirdly the arrangements for strengthening the budgetary powers of the European Parliament.

Hitherto the Parliament has exercised a purely advisory role on the Community's budget and its views are often overruled by the Council; under the procedure proposed by the Commission, the Parliament would be able to make amendments to the draft budget which would be deemed approved unless the Council within twenty days modified them by a five to one majority (each country having only one vote). If on the other hand the Commission agreed with the Parliament, only a four to two majority would be needed in the Council. It was pointed out at the time that these proposals had the effect of strengthening the position not of the Parliament but of the Commission as well. If the Commission could secure the support of the Parliament, the new proposals would make it easier to restore cuts initially made by the Council. Under the present position, the Council can vote the budget by qualified majority, i.e. the disapproval of two of the big powers France, Germany and Italy is enough to prevent passage. One country one vote and a four to two majority would enable the Commission and Parliament to get round this difficulty.

The response to the proposals was generally favourable everywhere, but in Paris there was anger at the Commission's audacity. There was never much prospect of agreement from the outset and deadlock came at the Council Meeting of 30 June. This was the last day of France's six-month occupancy of the chair and at midnight M. Couve de Murville offered to surrender the chair to Italy. However, the usual tradition that the chairmanship does not change in the middle of a meeting was maintained; France's partners may have regretted this when M. Couve de Murville used his position to close the meeting at 2 a.m. although everyone else wanted to go on talking. Major differences of opinion still remained, France, Belgium, Luxembourg and Germany being willing to accept temporary financial arrangements in agriculture for five years, Italy and the Netherlands only being willing to accept this for two years.

The boycott, which affected EEC, ECSC and Euratom, officially began on 6 July when the French Permanent Representative was recalled to Paris. For the next six months France did not attend any meetings of the Councils of Ministers nor any of the working groups and advisory committees that meet under Council auspices; France did, however, send representatives to a number of technical committees like the Management Committees for the various agricultural product groups. Not to have attended these committees would have meant that day-to-day decisions inconvenient to France might have been taken.

All the relevant chairmanships now having passed to Italy, it was decided that all meetings should be held. France was persuaded during this six-month period to take forty decisions *in absentia* by 'written procedure' but of course all the controversial decisions that had to be argued out at full meetings simply piled up.

All the other Community institutions like the Court of Justice, the Commission, the Parliament and the Economic and Social Committee carried on as usual and all attempts by France to settle any of her grievances outside the framework of the EEC were firmly and persistently resisted by her partners. During the October session of the European Parliament, there took place one of the stormiest debates so far and Gaullist deputies who tried to justify the boycott were simply shouted down. Nor did the French Government derive any comfort from the attitude of the various economic interest groups in France and the rest of the Community. In December de Gaulle faced four opponents at the Presidential election all of whom opposed his European policy; it is hard to be sure how much the crisis affected the result of that election, but the issues involved certainly had a full airing during the campaign.

At last in January 1966, the French agreed to meet the other five at Luxembourg in a private session (without the attendance of the Commission) and discuss their differences. The French grievances were in two parts—an unwillingness to accept transition to majority voting in the Council and a list of ten complaints against the behaviour of the Commission.

On majority voting the issue was straightforward: while not asking for the cumbersome process of a treaty amendment, the French nevertheless wanted the member Governments officially to commit themselves never to overrule any country when the *country involved considered* that its 'vital interests' were at stake. To this the other five would not agree, but the following form of words was selected, recording an agreement to differ:

(i) Where, in the case of decisions which may be taken by majority vote on a proposal of the Commission, very important interests of one or more partners are at stake, the Members of the Council will endeavour, within a reasonable time, to reach solutions which can be adopted by all the Members of the Council while respecting their mutual interests and those of the Community, in accordance with Article 3 of the Treaty.

(ii) With regard to the foregoing paragraph, the French delegation considers that where very important interests are at stake the discussion must be continued until unanimous agreement is reached.

(iii) The six delegations note that there is a divergence of views on what should be done in the event of failure to reach complete agreement.

(iv) The six delegations nevertheless consider that this divergence does not prevent the Community's work being resumed in accordance with the normal procedure.

The list of complaints against the Commission is a long one . . . It covers ten points and has come to be known as 'the decalogue'. Five of these points are particularly interesting and are illustrative of the way the Commission has tried to extend its influence and power.

In the first place the French demanded that the Commission should not unveil the tenor of its proposals to the Parliament or the public before they had been officially submitted to the Council. This was designed to stop the Commission building up public and Parliamentary support for some of its more controversial proposals before the Council could vote them down. While it was agreed that the practice would cease, this only applied to the official text of proposals and the Commission can easily get round the difficulty by making much more general 'statements of future policy' to the Parliament. Deputies clearly cannot be expected to exercise parliamentary control over the Commission without these statements.

Secondly, the French complained of the Commission's repeated tendency to ask for wider discretionary powers for themselves but to seek to limit the margin of discretion open to the Government when they had the task of implementing a Community directive. However, since the cure for this particular illness had been and will be in the hands of the Council itself, it seemed hardly fair to blame the Commission and the issue was dropped.

Thirdly, we must mention what has now become known as the 'striped pants clause'; this was the complaint that President Hallstein had been receiving Ambassadors to the Community in a ceremony patterned on the one used in the member States. Seventy-four countries now have diplomatic missions accredited to the Community. As they have arrived the question has naturally arisen of who should receive their credentials. The prerogatives here were officially divided between Council and Commission in 1959 but pressure of work has made it too difficult for the Council President to participate and the task has consequently been left to the Commission. The member States agreed that the Council should resume its share of these duties.

Fourthly, the French demanded that the Commission should observe 'a proper neutrality' about the policies of member Governments, in their public statements. There is nothing in the Treaty which requires this and it is only the French who wish to down-grade the Commission into a purely technical body. While the Commission is not 'party political' in the orthodox sense, it is a political body in the sense that it pursues its own policies which sometimes do not coincide with those of the governments, particularly of France. Several members of the Commission openly denounce the intransigence of particular countries when they are holding up agreement. France has been on the receiving end of this practice most notably during the boycott and during the aftermath of the veto on British entry. At the Luxembourg meeting, the governments agreed that their Chairman should convey verbally the Council's feeling that Commission Members should adopt restraint in their public statements. The Commission have noted this but there is no record or evidence that they have ever *agreed* to discontinue making political speeches.

Mostly this same desire to minimise provocative statements is behind the French complaint about lack of control over the information services, which as far as the EEC is concerned owe their allegiance to the Commission. This question came to a head towards the end of the boycott in December 1965, when the office in The Hague devoted a special double-page feature in one of its issues to a section of anti-Gaullist cartoons from various European newspapers. Although the issue was withdrawn after protests, the French determined that the Community's information policy should in future be decided by co-operation between Council and Commission. The other five countries agreed in principle, leaving the method to be used to be decided later.

After these minimal concessions, and an agreement on a future programme of work, the French Government agreed to resume its participation in the three Communities. In theory, there is no reason why the points that were settled could not have been agreed the day after the crisis began, but if that had happened the most important feature of the crisis would never have occurred, namely the clear demonstration by the French that unless they get their way on what they deem these issues of principle, they are prepared effectively to bring the progress of the Communities to a standstill. Few observers have any doubt that in similar circumstances the French would do it again; the result has been that although the ending of the boycott in January 1966, was hailed as a defeat for France, her five partners and the Commission have taken the point completely. No one wants a painful repetition of this crisis and while the threat remains, the Community is likely to be conducted within the limits that France has set. The passing of 1 January 1966 brought majority voting automatically into force under the Treaty but no one is going to risk using it against France. The most that could happen is that a non-French Chairman of the Council might call a vote on an issue in which his country alone is holding a minority view; the Dutch have talked about doing this, but if it were once tried, the likelihood is that France would, on principle, change sides, cast her four votes alongside the country in the minority and prevent the necessary qualified majority being achieved. The way the votes are weighted at present, this move would be successful in all cases except where the dissenting country was Luxembourg.

The Commission in this episode certainly overreached itself and has had the boundaries of its powers clearly delineated. With the benefit of hindsight it seems that it would have been better to have made some temporary arrangements for extending the financial regulations on agriculture and have let majority voting come into force before getting into a stand-up fight with the French. If majority decisions had first been taken on minor issues, France might have been forced to take her stand on much less favourable ground.

In spite of the range of powers, privileges and natural advantages which the Commission possesses, there can be no doubt that in a trial of strength the ultimate power lies not just with the member Governments but with any single Government. Doubtless Luxembourg could not hold the Community to ransom for long, but any other member Country could, if it chose to, ignore the spirit and the letter of the Treaty.* De Gaulle, for the time being, has won and

* The boycott was without any question a legal infringement of the Treaty of Rome. Article 5 says that 'Member States shall take all measures, whether general

as long as his political position is not undermined at home the trumps are likely to remain in his hand.

(Extracted from *The Common Market: The Conflict of Theory and Practice*, Hamish Hamilton, London, 1971, pp. 69–76.)

2.5 Mountains of Bureaucracy
RICHARD NORTON-TAYLOR

The Common Market machinery turns slowly and inefficiently on a pyramid of bureaucracy which, like all bureaucracies, is intent on preserving its authority and on trying to increase it. One of the vital cogs is, of course, the European Commission—staffed by *apatrides* or 'stateless men', as de Gaulle called them.

But the other essential element in the Brussels decision-making process is the Committee of Permanent Representatives comprised of ambassadors who are very much servants of their respective Governments. This committee, Dr. Dahrendorf complained in a controversial article in the West German press exactly a year ago, took decisions on nine out of ten issues that came before it. Ministers who, unlike the diplomats, are accountable to national Parliaments, are left to take one decision out of ten.

As the influence of authority of the Brussels bureaucracy snow-balls, so the authority of national Parliaments is declining. While the European Commission has a watchdog role over national Governments, the European Parliament's control over what happens in Brussels is virtually non-existent.

If the Foreign Office is really intent on pursuing secret diplomacy once the Community is enlarged, it would seem to have a perfect state of affairs already in existence to help it on its way.

But the mountain of Brussels bureaucracy is, as one long-time observer of the scene put it, rather like a huge Gruyère cheese. There

---

or particular, appropriate to ensure the carrying out of the obligations arising out of this Treaty or resulting from the acts of the institutions of the Community. They shall assist the latter in the achievements of its tasks. They shall abstain from any measures which could jeopardise the attainment of the objectives of this Treaty.'

are holes in it out of which leak over-classified documents or indications of a dispute between two or more member countries.

Six member Governments—frequently at odds—and a Commission with occasionally competing departments and ambitious commissioners, use the press and pressure groups for their own ends.
Below them there are a number of civil servants—certainly more than
in a national context—who see it as their duty to inform the press of
Community lobbies precisely because traditional methods of public
accountability are blocked.

All community decisions, whether they concern transport, social,
monetary, state aid or agricultural policy are taken in Brussels by the
EEC institutions. Many of the apparently minor negotiations and
agreements are carried out by officials from national Governments
and the Commission. But a great deal of these—insurance rules,
imports of textiles from overseas, for example—are at least as
important for certain sectors of the economy as the semi-public
annual marathon on the fixing of farm prices.

Community directives are sometimes issued by the Commission
itself; sometimes they have to be ratified by the national Parliaments,
but with the time limit and under the conditions laid down by the
Brussels institutions.

The Vedel report on the future powers of the European Parliament—the bulk of which has been laid to rest—suggested that one
reason for the cumbersome inefficiency of the EEC institutions was
that too many Ministers were playing to their national Parliaments
back home, that their freedom of negotiating manœuvre was limited
because they were always looking over their shoulders.

This may be the case for farm Ministers, whose lobbies are
extremely powerful in every one of the Six. But all too frequently,
EEC ministers present their Parliaments with *faits accomplis*. Vedel's
answer is that a single institution—the European Parliament—should
control Ministers when they are operating in the Community framework. Yet everyone knows this is not for tomorrow.

The role of the press and the role of Parliament varies from one
country to another. Running stories, and even a Community decision
which affects another country, are usually 'relegated' to the economic
pages of the 'quality' press. Sometimes they are ignored altogether.
But the Commission's objections to the Belgian Government's investment aid law earlier this year was splashed over the front pages of
the local press, although it is unlikely that the Commission's ques-

tioning last week of France's regional aid law will get similar treatment.

The French Government frequently treats the Community institutions with nothing short of cynical contempt. The Commission takes France to the European Court of Justice for breaking the rules of Euratom, the Community's nuclear agency, and questions its agreement to buy enriched uranium from Russia—but France quietly agrees to hold behind-the-scenes talks with the Commission and it is extremely difficulty to discover their outcome.

The Commission, the guardian of the Rome Treaty, does not want to lose its credibility, but there is no doubt that each of the Six has succeeded in bending Community rules to defend its national interests.

Given France's 'uncommunitarian' attitude and its attacks against the Community's institutions, it was ironic that President Pompidou decided to hold a referendum on his Government's European policy. It was doubly ironic when the referendum turned out to be a gross political failure.

France's European policy—in the fields of monetary or foreign policy, for example—has little to do with the EEC as seen from Brussels (and one suspects this broader French vision of a 'European Europe' is shared by Mr. Heath, although Britain will want to reform the Common Agricultural Policy which, to France, remains the main *raison d'être* for the Community's existence). The EEC is simply a convenient base on which to build. As France sees it, national sovereignty will be severely threatened if the European Parliament increased its powers, whereas a commitment to narrow exchange rate margins does not affect national sovereignty, if only because France's monetary philosophy traditionally has been based on fixed parities.

The degree to which national sovereignty is affected by the EEC, and the flow of information about policies worked out in Brussels, are related issues. Four years after Dr. Mansholt's plan to modernise agriculture was announced, well over a majority of Italian farmers questioned in a recent poll were unaware of the plan's existence. This was partly because the plan received scant coverage in the Italian press, but, perhaps more significantly, also because the farmers still regard their own Parliament, if not the local mayor, as the source of real authority.

For the first time, this year the German Government decided to present a 'report on European integration' to the Bundestag. The Dutch Parliament receives an annual report on the Government's past and intended EEC policy which is followed by a general debate. In other Community countries, the Government's handling of EEC questions is formally presented during a foreign affairs budget debate. If there is sufficient opposition to the Government record or future programme, a vote can be forced. Similarly an individual minister can be called to question during, for example, a debate on agriculture, or following a major EEC council meeting in Brussels.

But in most cases, a minister does not face his Parliament before he goes to Brussels; and when he returns, Parliament is faced with a *fait accompli*—the minister has bound his Government by negotiating a new agreement with his EEC partners which will form part of Community law.

Unless the minister himself informs Parliament in good time of his reasons for flying to Brussels, Parliament will be in a position to put pressure on the Government before a decision is taken only if it has been informed by the press or by sectorial pressure groups operating on the Community level in the Belgian capital.

Members of the European Parliament are the first to admit this and rely heavily on the press and their own individual contacts in Brussels to use one of the few powers of action open to them: putting written questions to the European Commission. Mr. Vredeling, a Dutch Socialist and one of the most active parliamentarians, frequently refers to press articles in his questions that cover a wide range of subjects from agricultural prices to anti-trust policy to conditions of sulphur miners in Sicily.

There are four important areas where the Commission itself has very real decision-making authority: agricultural trade, industrial competition, State aid and regional policy. But a host of other decisions on car insurance or the grading of eggs, for example, are taken quietly in the top floor offices of the Common Market headquarters.

If Parliament is threatened by the complexity of the growing business of government in a national framework, the same phenomenon will be exaggerated in the EEC framework when Britain joins the Community.

(Extracted from *The Guardian*, 28 July 1972.)

2.6 Agriculture and Transport Policies

LEON LINDBERG and
STUART SCHEINGOLD

Introduction

Agriculture is a story of action and success; transport is a story of inaction and failure. Yet there are many similarities between the two sectors that might lead us to expect more similar outcomes. In both cases the Rome Treaty provisions are relatively brief: eleven articles for transport and ten for agriculture, as compared with twenty-nine for the customs union. There are relatively few specific obligations to be fulfilled and most of these are temporary. Rather, the Treaty sets forth the general goals: 'The common market shall extend to agriculture and to trade in agricultural products . . . (and) shall be accompanied by the establishment of a common agricultural policy . . .', and that 'the objectives of the Treaty shall . . . be pursued by the member states within the framework of a common transport policy.' Some general policy objectives are then specified in each case, but the process of translating these into specific policies and rules is left to the Community's institutions. The Commission is to make proposals for action and the Council is to act on these by a unanimous vote during the first two stages of the transition period, and thereafter by a qualified majority vote. Both areas represent what we termed previously 'an obligation to engage in a joint decision-making process'.

Furthermore, achieving a common Community policy in each area was considered necessary if the general customs union provisions of the treaty were to work effectively.

Farming is of basic importance to the economies of all the six countries . . . and it was unthinkable to remove trade barriers for industrial goods and leave agricultural markets isolated. On the other hand there was no question of merely lowering or removing trade barriers on farm produce, since all the member countries have managed markets more or less heavily protected.[1]

Transport is of course a basic element in any economy, figuring to a large extent in the costs of all goods and of many services.

In 1956 the transport sector accounted for a fifth of the six countries' combined gross national product, and employed 16 per cent of all the workers in the industrial sector. Thus a uniform system of fair and undistorted competition in the transport sector is an indispensable condition for the successful merger of the separate economies in a common market. Equally, the development of the Common Market area as an economic unit depends upon the provision of a unified and adequate transport network.[2]

Not only is the kind of obligation involved in each case different from much of the rest of the treaties, but so is the type of content envisaged. In the case of the general customs union provisions of the EEC, and most of the ECSC Treaty, what is involved for the most part is removing existing obstacles to trade, such as tariffs and quotas, and agreeing not to reimpose them unilaterally. In contrast, agriculture and transport appeared to require the adoption of European-level policies that would apply everywhere in the Community and would replace national legislation. What this represents is a move to a higher degree of economic integration. Economists distinguish four ascending degrees of economic integration: a free trade area, a customs union, a common market and an economic union. As a customs union the EEC already represents a higher degree of integration than a free trade area, because it implies that the member countries not only eliminate internal barriers, but that they also apply a common tariff level in their trade with non-member countries. But the European Community goes further still. It has aspects of both a common market and an economic union. In a common market the members go beyond trade liberalisation to agree to permit factors of production such as labour and capital to move freely. Finally, an economic union

> combines all of the characteristics of a common market with an attempt to remove the stresses and distortions induced by differences in economic policy among the member nations. Consequently, in an economic union, national policies are to some extent coordinated and harmonised.[3]

Thus, achieving a common policy in agriculture and transport would represent the beginnings of an economic union. As such, it was likely to involve far more difficult technical and political problems than the essentially negative customs union and common market provisions. Government controls have been extensive in both areas and have led to very different patterns of public policy from one country to another. Both have had considerable strategic and political significance. Both involve a very large number of small private operators—owners of small farms on the one hand, owners of a single ship or truck on the other. Changes in policy as a result of European level activities are thus likely to affect a great many established interests and traditional ways of doing things.

In spite of these similarities, there could hardly be a greater contrast than between these two areas, as far as Community policy-making is concerned. Agriculture has been the outstanding success story of the European Community, an almost classic example of forward linkages, where a general commitment has activated an intensive political process whereby the scope of common action and the capacities of the institutions have all been increased. Transport, on the other hand, is primarily a dismal story of false starts, of politically inept Commission proposals, of persistent Council inaction, of divided government views and of an apparent drift in the direction of more nationally directed policies.

Explaining the Contrasting Outcomes in Agriculture and Transport

Previously we argued that differences in the ability of the European Community to produce decisions could be explained in terms of variations in the flow of demands and in the leadership available to process them. Our purpose here is to isolate the factors associated with success in agriculture and with failure in transport in order to illuminate the ways in which demand flow and leadership are related to decisions or outcomes that induce growth, that is, to forward linkages. Specifically, we seek to discover how and why the mechanisms of functional spill-over, side payments and log-rolling, actor socialisation and feedback were activated in one case and not in the other. We see this as a first step towards our eventual goal of hypothesising about the general conditions or causes of forward linkage and output failure.

[*Lindberg and Scheingold base their analysis on a 'systems' approach to the study of political organisations. This type of theorising focuses not so much on the actual decisions taken, but on the 'process'—the way the decisions are taken. In this particular case, the emphasis is on the 'flow of demands'—e.g. demands by the Governments that action be taken to produce a Common Agricultural Policy; and on the 'availability of leadership'—the way in which those demands were processed by the Community as a whole, both by the supranational institutions and by the national Governments.*

It is in this context that many of the terms used must be understood —e.g. spill-over, log-rolling, side payments, actor socialisation and feedback. These five are briefly defined below:

(a) Functional spill-over—*according to 'spill-over' theory, the process of integration is expected to pass from one sector of society to another in more or less automatic fashion until total integration is achieved.*

(b) Log-rolling *is a term which has been assimilated into the jargon of political science from the favourite sport of the American lumberjacks. This developed from the agility and nimble-footedness required to retain balance on the carpet of logs floating down a river. The slightest mishap or miscalculation could lead to death. The skills thus acquired were made into a sport in which two men, standing on a log in midstream, endeavoured to unbalance each other by 'rolling' the log. Its meaning for politics can be inferred— the maintenance of a dominant, stable position in a dynamic negotiating situation.*

(c) Side payments—*the process of buying in support from third parties for your position in a negotiating situation. The payments, which may take various forms not necessarily monetary, are incidental to the main negotiations. The support received, however, may affect their outcome.*

(d) Actor socialisation—*socialisation broadly conceived, encompasses all political learning, formal and informal, deliberate and unplanned, at every stage of life. In this context, the values and practices which socialisation mechanisms attempt to inculcate are those of the Communities.*

(e) Feedback—*information received about the results of action which, as an input at the next stage of decision-making, indicates whether subsequent action to achieve the given goal should be modified. Ed.]*

Demand Flow

Was there a clear difference between agriculture and transport in the numbers and types of political actors making or resisting demands on the system, in the nature of their interests in integration, and in the distribution of such interests among the actors?

In agriculture all Governments accepted the principle of a common or closely harmonised policy. There was a consensus that national agricultural policies had been generally unsuccessful in dealing either with problems of income maintenance and modernisation or with those of providing for a more efficient international division of labour in agricultural production. This consensus started with the interest groups concerned and extended to most technical experts and the responsible government officials. All were receptive to replacing national policies with a Community policy. The often enthusiastic espousal of a common agricultural policy by agricultural interest groups was especially crucial since farmers are politically potent in most Community countries. Several Governments manifested such a strong interest in achieving a common agricultural policy, most notably France and the Netherlands, that they were prepared to make it an absolute precondition for progress in other areas. In the case of General de Gaulle, a dramatic-political actor if there ever was one, these interests were sufficiently compelling to induce him to make use of a number of dramatic-political actions (threats, warnings, boycotts) to push the negotiations along.

Although there was reluctance in some circles, notably from German farmers' organisations, it was balanced or neutralised in each country by support from other groups or élites. No major political actor, either at a system or subgroup level, perceived the common agricultural policy to be *ipso facto* a threat to his own basic interests. What opposition there was could be overcome with side payments (as in the Kennedy Round) or by log-rolling (as with acceptance of a relatively high agricultural price level and special compensatory payments to German farmers who suffer income losses).

There was thus a high potential for the construction of a coalition of supporters of positive action in agriculture within each Community country and transnationally at the Community level. Both incremental-economic and dramatic-political élites made demands for action on the system based on calculations that their interests were better served in that way than by the national alternatives open to them. Furthermore, the overall distribution or patterning of their interest perceptions was essentially convergent, that is, all anticipated gains from different aspects of the proposed policy and few really expected to suffer irrevocable harm.

In transport the situation was very different. While there has been a rather vague and generalised interest in some kind of common transport policy, no major government or category of political actors (interest groups, for example) has perceived it to be in its vital interests that such a policy be rapidly developed. It is reasonably clear that so far no Government has felt itself under real pressure, either from transport interest groups or from other interest groups, including those representing users of transport facilities, to push strongly for positive action. Nor have governmental decision-makers or civil servants themselves taken the initiative to force the pace. Indeed, the Government with the largest economic stake in transport, the Netherlands, has been the one most opposed from the very beginning to the proposals made by the Commission. Opposition in the Netherlands has been nearly unanimous, with almost all actors agreeing that no action was to be preferred to what the Commission was proposing. The Commission's proposals have been somewhat more to the liking of the French and German Governments, but in neither case has there been very much enthusiasm for the kinds of proposals being made.

A consensus that there must be a common transport policy has simply not emerged. The sense of urgency generated over agriculture has been absent in transport. In short, Governments have tended to support the defensive positions taken by the national interest groups most concerned and by civil servants in the transport field. The rail-roads have been the persistent problem. These are government monopolies in each of the six, and they have been operated in a variety of uneconomical ways to give preference to favoured regions or sectors of the economy. It is not surprising that those with vested interests in the present policy would resist change, especially since the broad outlines of the new policy are not clear.

In retrospect, then, there seems to have been much less potential for forward linkage in transport because of the absence of a strong flow of demands for action into the system. Most interest groups and the civil servants concerned defended the *status quo*, and interest perspectives of the policies being proposed by the Commission formed a conflictual or divergent pattern rather than a convergent one. What one actor saw as possibly in his interests another saw as diametrically opposed to his.

The Availability of Leadership

If demand flow is the life blood of the Community system, then leadership must be seen metaphorically as the heart that distributes this vital substance to its cells and organs. Demand flow provides the raw material for activating the mechanisms of spill-over, log-rolling, side payments, actor socialisation and feedback. But this raw material must be exploited, combined, balanced, moulded. Functional links must be capitalised upon, bargains and exchanges proposed and accepted, socialisation and feedback mechanisms nurtured or stimulated. These are the functions of leadership, both national and supranational.

Can the agricultural and transport experiences also be distinguished on the basis of inputs of leadership? Let us first consider national leadership and its potential roles relative to demand formulation, the development of bargaining norms and the stimulation of support ... the concepts of demand flow and national leadership tend to overlap. A prime way in which governmental actors lead is by trying to move the system in some desired direction by developing public expectations and making demands on it. To move the system they must try to develop coherent national demands that can be transmitted to the Community. To do this they must simplify or reduce the often divergent interests and demands that may be generated within the national system. In the case of agriculture this has often meant supporting the demands of some (for example, efficient agriculture producers) against others (less efficient producers or consumers). It may also mean neutralising opposition by making active efforts to subsidise or indemnify those who fear losses from Community policies, as for example when the German Government offers special payments to farmers who would suffer because the German wheat price is lowered as a result of the common agricultural policy. We have already seen that in agriculture at least two Governments, those of the Netherlands and France, were insistent that an agricultural policy be passed, and they worked hard and persistently to accomplish that end. Although the Dutch and the French are at loggerheads in most other areas of Community policy-making, their interests in agriculture converged and therefore their leadership efforts reinforced each other. The German Government saw integration in agriculture as necessary for the continued progress of the Common Market and were hence willing not only to make sacrifices in terms of the bargaining settlement (transfer payments to France in the agricultural budget), but also to absorb domestic discontent with the policy and some of its effects. In transport there was little of this insistence upon action by governing élites and what there was was conflicting and cancelled itself out.

To the extent that Governments want something from the system, we may expect them to develop incentives to make the system work, as they did in agriculture. For example, the French under de Gaulle, although obstreperous and unpredictable in many other areas, by and large played the Community game in agriculture. They stressed how important the Community was for them; they accepted and indeed promoted partnership with the Commission in the policy preparation process; they were willing to compromise and take the other countries' interests into account; and they accepted proposals that increased the Commission's powers in agriculture. During the 1965–6 boycott they did not obstruct the functioning of the machinery of agricultural policy that was already in operation. In these ways they have nurtured and activated the socialisation mechanisms and all that they imply.*

De Gaulle, and other governmental leaders have also stimulated public support for the Community's efforts in agriculture, in part by the feedback mechanism and in part by evoking symbols that relate to the affective dimensions of integration.† Especially in France, but also in the other Community countries, governmental leaders have given much publicity to the common agricultural policy, and to how it promised to alleviate the problems of the farming population. It has loomed large in parliamentary debates and in electoral campaigns. Governmental action has thus facilitated the communication of information about the outputs, both actual and anticipated, of the Community system to the population at large and to farmers in

* De Gaulle was not always happy with some of the side-effects of actor socialisation and there is evidence of efforts to limit the development of pro-European constituencies in the French Government.
† [Affective dimensions of integration. *Generally, those facets of the integration of Europe which might be most favourably regarded by the nationals of the member states. In this case it refers to the stress placed by the French Government on the benefits to their agricultural community of the CAP.*]

particular. Although this was done primarily to stimulate support for the national Governments ('See how well we defend your interests'), its effect is also to help establish the authority and legitimacy of the Community system.

Governments have not had incentives to give priority to action on transport matters. As far as we can tell from the limited evidence available, log-rolling and side payment exchanges have not been actively sought. Bargaining has not nurtured the Community spirit. Nor have Governments publicised transport activity or emphasised it very much, except as a potential threat.

What was the role of supranational leadership in the two cases? We have suggested that for a number of reasons an active Commission is a necessary condition for successful coalition formation, that under some circumstances it can capitalise on disagreements within Governments or among them to create consensus for its proposals, and that even when Governments have been internally unified, and desire positive outcomes, they are seldom able to activate the Community system without the aid of the Commission.

These assertions seem amply supported by the events in agriculture. Most of the credit for building the coalition and for holding it together must go to the Commission and especially to the Commissioner in charge of agriculture, Sicco Mansholt. This is not to underestimate the significance of national 'leadership' in the form of pressure from the French and Dutch Governments. But Mansholt and his staff have operated with extraordinary skill to make the most of the leadership resources of the Commission, its special perspective, its 'power' of initiative and its technical expertise. Let us now illustrate how each of these was brought to bear at each stage of the policy process in the agricultural case, to activate coalition formation mechanisms and produce system growth.

As we have said, only the Commission can legitimately claim to be acting solely in the interests of the emerging 'new Europe'. National initiatives and policy proposals must always be somewhat suspect, since they are seldom divorced from individual national interests and ambitions. This gives the Commission the possibility of appealing to all groups who perceive any stake, whether economic, political or symbolic, in integration. To do this it must express and symbolise specific proposals and technical arrangements in terms of the broader goals of integration. The specific arrangements and decisions that make up the daily stuff of integration in any sector are not the sort of thing that fire the imagination, and unless they are cast in a broader context of an emergent European common interest, they will be relevant to only a narrow range of experts and interest group representatives. If the Commission is to help mobilise supporters outside this immediate specialised constituency, which it generally must do if it is to build the broad political coalition required for forward linkages, progress in a particular sector must be made to appear vital to integration *per se*. The common agricultural policy is a staggeringly complex mass of regulations that in and of itself practically defies understanding or even description. Yet Mansholt has succeeded in casting its overall goals in such a way as to keep agriculture at the centre of integration politics for ten years. Each successive step has been widely celebrated and acclaimed. Somehow, a great many groups and individuals have taken vicarious satisfaction in the steady advances made in agriculture. Mansholt has become perhaps the best known of the Commissioners—a real European personality, and indeed, a veritable European Minister of Agriculture.

Besides this broad constituency, the Commission must, of course, be able to appeal to those who are immediately affected by its proposals. In the case of agriculture this means above all the farmers. Commission proposals must be accepted by the Council of Ministers, and hence have to take into account the specific interests and needs of individual countries, and the balance of benefits and costs among them. Mansholt clearly designed his proposals for a common agricultural policy to serve the interests of those Community countries for which agriculture was already an important economic sector and which anticipated maximum gain from a rationalised, Europe-wide agricultural market. He also cast his lot with those in each country who saw the future in terms of a declining agricultural population, larger and more efficient farms and a major migration from the land to other occupations.

Mansholt not only took 'constituency' interests into account, but he also co-opted those interests into the decision-making process so as to give them a maximum sense of *participation* in the great European enterprise. In so doing, he went well beyond the standard consultation procedures usually engaged in by the Commission. He actively stimulated the creation of Community-level farmers' organisations (over 100 now exist). He consulted them at every stage of the process of preparing for changes of policy, thus forcing them to try to reach common viewpoints, rather than expressing six national ones. Each of the market organisation systems provides for official advisory committees representing farm groups, thus giving them a role in the routine decision-making process of the agricultural policy. It is no accident that Mansholt is so well known among European farmers, or that he has usually been able to count on their support when his proposals have gone to the Council of Ministers.

The Commission's ability to make proposals that will be taken seriously depends in part on its command (or potential command) of a technical expertise that is simply not available to any Government. The Commission is at the centre of a Community-wide web of communications, giving it the substantive and statistical information necessary to the formulation (and implementation) of Community-wide policies. Capitalising on this favoured position demands gathering around you a competent and cohesive staff that shares your goals and that understands the technical dynamics of the economic sector in question. Mansholt's success in this area has also been striking.[4]

One use the Commission has made of its resources of perspective and expertise is to incrementally time proposals so as to maximise functional spill-over. For example, in building a common agricultural policy, the Commission began with a proposal for a levy system that provoked little opposition precisely because, in itself, it involved no real policy changes. But once a levy mechanism was in existence, this increased the incentives to take the much more difficult policy decisions that were then implied. In a similar way, Mansholt's first substantive proposals were in the area of price policy, even though he had himself always been generally committed to an agricultural policy that relied on structural policy rather than price policy (that is, on increased efficiency and modernisation rather than high prices) as a guarantee of the long-term future of European agriculture. But structural reform ran too much counter to existing policies and would be much harder to get accepted on the European level. It was likely to succeed only if a price and commercial policy already existed. The shortcomings of this approach might then be expected to become apparent to everyone. The Community's butter surplus problem . . . is a case in point.

Besides bringing its resources to bear at the policy initiation and preparation stages, the Commission has also played a vital role at the bargaining and decision stages by acting to facilitate log-rolling and side payments. As we have seen, these are the vital mechanisms of forward linkages, whereby Governments seek the bargains and balances that integration inevitably involves. Experience has shown that six Governments meeting in the Council, each defending its own interests, find it extraordinarily difficult themselves to come up with that balance of gains and losses that can precipitate final agreement. Because it sits by right in most Council meetings, because it speaks with the voice of the Community interest and because its formal assent is required if its proposals to the Council are to be amended, it has become almost standard procedure to wait for the Commission to formulate the final package deal. And it is no exaggeration to say that it has been Commissioner Mansholt who has practised the art most successfully. On the basis of his long acquaintance with agricultural problems (he has been a farmer, a Minister of Agriculture for thirteen years in the Netherlands and a moving force in the UN Food and Agricultural Organisation), his understanding of the positions of each government, acquired through the negotiations and through his extensive travels in the Community, and the respect which all the negotiators hold for him personally, Mansholt has been able time and again to piece together the almost magical compromises that have marked the progress of the common agricultural policy.

If agriculture is a classic case of how much active Commission leadership can accomplish, transport is perhaps a classic case of what happens when leadership resources are not utilised.

In spite of policy differences and the problems inherent to the transport sector that limited possibilities for growth, and in spite of the absence of great pressures for action from the Governments, it does appear that there was in transport a sufficient potential for functional and political linkages for the Commission to build a coalition in favour of some sort of common policy (albeit more modest than in agriculture) had it acted with anything like the skill and imagination shown in agriculture.[5]

At the outset, there was more optimism with regard to transport than there was for agriculture. And as late as 1965, Jensen and Walter in their fine study wrote of the manifold pressures for action that existed:

The degree of economic specialisation is dependent upon the size of the market, and the size of the market is determined to a con-

siderable extent by the nature and costs of transportation. . . .
The many new, expanded needs and requirements brought about
by gradual economic integration should be met by favourable
rate structures and freedom from undue discrimination.[6]

The delays which have characterised the formulation of the
common transport policy during the first years of the EEC seem
to have been overcome to some extent. It may reasonably be
expected that the Commission's transport programme will be
fully realised during the remainder of the Transition Period.[7]

While we cannot demonstrate conclusively that there would have
been more progress had the Commission acted differently, we consider that a persuasive case can be made out of the sharp contrast
between its modes of operation in agriculture and in transport.

In the judgement of one commentator, the Commission did not
show in transport the kind of 'long-range vision and obvious independence'[8] so important in agriculture. Indeed, its original proposals
seem not to have been based on the kind of consultation and compromise with client groups and national Governments necessary if
a coalition of supporters is to be built. They have been totally
unacceptable to a small but important country and the Commission
has shown itself generally unresponsive to criticism, not only from
the Dutch, but from the Economic and Social Committee representing interest group opinion, from most private economists, and even
from a committee of five independent experts consulted by the Commission itself. German and French official opinion tended to shift
in favour of a different approach as action on the Commission's
proposals seemed blocked. But the Commission was seemingly
insensitive to all this and instead of taking the initiative and reshaping
its own proposals, it was the Council that finally 'suggested' that it
make new proposals to accommodate to the balance of interests that
existed in the Community.

There are some who argue that it is the Commission's whole
approach to transport policy that is at fault. Having decided to go
beyond a minimalist approach of simply trying to assure that discrimination in transport did not unduly distort competition in the
common market, the Commission failed to cast its net widely
enough. Its Action Programme envisaged an entirely new set of
balances in the transport market.

The overall philosophy ... is that the distribution of traffic between different forms of transport should be effected by the price mechanism, and controls on capacity and other institutional forms of protection ... should play a less important part. ... At the same time, the pressures which have artificially boosted or lowered costs of providing one or other types of transport services, are to be removed. Thus, the policy relies on two simultaneous adjustments: first, prices charged are to be brought more into line with actual costs of provision, and, secondly, financial costs incurred ... are to be brought more into line with the true economic costs of their operations. ...[9]

But the Commission's initial specific proposals were in one policy area only and would have affected only one kind of transport, namely road transport. As such, they demanded, as we have seen, a sacrifice on the part of one of the bargaining partners long before compensation could be provided in other types of transport or in other policy areas, or before the outlines of the overall policy and its balanced benefits and compensations would become visible.

Whether or not the programme as a whole is a desirable one, implementing it piecemeal may have dangers. There is a logic in all the proposals taken together, while some of them in isolation could have effects which are opposite to those desired. ... The precedence of some measures over others can so affect the present transport market that some undertakings may lose traffic because they have lost some institutional burden on their costs. ... There is also a long-term danger of proceeding to implement some of the measures on the assumption that the others, which complete the 'balance' will follow, and finding that agreement on these cannot be reached.[10]

Thus, in contrast to its practice in agriculture under the leadership of Sicco Mansholt, the Commission failed to articulate the general goals of a common transport policy in such a way as to create a general expectation of long-term gain that could compensate individual short-term sacrifices. In its specific proposals for action, it has persistently failed to discover the limits of the possible so that a coalition of supporters at the national level could be built. For example, Scheinman argues that the Commission had ample possibilities to mobilise users' associations in the transport field who presumably had more of a stake in getting a common policy than suppliers, but that no real effort was made to do so.[11]

As we have seen, side payments and log-rolling have been strikingly absent from the transport negotiations. The Commission did not respond in a creative manner to the objections of governments and groups to its initial plans, and it failed to play the role of broker by modifying and broadening its proposals so as to facilitate the construction of package deals.

References

1. Michael Shanks and John Lambert, *The Common Market Today—and Tomorrow*, Frederick A. Praeger, Inc., New York, 1962, p. 83.
2. Ibid., p. 95.
3. Finn B. Jensen and Ingo Walter, *The Common Market: Economic Integration in Europe*, J. B. Lippincott Co., Philadelphia, 1965, p. 7.
4. See Lindberg, 'Decision-Making and Integration in the European Community', *International Organisation*, Vol. 19 (Winter 1965), p. 208.
5. It is significant to note that the apparent progress made in 1968 coincides with the departure of the Commissioner formerly in charge of transport. With the new Commissioner has perhaps come a new set of tactics and strategies that may more closely resemble the agricultural pattern.
6. Jensen and Walter, op. cit., p. 141.
7. Ibid., p. 149.
8. *Common Market*, no. 7, November 1967, p. 276.
9. *Transport in the Common Market*, Political and Economic Planning Broadsheet, 29, no. 473, 8 July 1963, pp. 243–4.
10. Ibid., p. 244.
11. Lawrence Scheinman, *Transport, Bureaucracy, and Integration: Some Common and Uncommon Problems in Decision-Making* (forthcoming).

(Extracted from L. Lindberg and S. Scheingold, *Europe's Would-Be Polity*, Prentice-Hall Inc., Englewood Cliffs, New Jersey, 1970, pp. 141–81.)

2.7 Masters or Servants of the New Europe ?
ROGER BERTHOUD

The debate on the EEC's institutions is gathering pace as enlargement approaches. Everyone agrees that the Council of Ministers
needs to be made more efficient as a decision-taking machine. Everyone agrees that the European Parliament in Strasbourg needs to be
redeemed from its helpless obscurity and given some real powers of
control. But even the nine members of the European Commission
are divided over the future needs of that vast, elusive but vital
Brussels institution.

Interviews with four of the most prominent commissioners have
produced a richly varied range of responses. The basic division
within the Commission is between those who feel that it should
become more of a political factor in the Community, and those who
feel its strength lies in fulfilling its roles quietly but effectively.

Part of the trouble springs from the conflicting nature of these
roles, as France's handsome and brilliant Jean-François Deniau
(responsible for the enlargement negotiations and for development
aid) pointed out. The Commission is both the 'animator' or motor
of the community by dint of its right to make proposals to the
Council (which takes the decisions) and also the executor of resolutions enacted by the Council. It must guard the best interests of the
Community as a whole, without alienating the representatives of the
member States on the Council of Ministers. All too often the Council
and the Commission have been at loggerheads.

'The catastrophe has been the conflict in the past two or three
years between the two,' said M. Deniau. 'I hope that within the
enlarged community this conflict should disappear. It is in the Commission's interest hat the Council should work as well as possible.'

The Commission, he said, must produce reasonable and applicable
proposals. But a good secretariat could do that. The Commission
must therefore also have moral authority. 'It must be able to say to
the Ten: "No, that is not the right way for the long term, it's against
the Community's interest."'

There are those in the Commission, M. Deniau said, who see this
aspect of moral authority as the most important. They feel the
Commission should increase its role as animator, throw its weight

around more and become a spectacular political organ. But this would be contrary to its role as executant and source of *bonnes offices*.

Moreover, if it made a great political impact, it might find no agreement with the member States. 'It should show its moral authority on a certain number of major topics, not every week,' he said, 'The Commission cannot speak independently of the Council. It's no good if it does not speak with the Council's full backing . . . the aim is not to beat the member states, but to make them work together, to push them towards a compromise. It's difficult: unity has rarely been achieved in history by agreement rather than by military domination.

'An effective commission is essential for constructing Europe. Europe *à la carte* (i.e. based on *ad hoc* intergovernmental agreements) is Euratom—*une fausse belle idée.*'

M. Deniau, it will be deduced, is among those who believe the Commission should keep a relatively low profile. His much respected Italian colleague, Signor Altiero Spinelli (responsible for industrial affairs and research), stressed the Commission's role as a counterpoise to the Council, as the supranational element balancing national interests. Signor Spinelli, who spent ten years in Fascist jails, said: 'The Commission is the only permanent centre in the Community which has the ability to be supranational, to be obliged to have the common interests in mind and a *vue d'ensemble*. The Council and the permanent representatives have the opposite role, to insert their national exigencies into the common view. The Commission must be strong to be the partner of the Council.'

He thought this strength could be gained partly by appointing men of political weight to the next commission: the instinct of the good official as opposed to the good politician was to receive political indications and then act on them (though the French tradition is rather different). He hoped the British would put forward political heavyweights. To be collectively strong, however, these fourteen political heavyweights would have to have a measure of political homogeneity, and must draw up a list of political priorities. During the first two commissions (under Professor Hallstein and M. Rey) the programme was in the Treaty of Rome, with deadlines, transitional periods and all. The third commission had faced the challenge of enlargement but otherwise had had no programme.

It had never made a comprehensive study of the problems and isolated the priorities. Within the Commission it had simply distributed the roles established by previous commissions, without discussing their merits. Neither the Council nor the Parliament could settle the programme for the next two years. The Commission could and should. M. Deniau thoroughly agreed with this suggestion. He felt that summit conferences should only be held at times of major change.

Both men feared that a fourteen-man Commission would be unwieldy. If each Commissioner spoke for ten minutes—M. Deniau suggested that there should be more delegation of powers: the Commission as a whole reaching broad agreements, then leaving the Commissioner responsible to get on with it without referring back constantly. He saw the French *toi cadre* system as a possible model here. His Italian colleague felt that the Commissioners should be grouped into three or four big blocks; say, agriculture, industry, general economic policy, with perhaps foreign relations as the fourth. These sub-commissions would have their own internal balance, and full meetings of the Commission could perhaps be reduced to fortnightly intervals. He felt certain that a field as vast as agriculture, absorbing some 80 per cent of the Community's funds, would no longer be entrusted to one man (as it has been since 1958 to Holland's Mr. Sicco Mansholt).

Professor Ralf Dahrendorf, the West German sociologist, and Free Democrat responsible on the Commission for external trade and relations, is pessimistic about the Commission's future. 'I don't believe a Commission of fourteen makes sense at all,' he said, 'not even a Commission of fourteen ex-ministers or potential ministers. They would simply all look to their own constituencies. Fourteen Malfattis don't make a powerful Commission. A Commission of fourteen would simply strengthen the Council of Ministers.' He favoured a reduced Commission of three or four members, backed by a high level administration which did not mind being called technocratic.

Professor Dahrendorf was widely castigated last year for suggesting, among other things, in two pseudonymous articles in *Die Zeit* that consultation on the Davignon model, i.e. outside the framework of the Community, with close collaboration between senior officials from member capitals, was the thing of the future. The recent agreement to set up a short-term economic policy steering committee suggests that he had a point, though the Davignon committee's efforts to co-ordinate foreign policy have not been notably fruitful.

He feels it is a fiction that the Commission represents the Community viewpoint. 'What is the European interest, and why should we be able to define it better than others, for example, the Council?', he asked. He was convinced that as Europe became more and more important to its member States, they were bound to want increasingly to influence decisions themselves.

The stormy petrel of the Commission favoured instead the strengthening of the Presidency of the Council of Ministers and the appointment as suggested by President Pompidou, of European ministers to eliminate the present situation where professional diplomats (the permanent representatives in Brussels) take 'most of the important decisions'.

Most of these ideas would be anathema to Mr. Mansholt. Since I saw the Commission's veteran (it was the occasion when he first lashed out against Labour's attitude to British entry) Mr. Mansholt has succeeded Signor Malfatti as its President. He has made it clear to all that he believes the Commission should be more independent, and should exercise a high degree of moral authority. Perhaps because he himself was and is a substantial political figure, and has been the dominant personality in the Commission, he believes that strong, independent political figures of national stature will make a good commission. He would like them to be members of a political party (he is a Socialist) and committed Europeans to boot.

It is clear from this diversion of views that the new Commissioners will have many problems. They will have to be men with moral authority, yet effective administrators. They will have to be political figures in virtually the same class as the minister sitting in the Council, yet without the ministers' powers of decision. They will have to divide up their portfolios in such a way that they can get on with the job and keep out of each other's hair. They will have to pull as a team without setting up as opposition to the Council. They will have to combat a tendency for the task to be eroded by Davignon-type committees of top officials meeting fresh from the capital. They will have to be prepared for more parliamentary influence. They will have to reorganise the huge commission staff so there is more horizontal contact and less of the Prussian sense of hierarchy bequeathed by Prof. Hallstein. Above all, their President must be gifted with the power of leadership.

(Extracted from *The Times*, 28 April 1972.)

SECTION 3

Participation—Parliament, Parties and Pressure Groups

3.1 Introduction

The last section was concerned with the institutions of the communities, and their relations with member Governments. It is a world dominated by ministers, commissioners and bureaucrats. It leaves open such questions as 'Is there any role in the political process for those who do not hold official positions?' 'Are there opportunities for democratic participation?' In the Western democratic system the most obvious forms of participation are found through Parliaments, political parties, pressure groups and involvement in local governments. It is with these that this section is concerned. It is a long section not because parties and pressure groups are more important in the European political process than the formal institutions but because of the diversity of groups and their activities.

The extract from Bracher at the beginning of the section (pp. 99–104) presents a very broad picture in which he sees 'democracy' under challenge in the nation State, and even more so within the European communities. He writes that 'a newly minted European bureaucracy has gained a considerable advantage over the parliamentary organs'. He also notes that the different traditions of the individual states cannot be ignored in any attempt to create an overall European democratic system.

The scene having been set by Bracher, the next articles are concerned with the European Parliament and the political parties. The European Parliament has so far played a minor role in the development of the communities. If has certainly failed to live up to the hopes of the founding fathers, who saw the Parliament both as a means of exercising democratic control and a means of stimulating a sense of European unity. Writings about the Parliament therefore tend to concentrate either on its present ineffectiveness, or on plans for the future to give it new life and fire. For example, John Mackintosh (pp. 129–39) writes about the future and the possibility of greater effectiveness through co-operation with national Parliaments or through the introduction of more direct representation (the Stewart Plan).

The past ineffectiveness of the European Parliament can partly, but only partly, be laid at the feet of the national political parties. There are no European parties as such, although members of the European Parliament sit in broad party groupings and not national *blocs*. The European Parliament is drawn from members of the national Parliaments and hence from national parties. These national parties still concentrate their main efforts on exercising control or influence within their own national boundaries. In the main, therefore, they are opposed to a situation in which 'the formation of European political parties means that national party congresses will no longer have the last word' (Vredeling, pp. 105–9). Enthusiasm for a more virile European democratic process has always been tempered by the realisation that this can only flourish at the expense of some existing national powers.

While the relative ineffectiveness of the European Parliament is widely recognised and was amply demonstrated by the Italian failure to replace their members (Leich, pp. 110–12), the weakness should not be exaggerated too far. All national parties realise that whatever their views on the desirability of the community structure important decisions are being made there, outside the national political framework. The European Parliament gives at least some say in how these decisions are being made. This partly explains the behaviour of the Italian communists as explained in Leich's article (pp. 110–12), and Peter Wilsher questions whether the British Labour Party fully appreciated the implications of its decision not to send members in 1973 (pp. 122–5). Richard Norton-Taylor's piece about Henk Vredeling (pp. 126–9) shows how even a single individual, if he has the determination and skill, can use the existing parliamentary machinery to exert some influence.

The remaining articles and extracts are concerned with pressure groups. The flow chart (p. 144) connected with the extract on Industrial Representation (pp. 143–9) is generally applicable to the agricultural groups, described by Nielsen (pp. 149–57) and the trade unions with which Bouvard is concerned.

Sidjanski examines the pressure groups in general terms, pointing out that they concentrate their activities on the Council–Commission tandem in obvious recognition of where most power lies (pp. 166–73).

Like the political parties, the pressure groups face major problems of organisation and reconciling national and community interests. Sidjanski notes that the variety of interests within any single European group means that a confederal structure usually has to be accepted (p. 171), and Nielsen says of COPA that: 'Political cleavages are based predominantly on national antagonisms, but sectoral problems also provoke clashes of interest' (pp. 152–3). Despite these difficulties, pressure groups have been very active as Armstrong's article on lobbying shows (pp. 173–81). Perhaps two words of warning should be given before reading Armstrong's piece. First, as Armstrong himself says, 'there is nothing reprehensible about lobbying . . . so long as it does not degenerate into straight corruption'. Second, the amount of activity is not necessarily correlated with the amount of influence (Nielsen, p. 156).

European pressure groups are, however, alive and kicking in a way that European political parties are not. This leads to an interesting suggestion in Hartley's article that European parties will not be spawned by the national parties, but will develop from the pressure groups which he says 'are concerned with genuinely transnational issues' (p. 142).

The final article in this section takes a quick look at the implications for local governments of membership of the communities. The range of services affected is very wide, and Swaffield, who believes that 'local self government is a cornerstone of democracy', states that local authorities must be prepared to participate at all levels of community activity (pp. 181–6).

3.2 Democracy
KARL BRACHER

In all western democracies the question of whether the old and honourable institution of Parliament is still capable of exercising effective organisation and control over politics, and indeed of actively contributing to the making of political decisions, is becoming more urgent. Even more so is the question of whether it is still wise to submit complicated decisions in the economic, social and military spheres, which call for planning and continuity, to lengthy and often random discussions in the scarcely competent assemblies of parliaments, where a small circle of committee experts merely repeats its familiar dialogue. Is parliamentarianism still at all capable of reconciling democratic representation with correct decision-making, or does not the parliamentary process descend to mere formality and become a fiction when the great majority of the voting members of parliament can no longer understand the complicated problems? . . .

Not only is the development within states problematic. In addition, the supranational and international interweaving of many individual decisions has necessarily over-taxed and limited the capacity of national Parliaments. In recent years the development of the European institutions has demonstrated to how large a degree there has been a shift of policy from the parliamentary to the governmental and bureaucratic level: a newly-minted European bureaucracy has gained a considerable advantage over the parliamentary organs in those institutions; the supranational formation of policy has to a large extent been put under the jurisdiction of extra- and supra-parliamentary experts (e.g. the EEC Commission) and Governments (Council of Ministers); compared with this the merely advisory function of the European 'Parliament', which anyway possesses only a derivative and not an immediate legitimation through direct European elections, remains almost meaningless.

Two great areas of future problems arise from this diagnosis: on the one hand is the experience of practical and functional inefficiency, which requires a fundamental reform of the out-dated and unrealistic structure of parliamentary democracy; on the other hand is the fundamental criticism of the possibility and legitimacy of representative parliamentary government, with the revolutionary demand for directly democratic forms of control and decision-making through referenda or soviets. It is around the slogans of efficiency and participation that argument about the modernisation or transformation of democracy will take place in the next decades. The decisive question will be whether these postulates of practical efficiency and democratic participation are understood as competitive elements and stimuli in a parliamentary system capable of development, or whether they are placed in opposition to traditional liberal democracy as alternative, mutually exclusive models.

The demand for practical efficiency in the political system applies not only to the relationship of parties, Parliament and Government, but also above all to the increasing role of interest groups on the one hand and public administration on the other. In both cases, the 'non-political' expert and impartial planning are increasingly opposed to the claims to political decision-making and control made by Parliaments, and either infiltrate them or supplant them. This is very necessary for continually improved and rational organisation and planning in a complex, highly differentiated and sensitive society, which can as ill afford mere improvisation and dilettantism as can the modern economy and modern industry. The great objectivity and effectiveness of the 'non-political' expert, and of the impartially planning and rationally functioning, specialised bureaucracy in state and society is set against the wasteful political process of parliamentary democracy. But in consequence there appears the bogey of a pure technocracy, the rule of managers and officials, scarcely allowing of control and removed from the sphere of the parliamentary-democratic consensus. It is this antithesis between highly specialised expertise and the principle of democratic representation and co-determination which will continue to be a central structural problem of all Western parliamentary democracies. . . .

If decision-makers in the modern State are becoming ever fewer and the tendency to the rule of experts ever more difficult to control, then the future of democracy depends finally on whether we succeed in opening up new ways for the citizen to participate in political and social life which will raise him above the mere role of spectator. Parties, associations and local self-government are the media for this; improved political education seems to be their prerequisite. This is also true of the specialists on the planning and management boards. There, 'democratisation' and control would seem to be most easily possible, if all monopolistic and hierarchical consolidation of political decision-making were avoided, and room were made for the principle of truly free competition in the sense of competition based on achievement (K. Mannheim).[1] In reality there is no necessarily insoluble dichotomy between objectivity and politics, expertise and democracy. The precedence, *the primacy of politics must be preserved*. And here as before, parliamentarianism has its decisive function, more than ever in fact in the face of the increased demands of modern foreign, social, economic and military policy. Parliament and the parties which sustain it have as before a dual function: as an organ of the electorate, to concern themselves with the contact and co-ordination of the different areas of interests, expertise and politics; and further to guarantee frankness, readiness for compromise and competition, and the control of consultation and planning, to scrutinise them in the argument between Government and Opposition and to relate them to concrete political reality. . . .

. . . Increasing international interdependence and the creation of supranational institutions has given rise to the question, even outside national parliamentary life, how the tension between politics and planning, democracy and 'expertocracy' can be regulated in the sphere of European and, in part, Atlantic involvement. Here too an advancing, expanding bureaucracy of administrators and specialists faces inadequately participating democratic parliamentary institutions. The Commission and Council of Ministers of the European Economic Community are developing along these lines, while the parliamentary institutions are lagging far behind. Supranational exchanges of ideas and co-ordination do not disguise the small importance of the European Parliament so long as it lacks legitimation by direct European elections and only carries out unimportant advisory functions.

Here, too, it is important to recognise that expert planning needs political planning, needs parliamentary consensus and control, if it is to be effective and at the same time democratic. The visible economic and technical success of co-operation at bureaucratic level cannot remove these political insufficiencies. The negotiations between the EEC and Britain could be seen in this context. The entry of Britain may shift the policy of European unification from the bureaucratic to the parliamentary plane. Here—beside the French claim to leadership—lay one reason for the resistance of de Gaulle, who feared the disrupting effect on the economic and technical development of European co-operation of such a return to politics and parliamentarianism. Here, too, however, is to be found one reason for Britain's over-long hesitation, distrustful as she is of the political repercussions on the institutions of her own political system, itself so sanctified by tradition. . . .

The more a Europe of limited individual sovereignties reflects on its own role in the world, the more anachronistic a sinking back into national isolation appears. It is not only a question of economic and military potential. It is far more a political question. For like the external dangers to West European democracy, the internal threat of a multiple failure of parliamentarianism has not been removed by the swift recovery. For security and necessary reform, the states of continental Europe need a close association among themselves, and at the same time, association with the Anglo-American democracies, which have strong traditions and experience in the art of adapting a democracy to the new conditions of the industrial world.

If European parliamentary democracy has been discussed here and the similarity of symptoms and problems emphasised, there remain for consideration in conclusion the important variations in political reality. In Germany the experiences of the Weimar Republic and its breakdown form the point of departure for all debates on the relationship of Parliament, Government and bureaucracy. The pseudo-presidential experiments of 1930–33, which led to Hitler's dictatorship, justify mistrust of any attempts to limit the parliamentary system in favour of the administrative state. In France, on the other hand, the breakdown of classical parliamentarianism in the IVth Republic led to an almost diametrically opposed conception. While in both these cases the consequence is a modification of parliamentary democracy, in Italy, as in Holland and Belgium, we still see the older form of multi-party parliamentarianism confronted with the classic problems of disunion and the difficulties of coalition. These profound variations in European internal politics must be taken into account when assessing the future perspectives of European integration. The burdens of the past are different, and different also are the answers to the question of how stable government and administration can be combined with effective control. Very different traditions of centralism or federalism, especially in France and Germany, form an additional element of differentiation. The efforts at European unification tend to underestimate these problems; in consequence they may even intensify them. In this respect, too, the necessary creation of a really competent European Parliament is a long way off, and its position will be extremely difficult.

In fact the inner development of parliamentary democracy in Europe still takes place completely within the framework of the nation State. A political Europe would depend on a system of far-reaching compromises and renunciation of sovereignty which would submit the very co-operation of the Governments and the activity of a European bureaucracy to the real control of a common parliamentary system. For despite the experiments of de Gaulle's Vth Republic, parliamentary democracy has remained the fundamental form for the free states of Europe. Reforms and limitations are imposed upon it. But although frequently given up for dead, it holds its own; the many problems which have been discussed here have not prevented parliamentary democracy from outliving dictatorship again and again. If it has frequently broken down in the first instance, in the new states of Africa and Asia, it was as a colonial importation. Its prerequisite is a developed society. It seems scarcely likely and also scarcely appropriate that parliamentary democracies will be replaced by presidential systems of the American kind, as have been adopted with little success in numerous new states in South America. Presidential democracy is too closely linked with the special historical and social pre-conditions of the United States; its export could not answer European questions and would create new problems, as the hybrid form of the Vth Republic shows. In this respect the difference between Europe and the United States remains a reality which must be borne in mind for the future of European and Atlantic policy.

It was possible here to give only a short résumé of a few of the problems which must be taken into account for a realistic assessment of European democracy. Neither idealisation not pessimism is helpful. Certainly the burdens and crises of adaptation of parliamentary democracy are likely to be intensified in our swiftly changing political and socio-economic world. But they can be overcome if, in contrast with the period after the First World War, reform is understood as the strengthening of parliament's position and greater publicity for its work, that is, if reform is not confused again with capitulation to authoritarian, bureaucratic-official ideas of order or with utopian-bureaucratic-official ideas of order or with utopian-élitist, totalitarian ideologies of perfection, and if all over-eager perfectionists are reminded of Winston Churchill's well-known words, that the parliamentary system of government is the worst system of government there is, except for all the others.

Reference

1. K. Mannheim, *Freedom, Power and Democratic Planning*, Routledge and Kegan Paul, London, 1951.

(Extracted from R. Mayne (ed.), *Europe Tomorrow: 16 Europeans Look Ahead*, Fontana/Collins, London, 1972.)

3.3 The Common Market of Political Parties
H. VREDELING

A curious phenomenon may be noted within the European Community, and also in the negotiations on the entry of other European countries into it. This is the *absence* of any move towards European integration among the political parties in the member States. Rather surprisingly, an obstinate silence prevails in Europe and within the national political parties regarding this deficiency. One cannot help wondering what is the reason for this and what can be done to break this silence.

Outwardly the process of European integration presents in the main an *economic* aspect. The EEC Treaty is a classic example of this. The goal striven for is a customs union with a common policy in the economic sphere. Thus the first steps are being taken in the Community towards a common policy in a number of sectors (agriculture, transport, energy, external trade). Recently attempts have been made to link this sector-by-sector policy through the inauguration of a common economic and monetary policy.

In the social sphere, however, far less progress has been made. A common social policy is not one of the aims of the EEC Treaty. Consequently what there is in common in the social sector is of a secondary nature. Efforts are made through the European Social Fund to hold in check any adverse effects of the process of economic integration. The Community, however, lacks a social policy as such (that is, one actively concerned with full employment, a fair distribution of income and a bigger say for the citizen in macro-economic and micro-economic affairs). In education, cultural affairs, housing, town and country planning, control of the environment, local government, the administration of justice and other important sectors of every national policy the European Community lacks even the rudiments of common aims and of a common policy.

In so far as one can speak of a common approach by member States to external and defence policy, this is governed mainly by factors unrelated to the existence of the European Community. It should no doubt be noted that the first signs of co-operation in external policy can be detected, for example, in the Davignon Committee.*

* A Committee of the Foreign Ministers of the Nine which meets half-yearly to discuss the co-ordination of foreign policy.

The only conclusion that can be drawn from this is that the member States of the EEC are obstinately bent on confining co-operation to the economic sector and are not as yet inclined to extend such co-operation to other sectors.

European Parties and Parliament

Now how do the national political parties of the Six feel about all this? First it should be noted that these parties leave it mainly to their respective political groups in the national Parliaments to follow up the European integration process. These groups are brought in touch with EEC affairs only through their Governments. They themselves are not, apparently, directly involved. That in fact was the intention of the authors of the European Treaties. These make provision for the setting up of a European Parliament composed of national representatives appointed to sit there by their national Parliaments. In addition one of the aims laid down in the Treaties is the holding of direct European elections. Unfortunately they fix no time-limit within which these elections must be organised. Nor, in fact, have they ever been held. Although most of the national political parties have included European elections in their programmes, they have never made a real issue of them. As a result of all this the national political parties are brought only indirectly in touch with European questions—that is, through their Governments and members of national groups sitting in the European Parliament.

The European Parliament, however, has only an advisory role. Decisions are taken in the Council of Ministers of the European Communities. In the eyes of the national groups, members who sit in the European Parliament are of only limited importance. They are certainly of great help in shedding light on the obscure process of European integration. But they have no real say in policy-making. The result is that members of national political groups who play an important part in shaping domestic policy are practically never members of the European Parliament. The selection of representatives to the European Parliament is a negative process for two reasons. On the one hand national groups tend to put forward only second line politicians as candidates; and on the other, if influential national parliamentarians become members of the European Parliament or if lesser known figures—as often happens—discharge their European parliamentary duties with devotion and zeal and in so doing acquire national recognition, the time inevitably comes when they are called upon to assume a responsible post in national politics, either in the national Government or in Opposition. This may be beneficial to the national groups but the overall effect on the European Parliament is adverse. This phenomenon is due to the fact that the European Parliament has no political power.

Meanwhile the process of European economic integration is moving ahead. It is accompanied by the growth of transnational economic power groupings. The EEC is a paradise for industrialists. The creation of a huge market of 200 million consumers (close on 275 million after the accession of the four applicant countries) at a time of buoyant business activity is a political act by the Governments but it is also a 'give-away' with an unusually high goodwill value for business interests. (The British Government is having to pay a substantial price for a benefit it could have obtained for nothing in the early 1950s.) The Governments of the Six are working on the completion of this paradise. Almost all the measures taken in the Community are designed to eliminate obstacles to trade and distortions of competition. Even the free movement of workers helps to create a source of cheap labour. The Governments seem to have only one concern: to stem the influx of American capital. European capital is their ally. But does anyone believe there could ever be a real conflict between American and European capital?

The consolidation of political power is lagging far behind. The Council of Ministers is the only institution to embody real political power, but this merely serves the economic Common Market because economic strength seems to be the only objective of political power. Significantly the political power of the six governments, culminating in the Council of Ministers of the European Community, stems from the domestic political power of each Government which only exists by the grace of the national balance of political power. In the West European democracies, national political power rests with the governing political parties which are to some extent held in check by the Opposition. In the parliamentary democracies this national process of checks and balances is dependent on the system of free elections, i.e. on the fact that citizens are allowed to have their say.

There is, however, a real risk that the derived power of the EEC Council may become an independent factor on which the national political parties can exercise little influence even indirectly. The Council is the cuckoo in the nest of European integration. The national political parties are like the sorcerer's apprentice in their dealings with the Council. They have waved their magic wand in the national Parliaments to set the process in motion but they do not know the spell to control the Council's policy. . . .

The Causes of Reluctance

What are the principal causes of this internal resistance by the national parties to the formation of European political parties? Such resistance is not confined to the SPD.* It is particularly strong in the SPD because of the national character, adverse political experience in the past and the special political situation of the Federal Republic in Europe, but all political parties will show the same opposition when it comes to the point, and everyone realises that the formation of European political parties means that national party congresses will no longer have the last word. Perhaps this factor will not seem so very important to the ordinary party member who attends congresses, but it may appear vital to the party executive which often uses the decision-making process at the party congress to force through its own opinions and override its opponents. As but one component of a democratic European party, the national party executive would never have the last word, because a European party congress might come out against the decisions which the national party executive has been able to force through at a national congress.

The exercise of power will therefore be an important problem for European political parties. Power can be directly embodied in a national party when it is in Government and indirectly when it is in Opposition. But this is only possible at national level.

What is to be done when power is taken out of the hands of national authorities? This is already the case in the economic sphere in the European Community, and the same transfer of authority will soon be made in the monetary sector too. Power then shifts to the European decision-making machinery in the Council of Ministers. The national party still remains very close to the centre of power through its national Government representation; but the power it wields is less absolute. The Opposition is in an even worse position because attacks on a national minister after difficult secret negotiations in the Council—in which he will always claim to have defended national interests particularly successfully—are seldom popular.

* SPD—Social Democratic Party.

The supervisory powers of parties in Government and Opposition over the process of national Government are being eroded while the powers of the Council of Ministers are increasing. But since in a parliamentary democracy the national parties are the mouthpiece of public opinion and the channel of democracy in an elected parliament, this is a dubious anti-democratic process, especially as the Council of Ministers wields its increasing power without any form of supervision.

This process ought to give rise to serious concern among the leaders of the social democratic parties in the EEC member States. Unfortunately this is not the case. If the leaders of the national parties recognised the facts, they would surely be more willing to reach agreement on the creation of a political counterbalance to the concentrated power of the Council. However, they seem satisfied with their attempts to maintain power at national level. In general election campaigns they make all kinds of promises to the voters which they cannot implement once they are in government. This generally unintentional deception of the electorate is most apparent in small countries.

The average voter is not so clearly aware of the facts. He is not told the truth but when he reads the newspaper he gains a vague impression that the general election campaign is not really as momentous as his political party would have him believe. The result is a waning interest in national politics. Responsible people (especially in the younger age groups) are therefore adopting an increasingly reticent attitude to the supranational decision-making process in important areas of EEC activity. . . .

(Extracted from *Government and Opposition*, Vol. 6, no. 4, Autumn 1971. Also in Ghita Ionescu (ed.), *The New Politics of European Integration*, Macmillan, London, 1972.)

3.4 The Italian Communists and the European Parliament

JOHN FOSTER LEICH

On 12 March 1969, a qualitative change occurred in the composition of the European Parliament: newly elected Italian representatives took their places in the *Maison de l'Europe* in Strasbourg, and among these representatives were seven members of the Italian Communist Party (PCI). Thus, after twelve years of standing on the sidelines, first in outright opposition, then in a position of critical ambivalence and finally as applicants for admission, the largest communist party in Western Europe has accepted and endorsed the principle of European political and economic collaboration.

As Giorgio Amendola, the leader of the PCI group in the European Parliament put it in his maiden speech on 12 March:

> Our opposition [to the Treaty of Rome] did not mean that we did not recognise the necessity of economic and political cooperation among the European countries and regions. Nor, on the other hand, has our opposition ever reached the point of denying or ignoring the reality which was coming into being, the reality of a process of economic integration, even if this process has been concretely controlled by important American and European monopolistic forces.[1]

Despite the somewhat tortuous nature of Amendola's reasoning, on one point he is quite clear: the Italian Communists have joined the European Parliament for better or for worse, they plan to stay there and they plan to increase their influence on European affairs through their participation in the work of the Parliament as the quasi-legislative branch of the European Communities. More than a year has now passed since the PCI joined the European Parliament, and it is now possible to see somewhat more clearly the objectives which the Italian Communists hope to achieve through their presence in Strasbourg, and the tactics which they plan to employ to this end.

Much of the background of this new development on the European scene has already been covered in detail and with expertise by Donald Blackmer[2] and Werner Feld,[3] and only the major facts need be mentioned here. Like all the West European communist parties, the PCI voted against ratification of the Treaty of Rome; following the Soviet line the Common Market was an aggressive American–West tool for their domination of Europe and to re-enforce the North German Atlantic Alliance.[4] However, as early as November 1960, there were indications of a change in the attitude of the PCI, and a distinct divergence from that of the Soviet Union. At the 81-Party Conference in Moscow, the Italians argued that Western Europe was becoming increasingly prosperous and more and more independent of the United States, and that:

> ... increasingly close collaboration among the European monopolies required a revision of communist attitudes and action toward international bodies such as the Common Market.[5]

Indeed it was at the 1960 Moscow Conference that the question of communist representation in European organisations was first posed formally by the PCI, when they maintained that:

> The very act of denouncing the activities of the monopolies and mobilising the masses of the workers can be facilitated by the presence of the legitimate representatives of the working class in these organisations.[6]

In September 1962, the PCI's 'Theses for the Tenth Congress' spelled out the need to work within the European Economic Community (EEC) in order to reform what 'is now a political and economic reality with which one must come to terms'.[7] By 1966, the PCI was already pressing strongly for its inclusion in the renewed Italian delegation to the European Parliament, which was due to be elected in the near future.

Meanwhile, the communist-controlled Italian trade union confederation, the CGIL, had opened an office in Brussels in 1962, and the trade unionists were also demanding that they be given representation in the EEC consultative committees. The CGIL joined forces with its French counterpart in this initiative, and the two confederations were finally given seats on the new Economic and Social Committee in 1969. The French Communist Party, however, continued to maintain a negative attitude towards the European Communities.

The first concrete opportunity for the PCI to participate in an organ of the European Communities presented itself with the decision to renew the Italian representation in the European Parliament for the 1969 session, after a delay of six years. The rules of the Communities prescribe that each national Parliament shall decide how its representation in the European Parliament shall be determined. Presumably it reflects the political party composition of the national Parliament, and should therefore be renewed after each general election. This, however, was not the case in Italy.

The Italian rules for the selection of Italy's representation provide that the Italian Senate and Chamber of Deputies will each elect eighteen representatives. The first representation in 1959 excluded members of the PCI and the PSI (*Partito Socialista Italiano*), two of the largest parties in the Parliament, on the grounds that they had opposed the creation of the European Communities. However, by 1963, with the advent of the 'opening to the left', great changes had taken place in the configuration of the Italian political parties. The PSI had broken its united front with the Communists, and had joined the governing coalition.

Despite the fact that general elections were held in Italy in 1963, and again in 1968, the Italian representation in the European Parliament remained unchanged for over ten years. Fortunately— perhaps—the rules of the European Parliament require only that its members be members of their national Parliaments at the moment of their election. Thus, several Italian members of the European Parliament, who were not re-elected to the Italian Parliament in 1963, continued to occupy their seats in Strasbourg. As one commentator put it, the failure to renew the Italian representation meant that 'a large number of the delegates represented no one apart from themselves, or had simply died'.[8] Of the thirty-six original Italian members of the Parliament, only thirteen were still active by 1968.[9]

This lack of Italian representation was not only damaging to Italy's interests, it also meant a greater burden for the other members of the Parliament, who had to assume the Italians' share of committee work. What made the matter even more interesting was the fact that it was now Italy's turn to have the presidency of the Parliament, in the person of that country's former Prime Minister, Mario Scelba. According to informed parliamentary staff members, the European parliamentarians made the acceptance of Scelba's candidacy contingent upon a renewal of the Italian representation in the Parliament. Commission Chairman Jean Rey described as 'shocking and abnormal' the fact that Italy had not renewed her representation in the European Parliament for several years, while all the other five member countries had renewed their representations on the basis of each new general election.[10] Rey claimed that he could not understand why the communist party members who had seats in the Belgian, French and Italian Parliaments should be excluded from the Strasbourg Parliament.[11]

New Italian representatives were therefore appointed to take their seats at the beginning of the new session, in March 1969; and Scelba was duly elected President of the European Parliament for a one-year term. The new representation reflected rather accurately the actual distribution of seats in the Italian Chamber of Deputies, with perhaps some undue weight being inevitably given to the smaller parties, in order for them to be represented at all. Delegates of the nine Italian parties represented in the Rome Parliament were elected to the Strasbourg Parliament, and took their seats in the hemicycle of the *Maison de l'Europe* as follows, from left to right:

  7 Partito Comunista Italiano (PCI).
  1 Partito Socialista Indipendente d'Unità Proletaria (PSIUP), seated with the Communists.
  1 Independent, seated with the Communists.
  6 Partito Socialista Italiano (PSI). These included former Social Democrats who later in 1969 split off to form the Partito Socialista Unificato (PSU).
  1 Partito Repubblicano Italiano (PRI), seated with the Socialists.
15 Democrazia Cristiana (DC).
  1 Südtiroler Partei, seated with the Christian Democrats.
  2 Partito Liberale Italiano (PLI).
  1 Partito Nazionale Monarchico (PNM), seated with the Liberals.
  1 Movimento Sociale Italiano (MSI), seated with the Liberals.

A description of this change is complicated by two factors. In the first place, in theory there are no national delegations as such in the European Parliament, but merely members of the Parliament who happen to be designated by the member nations of the European Communities. The Rome Treaty provides that ultimately the members of the Parliament are to be elected in Europe-wide elections. Secondly, seating in the Parliament is by political groups and not by nationalities. Today there are four recognised groups in the Parliament: European Democratic Union (French de Gaullists), Liberals, Christian Democrats and Socialists. In order to qualify as a political group, there must be at least fourteen members who are sympathisers of a particular trend. The seven PCI members, and their two Italian and one French sympathisers, do not therefore constitute a group, but are listed as *non-inscrits*, or 'non-aligned', which both flies in the face of reason and places the communists under certain parliamentary disadvantages which they are quick to point out.

From the practical viewpoint, parliamentary groups are each given an office with a secretary and other facilities, and the group chairmen have in the past been consulted by the President for the purpose of deciding procedural matters, such as the day's agenda, and even more substantive matters, such as the selection of vice-presidents, which is customarily done on the assumption of a unanimous consent, once the chairmen have agreed. Such unanimity is now lacking, with the arrival of the communists and the sub-group status—so to speak—with which they have had to content themselves.

From the very first day they appeared at Strasbourg, the PCI members have complained loudly of a general and particular discrimination against the communists. As far as Italy is concerned, they maintain that they represent at least 26 per cent of the voters,[12] and with their allies $33\frac{1}{3}$ per cent, and that therefore they are entitled to several more than the nine seats (or 25 per cent of the Italian representation) which their technically non-existent 'group' now occupies. As far as the other five countries, members of the Community, are concerned, the communists are not represented at all.[13]

Needless to say, the PCI stands foursquare for direct proportional elections for the European Parliament, as do in fact both President Scelba and the Italian Foreign Office. Such elections would undoubtedly result in a greater communist participation, both as far as Italy is concerned as well as the rest of the six member nations. In the meantime, however, the PCI members of the Parliament, like Amendola, maintain the interesting thesis that they in fact are 'representing the communists of the other [five] countries, or at least a current of ideas and forces which is an essential element of European and worldwide reality. This reality can be fought against, but it cannot be ignored.'[14]

In addition to these organisational matters, Amendola was able in his maiden speech to set forth what during the following twelve months has turned out rather accurately to be the communist policy line in the European Parliament. According to Amendola, the

Common Market was an outgrowth of the cold war and led to a perpetuation of the political, economic and military *blocs* which divided Europe. In this fashion the EEC became involved in the crisis of NATO. The PCI is entering the European Parliament just at that point when the Parliament is finally recognising the existence of a crisis within the Communities. The crisis, says the PCI leader, is the direct consequence of the involvements of the European Communities on the side of the United States in a policy of competing military *blocs*. The idea of a third force has proved an illusion.

Amendola holds that European unity can only be achieved on the basis of two conditions: (1) the opposing military *blocs* must be liquidated and replaced by a policy of co-operation between European states of differing political systems, and (2) the forces of the left in all European countries must work for peace and social democracy. In addition, Italy must eventually become neutral and anti-imperialist, and the forced exportation of Italian labour must cease.[15]

When it comes to the constitutional position of the Parliament, the Council of Ministers and the Commission, the PCI position is not entirely clear. One has the impression that PCI representatives are more nationalistic than any other Italian group. However, this manifestation is not always consistent; and it is related to the PCI's attitude on the question of direct elections for the European Parliament.

As one of the PCI representatives, Leonilde Iotti, explained the Party's position to the writer, as long as there are no Europe-wide elections with universal suffrage for the European Parliament, the PCI will regard the European Communities as merely an economic union of limited objectives, which is not competent to take political decisions. Therefore, matters of policy must be referred to the individual Governments and ultimately to their respective Parliaments.[16] For example, the association agreements which the Commission has negotiated with Tunisia and Morocco should be submitted to the individual Governments for ratification according to their own constitutional procedures, and cannot be the subject of a resolution of approval or disapproval on the part of the European Parliament.

On the other hand, the PCI representative Silvio Leonardi found no inconsistency in claiming that the Commission should resign on the basis of the European Parliament's rejection of the Euratom budget.[17] Leonardi was somewhat off base here, as Commission President Rey was quick to point out, since it was the Council and not the Commission which had actually drafted the Euratom budget. But the PCI apparently wanted to make the point that the principle of the Parliament's right to consider a motion of censure should not be abandoned.

Again, on the question of the Communities' finances, the position taken by the PCI members in the debates at Strasbourg has not always been entirely consistent with Mrs. Iotti's formulation. Senator Giovanni Bertoli would like to see 'an immediate strengthening of the Parliament's powers in all matters in which the Commission has an autonomous power of decision, for example the administration of the EEC Social Fund'. Greater sources of financing are needed, and the Parliament should lay down guide lines for the expenditure of these funds.[18] Surely, greater independent sources of finance are bound to add to the supranational character of the Communities. However, the PCI standpoint here would be in line with their general claim that the European Parliament as the only organ in which the communists are represented, should exercise more authority in the Communities' affairs.

The most interesting development of the 1969–70 parliamentary year has been the growing function which the PCI has performed of acting as a sort of vanguard for Italian protectionist interests, especially where agricultural products and the fate of small farmers have been involved. A case in point is the debate which took place during the July 1969 session of the European Parliament on the creation of a common market in tobacco.

Among the six countries, it is only in Italy that tobacco is grown in any significant amount, and the production there has enjoyed the benefit of a high protectionist tariff for many years. On the other hand, the big cigar and cigarette manufacturers in Europe are largely concentrated in West Germany and the Netherlands. These understandably wish to decrease their production costs through the abolition of the Italian tariff and a closer association of cheap tobacco-producing countries, such as Turkey or the North African countries, with the EEC. In the course of this argument, the whole question of the effect of the use of tobacco on human life and the problem of the control of this use seem not to have been raised at all.

Originally it was thought possible to deal with this problem in the same fashion that the EEC had dealt with the question of a milk production surplus within the Six, which was not competitive with dairy products imported from outside the Six. In this case, the surplus milk was bought up, converted into dried milk, fed to milk cows, who in turn produced more excess milk, thereby starting the whole cycle over again.

The Agricultural Commission of the European Parliament saw the fallacy of this type of price support, especially when it was applied to a non-essential, or even harmful product, such as tobacco. Instead of purchasing all the surplus tobacco production of the Six, the Commission proposed that the tobacco producers, after negotiating their contracts with the manufacturers, be given a premium by the EEC which would guarantee an 'objective price' that would show exactly how much the protection of tobacco production was costing each year.

This proposal of course gave rise to fears on the part of the producers that, if they had to negotiate directly with one or two big tobacco cartels, they would be in a very unfavourable bargaining position, and ultimately even at the mercy of these big processors.

When the report[19] of the Agricultural Commission came to the floor of the Parliament on 3 July, the situation was tailor-made for an aggressive communist intervention on behalf of the Italian tobacco growers.[20] Leonardi and the PCI Senator Francescopaolo D'Angelosante were particularly critical of the *rapporteur* of the Agricultural Commission for this question, Astrid Lulling (Socialist) of Luxembourg. She had proposed that the displaced Italian workers be retrained during a period of two years. These sentiments were echoed by at least one Italian Christian Democrat, Mario Vetrone, and by Raymond Triboulet, a French de Gaullist.

This discussion was not without its drama. Senator D'Angelosante accused Mrs. Lulling of wanting to 'liquidate' the Italian tobacco workers. Mrs. Lulling loudly objected that no communist had the right to use the word 'liquidation' in this connection. For this she was called to order by President Scelba, who pointed out that not only the communists but other members of the Parliament as well were critical of her report. Shortly thereafter, in a moment of parliamentary confusion, Senator D'Angelosante apparently gave vent to the opinion that Mrs. Lulling had been 'paid by the German tobacco industry'. Upon being questioned by President Scelba, the senator admitted having made this informal accusation, which the President thereupon officially deplored.[21]

In addition to posing as the champion of the poor farmers in the Community, the PCI has also taken advantage of its presence at

Strasbourg to raise high the banner of anti-colonialism. At times, oddly enough, these two objectives seem to go hand in hand. For example, the PCI voted against the association agreements between the EEC and Tunisia and Morocco, on the grounds that they perpetuated the colonial status of these areas. Actually, these agreements also worked to the disadvantage of the Italian citrus fruit growers. In connection with these agreements, the PCI also raised the procedural question of approving a treaty which has not been ratified by the national Parliaments of the states concerned. Apparently a short while before, there had been a government-sponsored resolution in the Italian Parliament criticising the draft of the treaty with Tunisia and Morocco and recommending changes in it to the advantage of the Italian citrus growers. Once more the PCI was in the forefront of the defence of the sovereign rights of EEC member countries.[22]

Similar arguments were also applied in the case of the proposed agreements between the Community and the Central African countries, and between the Community and the countries of Latin America.[23] The PCI also objected to a ruling of the Commission which required that the Commission approve by a qualified majority any bilateral East–West trade agreements which the member nations may conclude.[24]

In the case of the common market for wine, the PCI's position was the reverse of the one they held with respect to citrus fruits. Here, of course, other member States, particularly Germany, wanted to regulate wine production in such a way as to favour the less efficient producers, especially those of the Rhine and Moselle valleys. The Commission proposed restrictions on overall production, no preference for producers in the member States and the authorisation of greater amounts of artificial sugaring—all of which measures would favour the German wine producers, with their shorter growing season and less consistent sunshine, and rebound to the disadvantage of the Italian producers. The PCI strongly opposed the Commission's draft, and in its opposition was joined by the rest of the Italian members of the Parliament.[25]

Finally, on the general political plane, the policy of the PCI has been quite clearly expressed. In three of his four interventions during the 1969–70 session, Giorgio Amendola made reference to 'il superamento dei blocchi',[26] to Europe's need to escape from the trap caused by the existence of the two blocs which were the result of the cold war. He also spoke of the need for a European security conference, as a means of 'overcoming the *blocs*'. Cassandra-like, he stressed the gravity of the crisis of the Community, which others refuse to recognise. No one will say that the king is naked. The Community, according to Amendola, is afflicted with an original sin, the fact of its birth in the cold war. What is needed is a critical reflection on the cause of the crisis, the relationship of the Community to the great powers. For this purpose, says Amendola, a European security conference would be a useful step, with the participation both of the United States and the Soviet Union.[27]

This brings us at long last to the basic question which this paper raises, but as yet had not satisfactorily answered: what it is that the Italian Communists hope to achieve from their participation in the European Parliament? Perhaps we can begin to find the answer to this question in the text of Palmiro Togliatti's testament, dictated as the long-time leader of the PCI lay dying at Yalta in August 1964.[28] Togliatti said at that time, not without a certain optimism,

> Objectively, very favourable conditions exist for our advance, both among the working class and among the working masses and in social life in general. But it is necessary to know how to seize upon and exploit these conditions. Therefore, communists must have great political courage, and must surmount all forms of despotism, facing and solving new problems in new ways, using operational methods which are adapted to a political and social climate in which continuous and rapid transformations are occurring.[29]

Togliatti's successor, Luigi Longo, gave a practical example of this flexibility when discussing the reasons for the PCI's desire to participate in the European Parliament, in a newspaper interview in 1966.[30] When the Common Market was formed, Longo said, the PCI was critical of it as an expression of great monopoly interests, whose control of the organisation would prevent the democratisation of the member countries. These fears, he said, were justified, however: 'Now . . . other political and social forces which used to and still do support the Common Market are much more critical of the Market's policy.'

Therefore, says Longo, a changed situation has arisen. The PCI, together with the French Communist Party [*sic*], recognise that the Common Market exists and is a reality which profoundly influences the economic life of all his members. For this reason, it is necessary to carry the PCI's action into the organisation itself, not with the objective of disintegrating or blowing up the Community—as some unfriendly critics erroneously pretend—but to fight within the institution for a new policy, for a policy not directed by the trusts and cartels.

At Budapest in 1968, Enrico Berlinguer boasted that

> The forces which can be used in the battle against imperialism today are limitless. But in order to realise this task effectively, the communists must regain their freedom of movement, in conditions and with objectives and methods of operation which are necessarily different from those of the past, with that same *larghezza di idee*, with that same creative courage as that of which the VIIth Congress was the model.[31]

Berlinguer's reference to the Seventh Congress of the Comintern, which in 1935 enshrined the policy of the Popular Front, is highly significant, and is probably the key to the PCI's behaviour in the European field, both at home and abroad. Togliatti's polycentrism, or 'unity in diversity', has in effect two faces: an international face which authorises the PCI to take initiatives in the European arena, which run counter to expressed Soviet policy,[32] and a national face whereby the party increases its prestige and acceptability at home by fighting for the defence of specific Italian interests in an international forum.

In a press conference upon his return from the first session of the European Parliament in which the PCI had participated, Amendola gave four reasons for his party's joining the Parliament: (1) to put an end to discrimination; (2) to gain direct knowledge of the Community and of the best means of effectuating a revision of the Treaty of Rome; (3) to establish relations with those forces of the European left which desire a revision of the Rome Treaty and co-operation among all the European states, both East and West; and (4) to undertake immediately the task of defending the interests of the Italian workers, the migrant workers, and the small farmers.[33]

On balance, these objectives seem to have been pursued rather closely during the first year that the PCI has been represented in the European Parliament.

References

1. *Journal officiel des Communautés européenes, Débats du Parlement européen,* ♯ *113, mars, 1969,* Service des Publications des Communautés européenes, Luxembourg, 1969, p. 38.
2. Donald L. M. Blackmer, *Unity in Diversity: Italian Communism and the Communist World,* The M.I.T. Press, Cambridge, Mass., 1968.
3. Werner J. Feld, 'National–International Linkage Theory: The East European Communist System and the EEC', *Journal of International Affairs,* Vol. XXII, no. 1, 1968, pp. 107–20; and 'The French and Italian Communists and the Common Market: The Requests for Representation in the Community Institutions', *Journal of Common Market Studies,* Vol. VI, no. 3, March 1968, pp. 250–66.
4. Blackmer, op. cit., pp. 152 ff.
5. Ibid., p. 175.
6. 'Promemoria della delegazione italiana alla commissione preparatoria', *Interventi della delegazione,* cited in Blackmer, op. cit., p. 173.
7. *L'Unità,* 27 April 1962, cited in Roger Salloch, 'Attitude of the Western European Communist Parties', *The Communists and the Common Market,* Radio Free Europe Research, Munich, 1967.
8. 'L'Italia nella politica internazionale', Vol. I, no, 1, May 1969, Istituto Affari Internazionali, Rome, 1969, p. 26.
9. Ibid., p. 10.
10. Press Conference, Brussels, 17 December 1968, RFE Special/ Dybvik.
11. Ibid.
12. In the last general election, the PCI polled 28 per cent of the vote.
13. *Journal officiel, Débats,* ♯ *113 mars, 1969,* loc. cit. Of course, the question remains unanswered as to whether the other parties actually want to be represented in the Parliament. We know, for example, that the French do not.
14. Ibid.
15. Ibid., pp. 39–40.
16. Cf. Silvio Leonardi, 'Un'alternativa per i Paesi del Mercato Comune', *Rinascita,* no. 27–3, 16, 1970, for a further amplification of this view.
17. *Journal officiel, Débats,* ♯ *116, juillet, 1969,* p. 51.

18. Ibid., p. 123.
19. *Journal officiel, Communications et informations, 12ème année, No C 97, 28 juillet, 1969*, pp. 49–79, gives the Commission's draft and the Parliament's proposed amendments.
20. 35 per cent of the supporters of the PCI come from the agricultural sector. Primarily they are *mezzadri* and *bracianti*, and many are or were employed by the protected tobacco planters. Cf. Joseph LaPalombara, *Interest Groups in Italian Politics*, Princeton University Press, Princeton, 1964, p. 95.
21. *Journal officiel, Débats, ♯ 116, juillet, 1969*, pp. 119 ff.
22. *Journal officiel, Débats, ♯ 110, juillet, 1969*, pp. 38 and 45.
23. *Journal officiel, Débats, ♯ 119, novembre, 1969*, p. 26.
24. Ibid., p. 47.
25. *Journal officiel, Débats, ♯ 121, fevrier, 1969*, pp. 146 ff.
26. *Journal officiel, Débats, ♯ 113, mars, 1969*, p. 8; ♯ *116, juillet, 1969*, p. 150; ♯ *119, novembre, 1969*, p. 16.
27. Ibid.
28. *Rinascita, No. 35–21*, 5 September 1964.
29. Ibid.
30. *L'Unità*, 29 May 1966, p. 1.
31. Cited in Luigi Longo's, *L'Unità del Movimento operaio e comunista*, Editori Ruiniti, Rome, 1968, p. 64.
32. Cf. George Schöpflin, 'Enlargement: The Soviet View', *European Community*, no. 140, November–December 1970.
33. *L'Unità*, 22 March 1969, p. 3.

(Extracted from *Journal of Common Market Studies*, Vol. 9, no. 4, Summer 1970.)

3.5 Does Wilson Know Where the Money is?

PETER WILSHER

Mr. Wilson may turn out to have jumped the gun a bit last week, when he contemptuously refused to send a Labour delegation to the European Parliament in Strasbourg after Britain's EEC entry on 1 January. Almost the same day that he chose to dismiss that much-abused body as meaningless and powerless, its members made their first serious effort to show that they have serious political teeth. And the ground they chose to fight on lies right at the heart of the Euro-political tangle—the control of the Common Market budget.

It is symptomatic of the abysmal level of the pro- and anti-market debate that very few people on either side (let alone in the street) could confidently say whether or not the EEC even had a budget, in the normal sense. They are dimly aware that Britain is expected to contribute vast sums to the support of undeserving French farmers, and that it hopes to get a bit back to help the beleaguered regions. But as to who draws up the estimates, who vets them, who has the power to vote or refuse the necessary taxes, or who checks that the money is being properly and efficiently spent, this remains (judging from the various parliamentary debates) a subject of almost total ignorance and apathy.

There is some excuse for this. Ever since 1958, the various national Governments which make up the EEC, with the Council of Ministers and (sometimes) the Brussels Commission, have conspired to pro-duce a complex and frequently chaotic sharing-out of financial responsibility. This is dispersed between themselves and the people in charge of particular areas like the Common Agricultural Policy, in a way that often seems deliberately calculated to deceive.

However, this is not, fortunately, the whole story. The fact of the matter is that the Community, however reluctantly, and with however much hair-splitting over the details, is committed, in some sense, to giving the European Parliament a bigger say in the raising and the spending of the Community's funds. And the form that this bigger say actually takes will in many ways define the sort of Europe we are joining—just as the decision to give Washington central taxing power, over and above that of the individual American states, ranks with the constitution and the Declaration of Independence, as a crucial factor in the development of the US.

The whole tangled story-so-far is lucidly and topically set out in a pamphlet published this weekend—David Coombes's *The Power of the Purse in the European Communities*.*

In general, as Coombes says, the EEC budget is still viewed, both by its officials and the member Governments, as a means of approving the receipts and expenditures of an ordinary international organisa-tion. 'It is, however, already more than this and will probably get increasingly like the budget of a national government in its political significance.'

* PEP, Chatham House.

The first question to come up was where should the money come from? Initially, the members put in contributions, more or less tailored to what they expected to get out of the EEC—the French notion of *juste retour*. But increasingly it has become accepted that, for the Community to function effectively it needs access to its own resources. This was recognised only very slowly. The Treaty of Rome gave it nothing at all, the Coal and Steel Treaty allowed merely a modest 1 per cent levy on production and a major row on the subject virtually halted all Brussels activity for nine months in 1965. It was only in 1970—at the same Hague meeting that cleared the way for British entry—that a substantial breakthrough occurred. For a 'provisional period', to the end of 1974, members' contributions are being gradually replaced by the income from levies on agricultural imports and the customs produced by the common external tariff.

This then gives way to a 'normal period', starting on 1 January 1975, when the Community gets, in addition, a share of the VAT revenue arising in each of the member countries. But there will still be some restrictions on the way the total can grow until the beginning of 1978. Only then will the money be truly the EEC's own.

This much is relatively clear. But the same could not be said for the extra powers which the Strasbourg Parliament, under the same Hague proposals (as later enshrined in the Treaty of Luxembourg), is to have over the cash. Every aspect of the matter—ability to set the rates, to find new sources beyond the initial three, to set new spending policies, or to vet, cut back or expand existing programmes—is completely up in the air. But to say that does not mean, it seems to me, at all the same as accepting the Wilson line. The functions of the Parliament will be defined only after a series of pitched battles; several of which have already been joined. But defined they will be—and, judging by last week's exchanges, where a French deputy threatened to bring about the resignations of the entire Commission (which is one fairly spectacular thing the Parliament can already do), they will be defined at a level significantly above zero.

One knotty problem to be ironed out concerns the typically serpentine Brussels distinction between 'obligatory' spending, arising out of Community policies (like agriculture), which are more or less specified under the treaties, and where, according to many officials and ministers, the parliamentary delegates should have no say, and the 'non-obligatory' remainder. If the size of the 'non-obligatory' sector can be made big enough—or there are provisions to enlarge it by political will—the European parliamentarians could still find themselves with a useful wedge, and considerable bargaining power.

The Luxembourg proposals, however, appear to go considerably beyond this. They lay down that the Parliament, in one of those marvellously open-ended EEC phrases, should have the 'final word' in budgetary matters from 1 January 1975 on.

Just what this means, of course, constitutes the main battlefield over which the Strasbourg power struggle will be fought during the next three years. It could be anything at all, from a purely symbolic blessing, like the Royal Assent in Britain, to a full-blooded right to amend, cut, increase or in the last resort, veto, the whole Community spending programme and the way it is financed. Few member Governments—certainly not Mr. Heath's—would go anything like that far in the direction of central parliamentary freedom. But on the other hand, few, even the French, would dare (or even wish) to press the purely symbolic interpretation.

There are plenty of other connected problems to be sorted out if Europe is to move from its present, rather incoherent group of national bargainers to anything resembling a centrally cohesive, federally-orientated, decision-making force. There is no European Treasury to ensure the economic and financial consistency of the dozens of different policies being pursued; there is no committee of public accounts to check that the faceless men of Brussels know how to get value for money, and so forth.

Whether the European concept is to mean much or little over our lifetime is fairly intimately tied up to the way such gaps are ultimately filled. The European deputies, backing Georges Senale in his motion of no confidence, take the view that they have a significant part to play in the process, and that the Commission, which has failed—so they say—to meet its deadline for putting up concrete proposals to this effect, should be displaced to make way for a more expeditious team. It may be shadow boxing—but I suspect that Wilson may come to regret his arrogant dismissal of the European Parliament's place in the scheme of things. After all, it does happen to be the only forum, in the entire spectrum of Community institutions, where party politics can still be practised. And why leave Heath with all the best tunes, and the money box as well?

(Extracted from *The Sunday Times*, 26 November 1972.)

3.6 Coming to the Aid of the Europarty Concept

RICHARD NORTON-TAYLOR

When the West German Bundestag was agonisingly waiting for a debate on the Ostpolitik treaties last week, and the Italian deputies were preparing for a new battle of coalition-forming, the European Parliament, in peaceful Luxembourg, discussed aids to the silkworm industry and freedom of movement for hairdressers.

Fortunately, Henk Vredeling, a Dutch Socialist MP, was there trying, as ever, to encourage his colleagues to inject life into the European Parliament's proceedings. Vredeling has been a member of the European Parliament since the Common Market was founded fourteen years ago.

He admits that 'he has spent the best years of his life there', but he says that the necessity for it has made it all worthwhile. 'Democracy,' he adds, 'is based on political parties,' and he sees his main task as getting the Socialist, or progressive parties in the Common Market to co-operate effectively with a common manifesto on the Community level.

Vredeling is famous in Brussels for his persistent use of the parliamentary question procedure. Week after week, he bombards the European Commission with more questions than all his 141 colleagues in the European Parliament put together. The word is that the Commission has two officials employed full time trying to answer them within the conventional two months' deadline.

Many of his questions, dealing with anything from agriculture frauds to the role of multinational companies or trade relations between the Community and China, are inspired by newspaper articles. But he also encourages his political colleagues and Dutch trade unionists to use him as an official channel.

And although the Commission is sometimes embarrassed—frequently irritated—by the steady flow of Vredeling questions, they can be used by some of the younger, more dynamic, officials in the Commission to fight against the bureaucratic timidity of their superiors.

On one occasion, an attempt by Community agricultural ministers to get out of a problem by adopting a strictly illegal compromise (illegal in that it was forbidden by the Treaty of Rome) was abandoned when the German Minister warned his colleagues 'what would a certain Vredeling say about this?'

Vredeling lays great store by the traditional 'nuisance value' of Parliament. Yet he is fully aware that this is limited. 'It will be more and more difficult,' he says, 'for national Parliaments to get a grip on the enlarged Community.'

Because the Community rules give the European Parliament specific—albeit extremely limited—rights when it comes to budgetary control, both the Strasbourg institution and his own national Parliament have, Vredeling admits, tended to concentrate too much on the issue of budgetary control.

But even there the complicated Community rules are open to more than one interpretation. While the Dutch insist that the European Parliament does have the right to reject the entire Community budget, the French say it does not.

Vredeling, of course, would like the ten* potential members of an enlarged Community to give the European Parliament the right to have a direct say in the formulation of policy at their October summit meeting.

But he is prepared to accept the power of a negative veto that would enable a majority in the European Parliament to block decisions made by the Council of Ministers. As far as the Commission is concerned, he says that the nomination of Commissioners should be the subject of internal debate of political parties as well as member Governments.

(A new enlarged Commission that is due to take office on 1 January next year should have at least five Socialist members—one British, Danish, Norwegian,* German, Italian and possibly one from Benelux as well.)

But Mr. Vredeling's main concern is with the failure of European political parties to face up to the reality of the Community. 'In 1958,' he said, 'I would never have thought that the integration process would move so quickly. But I am very much disappointed with the lack of political follow up.

'The parties, especially the Socialist groups, are very guilty of negligence. In the year 2000 historians will say this has been the failure of the so-called democratic parties. They did not see the reality, they didn't tell the truth to their voters and to the people.

* [The ten includes Norway, which rejected entry.]

'And there's an enormous lack of leadership, of leadership with vision. I think the Labour Party is a very good example. What Mr. Wilson lacks is vision. I know that one of the qualities of the British is muddling through, but . . .'

Vredeling, himself a trade unionist, accuses the Community's Socialist parties of not creating an adequate framework in which trade unions can co-operate on the European level.

'It's very difficult,' he says, 'for Europeans to accept that a majority could be formed by people with another language. Big business has gone much further. When AZKO (a Dutch chemical group) recently decided to close down some of its plants in the Netherlands, Germany and Belgium, it had no difficulty in saying that this was simply in the interests of the company. It's the same in Britain.'

Vredeling foresees that British entry will lead to a very painful regrouping of British industry. The trade unions will have to stop this, and the best way is for unions and progressive parties to co-ordinate at Community level.

AZKO's action provoked one of the few really meaningful debates (last month) the European Parliament has witnessed. As a result, the Commission promised to organise union and employer contracts in Brussels; AZKO promised to negotiate alternative measures, and unions have established an emergency liaison procedure whenever company decisions are taken that affects workers in several countries.

But Socialist parties, like unions, adds Vredeling, 'should always be where the centre of power is. It isn't in The Hague and it won't be in London, but in Brussels.' He is dead against the European Parliament sitting in Strasbourg. He wants the Parliament to meet in Brussels.

Over the past two years or so Vredeling has held behind-the-scene discussions aimed at forming what he calls a 'European progressive party' with a main Socialist stream, but including for example, the small Dutch D66 Party and the Italian Republican Party which is already associated to the Socialist group.

In the past, the German SPD has effectively blocked concrete moves towards the formation of a European progressive party. But once the Ostpolitik treaties are out of the way, Vredeling believes the SPD will adopt a more positive approach.

He points out that the Italian Communists and the Young Socialists in Germany, as well as the Dutch Socialist Party's new Left wing, have all accepted the Community as the 'framework of their political activity as a means to an end'.

(Vredeling personality claims the credit for convincing the Left wing of his own party. He told them one day that he was sorry to say that their views for development aid policy in the national framework were simply irrelevant. 'They became European-minded out of criticism.')

Henk Vredeling does not want a European progressive party to weaken existing national parties, and suggests that the Left and Centre political groups in the Community at first co-operate in a pragmatic way, concentrating for example, on a common social policy which is at the moment completely lacking.

He does not have any particular views on how members of the European Parliament should be directly elected short of as quickly as possible. Yet the elections (both national and European), he said, should be held very close together with the Socialists and their allies using the umbrella of a formal European progressive grouping with its own aims and objectives.

About the attitude of the British Labour Party, Vredeling is not very optimistic, fearing that if Labour wins the next election, it will adopt a restrictive and negative policy towards the Community and all its works. But, he said, Labour will be fooling its voters if it ignores Brussels, thereby neglecting their interests.

(Extracted from *The Guardian*, 16 May 1972.)

3.7 The House of Commons and the European Parliament
JOHN MACKINTOSH

. . . The final area covered by the existing institutions of the Common Market is that of parliamentary control. Normally it is assumed that this is solely a matter for the European Assembly. However, so long as the primary impulse in Community decision-making comes from the member Governments, the primary instrument of democratic control will be the national Parliaments. Each country will develop the methods of scrutiny of Community proposals and of controlling or influencing its representative on the Council of Ministers appropriate to its own parliamentary tradition. The Bundestag, with its emphasis on the expertise of its members and with its existing close intermesh with executive policy-making has devised one of the most effective methods of scrutinising EEC proposals. The other parliament of the Six original members of the Community which is equally vigorous is the Dutch Parliament.

The UK Parliament will have some difficulties in developing an adequate pattern of scrutiny because its tradition is against specialised committee work and is in favour of supporting strong executive powers, a tradition which it may want to modify when dealing with a European as opposed to a purely national executive.

In devising appropriate methods, the UK Parliament will have to consider the categories of proposals emanating from the Community rather in the same way as the Vedel Report distinguished between its List A and List B legislative proposals when looking at methods of increasing the powers of the European Assembly.* On all questions which involve the amendment of the Treaties, the creation of new areas of Community activity and the application to the UK of treaties negotiated by the EEC with third parties, the House of Commons ought to want full and immediate information and a debate on the floor of the House.

For regulations of the Commission which, when endorsed by the Council, have the force of law in the UK, the procedure must be different. Many of these regulations are minor matters, but some are of real importance. The most effective procedure would be for the House of Commons to establish select committees on each of the main areas of EEC activity: agriculture, industrial competition, trade relations and so on. Then, when the Commission makes a proposal, it could be considered by the appropriate committee before a decision was reached by the Council of Ministers. Indeed, in view of the 'open government' practised at Brussels, the select committees would probably be aware of how the Commission was thinking and of what was likely to emerge well before any such proposal was made. Then the committee could hear evidence from the home ministry and the relevant pressure groups. If it found that there were major issues at stake, the matter could be taken up by the backbench committees of the parties, the Opposition might request a supply day debate and ministers could be asked about their attitudes to the

* See page 138 below.

issues at question time. No minister would accept directions from a select committee or even from the House but this kind of procedure would inform the British public about what was happening and let the Government and the minister concerned form some opinion of the public's likely reaction to the proposal.

Then there is the category of directives made by the Commission and the Council which are binding as to their objective but do not specify the method of implementation. Up to the point of enactment by the Council, proposals for directives could be considered by the Commons in exactly the same way as regulations and pressure could be placed on the appropriate British minister to agree, to disagree or to amend. Once a directive is made, the procedure laid down for enacting the consequential legislation in Britain is set out in clause 2 of the European Communities Act. It allows the Government to proceed by statutory instrument but it would also be possible for Governments to legislate on such matters and to bring in the necessary bills as if they were emanating from the British Cabinet in the same way as other normal legislation. Alternatively, a convention could be established that the directive is published in a 'Green Paper' along with a discussion of its implications and various methods of implementation so that debate (and, possibly, scrutiny by the appropriate select committee) could take place before the necessary legislation was formulated.

Finally, the House of Commons will want to be informed about and may wish to examine and debate proposals for the draft budget and expenditure of the Commission before these proposals are adopted by the Council of Ministers.

It is not possible in the summer of 1972 to say how the Government and the Opposition front bench will react to this problem. It is their reaction that matters, not that of 'the House', as it has no method of acting apart from the Government; and, in cases of this kind, the Government will be reluctant to move without the agreement of the leaders of the Opposition. They may also not object to inactivity as it will be easier for Governments to negotiate with the other member States and the Commission if they are not closely scrutinised by the House of Commons. Indeed the practice of 'open government' and close observation by committees of elected representatives which is accepted in some of the original six members of the EEC is alien to the British tradition of a highly closed and confidential administration and a legislature where the chief task of the majority is to support the executive. Also, if new practices were brought in to permit maximum scrutiny of the proposals of the Commission, it would be impossible to confine these powers to the work of the Community; they would inevitably be applied to the purely domestic work of Whitehall. Similarly, the fact that whatever the British Government was saying to the Commission would become known more or less at once would soon lead to a demand by the Commons for fuller information about Whitehall attitudes and proposals on purely domestic matters.

As a result, it is by no means clear whether the two front benches will want to extend the powers of backbenchers to enable a proper scrutiny of the activity of the Commission and the Council to take place. If this scrutiny is permitted, it will represent a real gain for the House of Commons in areas such as agriculture and commercial policy from which it has been largely excluded in recent years. If Community affairs are handled in the same way as existing relations with EFTA or NATO are dealt with, and no new methods of supervision are devised, then this will accelerate the present dissociation of Parliament from the making of the important decisions which affect this country.

One other aspect of parliamentary control has to be noticed. Any effective system of control has to match the administrative system it is designed to monitor and therefore much will depend on the way Whitehall is organised to handle EEC affairs. This problem has not been thought through and the indications are that the Government may be content merely to expand the recent arrangements for the negotiations for entry, whereby the chief weight fell on the Foreign Office with the aid of experts from the other ministries. But when, after January 1973, it becomes necessary to answer parliamentary questions, there will have to be a decision as to which minister is responsible for Britain's relations with the Community. It may be that each minister will answer for his own area of jurisdiction and that the Prime Minister will deal with wider issues of principle. However, at present (July 1972), Mr. Rippon answers most of the questions and he is attached to the Cabinet Office. If this practice were to continue with a special minister responsible for most Community affairs and if he was located in the Cabinet Office this could lead on the one hand to the creation of a special Prime Minister's Department and, on the other, to a single European Select Committee of the House of Commons to examine all proposals emanating from the Commission.

An alternative would be for the British Government to leave responsibility for the various aspects of Community policy to the appropriate departmental minister. This solution would obviate the need for any special 'European Minister'. The Foreign Secretary would deal with all of the broader issues which affected foreign policy, the Chancellor of the Exchequer with economic and financial matters and so on. In this case, if there was to be effective supervision by the Commons, the appropriate organisation of the legislature would not be a single European committee but a series of select committees, one dealing with each of these functions and therefore with each of these ministers.

It is only possible, at this stage, to emphasise that it would be easy to devise the appropriate machinery and changes in the standing orders of the House. Failure to do so would leave Community affairs largely as a matter for bureaucrats and specialists, for pressure group experts and specialised journalists and would exclude any wider debate and any real element of public participation. On the other hand, to allow questions to ministers on what part they have taken in Council policy-making, to have a series of select committees discussing all Community regulations in their fields and to have regular and informed debates on the larger issues of EEC policy would do much to revive the waning influence and relevance of the House of Commons.

The European Parliament

A further series of difficult issues arises when the question of the powers and composition of the European Assembly is considered. Probably the most important matter is the powers of the European Parliament but, in the order of discussion here, membership should be examined first because it affects the organisation of the House of Commons. An issue of principle has to be decided. Is it better to have direct election to the European Parliament, thus creating a total separation between the members of the House of Commons and the members of the European Parliament; or should there be a method of indirect election which keeps an overlap of personnel, an intimate connection between the national and the supranational assemblies?

There are arguments for each solution. The case for separate direct elections is that only in this way will European issues be considered separately from national issues. In such elections the public would be educated while the MPs elected would gain a real democratic legitimacy. On the other hand, so long as the principal issues are settled by the member States, the national Parliaments will have the main task of influencing developments in Europe and of explaining them to the public. As the Community does more and as, it is hoped, the competence of the European Parliament grows, it is important not to permit a democratic gap to arise. This would occur if issues that are regarded as European are excluded from the area open to question and discussion by the various national Parliaments and if, on these issues, the European Parliament had not yet developed its capacity to examine and influence Community policy.

It is clear, therefore, that co-operation between the national and the European Parliaments is of great importance. European MPs who were also members of their domestic legislature could bring about this co-operation. They could, for example, alert the parties they belong to when matters which were of concern to them were being considered by the Commission. If the Commission had produced a proposal which was welcomed by the majority of the European Parliament, but was severely amended or just ignored by the Council, the European MPs, on returning home, could ask the ministers on the Council to explain their conduct. The disadvantage of such a close connection is that European MPs who were also MPs in their own countries would be elected on domestic tides of opinion and on the records of their parties at home, all of which would bear little or no relation to their record in Europe. On the other hand, it will probably be some time before decisions of the EEC will have enough impact on domestic electorates to produce real political warfare and party activity with the kind of percentage polls that such controversy arouses. It would be a pity to have direct elections before such interest exists, since the result would be a very low poll which would seriously undermine the credibility of the MPs who were thus elected.

There is also the problem of getting European MPs of an adequate calibre. To allow these members also to serve in their domestic Parliaments might persuade active and ambitious politicians to play a part, at least for some years, in European affairs, as they would not need to sacrifice their domestic careers. In Britain, the one solution to this problem that would be valueless would be to try to maintain a connection between European and British politics by giving the European MPs seats in the House of Lords. To have a worth-while contact depends on membership of the House of Commons where votes are cast, leaders are elected and party opinion is formed. Membership of the House of Lords permits none of these activities and would simply waste the time of European MPs to no advantage.

It would appear that for the foreseeable future, it would be a real gain for the British delegation to the European Parliament to be, at the same time, MPs at Westminster. After January 1973, the European MPs will have to be chosen from among existing MPs but to continue simply appointing British MPs in this way does raise certain difficulties, especially for the MPs concerned. Constituencies are becoming more and more demanding, and MPs are expected to be available most weekends; while membership of the European Parliament requires about a hundred days away from Westminster each session.

The 'Stewart Plan'

The proposals which go furthest in obviating these difficulties have been put forward by the Rt. Hon. Michael Stewart, MP. He has suggested that some six of the thirty-six British MPs come from the Lords. The rest would be elected by large regional constituencies at the same time as national elections were taking place. These thirty European MPs would therefore be full members of the House of Commons with the normal speaking and voting rights but they would be free from constituency pressures on purely domestic issues. To ensure that they could go at any time to the European Parliament, these MPs would be allowed to cast proxy votes at Westminster. But, being full MPs, some of them would make their mark in domestic British politics and move to a home constituency while domestic MPs who had concentrated first on home politics might well be prepared, at a later stage, to do five years in Europe as this would not cut them off from normal political life.

(One refinement should probably be added to the Stewart Plan and that would be to cut those elected by the regional constituencies to, say, twenty-four, the other six places being allocated to the six who were nearest to being elected in such a fashion as to ensure that the numerical result of an election in the 630 domestic seats was in no way altered by the election of the European members. This would prevent close results of the kind that took place in 1950 or 1964 being altered or affected by the return of the European members.)

This system would combine an element of direct election with over-lapping membership of the two Parliaments. If, at any time, it was desired to move to separate elections, the essentials of the Stewart Plan could be retained simply by holding the regional elections at times dictated by the state of politics in the European Parliament and not at the same time as British elections. The system would only become inoperable if the European executive became responsible to the European Parliament and it was impossible for domestic party divisions to meet the needs, divisions and conflicts which were occurring at the European level. But this is unlikely to happen in the foreseeable future and the Stewart Plan could be in operation by 1975.

If such a system were adopted and if the House of Commons established either a single large select committee on Community affairs with a range of sub-committees or a series of select committees covering all aspects of EEC activity, it would be important for the European members to serve on these committees. They would then be in a position to follow up issues that had been inadequately dealt with or had gone the wrong way in Europe by pressure on the appropriate British minister and through him on the Council of Ministers. If these proposals were carried through, it would be necessary to provide British MPs with proper office, secretarial and research facilities in order to let them keep abreast of the volume of business that would arise from this extra committee work and specialisation.

On the question of the site of the European Parliament, *The Economist* has suggested that each session should be held in a different country so as to publicise the work of the Parliament and bring it, in turn, closer to the political life of each member State. While this has some attractions, a legislature that wants to be taken seriously has to be based in the same city as the executive whose work it is trying to scrutinise. If Commissioners are to appear regularly in the European Parliament to answer questions and if committees are to investigate aspects of the Community's operations and to take evidence from European pressure groups, the Parliament must be in the administrative capital of the new Europe.

The Report of the Working Party on the powers of the European Parliament, set up by the Commission under Professor Vedel, was published in March 1972. It diagnosed the main problem, which is essentially that the Commission works within close limits imposed mainly by the Council of Ministers; and as the Parliament is supposed to scrutinise those actions the Commission takes on its own initiative, little scope is left to it. There is, as yet, no area of policy formation open to the Commission which is wide enough to merit the full-time supervision of an elected Parliament. And till there is such a degree of responsibility, elections to such a Parliament will not be fought over major issues; there will be no incentive to line up political forces which would, in time, coalesce into European parties; and there will be little coverage in the media and even less public interest in either the elections or the Parliament.

Strengthening the European Parliament

Despite this basically unfavourable position, it is still possible to strengthen the existing Assembly and to give it a more positive function. At present, when the Commission puts a proposal to the Council, it also goes to the Assembly, which then produces a report. But, by the time this is done, the original proposal will have been considerably altered by negotiations between the Commission and the Council so that the Assembly's reactions may well be of little relevance. The Assembly also has the right to approve or reject a small section of the Community's budget and it can, by a vote of no confidence, dismiss the entire Commission.

What is needed is to find useful functions for the Assembly which would add to its prestige, attract active and able members and make it into the kind of body which could exercise more influence if and when increased areas of consensus among the member States give the Commission a wider role. The Vedel Report argued that the Assembly should be given the power to approve the choice of President of the Commission. This might prevent the nomination of someone intended to slow down the pace of European integration and is a good suggestion. But there seems to be no reason why the Assembly should not be used to maintain a high standard on the Commission. It has the power to question Commissioners and this could be extended and supported by the power to pass motions of no confidence in individual Commissioners. Secondly, Governments could be asked at least to look to their members on the European Assembly before appointing their Commissioners.

The second useful function would be to use the Assembly to produce an 'all-European', as opposed to a national reaction to Commission proposals and to try to spread an understanding of overall European needs and policies among the member States. The Vedel Report sought to do this by recommending that Community legislation should be divided into two lists. The first (List A) dealt with major changes in the Treaties and in the membership or international relations of the Community and such items could not become law without the approval of the European Assembly. List B covered most of the areas of common action and, in this case, the Assembly could not refuse its consent but could hold up a proposal and ask the Council to reconsider its opinion. In general, the Vedel Report wanted all Commission proposals routed first to the Assembly, to be then, with its comments or amendments, put before the Council of Ministers—the refusal on List A or the 'suspensive veto' on List B taking place after the Council had reached its decision. A time limit of 1978 was set for all List B items being transferred to List A. It might have been possible for the Vedel Report to have added that where the Council simply refused to act on a Commission proposal, where it let an initiative die, the Assembly could, after a fixed period of time, demand an explanation from the Council.

The Commission accepted the Vedel Report as a reasonable approach to put before the Summit Conference due to be held in the autumn of 1972, though it disagreed with the division of legislation into two groups, wanting to give the Assembly the power of refusal on all items of legislation by 1975. The point of these proposals would be, as argued above, to make the Council take note of a European position or interest as well as just the reconciliation of national interests. The Assembly or Parliament would be inclined to back up the Commission as both institutions represent the European rather than the national approach; but this approach could be given extra strength by the activities of the European MPs in their national Parliaments. They could explain the European case in their own parties and legislatures and press ministers to explain why the Council was taking this or that position. It would be wrong and unsatisfactory to regard the national and the European Parliaments as being in competition; they should work together to enforce responsibility on executives whether operating on their own at home or together in Brussels.

(Extracted from the *Round Table*, no. 249, January 1973, pp. 23 ff.)

3.8 Transnational Political Forces
A. HARTLEY

Since an increasing number of economic decisions affecting many sections of European society will now be removed from the competence of national Governments and since, therefore, pressure through national political institutions will be likely no longer to produce the same effects as it once did, it would be logical for those who feel they have a grievance against the policies gestated in Brussels to organise themselves on an international scale. Such a trend, moreover, would correspond to the facts of contemporary economic life. The rise of the so-called 'multinational' company has created a situation in which it is outside the power of individual Governments to control the operations of the huge financial and industrial organisations which use their territory and affect the lives of their citizens both economically and socially. One answer to the multinational company is undoubtedly supranational regulations. But another might be the multinational trade union, and the British trade union leader, who recently said that, despite the policy of the Labour Party, he was eager for Britain to enter the European Community so that he could organise strikes on a multinational scale, showed himself alive to the possibilities of his time.

It seems fairly clear that, within the enlarged Common Market, labour can be expected to organise itself on an appropriate scale, though any institutional expression of working-class solidarity is liable to be delayed by the ideological clefts which divide European trade unions among Communists, Socialists and Christians. Rather than mergers or permanent arrangements for collaboration the more likely pattern will be one of *ad hoc* co-operation against individual multinational companies. Thus the makings of an alliance between British and Italian unions against Dunlop-Pirelli can already be discerned. The exact shape of events, indeed, is obscured by uncertainty over the extent to which Communist-controlled unions in France and Italy will be prepared to play down their political aims for the sake of more effective industrial action. Will the weapon of simultaneous strikes against all the subsidiaries of a multinational company be employed primarily against American-owned companies for reasons which have little to do with industrial conditions?

There is an undoubted danger here of killing geese which, however offensive to public and official opinion inside Europe by reason of their tax avoidance and the instability created by their transactions on the exchange markets, nevertheless do produce a substantial quantity of golden eggs. It is possible to imagine a trade union offensive against multinational companies of American origin which would be encouraged by a nascent European nationalism and end by causing a sharp crisis between the United States and Europe. And it might also be suspected that Communist trade union leaders would have strong political motives for bringing such a situation about.*

A farmers' lobby will be much easier to construct within the European Community than a united trade union movement. In fact, such a lobby already exists and there do not seem to be any ideological barriers to delay its incarnation in institutional form. European farmers have an immediate common peril to bring them together. Strong pressures exist within the Community to move towards a less inefficient agricultural policy and to keep food prices down. These forces can only grow in strength, aided, as they are, by American remonstrances from outside; and, in the process, farmers may feel that the advantages assured them by the Treaty of Rome will vanish out of the window. Whatever the rights and wrongs of the Common Agricultural Policy (and it was created in the light of social considerations which are ceasing to exist along with the small peasant farmer), there are the ingredients here of a fierce struggle of interests. For it cannot be imagined that a Europe, the greater part of whose population is composed of industrial workers, will accept forever restrictions on the import of cheap food from overseas. It would not be too hard to imagine the growth of a European movement, analogous to the nineteenth-century anti-corn law league, which would meet a correspondingly tough resistance from the farmers as it developed its campaign. The Common Market system has given lasting expression to a division of interest between the farmers and the rest of

---

* Perspectives of this kind are presumably what is meant by *New Left Review* when, in its latest number, it claims that 'entry will prepare the terrain for more advantageous class confrontations than those that occur within the old nation state framework'. This number, which is entirely devoted to a long article arguing the case for entry, is undoubtedly by far the most intelligent exposition yet to appear of the issues raised by the European Community for left-wing Socialists. One need not agree with its premises to find it the most serious discussion of the question which has appeared from that point of the political compass. See 'The Left Against Europe?', Tom Nairn, *New Left Review*, no. 75.

society, and it seems probable that, sooner or later, this will find political expression.

Labour and agriculture doubtless represent the areas in which interest groups conceived on a European scale will most immediately make themselves felt. But there are other possibilities. Consumer movements, for instance, should find collaboration within an enlarged Europe a profitable exercise and one which will increase their political influence. There might also be more disagreeable phenomena—pan-European protest against African or Asian immigration or a Poujadist rebellion of small businessmen and shopkeepers damaged by economic change—on the lines of the forces led, in France, by M. Nicoud.

Another interesting question is whether there will be any banding together of regional interests, any alliance of the enflamed feelings fostered in peripheral or backward areas of Europe. Already there are said to be links between the Breton nationalists, who have resorted to bomb-throwing over the last few years, and the Irish Republican Army (IRA). In the same way the partisans of *Occitanie Libre*, whose posters all over the south of France last summer denounced the 'exploitation' of the region by tourists, were also prepared to express sympathy for those struggling to 'liberate' Ulster. With a little care others could be added to the chain: Basque and Scottish nationalists, Welsh and Sicilian autonomists. It is not inconceivable that the less prosperous regions of Europe—especially those that feel their cultural identity threatened by economic and social change—may come to harbour militant political movements bent on obtaining equality with the wealthy central triangle of Paris, London and the Ruhr. One prophylactic against this ominous development would be an imaginative and generous regional policy on the part of the Community. Another would be direct democratic representation which would at least permit the regions to voice their grievances, though it would hardly guarantee them a remedy. Without some action the gap between 'developed' and 'underdeveloped' Europe may continue to grow and, with it, a difference of political structure such as can, at present, be seen between the North and South of France or the South and North of Great Britain. A contest between 'haves' and 'have-nots' expressed in regional terms might have disagreeable consequences for Europe's future, bringing with it local political instability and the creation of small *foyers* of chronic discontent.

European Political Parties?

Such problems should form the stuff of debate between political parties at the European level. Unfortunately, there is little sign that they will do so. Of all institutions within the countries of the European Community the political parties seem to find the greatest difficulty in broadening their horizon to co-operate with their opposite numbers in other countries. Even in a case where some similarity of policy and background exists such as that of the Labour Party and the German Social Democrats (SPD); the present relations between Herr Brandt and Mr. Wilson—not to mention the very different measure of their success during their years of office—show just how hard the establishment of common principles will be. Things are more delicate still when it comes to dealing with the French Socialists who can hardly be compared to the Labour Party at all in terms either of electoral clientele or ethos. In both France and Italy the working class is represented by those countries' respective Communist parties, and it does not appear very likely that the Labour Party will find suitable *interlocuteurs valables* in that direction. Nor are the Conservatives better off. They may get on all right with German Christian Democrats, but the Italians (fresh from their *aperture a sinistra*) are far too left-wing for them, and the average Conservative MP is not very much at his ease with the normal run of deputy from the *Union des démocrates pour la République* (UDR), the present incarnation of Gaullism.

One is driven to the conclusion, therefore, that European pressure groups of various kinds will make their appearance long before any type of organisation which could remotely be called a European political party. Indeed, when (or if) the European Parliament eventually comes to enjoy powers which require a clear expression of opinion on its benches, it is probable that embryonic European parties will spring rather from the pressure groups of the moment, which are concerned with genuinely transnational issues, than from the parochial political formations of individual countries. In other words, many of the characteristics of national political parties will be lost as European parties emerge. Some traces of origin will, of course, remain, but a new environment and new problems will have marked organisations designed for action on a European scale. The greater the powers of the European Parliament and the more directly it is elected, the further away will the state of mind of its members be from that of the parties which originally chose them. Conservatism or left-wing feeling (which it would be rash to call socialism) will remain, but many purely national features will have been eliminated. Co-operation between national political parties is likely to come about through their being forced into it by the need to decide issues in the European Parliament, but that in itself will ensure the creation of other and different formations, removed from their ancestors by the nature of their function and their abandonment of some of the most characteristic national traditions in the field of politics.

Thus the appearance of new political phenomena appropriate to the changing condition of Europe, the gradual transformation of international relations into the domestic politics of a new state, will not take place without some changes painful to those who are attached to their own political systems. The sacrifice required by a new union—to return to Oliver—is no doubt in the first place the leaving behind of well-tried institutions and familiar methods of government. Within the Europe of the Nine, if its affairs prosper, we can expect to see the old politics of state-to-state relations replaced by the new politics of unity, but this process will leave Europeans facing the unknown. There are few precedents for the daunting opportunity which they at present enjoy of making their own future, but it is in the light of this that future political activity within the Community must be judged whether it is to be creative work, residual attention to unfinished business or merely vain agitation. Yet it would be useless to wish such possibilities away or to succumb to vertigo before the acceleration of history. For better or for worse, Europeans are embarked on the construction of a new political system, and they cannot retreat now.

(Extracted from the *Round Table*, no. 249, January 1973, pp. 11 ff.)

3.9 Industrial Representation in the EEC

A. Channels of Communication

Although the Treaties provide for the formal consultation of industrial and other interests within consultative committees—the Economic and Social Committee, the Consultative Committee of the Coal and Steel Community—industry in the Communities has found

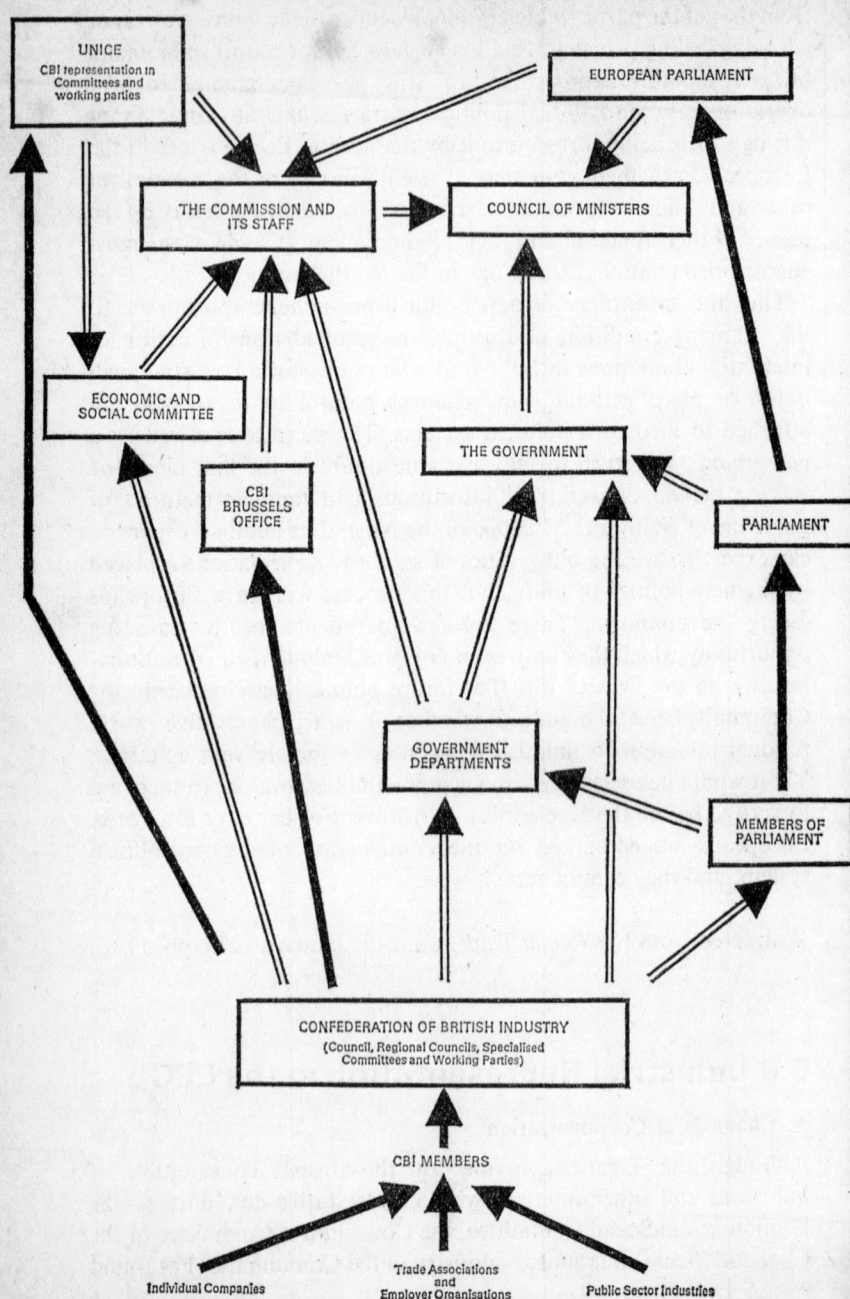

membership, direct participation

Informal contacts and Influence

UNICE
CBI representation in
Committees and
working parties

EUROPEAN PARLIAMENT

THE COMMISSION AND
ITS STAFF

COUNCIL OF MINISTERS

ECONOMIC AND
SOCIAL COMMITTEE

CBI
BRUSSELS
OFFICE

THE GOVERNMENT

PARLIAMENT

GOVERNMENT
DEPARTMENTS

MEMBERS OF
PARLIAMENT

CONFEDERATION OF BRITISH INDUSTRY
(Council, Regional Councils, Specialised
Committees and Working Parties)

CBI MEMBERS

Individual Companies

Trade Associations
and
Employer Organisations

Public Sector Industries

How the CBI keeps in touch with Community activity and represents the views
of British industry

it advisable and necessary to supplement this broadly-based formal consultation by forming interest groups in order both to provide a focal point for the Commission and its staff to consult on sectoral matters and to enable industry to ensure consideration of its interests in the evolution of Community policy.

There are now over 200 interest groups of various kinds, organised at a West European level (often with an inner group representing the EEC countries) or at Community level. These are effectively European level Trade Associations and they are normally consulted informally by the Commission where their particular industries are concerned. They have an important role to play in influencing Community decisions in view of the emphasis on bureaucratic rather than democratic procedures in Community law-making. For obvious reasons the Commission normally insists on a single contact point for each sector at European level.

However, these European level associations can only be effective to the extent that national associations are themselves effective both in their support at European level and as spokesmen for their sectors domestically. This is important as views can be satisfactorily represented at both national and Community level. Difficulties of representation can arise where at national level there are several associations in a sector which is covered by only one association at European level and, with this in mind, groupings have already been created in several sectors of UK industry. Clearly it is essential for the national associations to resolve together the problem of their representation at European level. Failure to do this could well result in a split national view at European level thus weakening its impact very considerably.

Industrial firms must recognise that if they are to influence the evolution of the EEC on sectoral matters, e.g. standards, safety regulations, tariffs, etc., they must ensure that national trade associations have the strength both to make their case to the UK Government, which in turn will make it in Brussels, and to ensure that their views are clearly heard at the appropriate European level association. On matters of general interest, e.g. public purchasing, restrictive practices legislation, influence is best exerted through general industrial bodies such as the CBI and Chambers of Commerce. These too have to speak clearly nationally and through their European level organisations—UNICE in the case of the CBI and the Conference Permanente in the case of Chambers of Commerce.

There are similar bodies representing the interests of public sector enterprises, agriculture, trade unions and other sectors of economic life.

The chart on page 144 shows the channels through which the views of industry may be represented.

While it does not claim to be comprehensive, an excellent list of European level sectoral organisations has been published by the Commission entitled: *Répertoire des organismes communs créés dans le cadre des Communautés européenes par les associations industrielles, artisanales et commerciales et de service des six pays; Associations de professions libérales, organisations syndicales de salariés et groupements de consummateurs.* It is in French, from HMSO, price £1·65.

B. Union des Industries de la Communauté Européene (UNICE)

(i) Membership

UNICE was set up on 1 March 1958 and is composed of the following central organisations which bring together the Employers' Associations from all sectors within each member State:

Belgium: Federation des Industries Belges.
France: Conseil National du Patronat Français.
Germany: Bundesverband der Deutschen Industrie; Bundesvereinigung der Deutschen Arbeitgeberverbande.
Italy: Confederazione Generale dell'Industria Italiana.
Luxembourg: Federation des Industriels Luxembourgeois.
Netherlands: Verbond van Nederlandse Ondernemingen; Nederlands Christelijk Werkgeversverbond.
United Kingdom: Confederation of British Industry.

(UNICE already maintains close contact with the industrial federations of the other acceding States which are expected to join UNICE later in 1972. As Greece is an Associate Member of the Community the Federation of Greek Industry has been associated with UNICE since 1962.)

(ii) Aims

The aims of UNICE are:
—to maintain and foster both the spirit and means of solidarity among its members;
—to encourage the building of an industrial policy in a European spirit;

—to be the official spokesman for industry in the member countries *vis-à-vis* the Community institutions on all problems of general interest or related to matters of principle concerning the common policy of the central federations of industry.

To achieve these aims UNICE:

—maintains permanent contact with the official institutions of the European Community;
—examines problems arising concerning the European Community;
—co-ordinates, as far as possible, the attitudes of the central federations of industry on all matters related to European integration and encourages common attitudes by surveys and exchanges of opinion.

(iii) Structure

(a) THE COUNCIL OF PRESIDENTS. The Council of Presidents is composed of the Presidents of the central federations of industry affiliated to UNICE and is the decision-making body of UNICE. It defines the general policy of the Organisation, gives directives to the Committee of Experts, and ratifies their work. The decisions of the Council require unanimous approval.

(b) THE GENERAL SECRETARIAT. The General Secretariat is managed by a General Secretary entrusted with the day-to-day running of UNICE and the execution of the decisions of the Council of Presidents. The General Secretary organises meetings of experts and interviews with members and staff of the European Commission and frequently undertakes preparatory contacts. He also keeps in contact with European Community officials and endeavours to collect and disseminate information on the activities of the European Commission.

(c) THE COMMITTEE OF PERMANENT DELEGATES. Each national federation has appointed a delegate who keeps in permanent touch with the General Secretary. These delegates form the Committee of Permanent Delegates which meets two or three times a month, with the General Secretary in the chair. The Committee of Permanent Delegates represents UNICE *vis-à-vis* the European institutions on matters of topical concern. Its special task is to follow the progress of the work of the European Commission. From the information available, problems likely to be of interest to European industry are selected. Examination of these problems is normally entrusted to appropriate Committees of Experts.

(d) THE COMMITTEES OF EXPERTS. To examine the various categories of problems related to the Common Market which concern industry, a number of Committees of Experts and Working Parties have been formed within UNICE. These are composed of representatives of the affiliated national federations and meet according to need. The secretarial work and the organisation of meetings are performed by the UNICE General Secretariat.

There are about thirty Committees and Working Parties of this kind, dealing in particular with the rules governing competition, economic policy, trade policy, aid to developing countries, tax problems, social matters and vocational training, transport, industrial ownership, licences, energy, scientific and technical research, small and medium-size industrial enterprises and statistics. (The list of these committees is kept by the Overseas Directorate of the CBI.) In addition, special committees have been set up in the fields for which the Treaties of Rome lay down special arrangements, e.g. in the problems of the agricultural and foodstuffs industries, and nuclear industry. To these may be added temporary 'ad hoc' groups set up to examine certain special problems.

(iv) Activities

The work of the Committees centres chiefly around the work in progress in the European Commission.

UNICE endeavours to make known the viewpoint of the whole of European industry on all important questions of integration. It is often consulted by the Institutions of the Community, but it also frequently takes the initiative when it undertakes a survey or decide on its official attitude. In addition UNICE performs the secretarial work of the Employer's Section of the Economic and Social Committee of the EEC. Here it acts as a co-ordinator and provides information.

UNICE also maintains close contacts, on the information level, with the European federations of each sector of industry, i.e. the European level trade associations.

On the international level, UNICE is in contact with industrial federations of other European countries and with international organisations such as UNCTAD (United Nations Conference on Trade and Development), UNIDO (United Nations Industrial Development Organisation) and BIAC (Business and Industry Advisory Committee to OECD).

C. The Permanent Conference of the Chambers of Commerce and Industry of the EEC

The Permanent Conference of the Chambers of Commerce and Industry of the EEC brings together the national associations of the Chambers of Commerce of all the Community countries and of those countries which are associated with it or have applied for membership under Article 237 of the Treaty of Rome. The ABCC has been a full member of the Permanent Conference since the UK signed the Treaty of Accession.

The General Assembly, consisting of Presidents and their experts, meets twice a year to approve the work of its technical committees and to adopt policy statements put forward by these committees.

The committees cover taxation, customs policy, economic and commercial policy, transport, regional policy, legal matters, finance, agriculture, training and distribution.

The Conference is guided by a Bureau of Presidents which in turn is advised by a Technical Committee. There is a permanent Secretariat in Brussels.

One of the main objects of the Permanent Conference is to influence the European Commission. To this end the Conference not only formulates views on the policies, Directives and Regulations proposed by the European Commission but also anticipates the work of the Commission at times and presses for action where this is required.

(Extracted from 'Signposts to the EEC', Confederation of British Industry, undated.)

3.10 European Groups and the Decision-Making Process
TERKEL T. NIELSEN

... A remarkable reshaping of the activities of interest groups has taken place since 1960, when some 80 European groups concerned to some degree with the agricultural sector could be identified as against some 130–40 today. Most are members of 'umbrella organisations'; the groups can be classified under the headings in Table 1.

The organisational structure of the European groups as well as their significance and power varies considerably. Some groups are well-organised institutions with an administrative apparatus, such as COPA and UNICE (the federation of employers' organisations) that perform a significant interest aggregation and provide an accommodation of different positions and demands; others are just weak bodies the activities of which rarely extend beyond acting as a post box between the Commission and the national member organisations. The agricultural organisations are among the most important groups.

TABLE 1* *EEC Interest Groups of Relevance to the Agricultural Sector*

Sector	Number	Central organization
Producers	15	COPA
Industry	55	UNICE/CIAA
Trade	38	COCCEE
Co-operation	9	COGECA
Trade unions	3	CISL/CISC
Consumers	3	Comité de contacte
Other sectors	10	
Total	133	

Three types of channel link the national organisations[1] to the EC authorities. One channel passes through the national governmental bodies, the traditional and well-known route; a second channel goes directly to the Community authorities where the groups try to exert pressure individually; by a third channel demands are funnelled through European groups which try to give priority to certain demands. During the early 1960s national groups seemed to prefer those channels which led through national Government organisa-

* Répertoire des organizations agricoles non gouvernementales groupées dans le cadre de la Communauté économique européenne; admission to the Répertoire is criterion of relevance.

UNICE = Union des Industries de la Communauté Européenne.
CIAA = Commission des Industries Agricoles et Alimentaires de l'UNICE.
[COPA = Committee of Professional Agricultural Organisations of the EEC.]
COCCEE = Comité des Organisations Commerciales des Pays de la CEE.
COGECA = Comité général de la Coopération Agricole des Pays de la CEE.

tions; but today at least some agricultural groups tend to put more emphasis on the route through the European groups. This trend may be related to the evolution of the CAP and parallels the development from the period of construction to the present phase of management of the CAP.

Committee of Professional Agricultural Organisations of EEC: COPA

As the agricultural umbrella organisation, COPA is the most important group. Its national member organisations are the central agricultural organisations and its organisational structure consists of five major components. The Assembly is the controlling body and consists of representatives from the member organisations; it is concerned largely with major policy options. The Presidium contains one elected leader from each member State. It represents COPA and by its power to approve the decisions of the specialised sections it occupies a central position. The group of general experts which assists the Presidium is composed of representatives from the member organisations (mostly from the secretariats) and apart from preparing the meetings of the Presidium it considers a number of general problems in line with *la philosophie du COPA*. The Secretariat had in 1969 a staff of seven people with professional qualifications and clerical assistants; it is the centre of communication within COPA and also between the member organisations and the Community authorities. Some thirty specialised sections, working groups of various kinds, are either directly part of the COPA organisation or are separate European groups (about ten). Their significance and independence of COPA varies considerably. Most are organised according to agricultural products; some deal with questions in the legal, structural and social field. It is an official goal of COPA to centralise all interest group activities in the agricultural sector.

COPA has developed its own procedure for reaching decisions. In response to measures initiated in the Commission the Secretariat sends a questionnaire to the member organisations (to the relevant specialised section) by which their positions are indicated. The members of the section try to reach a common position on the basis of the answers and reports from the Secretariat. The decision of the section is then transmitted to the general experts, who examine it and often make a set of 'observations' on the position. The next phase takes place within the Presidium which has to approve the decision before it is transmitted to the Community authorities as a note or a formal *prise de position*. Particularly important problems are discussed by the Assembly. Throughout the whole process the Secretariat plays an important role through its part in defining the questions to be considered within the various component bodies.

COPA can be considered a 'gatekeeper' in the Community system. Demands from the member organisations emerge from the COPA process with a rather different content. In 1964 COPA was unable to reach a common position on the fixing of the cereal price because of the divergent positions held by the German, French and Dutch organisations. This sort of situation which paralysed COPA no longer exists. Divergent positions in specific sectors are still to be found, for example in November 1968 the Dutch organisations added a rider to the COPA position on the intervention price for milk powder, demanding a lower price of 46·50 units of account (1 ua = $1) as against the COPA demand for a price of 48 ua per 100 kilograms. However, such dissension has become increasingly rare. The annual price review presents particular difficulties, but although divergent positions persist, compromises are usually reached. When in 1968 the Commission proposed to lower the intervention price for butter, COPA as a whole strongly opposed this. There is evidence that the mode of conflict resolution within COPA may be changing from an accommodation on the basis of 'the minimum common denominator' or 'splitting the difference' to an 'upgrading of the common interest'. In 1967 the national organisations put forward different claims for the annual price review, yet they succeeded in reaching a common position demanding a general price rise of 5 per cent. Moreover, in 1968, an agreement was reached to demand a *differentiated* rise of prices for each product concerned.

The initiative in agricultural policy generally lies with the Commission, and COPA responds to this stimulus. Thus the activities of COPA can be regarded as a process of feedback and response. COPA's behaviour is not always confined to a reaction; sometimes policy initiatives originate in COPA or its member organisations. For instance COPA has exerted considerable pressure upon the Commission to induce it to set up a new market organisation for sheep products, and the Commission is actually planning a proposal for the Council on this. The absence of voting procedures probably has a stress-reducing function; if compromises turn out to be impossible all points of view are presented to the Community authorities. Political cleavages are based predominantly on national antagonisms, but sectoral problems also provoke clashes of interests. On cereals and dairy produce disagreement is, by and large, attributable to national differences, while disagreement on structural problems stems from both national and sectoral antagonisms. In general, stable markets and a fixed policy seem to facilitate the possibilities of accommodation in COPA.

Co-ordination of views among member organisations of the same nationality is least developed in the Italian groups and most in the Dutch groups. One reason for the lack of co-ordination among Italian organisations may be ascribed to the fragmentation of Italian agricultural interest groups; conversely the three central Dutch organisations have established a joint international secretariat to co-ordinate their activities, and the Landbouwschap which comprises both farmers' organisations and trade unions facilitates the co-ordination of positions. In the majority of cases the representatives are competent to bind their organisations, but this has been more difficult in bodies where member States, rather than organisations, are represented. In respect of the overall configuration of power there is evidence that the Presidium and the major specialised sections are particularly influential, but so too is the Secretariat with its easy access to relevant information and numerous contacts with the EC authorities. Finally it must be underlined that the interest articulation of the member organisations through COPA is the basis of COPA's existence. Any threat to use other channels challenges the survival of COPA. In June 1968 COPA and the trades unions were strong enough to establish a collective agreement on hours of work for 300,000 agricultural workers in the EEC. . . .

European Interest Groups and the Decision-Making Process

COPA provides a good example of the activities of European groups.[2] The Commission is COPA's main target. The Secretariat of COPA has contact with all levels and practically all Divisions of DG VI* and with the Commissioner and his cabinet. On the whole direct personal contact is preferred, and the problem is to find the right man, one who takes part in decision-making, who has access to the relevant information and who has the appropriate authority. The most important contacts seem to be with people situated 'at the decisive middle level of communication and decision'[3] of DG VI, such as heads of Division. But in spite of good contacts with top

* DG VI—Directorate General VI deals with agriculture.

officials 'the real lobby', as one respondent said, exerts pressure at a relatively low level of DG VI.

COPA is represented by its specialised sections in the Consultative Committees in the various meetings organised by DG VI, and sometimes too in meetings with national experts. Examples of subjects considered in Consultative Committees are Community quality norms on barley for breweries and on cereal and rice prices, the determination of commercial centres for derivative intervention prices, and on the butter surplus. COPA is also consulted on general political problems; for example its general experts are responsible for COPA's opinion on the problems of the 'Medium Term Economic Policy'. While the specialised sections are primarily responsible for technical matters, the meetings of the Presidium which takes place every six to eight weeks with M. Mansholt and the top officials of DG VI cover key political issues. In the early years of the CAP these 'summit meetings' dealt with the general problems of the construction of a common policy, for instance the establishment of common market organisations in 1962 and 1963, and with a general exchange of positions. But today they tend to consider specific political options on for example the butter surplus or the memorandum on 'Agriculture 1980'. This plan was developed by a small *ad hoc* working group of top officials from DG VI (including the Commissioner) and COPA kept in touch with the problems at various stages, both through informal and confidential information at an early stage and through official consultations at later stages. Furthermore, recently the Presidium has been consulted on *avant-projets* for policy decisions.

A stable pattern of relationships between COPA and the Community authorities has developed. The first phase is to ascertain the new measures planned by the Commission on, for example, a market organisation for chicory, or on major changes in the restitutions for fats. COPA tries to be informed as early as possible. The next stage is the transmission of technical notes to the Commission indicating COPA's position. Then the Secretariat tries to discover the impact of the note on the Commission. Finally a formal *prise de position* is forwarded. Parallel to these activities the Secretariat and other COPA representatives exert pressure on officials at various levels in DG VI. Meetings may take place with experts from the Divisions; the problem may be considered in a Consultative Committee; or if it is an important problem the issue may be discussed at a meeting with M. Mansholt. While COPA is in contact with most major centres of decision in the Commission there are very few contacts with the Management Committees.

COPA and CIAA (representing the foodstuffs industry) are regarded by the Commission as the most important European groups in the agricultural sector. COPA is especially important for cereals and CIAA for dairy produce. In DG VI it is felt that the information passed from interest groups to Commission on dairy products is considered to be important, and in some cases even decisive; information on cereals is much less important, but occasionally decisive. Information on legal harmonisation is felt to have 'a certain importance'. Moreover it must be remembered that COPA is consulted far more intensively on 'technical' than on 'political' matters. Sometimes the transmission of positions and pressure exerted by COPA results in an *avant-projet* being changed. It is widely held in the Commission that its decisions would have been substantially different had it not been for consultations with such interest groups as COPA. In practice the Commission takes COPA's demands into account to the extent that they are compatible with the goals of the Commission, or as one respondent said, 'when the demands are realistic', adding that during recent years COPA's demands have become considerably more 'realistic' than in the early years of the CAP.

There is little contact with the European Parliament, although important views are communicated to it. Through overlapping membership and assistance to the agricultural representatives of the Economic and Social Committee, COPA devotes some efforts to influencing its opinions; but COPA considers the ESC relatively less important than it was in the early days of the EEC. Apart from communicating views and sending telegrams at the moment of decision of the Council sessions, there is little contact with the Council. On the other hand the agricultural groups at the national level exert strong pressure on national policy makers participating in Council negotiations.

Some Conclusions

The agricultural sector represents the most highly integrated area of Community activity. The common agricultural policy is implemented by a pattern of intensive intervention and a system of market organisations which have been in operation for a considerable period. Consequently stable practices and routines have been established. In this respect the agricultural sector is significantly different from other sectors which have not yet acquired such precise policies or become subject to regular Community management. Therefore, the patterns of decision-making outlined above cannot yet be regarded as typical for all sectors, either in terms of the behaviour of the Commission or in terms of interest-group activity. With the possible exceptions of the internal commercial market and social affairs, the access of interest groups to Community institutions has been less regular and less institutionalised than for agricultural groups.

It is difficult to assess the weight of influence exerted by the various participants in the agricultural decision-making process. A high degree of participation is not necessarily correlated with effective influence. For example, DG VI is very active at a number of levels, but its actual authority is heavily circumscribed both by the provisions of the Regulations and by the 'bureaucratic penetration' of the Commission by national representatives through the web of Committees.

It has been suggested that national agricultural groups tend to funnel an increasing number of demands through COPA at the expense of national channels. But as the national policy-makers are still of vital importance in determining strategic policy decisions in the Council negotiations, and since COPA has much poorer access to the Council than to the Commission, national groups inevitably continue to represent their interests through national governmental bodies. The question as to whether a national or a community approach predominates is thus partly a question of emphasis and partly a question of the kind of problem involved—for instance according to whether it is a political or a technical matter. COPA and the national agricultural groups act simultaneously at community level and national level. Although compromises in COPA are generally adhered to, the national groups may follow their own policy towards their respective governmental bodies. COPA has succeeded in reaching accommodation on significant and contentious subjects such as agricultural prices. Although deviating positions still occur they occur less and less frequently.

COPA approaches systematically all or nearly all major decision centres of the Community authorities with the Commission as their chief focus. The national groups are most important at the Council stage.[4] COPA can be said to exercise some influence on the way in which the market organisations operate and where COPA's demands are compatible with the goals of the Commission they seem to be taken into account. Very detailed decisions can hardly be influenced; and on major political options it can be argued that power is concentrated in the national Governments, although it is quite likely that COPA may have some influence at this level to the extent that it can maintain a united agricultural front. Consequently it can be argued that COPA has been more successful in influencing the way in which the CAP has been implemented than in influencing matters of detail or the definition of strategic policy options.

References

1. See Werner Feld, 'National Economic Interest Groups and Policy Formation in the EEC', *Political Science Quarterly*, Vol. LXXXI, no. 3, 1966, on the activities of the national groups.
2. On interest-group activities see Dusan Sidjanski, 'Pressure Groups and the European Economic Community', *Government and Opposition*, Vol. 2, no. 3, 1967; and Jean Meynaud and Dusan Sidjanski, 'L'action des groupes de pression' in *La décision dans les Communautés européennes*, Pierre Gerbet and Daniel Pepy (eds.), Brussels, 1969.
3. Karl W. Deutsch, *The Nerves of Government. Models of Political Communication and Control*, New York, 1966, p. 154.
4. Cf. Wilhelm Gieseke, 'Die berufsständischen Organisationen der Landwirtschaft in der agrarpolitischen Willensbildung der EWG', *Agrarpolitik in der EWG*, Theodor Dams et al., (eds.) Munich, 1968, p. 218, 'nur die systematische Einschaltung auf allen Stufen der Beschlussfassung bringt Aussicht auf Erfolg'. Dr. Gieseke occupies a high position in COPA.

(Extracted from 'European Groups and the Policy', Terkel T. Nielsen, *Government and Opposition*, Vol. 6, no. 4, Autumn 1971.)

3.11 Trade Unions in the EEC
MARGUERITE BOUVARD

From loose federations of national unions with limited resources at their disposal, the trade unions of the Six have developed European interest groups. Over the years, these groups have strengthened their structures and extended their aims to keep pace with European developments, and have forged close co-operation in promoting a European labour programme. By means of lobbying, publicity and participation in consultative bodies in the Community, these groups ensure a voice for the unions in the New Europe.

The trade union movements of the Community have offered unflagging support to the concept of European integration for the past two decades. When the three European Communities were established, a sufficient degree of consensus prevailed among the national confederations to form the basis of European trade union organisations functioning as European interest groups rather than as international organisations.

The European labour organisations created in response to the establishment of the Communities constitute a new political phenomenon. They are more cohesive than their international counterparts yet they are also heavily dependent upon their national membership for resources and leadership.

Socialist Trade Unions

Trade union support for European integration was already evident at the foundation in 1949 of the (Socialist) International Confederation of Free Trade Unions (ICFTU). In order to participate in the preparatory stages of the establishment of the European Coal and Steel Community and to ensure that labour's interests would be accounted for, the ICFTU established a Committee for the Schuman Plan to co-ordinate the activities of trade union delegates with those of government delegates to the Schuman Plan negotiations. These efforts were rewarded by the Paris Treaty provisions in the field of social policy and by the acceptance of trade union participation in ECSC institutions.

When the ECSC began to operate, the Schuman Plan Committee was replaced by a permanent organisation, the Committee of XXI, and when the European Economic Community (EEC) was established in 1958, the Socialist trade unions drew upon their years of European experience to establish the European Trade Union Secretariat. Through the Secretariat, the various labour confederations could draw upon each other's experience, and maintain permanent contact with the European institutions. Like its predecessor, it was a channel for the exchange of views and information between the trade unions and Community institutions.

Although this organisation was successful in performing lobbying and representation functions, its members felt a more centralised structure was needed to cope with an expanding Europe. To strengthen the structure of the European Trade Union Secretariat, to give its executive committee greater powers and to weld a closer relationship with its industrial committees, the Socialist unions (12m. members) revised their organisation. In April 1969 they drew up a new statute constituting the European Confederation of Free Trade Unions in the Community (ECFTUC). The general assembly of the Secretariat was transformed into a congress in which representation is determined not only on a national basis, but is also proportional to trade union strength. The ten industrial committees were granted three seats each for the first 500,000 members and an additional seat for each 500,000 members. In addition to having weighted representation, the congress takes its decisions by qualified-majority vote rather than by unanimity.

Labour is not interested in European unity for economic and social reasons alone. An enlarged Community would enjoy greater influence in international affairs. Therefore, the unions of the Six have always looked towards a larger Europe. The ECFTUC has maintained close relations with the labour unions of the European Free Trade Association (EFTA) through links with the EFTA Trade Union Committee, and representatives of the British Trades Union Congress (TUC) and the Norwegian and Danish members of the ICFTU have attended ECFTUC meetings as observers.

Britain's Trades Union Congress (TUC), after years of support for British entry into the EEC on acceptable terms, has taken a far more cautious line. As far back as 1964, the date of Britain's first application for Community membership, it established lines of communication with the ICEFTU's European Secretariat, and its Economic Committee and General Council have generally supported British participation in the European integration movement. At its 1971 annual assembly, the Congress opposed UK entry on the terms negotiated.

Christian Democrat Unions

In 1952, the World Congress of Labour (then called the International Federation of Christian Trade Unions) established a European Organisation (EO) as part of an overall plan for giving the movement a regional structure and for dealing with the European Coal and Steel Community, and subsequently the EEC. The fundamental aims of the EO include the pursuit of a supranational trade union policy, co-ordinating the action of its affiliates, representing the workers' interests in European institutions, and providing an information service for its three million members. In order to ensure the equal participation of the trade unions at European level, the EO maintains numerous contacts at all levels to gather information, prepare meetings, define the organisation's viewpoint and defend its position. These contacts include official encounters at ministerial level; contacts with the European Commission and its services; with the European Parliament; and unofficial contacts with the European Commission administration and various European personalities.

Like its Socialist trade union counterpart, the EO revised its statutes in 1969, and set up a European Confederation of Christian Trade Unions to help ensure that European integration would be a major concern of the national confederations. The main organisational changes consisted of converting the biennial conference, a deliberative assembly, into a congress with power to take decisions and set guidelines for co-ordinated action. All organs of the new confederation take decisions by majority vote rather than by unanimity, and annual conferences of the national confederation and international trade secretariat help to achieve co-ordinated policies and adopt measures for improving the organisation's financing.

Communist-Oriented Unions

Until recently, World Federation of Trade Unions (WFTU) affiliates in the Six were staunchly opposed to European integration and mirrored Soviet hostility to Western European trade unions. Apart from unleashing intermittent barrages of propaganda, the French CGT (1·5m. members) and the Italian CGIL (2·5m. members)—the two Communist-oriented labour federations—did not establish their own liaison bureau in Luxembourg to maintain contact with the

ECSC High Authority, nor did they ask for representation in the Workers' Group of the ECSC Consultative Committee. However, when the EEC was established, the Italian federation reversed its attitude and sought to establish an official presence in Europe, despite the opposition of the WFTU and the French federation.

One of the numerous attempts at reconciling the orthodox French CGT and its Italian counterpart resulted in the creation in 1958 of a Trade Union Committee for Co-ordination and Action within the EEC. After three or four meetings, it quietly expired, its sole achievement being a series of policy statements seeking to neutralise CGT–CGIL divergences in the Community.

The Italian CGIL has more to gain from the Community than other WFTU members, because the Common Market has had a beneficial impact on the Italian economy. If the CGIL adhered to the strict opposition of the WFTU towards the Community, it would lose considerable following and risk isolation both domestically and in Europe. Therefore, it repeatedly renewed its attempts to establish a Secretariat for Europe with the French CGT. A breakthrough towards this goal was the CGT's domestic success in achieving some accommodation with moderate groups in 1956. This marked the end of the French CGT's isolation in Europe and resulted in the establishment of a joint CGT–CGIL standing committee in the Belgian capital.

The Geneva and San Remo conferences of the French and Italian Communist leadership had modified attitudes and tactics in the French Communist movement. As a result, the French Communist Party (PCF) accepted polycentrism (i.e. that Communism should not be centred on Moscow alone), most of the Italian positions in Europe, and co-ordination of trade union activity on a European scale. Once the Communist parties officially claimed their right to full representation for their parties in the European Parliament, the trade unions followed suit and initiated serious attempts to achieve representation on the Community's consultative organs. With poly-centrism formalised in a regional organisation of Western European Communist parties and in a trade union bureau in Brussels, the Communist unions could protest against their exclusion from the Community institutions as discrimination. Two years later, in 1967, the Standing and Action Committee was transformed into a perma-nent Liaison Bureau.

Since then, the main activities of the Bureau have focused upon producing broad policy statements on European integration which would appeal to all labour groups and thus help to create a common trade union front in Europe. The Liaison Bureau was officially recognised by the European Commission in 1969 and now participates, along with its Socialist and Christian Democrat counterparts, in the meetings and conferences organised by the Commission between the unions, employers' organisations and Governments. Both the Socialist ICFTU and the Christian Democrat WCL affiliates have accepted this participation, however grudgingly.

A Common Front

Trade union plurality in the Community reflects varying international allegiances and has thus far prevented the formation of an organised common trade union front in the Community. However, these divisions have diminished in recent years and a common desire to influence the policy process within the Community has inspired co-operation among the European trade union secretariats. Since lobbying and publicity are the chief means by which labour organisations can exert their influence within the EEC, the unions have sought to increase their strength by co-ordinating their attempts to gain access to the Council of Ministers and by defining common programmes.

From initially divergent stands on Community affairs, the Christian Democrat European Organisation and the Socialist ECFTUC have developed common policies on the institutional structure for an enlarged Community, on social affairs and on the need for a greater degree of democracy in Europe's political and economic structure. The unions are concerned with the fact that, in the process of European integration, key national decisions are often taken in Brussels where labour may have marginal influence. They have, therefore, instituted the practice of close collaboration in developing and promoting European platforms favourable to labour.

Labour wishes to participate in European policy-making. It enjoys representation on the Community's consultative bodies, and good relations with the European Commission. Therefore, it wishes these organs to serve as key sources of policy. For years, the trade unions have called for the creation of a directly-elected European Parliament enjoying true legislative and budgetary powers, a Commission exercising supranational power, responsible to the Parliament, and a Council of Ministers taking decisions by a qualified majority.

Current Programme

The political goal of the labour movement is an enlarged, strengthened and democratised Europe. In addition to these long-term policies, the unions have developed a programme to be realised within the current Community framework. Basically, it aims at the upward harmonisation of living and working conditions, the achievement of full employment and the democratisation of relations within the firm.

Harmonisation can be accomplished through the traditional route of autonomous collective bargaining and through European policies. Some unions suggest a Community incomes policy to advance economic growth and improve the distribution of income. They believe that a well-conceived incomes policy could avoid the inflationary consequences of rising demand and provide a more equitable share of income for weaker groups, if accompanied by common monetary, budgetary and general economic policies. In order to complement their recent moves on the national level in the European setting, some unions would like to see the establishment of a Community policy on capital-sharing, and profit-retention plans included in a European incomes policy.

Another avenue to the upward harmonisation of wages and labour costs is through the development of European trade union programmes to serve as guides for national collective bargaining.

Community-level collective bargaining is on the unions' agenda for the near future. The ICFTU's European Federation of Agricultural Workers Union in the Community has been a pioneer, for it was a partner in the first collective agreement negotiated at the European level. In 1968, it signed, along with the farmers' representative body, COPA, a European agreement on the harmonisation of working hours for full-time agricultural wage-earners. Although the agreement is not directly applicable in the Six and is more in the nature of a recommendation, the unions consider it as a first step towards genuine collective bargaining.

The metal-workers' committee of the ECFTUC has been instrumental in establishing contact between the trade union representatives of the various branches of multinational companies and the central management for the electronics industry (Philips at Eindhoven), the automobile industry (Fiat-Citroën-Berliet) and the aerospace industry (Fokker-Vereinigte Flugtechnische). The Committee is pursuing the triple aim of initiating talks with the central management of these companies, co-ordinating national collective bargaining and concluding collective agreements.

The democratisation of relations within the firm, and especially within multinational enterprises, is one of labour's chief goals. The ECFTUC's committee on the democratisation of the economy has carried out extensive studies on current proposals for co-determination in the member countries of the Community. On the basis of its findings, it recently drew up, along with the EO, a position on the proposed European Company. Labour seeks to ensure that European companies allow co-determination, equal representation for labour and capital in management, and the workers' right to information on the state of the firm. The trade unions were partially successful in ensuring that provisions for co-determination were included in the Commission's proposal on a European Company.

The unions are working for the adoption of a Community employment policy that would ensure full employment by protecting the individual worker against the effects of technological change. The trade unions have always laid particular stress on the need for vocational training and retraining programmes to ensure that the workers will have the possibility of constantly acquiring new skills; and on European social welfare schemes to protect workers against loss of employment through technological or organisational changes in the firm. They would also like to see Community modernisation plans create new opportunities for employment in depressed regions, and have long urged the revision of the European Social Fund so that it can operate in close co-operation with the European Investment Bank to this end.

Lobbying

Labour has intertwined its official and its lobbying activities through its participation in the Community's consultative organs, and has also pressed its claims through the institutional channels of political parties in the European Parliament, the European Commission and national cabinets.

The presence in the rule-making structure of a member of European labour groups—or of a sympathetic and interested individual—constitutes another channel of access to Community decisions. The unions obtained a representative of labour on the unified Commission—Wilhelm Haferkamp—and have forged close relations with Commission members responsible for social and agricultural affairs. The Commission's consultation of the trade unions in various stages of drawing up proposals is more important to them as a means of exerting their influence than their representation on consultative organs, for it engages them in the policy-making process at an earlier stage. But unions rate both procedures as inadequate.

Labour representatives participate in the consultative committees for implementing the mobility of labour, and for vocational training, and in the Committee on the European Social Fund. The European labour secretariats also maintain regular contacts with the political groups of the European Parliament and submit detailed viewpoints to them before debates on labour matters. Co-operation is facilitated by the fact that a number of European Parliament deputies are either sympathisers of the labour movement or trade union members. The system of yearly hearings on social policy instituted by the European Parliament in 1967 has added a further dimension to labour's attempts to gain a platform.

Although labour's formal and informal relations with Community institutions have generally proved a useful channel, it has encountered some difficulty in establishing continuous working relations with the Council of Ministers. However, labour has scored a recent success in its efforts to gain a voice in the key decision-making organ of the Community. Following the employment Conference held in Luxembourg in April 1970, the Council of Ministers of Social Affairs set up a Standing Committee on Employment on 14 December 1970. The Committee serves as a framework for continuous consultation among the social partners and the Governments in order to achieve the co-ordination of national employment policies within the framework of Community goals.

The background to this decision is the existence of serious shortages of skilled labour in the Community, inhibiting economic expansion. The Committee's task is to lay the groundwork for future decisions in this area. Its creation was an important concession to the unions, which have frequently complained that their opinion is sought when it is too late to influence decisions significantly. The social partners have an important voice in proposing the agenda for the Committee and enjoy equal representation.

(Extracted from *European Community* no. 4, April 1972, pp. 22–4.)

3.12 Pressure Groups and the European Economic Community

DUSAN SIDJANSKI

The development of the power of the European Economic Community has given rise to a reaction from those interests which are most directly affected. In order to make sure both that they are informed and that their interests are represented and defended, the various groups concerned have been led to create for themselves new structures at the level of EEC. A parallel relation has thus emerged between the official powers of EEC and the private powers affected by it. These groups, formed on the European level, naturally have neither the solidity nor the effectiveness of professional representation on the national level. Moreover, since such groups are themselves a part of the process of evolution of the political structure, they adapt themselves readily to new political circumstances. But if these European professional organs are not comparable to the national groupings, they cannot be seen as similar to the international associations. They are more numerous—350 to 400 gravitate towards the European Community. Their action is both more intense and more concrete than that of the international associations, and corresponds to questions with which the community is concerned.

On the whole, the birth of new groups, as well as the strengthening of the weak links which existed before, was, and is, caused by the emergence of a new centre of decision at the continental level. In turn, this centre of decision needs to win over and to consolidate support.

The Four Phases of Formation

Roughly speaking, the emergence of the socio-economic groups within the regional European framework has passed through four phases:

The first wave appeared when the Marshall Plan and OEEC were launched. Ninety new organisations were set up to establish relations between the interests and OEEC (today OEDC); sixty of them were formed between 1948 and 1957. But they were mostly groupings with a very loose structure, mirroring in this sense the loose powers with which OEEC and later OEDC were invested. The main purpose of these organs was to ensure that information was transmitted in two directions—from the organisation to the members of the groups and from the groups to the organisation. These can best be described as potential pressure groups.

The second wave appeared during the setting up of ECSC itself, from 1953 onwards. It was limited, but more intense, as was ECSC itself. About ten new organs, grouping together the main interests saw the light of day: in 1953 the federation of the iron and steel workers of the European Communities (FEDEREL), the liaison committee of the European metallurgical industries, the committee for study of the coal producers (CEPCEO), the club of the steel producers, as well as two European specialised offices of the confederation of free trade unions and of the confederation of Christian trade unions were set up. These groups were not content simply to inform and be informed, but tried to intervene in the decision-making process of ECSC.

The third wave arose with the entry into action of the European Economic Community in 1958. It was vaster and had more profound effects. From then on, the creation of multiple professional organisations began in earnest. Following the example of EEC itself, these organisations were concerned with the main sectors of economic and social activity. Some, such as the union of the industries of EEC (UNICE), COPA (committee of professional, agricultural organisations of EEC) and the trade unions' secretariat of the Six came into being the moment the institutions of EEC were formed; others, such as the committee of consumers and interprofessional or specialised organs (COMITEXTIL) were set up at the same time as and according as the regulatory powers of EEC began to take effect and to influence various interests. Sometimes the formation of these organs was spontaneous. Sometimes it was prompted by an invitation or even by some pressure from the Commission, as in the case of the consumers' organisations. Whatever their origin their action in the field of simultaneous information and consolidation between the members and exertion of influence corresponded to real needs. The form of these groups and the intensity of their action varies from case to case, the best structured organs often being those whose interests are most directly affected or threatened. In short, whatever the original motivation of these professional groups, they all have, in various degrees, the object of bringing pressure to bear on the authorities of the European Community. For it is true to say that the European

Community does not have all-embracing political powers. It can only use a still imperfect political procedure, taking decisions in the last resort. Moreover, these procedures, contrary to what happens in national politics, apply only to certain specific economic and technical matters.

The fourth wave which again was a weaker one, coincided with the emergence of the European Free Trade Association (EFTA) of which fifteen professional organisations are members. However, the national groups have not felt any urgent need to be reconstituted in this intergovernmental organisation because, as in OEDC, they can use the classic, intermediary channel of their own Governments. This channel of influence suffices them because the decisions of the new centre of decision-making—the Council—are taken with the participation of national representatives.

Of course, the formation of the European Economic Community has created a new situation. The powers of the Community no longer belong exclusively to an intergovernmental institution. They are the result of an organic and often obligatory collaboration between the Council and the Commission. To the extent that the Commission fulfils an autonomous function, either by taking its own decisions or by working out proposals for the benefit of the Council, it becomes a centre of special interest for the groups. The tandem, Council–Commission, is the central mechanism of EEC and this centre of decision naturally attracts the groups. Certainly, the groups do not completely ignore other bodies such as the Economic and Social Committee. But in so far as it carries no effective weight in the decisions of the Council and of the Commission, the groups treat it rather as a future than as a present channel of intervention. Their relation with the European Parliament is even more ambiguous since, for the time being, it is only an indirect conveyor for resolutions which produce no results. . . .

Birth of the Professional Structures

The acts of the institutions of EEC differ from their counterparts in the other organisations in that not only are they binding and compulsory but they also have direct results. That is to say, they bring pressure to bear directly on groups and individuals without passing through the apparatuses of the respective states. A direct relationship is thus established between the Community organs and groups or individuals. No wonder that in these circumstances the groups should have tried to set up a defensive mechanism against the power of EEC. Over and above the protection and the resources with which they are already supplied they strive to counterbalance this power by endowing themselves with permanent structures on the scale of EEC. Organised action of the groups is correlated to collective action by states and by the Commission, with the result that the current is no longer all one way, but flows from EEC towards the groups as well as the other way. The network has become much more complex than was foreseen by the Treaty of Rome; influences work in many directions between the principal elements—the institutions and the states—and various groups and many groupings have grown up alongside them.

The more important, immediate and autonomous the powers (as exercised by the autonomous institutions), the more probable it is that the groups will try to organise themselves at the level of these powers. There is a certain parallel to be drawn between the degree and the nature of these powers, on the one hand, and the structure and action of the groups on the other. Besides, the creation of these European groupings is a proof of the importance of these powers. The groups do not act gratuitously. When they establish a network of structures and of action, it is because they are trying to satisfy a real need. In order to be effective, their action is directed solely at the real power-centres. If the groups try to influence the Commission, it is a sign that the Commission fulfils an important function in the formation, execution and control of decisions. The action of the groups on the Commission is the tribute paid to its genuine importance.

However, it would not be correct to rely solely on this explanation. If the groups answer to a need—and their survival and development prove this—their creation or their reinforcement are often, at least in part, the work of the Commission. It is clear that the Commission has defined its policy, which consists in consulting preferably or exclusively the professional organs which act at Community level. By refusing in principle to consult the national associations, the Commission has forced them to produce common organs. Two main criteria seem to guide the policy of the Commission: the representativeness and the autonomy of the organs of the Six. Thus, a committee can form part of a larger association, grouping the Six and the Seven, but it must show a sufficient degree of independence. In addition to this indirect pressure, the Commission has been sometimes the driving force: the consumer's committee is the result of the initiative of M. Mansholt who also played a part in the establishment and strengthening of the structures which group the activities connected with agriculture.

The motives behind this active policy of the Commission are many, of which the most important are:

1. The Commission prefers to avoid intervention in the interests of professional bodies; problems should be discussed by the groups themselves within their common organs, which should then present the institutions of EEC with agreed positions or take note of disagreement among their members.

2. The Commission also needs these organs not only to obtain technical information, but in order to use them as a network of information on the problems of the Community.

3. In this way a sphere of support for its activity is formed around the Commission. During the recent crisis in the Economic Community, most of the groups adopted positions favourable to the Commission and rose in defence of the Community when it was seriously threatened.

4. Lastly, and by way of exception, the Commission can sometimes try to influence Governments by using the national groups which are members of the European organs.

Up to a point, the preparation by the Commission and the adoption by the Council of the list of exceptions for the 'Kennedy round' provide a notable example of this procedure.

When speaking of the activity of the pressure groups, one thinks not only of a unilateral pressure, but also of the influence which institutions exert on the groups, or through them, on the national centres of power. It would be difficult, however, to say which of these two counter-influences is stronger. The action of the groups is conditioned by circumstances, by the relative importance of the respective group and by its position with regard to other groups. . . .

Conclusion

In principle, for a group to be able to act, it must have a clear view of the desired goal and it must be able to count on the support of its members. This double will is expressed in many organisations by the requirement of unanimous agreement of their members, an agreement which reflects the configuration of forces enabling the member groupings to act. Indeed, the European organisation generally takes a confederal form, which provides the best guarantee for the protection of the particular interests of its members. And yet this confederal form acts as a brake on the efficient functioning of a European group: COPA, for instance, was paralysed during the discussions of the question of the uniform price for lack of unanimity. This is why the groups have adopted in practice and often in their statutes, the rule allowing the expression of minority opinion, together with that of the majority. Thus the functioning of the group is assured, without a brutal suppression of differences of opinion. More and more frequently the groups present an agreed opinion. In exceptional cases, this unity of action can be assured by reference to the qualified minority. The statute of COCCEE, for instance, incorporates this principle for its own organ of decision, basing itself upon article 148 of the Treaty of Rome.

The central groupings concentrate more often on action of a general character, and leave more specialised activity to sectional or subsectional groupings. UNICE acts as the authorised spokesman for the industries of the Six on all problems of general interest, or on those problems which touch upon questions relating to the common policy of the central organisations which are members of it. In so doing, UNICE does not try to cover all industrial activities, but retains for itself questions of common policy or of general interest. The specialised federations are all free to organise themselves and to act in their own field.

Specialised action is within the competence of technical organisations. In COMITEXTIL the general activities of the textile industry coexist with the particular interests of the sectors. Cotton, for instance, does not necessarily take up the same position as wool. Each of these sectors can make its own approach to the Brussels authorities. At the level of common textile interests, the organisation of the entire branch intervenes. It is clear that in reality, both at the level of the central organisation and of the intermediary or specialised ones, many combinations and much friction and opposition can arise. Without venturing on generalisations, one may say that the predominance of specialised organisations bears witness to the effectiveness of limited technical action. General action is difficult to define, and general agreement is often the result of compromise. To the extent that action directed to general questions is vague and fluid, it has less chance of exerting real influence. A proposal to regulate beer or jam suggested by European organisations has a better chance of being adopted by the authorities of EEC than a general trade or anti-trust policy proposed by a central organisation. In the actual state of European integration, influence is exerted more effectively in the domain of technical matters than on general questions.

Finally one may raise the question of the relationship between the groups and the political parties, and their respective activity. The political parties have established only weak and ineffectual links, except for the socialist parties of the Six. This prolonged absence of the parties from the European political stage may lead to a lack of balance favouring the interest groups, with serious consequences for the future of European democracy. This situation is easily explained in the light of the parallel between the powers of the Community and the groupings at the same level: to the extent that the European Parliament lacks real power, the parties do not feel the need of wide-scale common action at the Community level and are content with a token presence in the Community. Indeed, their action is geared mainly to their national policies.

At the same time, some professional groupings, organised at the European level, occasionally give the impression, in their general declarations, of wishing to promote a political idea. This is why the European trade unions, as well as other groupings, periodically demand that the power of the European Parliament should be enlarged. But the situation is still far from clear. Both functions and powers are more intertwined and more fluid than on the national plane, where the action of pressure groups and of political parties occurs within a framework both global and better defined.

Within the Community, the structures of powers and of groups are in process of transformation. Moreover, the position is even more complex because a new scale is superimposed upon the national and local levels. But this new scale has not yet acquired the powers and the articulation of a national community. Indeed, in spite of a certain shift the principal and original power remains in the national units and groups. And the European groups attempt to maintain a minimum of co-ordination and common action between them. It appears that both in matters of policy reserved to the states, and in economic and social matters, the division of functions and activities in the European Community is still fluid and obscure.

Tendencies such as have been described here can develop in a variety of ways. However, to the extent to which developments continue in practice in the direction outlined here and to the extent to which the powers of the Community are enlarged, especially through the strengthening of the European Parliament or through the creation of an effective Senate, the division of functions between the future political formations and the pressure groups will tend to become more precise. For the moment, the groups, but above all the parties, tend to play only a marginal role in supporting integration. Active power is concentrated in the member States and in the central Council–Commission tandem of the European Communities.

(Extracted from *Government and Opposition*, Vol. 2, no. 3, Summer 1967, pp. 397–416. A fuller version is also in K. J. Twitchett and C. A. Cosgrave, *The New International Actors: The UN and the EEC*, Macmillan, London, 1970, pp. 222 ff.)

3.13 The Brussels Lobbyist at Work and Play

LINDSAY ARMSTRONG

Ten in the morning, in the office of a Brussels lobbyist a stone's throw from the European Commission headquarters. The phone rings. On the other end of the line is the familiar voice of an EEC official. 'Morning, Joe Bloggs here, I've got to go to Rome next week for the Commission. Can you suggest a good hotel?'

The lobbyist has got the point. 'Of course. But let me get on to my colleagues in Rome. I am sure they would be delighted to organise your stay.' 'That would be very good of you. I'll expect to hear from you.'

But the lobbyist is not going to let the opportunity pass: 'Let's have lunch together today or tomorrow. I have been meaning to get in touch. I've got something I'd like to talk over with you.' And a meeting at their usual restaurant is arranged.

The main task of a permanent Brussels lobbyist is to be the eyes and ears at the EEC of the group he represents. He has to alert his employers to ideas and proposals being cooked up inside the

Community headquarters, so that they have plenty of notice to defend their interests by intervening with the Commission or with their own Government.

'As far as we are concerned,' explains one lobbyist who is particularly experienced and active, 'everyone is equal when it comes to getting information. A doorman or a secretary can be just as useful as a director general (a senior EEC civil servant). We can't afford to discriminate between nationality or sex. No one is more Community-spirited than we are.'

Being an experienced lobbyist implies having at least one 'safe' official in each Commission directorate who can be asked any question urgently without beating around the bush. New arrivals should count on spending a year at lunches and cocktail parties, giving Christmas presents and doing favours, making courtesy calls, spending evenings playing bridge, and riding, playing football and tennis (the three favourite Brussels sports) before reaching this happy state.

Lobbyists (and some EEC officials as well) have recently discovered the delights of a few lengths of the Poseidon baths before breakfast since that is where Altiero Spinelli, the industrial policy commissioner, is to be found at seven every morning.

A good lobbyist never moves without the Trans Europ Express timetable and a toothbrush. Not a few EEC officials head for home in Paris, Amsterdam and Cologne every weekend, and there's no better place for broaching a subject than over a glass of whisky in a TEE bar.

The Need for Lobbies

Provided it is kept within honest limits, there is nothing to be ashamed of in the lobbying system that has grown up around the EEC as around national seats of power. And it has a positive value. More than most, the European Commission needs to be kept in touch with the various sectors of the economy—in six and soon ten countries.

Community officials like to feel too that the eyes of the economic world in the EEC countries are fixed on them. They need this to feel that their work is appreciated in everyday business life, and to rid themselves of the widespread feeling in Brussels that they are working in a vacuum.

They are also hungry for concrete ideas which would allow them to take action. The lobbies know this and the commission's telexes hum with incoming memoranda, answers to queries and suggestions from all over Europe.

Those responsible for framing Commission policy are perfectly ready, as a matter of policy, to hear what the lobbies have to say. At present, however, the situation of the pressure groups is somewhat ambiguous. Officially, the Commission only recognises the organisations which incorporate six national organisations in a single body. But there are in reality, hundreds of pressure groups—from industry, farming, banking and many other sectors—which have set up shop in Brussels. They range from the Union of EEC industries (UNICE), which represents the whole of Common Market industry, to the European federation of dried fruit, spice and honey importers, via the international secretariat of chemical industry associations, the committee of EEC wholesalers and retailers, the EEC banking federation, and the international union of craftsmen, small and medium companies. There are Europe's nurses and the liberal professions. There are the trade unions. There are the agricultural and the transport organisations, which are among the most active, the best organised and the best represented of all the Brussels lobbies. And, of course, individual firms have their men there too.

Theory and Practice

All these organisations are regularly consulted by the Commission. But these consultations are sometimes more of a formality than anything else. 'When they come to see us,' one highly placed official in Brussels complains, 'these organisations rarely present a united front unless they want a customs tariff increased or a quota set. They are rarely in a position to present more constructive suggestions. By continuing to consult them, we are trying above all to force them to have a real existence.'

But the lobbies cannot be expected to be more Catholic than the Pope. They know very well that the Commission, in most matters, only has the power to make suggestions and put policy into effect, while the basic decisions are taken elsewhere—in the national capitals or in the Council of Ministers. This forces the lobbies to take the same route—and in practice the Commission too.

A specimen of what happens is the proposal, prepared by the directorate for industrial affairs, for the development contracts that could be placed by the Community in certain advanced technological fields.

The directorate consulted forty or so large industrial firms before—and then mainly for sake of appearances—consulting UNICE.

Playing one pressure group off against another and then intervening as umpire between them is one of the Commission's tactics for attaining its goals in the free movement of goods, agricultural policy, industrial policy, etc.

One of the current battles is between an alliance of the Commission and French, Belgian and Dutch brewers on one side and German brewers on the other. At present German beer, by law, contains nothing but water, hops, malt and barley. The Commission, in the name of free movement of goods, is proposing to authorise the sale everywhere of beer made with additives as well (as is already the case in Belgium, France and the Netherlands). The German brewers have been campaigning vehemently in Bonn and in the European Parliament to maintain the *status quo*, but they seem to be losing.

The Strategy of Lobbying

Pressure groups obviously have to adapt to the way and form in which Community decisions are taken. Certain decisions—on agricultural issues, for example—take the form of regulations themselves directly applicable in the member countries. Here the most logical lobbying strategy is to defend individual interests with the national Governments, and common interests at the level of the Commission and, if need be, the Council of Ministers. Since the different national lobbies are really defending a common position this makes for effective pressure on Brussels.

But some decisions are made in the form of directives to member States. Here each State is itself responsible for application of the directive within its frontiers. The lobbies act differently here because they have many ways of delaying application of such directives, or of ensuring that the national regulations supposedly putting the directive into effect are not really in conformity with it.

Take transport: in 1969 a decision was taken that lorry drivers should not work more than eight hours a day. Certain member States are still not applying this. Worse still, Belgium, which had started to apply it, dropped it in the face of pressure from transport interests.

The pharmaceutical industry appears to be another hard nut for the EEC to crack. Since the beginning of the 'sixties the Commission has put forward five proposals which all in one way or another tried to promote free movement of pharmaceuticals. Only one has been adopted by the Council of Ministers.

Back in 1965 the Council adopted a proposal on the mutual recognition of authorisations of medicines for sale in EEC countries. Seven years later Belgium is the only country to have passed the necessary legislation. The reason, according to EEC officials: application of this directive in certain countries would have deprived many of the goods currently on sale of their claim to be of therapeutic value.

The battles on problems of standards are often fierce. The most spectacular fight has been over windscreens. Over the last few years two groups have been doing fierce battle to win the Commission over to their ideas. Monsanto has been fighting for compulsory introduction of laminated windscreens (it has the patent for the product which holds the two sheets of glass together). Saint-Gobain has been pleading for toughened windscreens (it is Europe's principal producer).

Six years ago the Commission's civil servants came out in favour of the laminated windscreen which Brussels thought was dearer but safer. But the proposed directive gathered dust in the drawers of Guido Colonna di Paliano, the Italian member of the Commission who was responsible for industrial policy at the time. In the meantime Saint-Gobain has strengthened its position and the file may be about to be dusted off again.

The Commission's Real Powers

There are areas where the Commission has more real powers and where it becomes vital to follow closely what is happening in Brussels. The European Development Fund, which annually disburses hundreds of millions of dollars, is one. The Commission is also becoming increasingly influential in anti-trust matters. Last but not least, the Commission sets the levels of agricultural levies and export repayments.

Particularly strong pressure is exerted on the European Development Fund, which channels EEC aid to associated African countries. Naturally the EDF can provide important political support for an African Government. And it is a key factor in the plans of European firms which are after big contracts in developing countries.

Everyone starts to act when the time comes to convince one African Government or another which is receiving Community aid that it should call upon one particular firm. There is even a group of low-level officials who are well known for being 'remote-controlled' by certain national firms and 'whom we have our eye on', says one of those responsible for the EDF.

The problem of outside groups influencing officials is a difficult one. It is perfectly understandable, in fact, that an official who always works on the same subject should end up taking sides and losing the objectivity required of him. This is one of the reasons why Willy Schlieder, director general for questions of competition, has reorganised his section by function rather than by product.

Farming and Transport Lobbies

Unquestionably the most active lobbies in Brussels are the farmers' and the transport organisations. The former are there because there is an EEC farm policy, the latter because there isn't a transport policy—and they don't want one. Representatives of both these groups are everywhere, hovering round the Council of Ministers' conference room, in restaurants used by EEC officials and in the corridors of the European Parliament.

The farmers especially are never at a loss as to how best to press their case: no one in Brussels (or further afield) has forgotten the occasion last year when they drove a cow into the room where the Ministers of Agriculture of the Six were meeting. The farmers' Comité des Organisations Professionnelles Agricoles (COPA) is by far the most energetic and effective of all the officially accepted lobby groups in Brussels. Its spokesmen command attention. Jean Deleau, for instance, COPA's vice-president, is a jovial little man, looking a bit like Khrushchev, and every inch a typical French farmer. His associates say he's as 'cunning as a monkey', and none have forgotten the blasting harangue he delivered during the farmer's demonstrations in Brussels in March 1971.

Another COPA star is the Italian Mario Vetrone who doesn't have Deleau's talent for public speaking but works no less effectively around the European Parliament. There's also Claude Dumont de Chassart, nicknamed the 'blue-blood beet-grower' and the German farming representatives, referred to as the 'German barons' because, in fact, some of them really are aristocrats.

Quite different to the COPA but at least as powerful is Unilever, a name often heard in Brussels. The Anglo-Dutch firm is rightly or wrongly considered a sort of grey eminence behind the Government in The Hague, and therefore behind the whole Common Market; people speak of Unilever as an occult and irresistible force.

On one occasion, the former French Minister of Agriculture, Edgard Pisani, thought he saw a Unilever man sitting as an expert in the Dutch delegation opposite him during a discussion on margarine. Pisani protested, and rather than risk a scene, the Dutch chose to ask the 'suspect' to leave the room.

The Community's rules on imported fats are often quoted as an example of Unilever's power, and have helped to earn the firm the title of 'the seventh member of the Common Market'. Almost the only major imported agricultural products that are not subject to the EEC customs levy are oil-cake and soya beans. If one asks why, the usual reply (and nobody has disproved it) is that these products are among the major raw materials imported by Unilever which, for once, finds itself sharing the same interests as the US agricultural lobbies. The losers in this case, of course, are EEC butter producers.

Compared with Unilever, whose headquarters are not far from Brussels and which hardly needs to keep its men permanently in residence, the Italians are much worse off and therefore probably have most pressure groups in the Belgian capital. One Italian lobbyist laments: 'Belgian industry is on the spot, the Germans and Dutch work hand-in-hand with their Governments, while French industry is backed by a thoroughly efficient civil service. As for us, we are far away and Italy's civil service is inefficient.'

Among the many Italian groups with lobbying offices in Brussels are Fiat, Pirelli, the state-owned IRI and IMI, and Assider, the federation of the Italian steel industry. They have a double task: keeping abreast of what is going on in the Community and making sure that pressures applied on the Italian Government in Rome don't somehow get lost on the way to Brussels.

If the right diplomatic instructions do not come through from Rome, as often happens, the Brussels lobby people get on to their Italian headquarters to apply pressure on the Government, while at the same time letting it be known as best they can in the committee of permanent representatives of the EEC countries that 'something is on its way from Rome'.

Companies from other EEC countries generally have one or two executives who make regular visits to Brussels to keep their contacts warm. In many cases these 'EEC specialists' have actually previously worked for the Commission or in the secretariat of the Council of Ministers.

The Italian baby-food firm Plasmon, for instance, was able to get meat for use in homogenised baby foods exempted from import levies, thanks, in part, to the fact that the firm employed a former EEC official.

British and American firms too have long since got the message and chosen Brussels as the site for their European headquarters—and not only because of its convenient geography or the tax advantages offered by the ever-hospitable Belgian authorities.

The Lobbyists are Necessary, but . . .

There is nothing reprehensible about lobbying; on the contrary, it is a necessary part of democratic processes, so long as it does not degenerate into straight corruption. But no particular lobbying interests should have excessive influence compared with others.

There is, for instance, no doubt that the consumers' lobby, in the shape of the Comité de Contact des Consommateurs de la Communauté Européenne has far too little influence. The organisation's general secretary, Jacques Semler-Collery, readily admits that 'the consumer groups only woke up to the need for a lobby when business and the unions were already well entrenched'. He also admits that the various consumer groups lack co-ordination among themselves. 'Still, I think it's scandalous that the Commission has only a tiny three-man department looking after consumer interests,' he says.

Semler-Collery and his consumers are not the only people to complain. For a number of years, the Commission has been sensitive to trade union charges that the Common Market is being built up solely for the benefit of big business. So it now has a tendency to listen attentively to what the unions say on such major things as the 'European company' law or minor ones like the forthcoming conference in Venice on the theme of 'Industry and Society'.

As a result, the Commission has lately been under fire in turn from business organisations in the EEC countries. Though it has to be admitted that the business organisations are not always in agreement among themselves; hence their difficulties in making UNICE an effective organisation.

Fundamentally, however, the EEC Commission looks upon all these various pressure groups with a benevolent eye. After all, they are living symbols of its power and influence. The Commission could indeed parody Descartes and say, 'I am lobbied, therefore I exist.'

(Extracted from *Vision*, March 1972, pp. 46–50.)

3.14 Local Government: Feeling the Impact of Entry

JAMES SWAFFIELD

Local authorities will feel the impact of Community membership in three ways. First, generally, as employers, and as spenders of a large share of public money on goods and services that are affected, in varying degrees, by the Community's action to eliminate trade barriers and to achieve free movement of capital and labour.

Second, they will feel the impact specifically, as providers of statutory services and as enforcement agencies responsible for administering the law at local level in matters affecting the health, safety and fair treatment of the public; and third, politically, as representatives of specific localities which are liable to be affected in terms of employment, investment, development, communications, etc., by decisions of the Community.

In the first category, there are many Community measures which will have an effect on the way in which local authorities conduct their business. An obvious illustration is the introduction of Value Added Tax, although we are assured that this would have come in due course whether or not Britain joined the Community: the determination of the areas of local government activity to be exempt of VAT or zero-rated, and the working out of the administrative and accounting implications in respect of both commercial and non-commercial transactions, are receiving a good deal of attention from the Associations and the accounting bodies.

There are also some specific common rules for procedures for awarding public sector contracts both for works and supplies, the first of which relating to public works contracts have recently come into effect within the Community. Public works contracts worth over £410,000 have to be advertised in the Official Journal and their award is subject to strict procedures designed to ensure that contractors from any of the member States have an equal chance of competing; the public supplies contracts Directives have not yet been adopted but they will apply similar common rules and the proposed threshold at which they will bite is the low contract figure of £25,000 (though this may still be increased in accordance with views expressed by the European Parliament and other bodies). These measures are likely to be drawn to the attention of local authorities by departmental circulars.

A major step towards the achievement of a single Common Market provided for in the Treaty of Rome is the objective of the free movement of workers among member States and free access to employment in all of them. Two general programmes of work are currently proceeding, one dealing with establishment and one with the supply of services, and the intention is to specify the discriminatory restrictions based on nationality which are to be removed and to achieve a degree of equivalence of professional qualifications in the different countries. The Treaty of Rome specifically provides that legislation on free movement of workers 'shall not apply to employment in the public service' and that the provisions relating to freedom of establishment shall not affect occupations 'which involve, even occasionally, the exercise of official authority'. It is at the moment left to member States to determine what constitutes such employment or occupations and the question whether all or only some local authority employments, as well as a number of other borderline cases, are to be included is currently under consideration. While there is now little movement of nationals of member States within the Six, and the prospect of such movement within the enlarged Community on a large scale also seems unlikely, both unlimited freedom of movement and excessive restrictions under the public service provision could be to the detriment of local authorities and so must be carefully watched.

Local authorities will also be generally affected by Community membership in their capacity as users of motor vehicles. Harmonisation of construction and use regulations will affect manufacturers more than users, though they will have to be borne in mind in specifications for special vehicles. Community requirements on drivers' hours and records and the compulsory fitting in due course of tachographs will affect some local authority vehicles, and although many vehicles used for the public services are exempt from the general requirements, alternative provision will no doubt be needed to cover these exempt classes.

Among Community matters which will affect local authorities specifically in their capacity as providers of statutory services and as enforcement agencies responsible for administering some parts of the law at local level, mention must be made of housing and a number of matters in the public health and consumer protection fields. Although there is no Community housing policy as such, there is a Regulation requiring equality of treatment for all EEC nationals in the allocation of housing accommodation, which will preclude housing authorities from applying any nationality qualification for their housing lists to any nationals of EEC member States. There is also the possibility of loans at reduced rates of interest under the resettlement provisions of the ECSC Treaty, though it is difficult to see what benefit can be derived from these in the context of current UK housing legislation.

On the public health and consumer protection side, Community legislation is much further developed as a result of the common agricultural policy, and a number of changes are likely to be necessary in current requirements for the compositional testing of liquid milk, meat and poultry inspection, and standards for fertilisers and animal feeding-stuffs, which will affect the activities of public health inspectors and other local authority officers and may increase their work-load. The Ministry of Agriculture, Fisheries and Food are currently consulting the Associations and a wide range of other interested bodies on the implications of these various Community requirements and it is not impossible to foresee a time when there will be not only common requirements but also harmonisation of enforcement arrangements, at which point local authorities will wish to be involved at a very much earlier stage of the consultation process.

However, it is perhaps in their political and representative capacities that local authorities will be most deeply affected by Community membership. Some Community measures—and progressively more as time goes on—will have direct effects upon whole local communities and regions as such, just as some national measures do at the present time. In this area it is critically important that local authorities should be aware of the workings of the Community and their scope, be able to convey this understanding to their constituents and have access to appropriate means of influencing Community institutions. Developments in the Community's agricultural and industrial policies, and the evolving environmental policy, come into this category. While local authorities have no intrinsic responsibility for particular industries or particular forms of agricultural production, they cannot but be interested in the fortunes of local employers, All these matters are, of course, interconnected, and common aspects are to be found in two general fields to which the Commission ascribes particular importance, transport and regional policy.

Transport policy comprises a number of technical issues such as drivers' hours, motor vehicle standards, insurance requirements, etc., some of which have been mentioned earlier, but the most important aspect in the development of a common policy as such is the Commission's proposal for the adoption over a ten to fifteen year period of a common system of charging for the use of road, rail and inland waterway transport infrastructure, intended to promote fair competition between the different modes. The first stage would be a common system of taxation for motor vehicles under which ultimately the total amount of vehicle and fuel taxes falling on any class of vehicles would relate specifically to the infrastructure costs caused by that class. The final objective is that the contributions paid by transport users in taxes and charges should be in balance with the amounts actually spent by public authorities in the provision and maintenance of the infrastructure: pending the achievement in full of this objective, railway undertakings may in the meanwhile be entitled to compensation where they can show that they are having to compete with road or waterway services being subsidised from public funds. The achievement of true infrastructure charging may have fundamental effects upon the organisation and use of transport and the Commission realise that changes must be spread over a number of years. Without doubt, authorities struggling with the problems of urban and inter-urban traffic will have much to contribute to the development of common policies in this sphere.

The Commission's Memorandum on regional policy was submitted to the Council of Ministers in October 1969 and the major decisions on it have yet to be taken. Although a European regional policy is not specifically referred to in the Treaty of Rome, the preamble states that one of the basic aims in setting up the Community was 'to ensure harmonious development by reducing the differences existing between various regions and the backwardness of the less favoured'. Although the Council of Ministers has as yet fought shy of adopting the Commission's proposal for the setting up of a permanent Committee on Regional Development to review the situation in regions 'for which the establishment, extension or execution of regional development plans is particularly urgent' and of national plans for dealing with these regions, it has so far taken two groups of decisions on more limited aspects. First it has adopted a Regulation limiting aid to new investment in the central regions of the Community to 20 per cent of the value of the total investment and requiring that aid to be clearly quantified; secondly there has been an overhaul of the European Social Fund to enable aid to be given for training, re-training, encouraging the mobility of labour and promoting better opportunities for employment in backward regions. More recently, the Council has agreed in principle that the Guidance Section of the Agricultural Guarantee Fund may be used for regional development projects and has asked the Commission to make firm proposals for the establishment of a regional development fund or some other appropriate instrument.

This survey of the major aspects of Community activity of which local authorities will need to be aware should perhaps conclude by drawing together some thoughts of the relationships that should exist in future between local government, central government and the European institutions. If the national Government of a country as small and apparently homogeneous as the United Kingdom attracts criticism of taking a sectional, London-orientated, civil service view of national problems, how much more must a European bureaucracy be in danger of seclusion in its ivory tower. The Commission is aware of this problem and, as has already been mentioned, goes to considerable lengths to undertake consultations with a wide range of interested bodies. The fact that these bodies must for practical purposes be Europe-wide may tend to create in them too a certain isolation though the pressure of relations with their constituent bodies, if incorporated in a satisfactory two-way flow of information and opinion, should combat this trend. Other pressures upon the Commission from the outside world are, of course, provided institutionally by the European Parliament and the Economic and Social Committee. The indications are that local government should, both for its own sake and in the interests of the development of the Community as a democratic structure, forge close links with all these bodies.

It is important that views represented to the Commission should be based upon sound technical knowledge and evidence in the same way as views expressed to national Governments. This can only be done through the established national Associations of local authorities, who should ideally find a way of associating their technical expertise and the resources at their disposal through their membership with the enthusiasm of those active in IULA and CEM. Over and above this liaison machinery which is being set up in Brussels, the suggestion has not infrequently been made in the past that there should be a larger grouping representative of local authorities in Europe to act in a consultative capacity in the way that the Economic and Social Committee does for the groups from which its members are drawn. The European Conference of Local Authorities fulfils this role in regard to the much more limited sphere of action of the Council of Europe and has itself in the past claimed recognition as the representative body for local government in Europe. If such a body were to have any institutional relationship with the Commission in Brussels, it would have to be a separate creation from that of the Council of Europe, although much reliance would doubtless be placed upon experience gained in the Strasbourg assembly.

It is necessary to lay stress upon direct links with the Commission if local government is to exert a positive influence upon policy. Once Community legislation has reached an advanced state of drafting and is before the Council of Ministers, at which late stage only are Government departments in a position to undertake consultations at national level, it is much more difficult to achieve anything more than technical changes. The established procedure will continue to be necessary: but if local authorities are to play a dynamic part in the development of Europe, in the belief that local self-government is a cornerstone of democracy, they must be ready to participate at all levels.

(Extracted from the *Municipal Review*, January 1973.)

Community Law and National Sovereignty

4.1 Introduction

The first piece in this section is an extract from the European Communities Act, 1972, and sets the general legal context of Britain's membership of the European Communities (pp. 189–92).

The second extract is taken from a much longer article by Bebr (pp. 193–7). In this extract Bebr places the law in the context of the Communities' objectives and institutions. The point is clear—the law cannot be set apart to be examined in isolation, for it is inexorably caught up in economic and political developments. Bebr also notes that there may be conflict between Community Law and the laws of the member States, and that the legal powers that exist in the Community operate through the courts of these states. In doing this he has raised two broad questions which are examined in the remaining articles—'Who makes the laws?' and 'Who administers it?'

Fawcett's article on parliamentary sovereignty in Britain is mainly concerned with the question of the source of law—who makes it?). He first states that the 'sovereignty' of Parliament 'is its power to make supreme law', but he concludes the article by speculating that entry into the EEC would plainly limit the areas in which Parliament is 'wholly free to legislate for the United Kingdom'. As Fawcett's article was written before the publication of the White Paper, his conclusion must be revised because the central provisions of the Treaty were not incorporated in a statute as he said would be necessary. (See section 4.2, pp. 189–92 below.)

Although his major concern is with legal-cum-constitutional issues, Fawcett, like Bebr, recognises that these cannot be divorced from political considerations. He shows that when the question is asked whether the United Kingdom could leave the Communities a narrow legal answer is inappropriate. Professor Wade (pp. 204–6) is also concerned with the source of law in his article. He recognises that a new legal order has been created so that we are now subject to the

Community as well as national law. He also touches on the question of 'Who administers the law?', for he notes that despite the existence of a European Court 'Community law can be given concrete application only by the decision of domestic courts.' The judges in national courts are therefore playing an important part with their counterparts in the European Court in shaping the new legal order.

The issue of national sovereignty in the Communities is examined further by Scarman (pp. 206–10). He comments that the nature of the Community law may alter significantly the constitutional role of the courts in this country. 'In the future,' he writes, 'the courts will have in some fields of their work to abandon the attitude of "subservience".' In doing this their activities could well affect the work of civil servants and the legal profession. Public administration will probably have a stronger legal emphasis, while the courts will be moving into an uncharted sea in which they will be required to decide whether statutes are constitutional or unconstitutional.

Bresler helps to bring law to life by writing about individual cases. He relates these cases to general issues by looking at the procedures used in the European Court (i.e. by asking '*How* is the law administered?' as well as by whom) and by returning to the old question of sovereignty.

It is clear from all these articles that entry into Europe poses anew one of the profoundest of constitutional-cum-political questions: 'Where does sovereign power lie?' Or is this a meaningless question? Some, like Uwe Kitzinger, would argue that sovereignty in the sense of having an ultimate authority is a myth. He examined the three most common claimants to sovereignty in this country—the law, Parliament and the people. He challenged each of them. The law he said only institutionalises decisions. It does not make them. The Parliament, the law approver, is likewise circumscribed and cannot control the day-to-day activities of the executive or the judiciary. Kitzinger said that the claim that 'the people' were supreme failed to identify where decisions were taken, and to recognise the constraints which surround the effective powers of any group, even a majority. 'So who is the sovereign now?' he asked. 'Or isn't it rather that in this modern world there is not any*one* who has the supreme power of decision, independent of anyone else's power of decision, off with his head? Our whole democratic system is a complicated, constantly shifting, purely momentary equilibrium of different forces, operating in different ways in different sections!'[1] Kitzinger's view certainly lends itself to the complex inter-relationship that has been established between and among the institutions of the Communities and the member States.

Mitchell (pp. 220–5) supports Kitzinger's scepticism about the usefulness of the concept of 'sovereignty'. He sees it as a 'mischief word of no certain and universal meaning'. After emphasising the novelty of the community process, he writes of the interpenetration or intermingling of authorities between the communities and the member States. For this to work he says that legal theories of the past must be abandoned.

The need to adopt novel approaches is underlined in the final article in this section by Albrecht Düren. This concerns the challenge to the concept of state sovereignty which comes from the growing power of multinational companies. Düren looks at these giant corporations as a legal and political problem for the whole world, not just Western Europe. He concludes that far reaching structural changes in company law and in governmental social policies will be required if these economic giants are to play their full part in the future progress of society (pp. 225–33).

Reference

1. Uwe Kitzinger, *Britain and the Common Market*, British Broadcasting Corporation, London, 1967, p. 69.

4.2 European Communities Act 1972 Part I Sections 2 and 3

General Implementation of Treaties

2.—(1) All such rights, powers, liabilities, obligations and restrictions from time to time created or arising by or under the Treaties, and all such remedies and procedures from time to time provided for by or under the Treaties, as in accordance with the Treaties are without further enactment to be given legal effect or used in the United Kingdom shall be recognised and available in law, and be enforced, allowed and followed accordingly; and the expression 'enforceable Community right' and similar expressions shall be read as referring to one to which this subsection applies.

(2) Subject to Schedule 2 to this Act, at any time after its passing Her Majesty may by Order in Council, and any designated Minister or department may by regulations, make provision—

(*a*) for the purpose of implementing any Community obligation of the United Kingdom, or enabling any such obligation to be implemented, or of enabling any rights enjoyed or to be enjoyed by the United Kingdom under or by virtue of the Treaties to be exercised; or

(*b*) for the purpose of dealing with matters arising out of or related to any such obligation or rights or the coming into force, or the operation from time to time, of subsection (1) above;

and in the exercise of any statutory power or duty, including any power to give directions or to legislate by means of orders, rules, regulations or other subordinate instrument, the person entrusted with the power or duty may have regard to the objects of the Communities and to any such obligation or rights as aforesaid.

In this subsection 'designated Minister or department' means such Minister of the Crown or government department as may from time to time be designated by Order in Council in relation to any matter or for any purpose, but subject to such restrictions or conditions (if any) as may be specified by the Order in Council.

(3) There shall be charged on and issued out of the Consolidated Fund or, if so determined by the Treasury, the National Loans Fund the amounts required to meet any Community obligation to make payments to any of the Communities or member States, or any Community obligation in respect of contributions to the capital or reserves of the European Investment Bank or in respect of loans to the Bank, or to redeem any notes or obligations issued or created in respect of any such Community obligation; and, except as otherwise provided by or under any enactment—

(*a*) any other expenses incurred under or by virtue of the Treaties or this Act by any Minister of the Crown or government department may be paid out of moneys provided by Parliament; and

(*b*) any sums received under or by virtue of the Treaties or this Act by any Minister of the Crown or government department, save for such sums as may be required for disbursements permitted by any other enactment, shall be paid into the Consolidated

Fund or, if so determined by the Treasury, the National Loans Fund.

(4) The provision that may be made under subsection (2) above includes, subject to Schedule 2 to this Act, any such provision (of any such extent) as might be made by Act of Parliament, and any enactment passed or to be passed, other than one contained in this Part of this Act, shall be construed and have effect subject to the foregoing provisions of this section; but, except as may be provided by any Act passed after this Act, Schedule 2 shall have effect in connection with the powers conferred by this and the following sections of this Act to make Orders in Council and regulations.

(5) The limitations on the legislative power of the Parliament of Northern Ireland which are imposed by section 4 (1) (4) (treaty matters) of the Government of Ireland Act 1920 shall not be construed to prevent that Parliament, on matters otherwise within their powers, from enacting provisions for any of the purposes mentioned in subsection (2) (a) and (b) above; and the references in that subsection to a Minister of the Crown or government department and to a statutory power or duty shall include a Minister or department of the Government of Northern Ireland and a power or duty arising under or by virtue of an Act of the Parliament of Northern Ireland.

(6) A law passed by the legislature of any of the Channel Islands or of the Isle of Man, or a colonial law (within the meaning of the Colonial Laws Validity Act 1865) passed or made for Gibraltar, if expressed to be passed or made in the implementation of the Treaties and of the obligations of the United Kingdom thereunder, shall not be void or inoperative by reason of any inconsistency with or repugnancy to an Act of Parliament, passed or to be passed, that extends to the Island or Gibraltar or any provision having the force and effect of an Act there (but not including this section), nor by reason of its having some operation outside the Island or Gibraltar; and any such Act or provision that extends to the Island or Gibraltar shall be construed and have effect subject to the provisions of any such law.

Decisions on, and Proof of, Treaties and Community Instruments etc.

3.—(1) For the purposes of all legal proceedings any question as to the meaning or effect of any of the Treaties, or as to the validity, meaning or effect of any Community instrument, shall be treated as a question of law (and, if not referred to the European Court, be for determination as such in accordance with the principles laid down by any relevant decision of the European Court).

(2) Judicial notice shall be taken of the Treaties, of the Official Journal of the Communities and of any decision of, or expression of opinion by, the European Court on any such question as aforesaid; and the Official Journal shall be admissible as evidence of any instrument or other act thereby communicated of any of the Communities or of any Community institution.

(3) Evidence of any instrument issued by a Community institution, including any judgement or order of the European Court, or of any document in the custody of a Community institution, or any entry in or extract from such a document, may be given in any legal proceedings by production of a copy certified as a true copy by an official of that institution; and any document purporting to be such a copy shall be received in evidence without proof of the official position or handwriting of the person signing the certificate.

(4) Evidence of any Community instrument may also be given in any legal proceedings—

(a) by production of a copy purporting to be printed by the Queen's Printer;

(b) where the instrument is in the custody of a government department (including a department of the Government of Northern Ireland), by production of a copy certified on behalf of the department to be a true copy by an officer of the department generally or specially authorised so to do;

and any document purporting to be such a copy as is mentioned in paragraph (b) above of an instrument in the custody of a department shall be received in evidence without proof of the official position or handwriting of the person signing the certificate, or of his authority to do so, or of the document being in the custody of the department.

(5) In any legal proceedings in Scotland evidence of any matter given in a manner authorised by this section shall be sufficient evidence of it.

(Extracted from Cmnd. 5179, HMSO, London, 1972.)

4.3 Law of the European Communities and Municipal Law

G. BEBR

1. Nature of Community Law

Before examining the relationship of Community law to the municipal law of member States, its legal nature should first be examined. This may perhaps be best demonstrated in a pragmatic manner in the light of the objectives, powers and institutions of the Community.

Community Objectives

The long-term, and certainly rather distant, objective of the EEC Treaty is a gradual development and establishment of a common market envisaged as an economic union which would ultimately integrate the national markets of the member States.[1] This gigantic task is to be attained, according to the Treaty, by a gradual establishment of a free movement of goods, persons, services and capital across the national boundaries of the member States.[2] To assure a free movement of goods, customs duties and quantitative restrictions and measures having their equivalent effect are to be abolished and a common customs tariff[3] and a common commercial policy towards third States established. A mere elimination of these trade barriers could not ensure this freedom of movement unless it was accompanied by free competition in inter-State trade and by harmonising the relevant legislation of the member States which may hamper it.[4] A common agricultural[5] and transport policy complete these basic principles.

The realisation of these aims alone, conceived as factors of integration, could hardly release effects powerful enough as to bring about an economic union. The structure of national economies may well withstand such an integrating impact. The Treaty requires, therefore, among its fundamental principles, a co-ordination of economic policy of the member States.[6] Significantly enough, as to the aims in the fiscal, monetary and social field, which are no less relevant for a progressive integration, the Treaty remains rather reserved and general.

Community Powers

A mere traditional co-operation among the member States could have hardly achieved this wide range of aims which are instrumental in establishing and developing a customs union and leading ultimately to an economic union. Independent Community powers, however limited, have, therefore, become indispensable. Within the limits set by the Treaty, the Community has its own, specific powers which reach out into the traditional competence of the State.

Depending on the respective field of application, the Community powers differ, of course, in their scope and intensity. Whereas they are extensive, to the point of being exclusive, in the field of customs duties, quantitative restrictions, agriculture, competition or State aids, to cite only a few examples, they are modest and inconspicuous in the field of economic or monetary policy.[7] In the first instance, the Community powers are particularly powerful as they may reach, in the form of a regulation, directly into the national legal orders of the member States. In the second instance, they are hardly more than an obligation of the member States to co-ordinate their policies in the respective fields. The nature of the Community objectives and of the subject matter to be regulated explain why the Community law, i.e. the Treaty and Community acts, are applicable to the member States as well as to individuals.

The EEC Treaty provides for three different forms of binding acts, the force and content of which widely differ.[8] In this sense there is a certain gradation of powers as expressed by the different Community acts. A regulation is the most powerful act typical of the Community legal order. It is binding in every respect and directly applicable throughout the *entire* Community without any intervention whatsoever on the part of the member States. It may impose obligations or confer rights on member States and individuals alike. By its content a regulation is a veritable Community law. Compared with a regulation, a directive is less powerful, as it binds only the member State addressed and that only as to the objectives to be attained, leaving the choice as to the proper form and means of execution to the competent national authorities. A decision is binding in every respect on the person to which it is addressed, be it an individual or a member State. In some instances the Treaty itself determines the form of the Community act to be taken; in others the Treaty leaves it to the discretion of the competent Community institution to choose for itself the appropriate form of the act.

Community Institutions

The powers of the Community logically require Community institutions to exercise them. Without examining the Community institutional structure at any length, it suffices to say for our purpose that the Community legislative process is carried out by an original interplay between the Commission, the truly independent Community body, and the Council of Ministers, a body composed of the representatives of the member States. At the risk of generalisation, it may be stated that the basic Community powers rest with the Council. However, and this is an essential institutional feature, the Council is restricted in its powers in so far as it may act, as a rule, only on the proposal of the Commission, which reflects Community interests as a whole. The role of the Commission in this process should not be underestimated. A proposal of the Commission carries great weight in this process in so far as the Council may disregard it only when acting unanimously.[9] Thus the Commission exercises its impact on the content of the Community act to be taken by the Council. Even though the Commission is primarily to apply Community law, it has nevertheless its own powers of decision in specific instances. It is quite typical of the Community legal order that it is the Commission which is to watch over compliance with Community obligations by member States or individuals.[10]

The exercise of the powers of the Community by its institutions would be inconceivable without judicial control. Generally speaking, the Court of Justice is exclusively competent to ensure the legal exercise of the powers of the Community by its institutions; the observance and execution of Community obligations by member States or individuals; and the uniform interpretation of Community law by municipal courts of the member States.

Conclusion

The objectives, the powers and the institutions of the Community suggest already that there is hardly any basis for comparing the EEC Treaty with a traditional international treaty. Community law is, in a sense, an autonomous legal order to which not only member States but individuals as well are subject.[11] A long-term process of integration, as outlined by the Treaty, would be impossible if not guided and fostered by a continually developing Community law, by a progressive Community legal integration. Thus even in legal fields the Treaty displays its own, inherent dynamism. This brief introduction may make it clear that to classify the EEC Treaty as any other international treaty would do violence to its true legal nature and rob the Community of its very foundation. It appears, therefore, misleading to view the relationship of Community law to municipal law along the traditional lines.

2. The Relation of the Law of the European Communities to the Law of the Member States

The gradual development of the European Communities prompts municipal courts of the member States to apply Community law more and more frequently. Applying it, municipal courts have had in a number of instances to rule on its conflict with municipal law in general and with constitutional law in particular.

At first sight this question seems to pose no particular problem. Municipal courts have always interpreted and applied provisions of international treaties and agreements. And depending on the respective constitutional provisions they may have upheld the supremacy of international treaties over conflicting municipal law.

The law of the European Communities undoubtedly reveals some very original features. Its relationship to municipal law raises, therefore, different problems from the relationship of traditional international treaties to municipal law. It is, therefore, not surprising that municipal courts may have difficulties in finding a reliable basis for resolving such a conflict.

The relationship of Community law to the law of the member States covers a wide range. It concerns not only the relation of the Treaty provisions to municipal law but that of the various Community acts as well. Particularly regulations which are binding in every respect and directly applicable in each member State, may conflict with municipal law—an unusual kind of a conflict indeed, up to now hardly envisaged.

This conflict may present itself in two different situations. The Community law may conflict with a *preceding* municipal law—a conflict the resolution of which hardly poses particular difficulties. But the Community law may also clash with *constitutional* provisions or with a *subsequent* municipal law. The resolution of this conflict is difficult in so far as most constitutions contain no appropriate provisions. This general observation may sufficiently reveal that the relationship of Community law to the municipal law of the member States is of a special nature, raising new problems which may call for a new solution.

References

1. EEC Treaty, art. 2.
2. EEC Treaty, art. 3. For a critical analysis of the objectives of the EEC Treaty see Dabin, 'Au-delà de l'union douanière, l'union économique', in Institut d'Etudes Juridiques Européennes de la Faculté de Droit de l'Université de Liège, de l'Union Douanière à l'Union Economique, 96, 1970.
3. As of 1 July, 1968, customs duties in the intra-Community trade were abolished and a Common Customs Tariff established, EEC Commission, Second General Report on the Activities of the Communities 1968, pp. 20–3, 1969.
4. EEC Treaty, art. 3 (f), (h).
5. Common market organisations for various agricultural products were established, EEC Commission, First General Report on the Activities of the Communities 1967, pp. 131–45, 1968.
6. EEC Treaty, art. 3 (g).
7. See Resolution of the Council of 22 March 1971, concerning a gradual realisation of an economic and monetary union, 14 Journal Official des Communautés Européennes (J.O.), C 23/1.
8. EEC Treaty, art. 189.
9. Ibid., art. 149.
10. Ibid., art. 169.
11. Preliminary Ruling No. 26/62 (van Gend & Loos), 9 Recueil de la juris-prudence de la Cour 1.23 (1963).

(Extracted from the *Modern Law Review*, Vol. 34, no. 5, September 1971.)

4.4 The Issue of Parliamentary Sovereignty

J. E. S. FAWCETT

In the sovereignty of Parliament, as in most factors of social cohesion, there is an element of myth; and in times of challenge, such as the prospect of entry of the United Kingdom into the EEC, this myth becomes a point of defence and a route of escape. It is worth, then, inquiring into it.

The sovereignty of Parliament is its power to make supreme law, and it is generally seen as having two essential features. First, a statute duly enacted[1] is good law, in that it cannot be declared invalid by the courts on any ground; for example, that its provisions are contrary to constitutional law, or to the common law,[2] or to international law. Secondly, a statute may, expressly or by implication, be amended or repealed by a later statute; or, as it is often put, Parliament cannot bind its successors.

We must first look at the logical puzzle which these features present, a puzzle noted by Lord Bacon. Suppose, he said, that Parliament enacts a statute providing that no statute shall be enacted for seven years, but that a later statute is enacted within that period. If the earlier statute is good law, then the later cannot be, in which case the second principle of sovereignty is invalidated; but if the later statute is good law on the basis of the second principle, then the earlier statute is invalidated contrary to the first principle. It will not do to say that the earlier statute is operative until repealed, for it can operate only at the moment of the enactment of the later statute.

The key to the puzzle lies in the fact that there are two kinds of statute: those which make rules of substantive law and those that enact rules for the making of law. It is in the enactment of the second kind that the sovereignty of Parliament can be limited, so that the grandiose statement that Parliament cannot bind its successors, made without qualification, takes on the role of myth.

We have, then, to apply this distinction to the implementation of a treaty of a special kind. For the Treaty of Rome requires, if it is to work, that a number of its provisions must be made part of the law of the member States of the Community. Further, it establishes certain organs, which may make law for the Community by way of Regulations and Decisions.

The implementation of the Rome Treaty would thus take a number of forms in the United Kingdom. It would, like all United Kingdom treaties, be ratified by the Crown, but, to make its acceptance fully operative under the law of the United Kingdom, Parliament would have to incorporate at least its central provisions in a statute.* Parliament could then go on to provide in various ways for the implementation of Regulations and Decisions, promulgated by the Community organs and addressed to the UK or all member States. It could enact each one as it was issued, as a separate statute; or it might by general statute authorise the appropriate Ministers to implement such Regulations or Decisions by Orders in Council or other subordinate legislation; or it might enact a single statute providing that they should take effect as part of the law of the United Kingdom, directly and automatically upon their promulgation, without requirement of further Parliamentary or Ministerial action. Similar methods could be used to give effect to decisions of the Communities' Court. Parliament might also use these methods in combination. We can perhaps ignore the first, as, given the very large number of Regulations or Decisions that will be involved, it is hardly feasible.

Now we notice that these ways of incorporating what is loosely called Community law into the law of the United Kingdom show in turn an increasing measure of delegation of law-making authority, or self-limitation of its sovereignty, by Parliament. Thus while, in adopting the first two methods, Parliament would retain ultimate control of Community law-making in the United Kingdom, by the third way the Community organs would, in the particular fields in which they were competent, become in effect direct law-makers for the United Kingdom.

Among the arguments made against the entry of the United Kingdom into the EEC is the assertion that it would somehow infringe or limit the sovereignty of Parliament or the sovereignty of the United Kingdom itself. And, in particular, it is said that acceptance of the Rome Treaty is, under its terms which are in this respect unlike those of most treaties, intended to be irrevocable. These arguments have both legal and political bases, which we may look at in turn.

Legally, three questions are posed here about the sovereignty of Parliament. Can Parliament by statute confer on the Community organs law-making authority in the United Kingdom? Could it

[* This has not happened—see Introduction to this section p. 187.]

revoke such a statutory transfer of authority by a later statute? Could it amend or repeal any statute or order giving effect to a standing Community Regulation or Decision, or annul such Regulations or Decisions if they had already been given direct effect under the law of the United Kingdom?

Can Parliament by statute confer on the Community organs law-making authority in the United Kingdom? The answer to this question is, on the best authority, Yes. Three instances may be described of the recognition that Parliament may abandon its law-making authority in favour of another legislative body, or may delegate or in effect transfer certain law-making authority to it. By 'another legislative body' is meant a body comparable in law-making function and authority to Parliament itself; in other words, we are not concerned here with subordinate or delegated legislation in the ordinary sense, by Ministers, municipal authorities or other public agencies.

The first instance is the *Government of Ireland Bill* introduced by Mr. Gladstone in 1886.[3] The effect of the proposed establishment of an Irish legislature was much debated both inside and outside Parliament, and what is interesting is that not only Sir Robert Finlay, the Attorney-General, but also Dicey and Anson, with their great authority, were agreed that the Bill would give legislative independence to Ireland *beyond recall*. The second, and in practice more decisive, instance is the *Statute of Westminster, 1931*, s.4. This provided that no future Act of Parliament of the United Kingdom was to extend, or to be deemed to extend, to a Dominion, as part of the law of that Dominion, unless the Dominion had requested and assented to such an enactment. Two points must be noticed: first, the provision is dealing with the operation of a statute as part of the law of a Dominion, and says nothing of the effect of such a statute under the law of the United Kingdom; secondly, it requires in effect not the usual three but four assents, of Queen, Lords, Commons and the Dominion, to such a statute. In short, it is a case of the law-making process being itself altered.

It is plain not only that Parliament may so alter its own legislative process, but that succeeding Parliaments will be bound to observe the changed procedure in enacting statutes, to which the procedure applies. A succeeding Parliament may, of course, change the procedure again, but here another rule of law enters in: that Parliament cannot effectively legislate for territories that are not part of the United Kingdom, its islands or dependencies. If, then, Parliament were, for example at the instance of the Province of Quebec but not with the assent of Canada, to enact a statute to become part of the law of Canada, it would not be an Act at all any more than an Act assented to only by the Queen and House of Lords. If Parliament, however, first amended the *Statute of Westminster*, s.4, and then enacted the statute for Quebec, it would be defeated by the rule, *as far as Canada is concerned*, that Parliament cannot legislate for independent States—and the members of the Commonwealth are no exception[4]—save in so far as they agree to accept such legislation. It may be that the courts of the United Kingdom might regard themselves as bound to treat a statute, so enacted after repeal of the *Statute of Westminster*, s.4, as good law in the United Kingdom, but this could have only the most limited effect. Indeed, this approach would belong wholly to theory and not to reality.

These two instances are offered by way of analogy in that they show that Parliament has, in the one case, contemplated, and in the other effected, a final transfer of law-making authority to another legislative authority. Dicey, with the first case in mind, observed that Parliament can divest itself of authority in two ways: 'It may simply put an end to its own existence . . . It may again transfer sovereign authority to another person or body of persons.'[5] But these cases differ from that envisaged in our question in that they represent a total surrender of sovereignty. Closer to a transfer of law-making authority to the Community organs[6] is a third instance, exemplified in the *United Nations Act, 1946*. Here there has been no change in the law-making process by Parliament, but the use rather of the second method, described above, of implementing the decisions of an external authority binding on the United Kingdom through its acceptance of the UN Charter. Security Council decisions, calling for economic sanctions under Article 41 of the Charter, are binding on members of the UN under Article 25. The *United Nations Act, 1946*, recognises this, and authorises the Crown to take the necessary action by Order in Council to implement any such decisions. The only decision of the Security Council under Article 41 so far has been to impose sanctions against Rhodesia. The fact that these sanctions have been applied by the UK, not under this Act, but under the *Southern Rhodesia Act, 1965*, does not qualify the *United Nations Act* or alter its character as a statute clearly implementing the decisions of an external authority having legal and administrative consequences for the United Kingdom. The United Kingdom might fail to implement, or implement inadequately, Security Council decisions: this would involve the obligations and sovereignty of the United Kingdom, but have nothing to do with the sovereignty of Parliament.

Could Parliament revoke such a statutory transfer of authority? And could it amend or repeal any statute or order giving effect to standing Community Regulations or Decisions, or annul these if they had already been given direct effect under the law of the United Kingdom? The answers to both these questions are essentially the same: legally, Yes in the United Kingdom, No in the rest of the EEC; politically, Yes on certain conditions.

It has been suggested above that Parliament might enact a statute, which authorised subordinate legislation to give effect to Regulations and Decisions of Community organs or which declared that these should become directly and automatically part of the law of the United Kingdom. In either case, a succeeding Parliament could, on our principles of the sovereignty of Parliament, repeal that statute. The repealing statute would be good law in the United Kingdom, but, in so far as it was contrary to the Rome Treaty, it could not be recognised or applied by the Communities' Court and would have no legal effect in other EEC countries. Here the obligations of the United Kingdom itself would be in issue, as a party to the Rome Treaty and a member of the EEC. Formally, the non-observance or breach of provisions of the Rome Treaty involved could be referred for decision by the Communities' Court; materially, it might become a matter of political negotiation and settlement.

Viewed politically, such a repeal by Parliament of statutes implementing Community law might point to and entail withdrawal from the EEC; and in an extreme case it might be treated as withdrawal in effect. Here it is sometimes suggested that, because the Rome Treaty makes no provision for the withdrawal of a participating country, entry to the EEC is irrevocable and that this fact infringes the sovereignty of Parliament: in other words, the statute accepting the Rome Treaty and membership in the EEC could not be repealed.

While it is true that institutions such as the United Nations and the EEC are by their very nature designed to be permanent,[7] it does not follow that membership cannot be terminated. Not only may members be expelled from the UN under Article 6 of the Charter, but the voluntary withdrawal of Indonesia and her subsequent re-entry were not regarded as in any respect inconsistent with the Charter. Similarly, withdrawal from the EEC is neither contemplated nor excluded in the Rome Treaty. Further, Article 235[8] could, it would appear, be used to expel a member of the Community, if it pursued policies so divergent from the Treaty as to compromise the objects of the Community.

Entry into the EEC would plainly limit the areas in which Parliament would remain wholly free to legislate for the United Kingdom. But the purpose of this Note has been to show that, whether or not that limitation is *politically* acceptable, the argument that Parliament cannot accept such limitations for legal and constitutional reasons is not well founded.

References

1. Viz. generally by assent of the Queen, Lords and Commons. Certain statutes may be enacted by assent of the Queen and Commons.
2. The principle, enunciated by Sir Edward Coke, that the common law has a power 'to control acts of Parliament and sometimes adjudge them to be utterly void'—*Bonham's Case* (1608), Co. Rep. 118a, did not win general acceptance.
3. For a full account see D. V. Cowen, *The Foundations of Freedom*, Oxford University Press, Cape Town, London and New York, 1961, pp. 181–4.
4. See, for example, the *Nigeria Independence Act, 1960*, s.1.
5. *Law of the Constitution*, 9th Ed., pp. 68, 69.
6. For example, under the Basic Law of the Federal Republic of Germany, the Bund may by legislation transfer authority (*Hoheitsrechte*) to international institutions: Article 24(1).
7. Article 240 of the Rome Treaty provides that it shall be of indefinite duration.
8. The careful limitations imposed on the taking of action under Article 235 strongly suggest that it is designed for extreme situations.

(Extracted from *The World Today*, Vol. 27, no. 4, April 1971, pp. 139–43.)

4.5 The Judge's Dilemma
PROFESSOR H. W. R. WADE

Sovereignty was sure to play some part in the Common Market debates, but it is strange that it has loomed so large in the speeches of left-wing opponents of entry. There would seem to be no shortage of ammunition for socialist opposition to an international policy of liberating the forces of supply and demand, reducing subsidies and discriminatory taxation, restricting state trading monopolies and so forth. But the Opposition seems more disposed to make an issue out of sovereignty. Perhaps it is because they are playing it up that the Government is playing it down. Official spokesmen have skated lightly over the subject in the debates, maintaining that the European Communities Bill involves nothing very out of the ordinary constitutionally.

There is nothing new in abdicating sovereignty—the dismantling of the British Empire was a gigantic exercise in exactly that. But it is undoubtedly revolutionary for this country to accept as law, in advance and automatically, the dictates of the Community's executive organs, the Council and the Commission. Acceptance of the European Court is in form less revolutionary, but may have even more profound repercussions. For the court has proclaimed on many occasions that the Treaty of Rome does not, like ordinary treaties, merely impose obligations on the signatory states: it has brought into being a 'new legal order', i.e. a body of 'community law' which must, if community is to mean anything, apply *proprio vigore* in all member States and take precedence over their internal law in any case of conflict. When there are ten member States* there will be eleven legal systems. How can room be found for an eleventh system in this legal game of musical chairs?

Community law can be given concrete application only by the decisions of domestic courts. The courts of the Six have been making heroic efforts to assimilate the 'new legal order', for example by holding that levies or taxes imposed by their own Parliaments, but condemned by the European Court, are not legally payable. In 1968 a French decision marked a set-back: the Conseil d'Etat refused to

[* As Norway did not join, this should read 'nine member states and ten legal systems'.]

disregard a French law allowing duty-free entry to Algerian semolina, although Algerian imports were by pre-existing community law subject to the common external tariff.

And now Germany has discovered that community law may conflict not only with ordinary domestic law but with the German Constitution—and what is more, with its guarantees of basic human rights. The European Court has not flinched from holding that even here community law must prevail. A German administrative court has rejected this decision and the case is now before the German Constitution Court. Must a member State submit to having its constitution amended—something its own Parliament may be unable to do—by a body of Eurocrats in Brussels? If the answer is yes, the revolution is profound indeed. If it is no, there will be no comfort for Britain. Being the only member with no formal constitution, Britain alone will have no sacrosanct preserve of fundamental community-proof law.

It is obvious, at any rate, that community law makes much greater demands than were mentioned in the White Paper of 1967,[1] which said merely that after the initial adjustments Parliament would have to refrain from passing legislation inconsistent with the Community law, and that this would involve no constitutional innovation. The key question for Britain is what will happen if some future Act of Parliament produces an irreconcilable conflict, as in the French semolina case. It is unrealistic to suppose that this will not happen.

The present Bill can and does make Community law prevail over existing Acts of Parliament. It also expressly attempts to make it prevail over future Acts, by a few words in clause 2(4) awkwardly wedged in the middle of a long sentence about other things, as well as by some words coyly lurking in brackets in clause 3(1). But here it falls foul of the classic principle of Parliamentary sovereignty, which ordains that no Parliament can bind its successors. Where two Acts of Parliament conflict, the later Act must always prevail. Whether the conflicting provisions are express, or implied is immaterial, provided that the conflict is irreconcilable. It is useless for the earlier Act to say that it shall itself prevail. This is the same as saying that it shall be unrepealable, and it is fundamental that every Act must be repealable.

The one thing that our legally omnipotent Parliament cannot do is to fetter its own continuing sovereignty itself. It is therefore inherent in the whole problem that nothing that the present Bill can say can make any difference.

It follows with equally inexorable logic that Parliament cannot dictate to the courts how they are to treat future Acts. The allegiance of the judges to the Parliament of the day is a political fact, which previous Parliaments are powerless to alter. But the judges can alter it—just as they did, without any strictly legal warrant, in transferring their allegiance from the Parliament of James II to the Parliament of William III. Then there is a true revolution, a shift in the political basis of the legal system.

Some lawyers argue that this may happen again with the EEC, and that the judges may spontaneously accept Community law as paramount even in opposition to later Acts of Parliament. But this is a political prediction which no purely legal argument can justify, and which most lawyers would regard as somewhat fanciful, at present at any rate.

The Government can therefore justifiably claim that Parliament's ultimate authority will remain unimpaired. But they have put themselves into a dilemma by attempting to fetter it by their own Bill. Either the Bill's provision about future Acts is meaningless in any case of real conflict; or else the Government is assuming that there will be a constitutional revolution of just the kind it is at pains to deny . . .

Reference

1. Cmnd. 3269.

(Extracted from *The Times*, 18 April 1972.)

4.6 The Coming Challenge to Parliament's Powers

SIR LESLIE SCARMAN, Head of the Law Commission

Certain changes now becoming manifest in the political field may within the next ten or twenty years transform the law and administration of the country. In particular, they may bring about a wholly new relationship between the legislature, the executive and the courts.

Put shortly, we may, without realising it, be on the brink of the most radical constitutional change since Parliament asserted its sovereignty in the seventeenth century.

For the past 300 years no one has sought to challenge parliamentary sovereignty: nor has anyone doubted the wisdom of maintaining its absolute power uncontrolled save by Parliament itself. But the second half of the twentieth century may well see just such a challenge.

The Treaties establishing the European Communities will be constitutional documents that Parliament acting alone will be unable to alter or amend: short of the sanction of withdrawal from the Communities, Parliament must accept the Treaties and the directly applicable law made under them.

Community law, consisting of a body of law enacted by institutions other than Parliament, will have to be integrated and applied within the Kingdom by our courts under the guidance of the European Court, which will be the ultimate and authoritative interpreter of the Treaties, and the regulations and direction of the Market. Thus, the Treaties will have something of the nature of a constitutional statute in a federal State, being incapable of amendment or alteration save by procedures laid down in the Treaties themselves. And, though Parliament and the Government will have influence through representation and in some cases a veto, they will not by themselves be able to control this law-making process.

No doubt both these developments can and will be accommodated in a statutory formulation which accords with the theory of Parliament's continuing sovereignty. But in practice it will be otherwise.

In the field of Common Market law it is certain that the courts will have to assume the burden of interpreting and applying legislation that may be in conflict with statutes made by Parliament.

The possibility of an independent role for the courts in the interpretation of constitutional provisions, a role which could in turn lead on to their application and enforcement independently of the will of Parliament, is sufficiently revolutionary to call now for preliminary study.

Since the seventeenth century the British Constitution has proved very successful in avoiding conflict between the three organs of government. The success is due not so much to the fact that the Constitution is unwritten—though that helps—as to the basic principle of the sovereignty of Parliament. The executive can act efficiently only so long as it retains a majority in Parliament, while the

Courts ?

courses are, to borrow a phrase of Lord Denning, 'subservient' to the will of Parliament. The courts do what they are told to do by Act of Parliament.

Although the subjection of courts and government to the will of Parliament is very well known, its implications are not. Because of it English law draws no distinction between public and private law. With the possible exception of the 1688 settlement and the Act of Union, there are no basic constitutional documents. The courts are not required to interpret or apply or safeguard the Constitution. The Constitution cannot be reviewed by the courts for the simple reason that it is not to be found in any statute: it resides in the practices, conventions and standing orders of Parliament, a review of which, if a judge were foolish enough to attempt it, would lead him rapidly to the Tower, there to purge his contempt.

A further implication is that the courts represent no threat to the policies of the executive. So long as the executive retains its Parliamentary majority, it can by Act of Parliament ensure that the courts act consistently with its policies. The executive must, of course, obey the law, which draws no distinction in this regard between public official and private citizen: but there is no Constitution which it is the duty of the courts to see is not infringed by executive or legislative act.

The imminence of the arrival in English law of constitutional or constitutional type enactments, by ending in fact, if not in theory, Parliament's power on all occasions and whenever it chooses to legislate as it alone thinks fit, means that in the future the courts will have in some fields of their work to abandon the attitude of 'subservience'.

Occasions will arise when it will be the duty of a court to declare the law of the constitution. Though the technique will superficially be one in which the courts are already well versed, i.e. the interpretation of statutes, the business being done will be more profound. The courts will be developing a control system based on written constitutional documents, interpreted and applied by the courts.

This will be no less than the beginning of a system of public law. And the beginning is near: for when the European Communities Bill becomes law; our courts will be required to administer a body of Community law based on a constitutional document, the Treaty of Rome.

The alarmists can say that in this strange new world of public law there will be the possibility of a conflict between courts and Parliament though its emergence, at least in the early stages, is far from likely. This is, of course, true. But I suspect we may safely leave to the day that it arises the problem of conflict between a directly applicable rule of the Common Market and a subsequent Act of Parliament. Yet the theoretical possibility of such a problem arising is an indication of the changes that are coming.

We may assume that the British in accepting into their law a system of public law will not have lost their native taste for compromise and that all three organs of government—Parliament, the executive and the courts—will co-operate to make the new system work. Yet inevitably there must come a new relationship. In preparing its own legislation Parliament will have to pay heed to the constitutional statutes and the interpretation put upon them by the courts, and will have, in particular, to bear in mind that Parliament will not always be able by its own act to amend them.

The impact upon the administration of the emergence of a genuine public law based on constitutional statutes will be as profound as upon Parliament. Ministers and their civil service advisers will find themselves more directly concerned with the law than they are now.

The sovereignty of Parliament has meant that Ministers and their advisers have exhibited in their daily work a total commitment to Parliament, conscious that, so long as their policies were satisfactory to Parliament, they had nothing to fear. Their attention to the law has never really gone further than the regard necessary to keep the department out of the courts. The law was never a threat to long-term policy, for Parliament could always reverse the decisions of the judges.

But in future a more sophisticated, perhaps a more constructive, attitude will have to be adopted. The administration will become aware of the finality of some judicial decisions that the Parliamentary system by itself will be helpless to undo. More positively, Ministers and their advisers may come to realise that the legal system can offer, as a matter of public law, rulings that will assist in the creation and formulation of policy.

Perhaps some lessons of policy can be learnt from the way the Attorney General of the US seeks the guidance on constitutional questions of the Federal courts and ultimately, the Supreme Court. But the urgent task will be to recognise the machinery of the public administration so as to meet the challenges posed by the development of a system of public law based on constitutional enactments interpreted and applied by the courts. It will be necessary to strengthen the legal resources of the governmental machine.

We may even have to abandon the essentially non-legal character of the Civil Service and welcome the lawyer into the higher echelons of the administrative branch of the service, as other countries do, on a much larger scale than we have ever contemplated.

In Canada, as in the US, one finds strong legal departments at the centre supported by legally-trained and qualified men at all levels in the policy departments, whose work is not limited to exclusively legal questions, but is used in the formulation as well as the application and enforcement of policy.

But, if a system of public law such as I have envisaged comes, the major challenge will be to the legal profession and the courts. For the first time, we may find ourselves requiring the courts to pass judgement on statutes, the question being whether they are constitutional or unconstitutional. It is clear that a radical reappraisal of our traditional methods of statutory interpretation would be needed.

Within the limited field of the Common Market a new approach will be called for as soon as we enter. The European Court is likely to establish and develop an approach to Community legislation very different from the traditional approach of our courts to Acts of Parliament. There is to be found in decisions already given by that court a greater emphasis on the policy as distinct from the letter of the law—a trend no doubt encouraged by the fact that the official letter of the law will be in six languages.

Our courts, since they must accept the guidance of the European Court, will have to adopt the more positive Continental approach to the policy of a measure when interpreting and applying it, and will have to overcome their native disposition to take refuge in the proposition that policy is not for the courts to consider.

In the subterranean waters of our legal administrative system there are flowing currents that may carry Parliament, the administration and the courts to places hitherto unexplored by them. It will not happen at once, but as this new public law emerges the judges will be required not only to interpret and apply it, but also to consider and construe other legislation in the light of it: the passage from statutory interpretation, which will henceforth become the major legal technique, to statute invalidation, may be shorter than some suppose.

(Extracted from *The Observer*, 16 July 1972. Based on a lecture to the Royal Institute of Public Administration.)

4.7 Our European Judges
FENTON BRESLER

The scene is totally alien. An elderly German barrister, in professional black robe and white bow tie, is droning on in German, his voice tired and old and without the slightest expression. Through my earphones I hear an instantaneous translation into French: the voice is younger, brighter, no doubt translating impeccably—but without any stress, accent or punctuation. The effect is drear and soporific.

Facing the elderly German, hunched over his lectern, sit seven grey-haired men in splendid deep red robes slashed with black velvet facings. Four are listening through earphones; three apparently understand German. But none seems very alert. One judge yawns, another sits back with his eyes closed. Throughout the barrister's sixty-minute speech, only one judge takes a very occasional note. Not once is the barrister interrupted by a single question from the Bench.

Yet this is the highest court in Europe. This is the Court of the European Communities at Luxembourg. When Britain goes into the Common Market, this large anonymous modern courtroom, with its great multi-coloured tapestry down one whole wall, its thick grey carpet and green-topped desks—or the even more elaborate court-house now in course of construction on the hills overlooking the city —will take over from the House of Lords as the supreme British legal tribunal for all matters touching on Common Market Law.

The case at present before the Court—remitted from the Hamburg Fiscal Court in West Germany—is a perfect example of the kind of dispute that the Luxembourg Court could next year be hearing from Britain.

It was all about Customs duties and refunds due from a member State on goods exported out of the European Community. To ease the discrepancies between world sugar prices and Community prices, the European Commission—the Common Market's Whitehall-like administrative authority based at Brussels—has made Regulations establishing levies on sugar imported into the Community from outside countries and providing for a refund on exports to outside countries on sugar grown within the Community. Refunds are to be paid by the member State on whose territories the Customs formalities for export have been finalised—and application for refund must, except in exceptional circumstances, be submitted within six months of finalising export formalities, which include submitting an exit certificate from the last member State through which the goods have passed. All this is contained in the Commission's Regulations which, by virtue of the Treaty of Rome, legal linchpin of the whole Community structure, have immediate binding effect on all member States.

What happened in the present case—as the elderly German lawyer's lone voice intoned to the Luxembourg Court—was that his clients, a firm of West German sugar exporters, shipped in October 1968 from Hamburg to Genoa 75,000 kilogrammes of sugar for use on ships. They at once made a preliminary application for refund to the West German Customs authorities on a form supplied by them—claiming that the sugar would soon be arriving at Genoa and thereafter go outside the territories of the European Community on ships plying from that Italian port.

The sugar arrived in Genoa within weeks. But it was not until April 1969 that the Italian authorities, with the delay which seems an inevitable part of life in that country, sent the West German shippers an exit certificate, declaring that as of 1 April 1969, the goods had finally left the geographical territories of the Community. The following month the shippers sent the West German Customs authorities a copy of their original preliminary application form dating back from the previous October together with the exit certificate—and asked for their money. But the Customs authorities refused to pay—on the ground that the application form contained a printed time-limit—that all refund claims must be submitted within six months. From October to May was seven months!

The shippers felt they were being cheated of their money. So they sued the West German Customs authorities for their refund in the Hamburg Fiscal Court, and—since a question of Community Law was involved—the Fiscal Court judge remitted the matter to Luxembourg for a ruling.

The question, therefore, to be argued, was the extent to which—if at all—the Customs authorities of a member State could limit the effect of a Common Market Regulation by inserting further administrative conditions in their forms. Undoubtedly, they were entitled to regulate their own administrative processes according to their own national law. But which was to prevail: Community Law or West German national law? If the Commission's Regulations applied, with the six-months' time-limit dating from the Italian's exit certificate, the West German shippers were entitled to their refund. If West German national law applied, with the six-months' time-limit dating from their original preliminary application, they were hopelessly out of court. On which side would the seven Luxembourg judges come down?

When the elderly West German lawyer wearily finished speaking, up got a much younger, brighter lawyer appearing for the West German Customs authorities. He had a different style: he harangued the silent judges as if they were a jury. They seemed no more or less impressed by his arguments than those of his predecessor. But at least they all now looked awake. He argued strenuously—in German—for the right of every member State to govern its own administrative procedures.

Finally, a young Belgian lawyer addressed the Court—also in German—on behalf of the European Commission. He limited himself to a short, none too forcibly delivered plea that the Commission's Regulation should prevail since Community Law was supreme in this field.

All three speeches were over in less than two hours. Not once had any member of the Bench interrupted or asked a single question. In a British appeal court, counsel is accustomed to having his arguments honed and his mind sharpened by an almost continuous dialogue with the judges.

But not so at Luxembourg. The style is totally different. In the West German Customs case, all three parties had already delivered written statements of their case. They were arguing from a brief already known and considered by the Court. Only at the end of the speeches did M. Robert Lecourt, the French President of the Court, invite his colleagues on the Bench to ask any questions. One judge accepted. He put his question in French. It was instantly translated into German by one of the battery of multilingual experts sitting behind me in a sort of cinema projectionist's box. The elderly barrister replied in German, simultaneously translated into French. And that was it! The 'oral procedure' stage was completed.

'It is not much more than a courtesy to the parties,' I was told. The Court at present has four official languages, always tactfully listed in alphabetical order: Dutch, French, German and Italian—with English to be added as from 1 January next. The claimant has the right to use his mother tongue, and the lawyers for the Commission usually respond in the same language. The judges are not themselves multilingual except that they all use French—which is the language they use for their own private deliberations. 'For them to intervene with frequent questions—which would then have to be translated— during the "oral procedure" would cause tedious delays,' I was told.

Advocacy, as we know it in Britain, does not exist at Luxembourg. There is no chance for silver-tongued counsel to persuade or charm. Decisions are reached largely on the judges' own reading of Community Law, unaffected by the eloquence—or otherwise—of counsel.

In due course, some time after I left Luxembourg, the Court gave judgement—in favour of the West German shipper. They upheld his right to claim his refund. Community Law prevailed over West German national law and procedures.

The case was remitted to the Hamburg Fiscal Court for the national judge to give judgement in accordance with this ruling. Following usual procedure, the question of costs was also left for him to decide.

The Luxembourg Court is staffed by seven judges chosen for renewable six-year terms from among the member States by common consent of the existing six member Governments. Each state does not have to have at least one judge on the Bench, although this is currently so. There are, in fact, two Italian judges at the moment.

The President of the Court is merely 'first among equals', and has no casting vote. Unlike the House of Lords or the English Court of Appeal, there are no dissenting judgements. The Court's decisions are taken by a simple majority in secret, and only one judgement is given.

There is a different *rapport* between Bench and Bar than is found in this country, and British lawyers will need to adjust to this. In Britain, every judge has at one time been a practising barrister or advocate (or occasionally solicitor), before going on the Bench. On the Continent, judges are of a different pattern. They have never practised independently as lawyers in their own right. As young men, they joined the judicial service of their state at the bottom rung of the judicial career ladder and they have slowly climbed to its top: as bigger and better judges. They are a separate breed of men from those who have chosen the more demanding or exciting way of life of a private lawyer.

So too have been the two Advocates-General of the Court. They are a sort of standing *amicus curiae* ('friend of the court' we would call them in English) supposed objectively to summate to the Bench in open court all the contending arguments, and submit a suggested final conclusion. They share the workload: one Advocate-General to each case. Currently, they are a West German and a Frenchman—and like the Court's judges themselves, they have known only civil service existence, usually as judges in their own home countries.

The Court's role under the Treaty of Rome is to 'ensure the observance of law in the interpretation and application of the Treaty'. Its judges and staff are all dedicated 'Europeans' in the sense of 'Community Europeans'. Once we are in the European Community, the Court will be asserting our right as fellow-Europeans—at least that is the theory.

In practice, during its fourteen years of existence, the Court has at times been timid; at times bold. The physical amount of its work is surprisingly small. In no single year has more than one volume of law reports been needed to house its annual output of decisions: the Queen's Bench Division of the English High Court of Justice needs two volumes every year for itself alone. But in 1971, from the whole of the European Community, only ninety-six new cases were registered at the Luxembourg Court.

The impact of the Court comes from the nature and importance of its decisions, not their number.

The Court operates in two main ways. Private individuals, companies and member States can sue the Commission or European Council itself direct at Luxembourg. In theory, a British citizen will have greater rights to sue the European Commission or Council for annulment of a regulation or directive that affects him 'directly and specifically' than he enjoys in English domestic law to sue, for instance, the Department of the Environment. Article 173 of the Treaty of Rome specifically empowers Community citizens to challenge directly at Luxembourg all legislative or administrative acts of the Commission or Council—and already over 3,000 regulations exist—that constitute a breach of the Rome Treaty or a 'misuse of power'.

But here the Court has shown itself timid. It has applied rigorously the *caveat* to Article 173 that private individuals or business houses can only complain of a Commission or Council regulation or directive if it 'is of direct and specific concern to him'. So that when, in 1970, several French undertakings sued the Commission for annulment of regulations fixing compensatory payments of flour exports after the devaluation of the French franc, the Court non-suited the claimants because the regulations were of general effect and not directed at any individual firm. In 1971, there were only ten direct actions brought by private parties at Luxembourg from the whole Community: in 1970, there were nine.

As for member State suing member State for alleged default in their obligations under the Treaty, this simply has not happened. Governments have preferred to deal with this sort of issue at the political rather than a legal level—including President Pompidou's threat in June 1972 to consider complete French withdrawal from the European Community unless the other member States came to heel and stopped squabbling over a concerted economic policy.

There have been a few cases over the years of member States suing the Commission, but the record does not show a robust independence by the Court. In 1971, for instance, there were two cases of this nature. In the first, the Dutch Government sued the Commission for alleged failure to uphold the interests of the Community because the Commission had refused to issue a recommendation to the French Government prohibiting certain state aid to the French iron and steel industry. In the second case, the West German Federal Republic sued the Commission for an alleged breach of Article 125 of the Treaty of Rome in that, in settling the annual accounts of the European Social Fund for 1969, it had demanded from the Federal Republic contribution at the rate of the revalued Deutsche Mark instead of the pre-revaluation rate (more advantageous to the West Germans). Both actions were dismissed by the Luxembourg Court as 'inadmissible'—and both Governments were ordered to pay the Commission's legal costs.

The Court also sits occasionally as an appeal court when the Brussels Commission imposes fines—recovered through the legal enforcement agencies of the member States—on Community firms guilty of breaches of Community regulations. There too, one has the uncomfortable feeling that the dedicated European idealists of Luxembourg tend to stand shoulder-to-shoulder with the dedicated European idealists of Brussels against all outside comers.

The second way the Court operates is by way of remittance from national courts. Here is the respect in which Luxembourg is likely to have the greatest effect on British everyday life after British entry into Europe—and where, as in the West German customs case, it has not been timid to uphold rights conferred by the Community, even as against or in defiance of national laws. To many this will seem the obverse side of the 'Europeans against the Rest' mentality—with ironically beneficial side-effects for Community nationals.

Article 177 of the Treaty of Rome states that any national court—however lowly—when dealing with a dispute involving a question of Community Law may, at its own discretion, remit the case to Luxembourg for the European Court to give an authoritative ruling on the Community Law aspect. Furthermore, if the case gets to the highest national court of appeal without any reference, that court *must* itself remit the case to Luxembourg. The British House of Lords would be under this legal obligation.

'Preliminary rulings under Article 177,' as they are called in the jargon of the Luxembourg Court, are the Trojan Horse by which this polyglot legal body could enter into the citadel of British law. And already the possibility is causing misgivings.

At a conference in London in March 1972, British law lord Lord Diplock warned that cases sent from British courts to Luxembourg should first be put through some form of filtering process. 'The many lay tribunals in England and Wales would be incapable of deciding if an issue necessitated an interpretation of Community Law,' he said. He feared that magistrates might be persuaded to remit a case to Luxembourg by a lawyer who wanted to delay proceedings for his client.

Indeed, if Article 177 were strictly enforced throughout the European Community, the Luxembourg Court would need to sit 365 days a year, in 24-hour daily sessions and with at least four times as many judges. In fact, there has been no avalanche of 'preliminary rulings'. Why? Because national judges and magistrates have chosen not to remit! You can bring a national court to water—but you cannot make it drink. In 1970, there were only thirty-two 'preliminary rulings'. In 1971, the number crept up to thirty-seven. And this from a total Community population of 187 million people!

But it would be misleading to confuse quantity with quality. 'Preliminary rulings' may be comparatively few, but their effect and importance can be great. I am convinced that by this time next year British lawyers will be arguing at Luxembourg—on reference from a British court. In May 1967, the Wilson Government brought out a White Paper, *Legal and Constitutional Implications of United Kingdom Membership of the European Communities*. Despite Mr. Wilson's own mental gymnastics later, the White Paper stands as an accurate assessment of the effect on British law of entry into Europe. It specifies the fields covered by Community Law: 'Customs duties, agriculture, free movement of labour, services and capital, and the regulation of the coal and steel and nuclear energy industries'. It also summarises the 'principal fields' in which Common Market regulations will have immediate and direct internal effect in Britain: 'Restrictive practices and monopolies, movement of workers and social security of migrant workers, agriculture, transport and the regulation of the coal and steel and nuclear energy industries'.

Within these categories, which is to say within the nation's entire industrial and commercial existence, 'preliminary rulings' will become a factor that forward-looking executives and alert-minded lawyers will both have to take into account. As Dr. Jean Stoll, head of information at the Luxembourg Court says: 'People should not get the impression that it is only big companies that are involved in cases before the Court. They are often medium-sized firms and family businesses.'

Take the case earlier this year of Signora Leonisio, an Italian farmer with a smallholding near Lonato. In order to reduce the surplus of milk and dairy products within the European Community, the Council and the Commission issued in 1969 regulations encouraging the slaughter of dairy cattle. As an incentive, the Council provided, by Regulation 1975, that premiums would be paid, to all owners of cattle who undertook to slaughter all their dairy cows by 30 April 1970. Half the premium was to come from Community funds, the balance from member States.

The Regulation specified that for herds of between two and five cattle, the premium was payable on receiving proof that the owner had complied with its terms, i.e. that he had slaughtered all his dairy cattle by 30 April 1970.

Signora Leonisio complied with the regulation. But after over a year she was still without her premium.

So she sued the Italian Ministry in her own local county court. Counsel for the Ministry did not dispute that she had honoured the Regulation. He did not deny that the Government owed her the money, but he said that the Ministry could not pay because the Italian Parliament had not as yet appropriated any funds for that purpose!

The Lonato judge decided, of his own volition, to suspend the proceedings while he referred to the Luxembourg Court the questions (1) whether, in Community Law, Regulation 1975 was a regulation that had direct and immediate effect in the member States of the Community, and (2), if so, whether it created a right for Italian nationals to claim payment of sums due to them under the Regulation—irrespective of how the Italian Ministry was to find the money to pay it.

In May 1972, came the Court's judgement: Regulation 1975 *was* directly applicable. It created rights for individuals which the national judge was under obligation to uphold. Payments to creditors accruing from such regulations become due once the perquisites laid down in the Regulation have been complied with, and cannot be made subject to other rules of implementation—such as, that the national Parliament has not yet appropriated the necessary funds. Regulation 1975 was of binding effect in Italy, and the Italian judge had no alternative but to give judgement in accordance with it.

Much has been said both by critics and apostles of British entry into the European Community on 'Loss of Sovereignty'. Lord Hailsham, the British Lord Chancellor, has claimed in a speech at the Grotius Dinner of the British Institute of International and Comparative Law in London in May 1972 that our going into Europe 'would not diminish the sovereignty of the British Parliament'. Yet as long ago as 1963 the Luxembourg Court was proclaiming that the Rome Treaty and Community regulations and directives conferred directly upon citizens in member States 'individual rights which the courts of the member States should protect'—even against the laws of their own Parliament. Within days of Lord Hailsham's speech, M. Henri Mayras, the French Advocate-General at Luxembourg, was quoting to the seven judges in open court one of their own earlier decisions, in which they ruled: 'The Rome Treaty instituted a Community of unlimited duration, endowed with its own institutions, legal personality and capacity, international representation and, last but not least, *real powers stemming from a delegation of sovereignty from member States to the Community as such*' (my italics).

This principle has already been so effectively inculcated into the minds of national judges on the Continent—largely by means of 'preliminary rulings'—that the highest national court of appeal in Belgium, the Cour de Cassation, has itself—without even needing to refer the case to Luxembourg—ruled that the Belgian Ministry of Economic Affairs must reimburse a Belgian company nearly 60 million Belgian francs exacted by the Belgian Ministry on imports of dairy produce contrary to Community Law—despite a specific law passed by the Belgian Parliament that the sum should not be recoverable.

The Belgian Cour de Cassation said in its judgement of 27 May 1971 words which their legal lordships in our own House of Lords would do well to ponder: 'The treaties which created Community Law have established a new legal order for the benefit of which the member States have limited the exercise of their sovereign powers in the spheres dominated by these treaties. . . . The effects of the Law of 19 March 1968 are stopped in so far as it was in conflict with a directly inapplicable provision of international treaty law.' . . .

(Extracted from the *Weekend Telegraph*, no. 412, 22 September 1972.)

4.8 The Governance of Europe—a New Dimension in International Relations
PROFESSOR J. D. B. MITCHELL

. . . International law starts from the hypothesis of the acceptance of the concept of the sovereign state, Community Law starts from the hypothesis of the denial of that concept in relation to its Members.[1] It is nevertheless unsatisfactory to continue the discussion on this theoretical level. It is unsatisfactory in the first place because the word 'sovereignty' is itself a mischief word of no certain and universal meaning. If by it is meant that the State retains its full uninhibited freedom of action then the concept is one which can serve as the foundation for international anarchy and not for an ordered system of international relations. If by it is meant that a State may resile from the consequences of obligations which it has accepted, then few with any feeling for morality can accept the term. An international order in any event therefore requires a limitation of the concept and one should be wary of any who use the phrase in this context. It may be merely a veiling word for nationalism of a retrogressive type, and for myself I would rather be a doorkeeper in the house of the Lord than a tatty cock upon his own dunghill. It is also unsatisfactory, for such a theoretical discussion obscures realities . . .

. . . the shape of the new system in Europe is dictated not by theory, but by practical and functional considerations related to ends and means. The result is a system which is new on the international scene and which is new in political theory. On the one side the novelty is to be found in the creation of a new entity, itself capable of acting on the international scene and binding its Members. The British negotiations are with a Community and not with Six Governments.[2] It is clear, too, that while in traditional international law the formation of new rules is essentially consensual or contractual, within the Community system the process is truly legislative, as indeed it has to be if policies are to be implemented rather than simple compromises are to be merely adopted and recorded and then only by painfully slow steps. At least in degree, but probably in kind, the implementation of the law differs markedly from traditional concepts. The universal applicability of regulations is one mark of this change, but the concept of the direct effect of Community law, which also involves the supremacy of that law, goes well beyond traditional doctrine. So does, too, the place accorded to the individual within the Community legal system vastly exceed that accorded elsewhere in any traditional system of international law. When the words *securité juridique* are used they imply, for the individual, the availability of means of protection both against the Government of a member State and against the Community itself in order to ensure the observance of Community rules,[3] or even of general fundamental principles. In this way the intent is to ensure that the full economic effects are obtained by its citizens evenly throughout the whole Community. It is, moreover, a protection which is accorded not merely to the individual but to other public authorities within the state, who thus regain a possibly important element of autonomy.[4] All of these changes find their reflection in a new institutional structure. In place of a secretariat there is found a completely Community organ, the Commission, given a fundamental right of initiative, essential to the task of formulating a truly Community policy. The Council of Ministers is a Community organ in law and, indeed, also in fact, even though the factual element needs to grow, and even though it also serves as the connecting link with the member States. These changes were inevitable, for it is just not true to argue that, without other changes, 'the unity of Europe will in the end be achieved by European Governments forming the habit of working together'.[5] All history demonstrates that this habit of working together is not strong enough, unless that habit is fortified by being contained within a system. It is equally clear that if one is speaking of 'unity' there is an obvious need for a body which thinks primarily in terms of the whole and not of the parts. This is especially important, for otherwise the occasions of working together tend to occur in matters which are not fundamental, or simply relate to prestige projects attractive at first sight to Governments but which are the least important in the long run, but are also those which in the short run are most likely to produce friction.[6] Those habits alone cannot enable Governments to cross essential thresholds; a leap, a new pattern, is required . . .

[*Within the new pattern Mitchell states that interpenetration or intermingling of authorities must take place. This will avoid the Community becoming a remote isolated authority. The Community institutions must interact not only with the Government of member States but with regions, private organisations and individuals. When the Coal and Steel Community reaches out to help in the redeployment of labour it reaches out to the town or region directly affected!*]

. . . If the interpenetration occurs in the process of decision-taking it occurs even more significantly in the execution of decisions, for each one of the traditional arms of government assumes a new character and consequently in some sense a dual responsibility. While it remains true that in some senses the member States themselves do not become agents of the Communities and may, indeed, in agreements under Article 220 of the Treaty of Rome be said to be still masters or parents of the Communities, yet State agencies may become the agents of the Communities. Administrations act on behalf of both member State and Community. The national legislator equally may, in particular cases, become part of the process of legislation in a Community sense, and, in addition, in his general activity must also have regard to the society or Community of which he is, by voluntary act, a member.

But if I may, since I am by training a lawyer, I would like to emphasise the importance of this change for judges, for in the end of the day much depends on them. In the last resort, granted the independence which they enjoy, and which any administration must respect, it will lie with them to determine whether the system will work as well as it can and whether individuals shall be allowed fully to enjoy those rights and benefits which Community law confers, or whether they will frustrate that system and deny those rights. It must be emphasised that such is the interpenetration of legal systems that benefits arise for small folk as well as large enterprises, and thus no court can close its eyes to this law. The problem which faces judges and lawyers can be wrapped up in the language of legal technology, speaking of monism, of dualism or even in yet more mystic uses of the word 'sovereignty'[7] yet in the end of the day the problem resolves itself into the terms of harsh reality that I have used. The fact of this new dimension causes traditional concepts to be rethought. That was its purpose. Thus, legal theories based exclusively upon the concept of the nation state must change. The treaties have taken the wisest but most dangerous course of not creating an ultimate central court which finally applies Community law to all and sundry. In substance, the European Court of Justice only 'applies' Community law to member States and Community institutions,[8] and for them no other solution was possible. For the rest, it interprets Community law and leaves its application to national jurisdictions of all levels. The risk is taken that those courts may not fully appreciate their dual role. It is a risk which had to be taken to avoid excessive and costly centralisation in an area of activity which has a manifold importance. It had also to be taken out of respect for long established jurisdictions, in the hope that thereby their ready collaboration in building a polity would be secured, for here law has a truly formative role. Indeed the Court at Luxembourg has constantly emphasised its respect for other courts. On the other hand those courts must for their part respect the dual system of law within which they must work. In that the role of the judge is not betrayed. It is betrayed within this system when by a judge's will Community law is denied its full effect. It is at this point that this concept of interpenetration assumes for the moment its greatest importance in making national courts the instruments for the enforcement of Community law, for in allowing direct effect to that law it is probable that the whole system may most easily strike roots. Without that effect considerable obstacles could remain.[9] I have emphasised this matter for it is in this context that the lawyers in the United Kingdom, together with lawyers in some of the existing member States, may find the greatest challenge to their imagination, and thus the greatest stumbling block. When the system is seen as I have described it it is the judge who fails, save *per incuriam*, to apply Community law, who oversteps his role, and opposes himself to the constitutional system of which he is part . . .

References

1. Pescatore 'L'apport du droit communautaire au droit international public' (1970) *Cahiers de droit Européen*, 501.
2. Of course the adhesion of new Members presents special problems. The more normal situation is to be found in Article 228 of the Treaty of Rome which ends 'Agreements concluded in the manner laid down above shall be binding on the institutions of the Community and on member States.'
3. Clearly there are limits to this availability, especially at the highest and most general level. Nevertheless, within this system, the United Kingdom citizen could have more and more easily legally enforceable rights against Community decisions than he has against his own Government, and his remedies under Article 215 (second paragraph) of the Treaty of Rome would have a much broader base.
4. Aff. 2/68 *Ufficio Imposte di Consumo Ispra c la Commission* XIV Rec. 635 at 640.
5. Mr. Edward Heath, 'Realism in British Foreign Policy' *Foreign Affairs* vol. 48 (1969–70) 39 at 42. 'In my judgement the unity of Europe will in the end be achieved by European governments forming the habit of working together. Public and Parliamentary opinion works upon governments, but in the end it is governments, elected ministers and their officials, who take the decisions. Confection between Governments is the only lasting cement for the unity of Europe.' It is not true, unless governments are contained within a framework which forces them to be responsive; otherwise the forces of inertia within Governments (each of which thinks only of itself in the first instance) are too strong.
6. The small success of European space projects demonstrates all these difficulties. The limitations of this form of co-operation are clearly and rightly seen by Mr. Heath, *Old World New Horizons*, pp. 42–7.
7. I refer, of course, to the doctrine of the Sovereignty of Parliament which here is frequently misunderstood and exaggerated in importance, see Mitchell 'L'Adhension du Royaume-Uni aux Communautés', *3 Cahiers de droit européen*, 1970, p. 25.
8. This is not entirely true in relation to decisions under the cartel regulations, though even there it is not false, for the Court is acting to correct or uphold another institution—the Commission.

9. The difficulties which Lindberg and Scheingold *Europe's Would-Be Polity*, Prentice-Hall, Englewood Cliffs, New Jersey, 1970, p. 132 discuss can at least be met to some extent by these techniques.

(Extracted from 'The Governance of Europe—a new dimension in international relations.' Lecture delivered at Heriot-Watt University on 24 November 1970 by Professor J. D. B. Mitchell. (In *Britain and the International Scene*, The Heriot-Watt University Lectures 1971 (Heriot-Watt University Press, Edinburgh, 1971.))

4.9 Multinational Companies as a Political Problem

ALBRECHT DÜREN

Far-reaching structural and social changes are required if the economic giants are to play their full part in the progress of democratic societies.

Modern industrial production, whether of sophisticated individual items or of mass products such as motor-cars, demands large markets. (The same applies to a number of service industries.) The method of selling the surplus output after saturation of the domestic markets by means of direct exports is no longer adequate when 40 to 50 per cent or more of home production is exported. The minimum requirement is the setting up of a sales office, at least in the most important foreign markets. Many of today's industrial products need intensive service, and it is often only a short step from a sales office via a service station to a manufacturing plant. If production is embarked upon in more than one important foreign market, the next logical step is to move on promptly to a corporate strategy involving planning and operating on a worldwide basis.

For an outsider, the stages of the development of the concern from investment in foreign assembly plants by way of sophisticated production abroad to international management of the parent company and finally international ownership of the concern are not always easy to distinguish. Worldwide activities by themselves are not enough to make a concern truly multinational. Up-to-date forms of co-operation in research, development, service, selling, etc. are stages that can be reversed at any time. But when an increase in the capital of the co-operating firms is called for, more thorough-going integration beyond the limits of the contract of co-operation becomes necessary, including long-term contractual obligations. In most cases interlocking capital arrangements are made, principally through the exchange of already existing shares.

The extraordinary development of world trade after the Second World War, based on a world currency system which worked relatively well for twenty-five years and on the General Agreement on Tariffs and Trade (GATT), has led to an enormous increase in the number of companies operating beyond the borders of their own countries and having subsidiaries abroad.[1] The process of industrial concentration promoted by the development of modern technology has not stopped at national boundaries. A combination of wage increases with rapidly rising costs for research and development, on which in turn the industries with particularly high growth rates depend, furthers concentration beyond the national framework. This trend was spearheaded by US companies: equipped with a large production apparatus and abundant capital and supported by the latest technological developments, they found the American market too small and were attracted both by the seemingly limitless demand for imports on the part of the countries devastated by the war and by the development needs in States newly released from colonial dependence. At the same time, the continuous rise in US wages and living standards narrowed their competitive advantage on their home market and abroad, particularly *vis-à-vis* Europe and Japan, whose enterprises were quickly recovering lost ground.

The growth of the 'giant' concerns[2] has roused various apprehensions. The supporters of the Marxist theory of increasing industrial concentration and rising poverty regard it as grist to their mill when the trend towards further industrial concentration in the developed countries is contrasted with the Third World where the growth of the giant concerns is even more disproportionate. This leads to alarmist forecasts, according to which a few hundred firms will represent about three-quarters of the world's industrial production by 1980.[3]

Lack of International Company Law

A purely economic approach does not lead to a satisfactory analysis of the problems of multinational companies. The terms 'international or 'multinational' do not give any indication of legal status; they merely describe a certain outlook and strategy. International private company law does not exist at all; even 'international' private law is national. A public limited company as a corporate body, its internal structure, and all regulations governing its legal competence are subject to national law only. Even when a company spreads its production over many countries and integrates itself fully into these markets, sells its products as domestic goods, appoints foreign nationals to the management of its subsidiaries and tries to raise capital from the different national sources available (like, for instance, General Motors, Ford, IBM), the combined concern, including the subsidiaries established in the different countries, is subordinate to the top organisation, which is subject to a particular national law. The shareholders' rights, obligations and influence are governed by this law, although the shares can be marketed on the stock exchanges of different countries.

Even in the EEC, where trans-frontier co-operation is frequently practised as a result of the process of economic integration, the position has not yet been reached where Community law overrides national company law. Should a company with registered offices in more than one country be formed today, it would be governed by two or more national laws. No satisfactory answer has been found so far to the question of which law would apply for particular cases, since the company would not be able to form a supervisory board in compliance with the law of both countries at the same time. As they stand today, the rules of international private law do not allow for the 'internationalisation' of the problem; one legal system must yield altogether if there is to be no clash between the two systems. In the same way, mergers and take-overs are impossible on an international level. Syndicate contracts are illegal under most countries' law and can be concluded on an international basis only in a very few cases. The same applies to inter-company agreements (profit and loss pooling agreements, agreements on control or transfers of profits).

It is not necessary to spell out how the lack of Community legal regulations is impeding the process of European integration. Though the structural adjustments which are a natural consequence of advancing European integration frequently necessitate important changes, for example a transfer of the registered office, these have hitherto only been possible within the scope of national law. The lack of common tax legislation is particularly inhibiting and renders mergers of firms with equal legal rights in different countries practically impossible. With regard to the creation of a European company, which has been attempted for many years now,[4] the aim should therefore not be to improve the national company laws which are encumbered by hundreds of years of history, or to initiate a new type of company based on 'harmonised' law in all the EEC countries; what is required is the creation of a new company law of truly international character. This means that extensive concessions and agreements have to be reached by the legislators of all the participating nations on those issues to which different regulations apply at present. It is enough to refer in this context to the German principle of worker participation in decision-making (*Mitbestimmung*), and especially to the German trade unions' persistent efforts to widen its application as in the European Coal and Steel Community, to show that there is still a long way to go. Attempts to harmonise differing company laws within the EEC also run up against similar difficulties.

When agreements between two partners have nevertheless been reached, as in the case of the steel firms Hoesch/Hoogovens, this has been made possible by the readiness of both to make concessions in favour of unusual operational or purely locational advantages in an industry subject to worldwide and rapid structural changes. By distributing the seats in their top supervisory board according to nationality Hoesch/Hoogovens have avoided the problem of equal representation of employers and employees as practised in the German coal and steel industries.

But this particular case cannot be a model for general developments. Nor can the stratagem of a holding company be a substitute for Community company law; determination of the firm's domicile and thus of the law governing the executive responsibilities of the leading holding company raises complex problems, not least as regards taxation. For this reason Agfa/Gevaert had to create a 'double' holding company, operating without a main head office and developing new methods of uniform management for the whole concern (i.e. not just for research and development). In the eight years since these two firms merged, it has been possible not only to co-ordinate their general business policies, especially production, research and development but also, thanks to flexible decisions by management and staff representatives, to overcome the handicap represented by the still quite different social and political systems in

Germany and Belgium. From a legal point of view, however, the situation is by no means satisfactory.

Within the EEC, where the accession of Britain with her highly developed industry and company law might make it even more difficult to harmonise the legal systems,[5] developments have practically come to a standstill since Professor Hallstein's term of office expired. Germany's partners recognise that her company law is in certain respects highly developed, but they are not prepared to adopt her regulations on worker participation; at the same time a retreat from *Mitbestimmung* is out of the question for the German Government. Thus finding alternatives and ways out is becoming a fine art, and possibilities of co-operation without far-reaching legal reforms are being canvassed. Slightly more promising than pure *ad hoc* consortia, the *groupement d'intérêt économique* popular in France is held up as a legal formula which ought to become EEC law. These makeshift arrangements may be accepted while there is no real progress in the harmonisation of European law; but they are only applicable to such functions as research and development, purchasing and selling. As soon as joint production is in question, the problem of Germany's participation regulations, which her partners refuse to accept, becomes pressing. The way to permanent solutions is thus blocked.

Political Objections

Although the lack of a legal framework has not prevented the establishment or development of multinational enterprises, it has generally stood in the way of reaching optimum solutions. But, what is more important, an increasing number of observers feel disquiet at the way in which the big concerns seem to develop—precisely because the evolution of legal regulations is not keeping pace with economic development. The greater the dislike in Western countries of the existence of autonomous spheres of action and of the increasing complexity of technological-economic progress which demands delegation of power and the institution of checks and balances, the stronger the misgivings about a situation in which the giant concerns carve out for themselves control-free areas and exercise power that can be checked only by competitors in the market, if at all.

The head organisation of a multinational enterprise is, of course, subject to a particular national law but, by its very nature, this law derives its aims and methods of control from the national framework. There are widespread doubts about the effectiveness of controls for worldwide operations based on one particular national law. Previous experience with the International Court of Justice and the Court of Arbitration at The Hague does not encourage faith in the effective administration of international law. Though interventions by the US Secretary of Justice, with strong anti-trust legislation at his disposal, have frequently obstructed individual schemes on the part of American combines, they have not succeeded in eliminating doubts about the capacity of the national administration or legislation to cope satisfactorily with multinational concerns.

The main objections can be summarised as follows:

(i) The most frequently heard criticism concerns tax evasion, such as manipulation of internal costings and incorrect distribution of expenses and overheads within the different components of the whole enterprise. The fairly tight network of agreements on double taxation and the experience of the revenue authorities over the years in handling companies operating on an international basis should be able to allay such fears. But the various national tax systems have different objectives, especially when industrialised and developing countries are compared. Raymond Vernon's suggestion that the United States should help to develop bilateral tax regulations, recognised by all members of the OECD, to demarcate revenue and costs as between different branches of a concern is valuable but does not promise an early solution of the problem.[6]

(ii) The problem becomes even more difficult as regards international money and capital flows. The erosion of the Bretton Woods system over the past five years has forced many basically liberal-minded Governments and central banks to keep a close watch, and even to impose controls, on the movement of money and capital belonging to their nationals and companies. The deployment of individual branches of a multinational enterprise—as far as current transactions and investments are concerned—depends more on the interests of the company or its subsidiaries than on the wishes of national Governments, especially since the latter are not expressed in clear legal regulations. During periods of international monetary crisis this can lead to severe disagreements, if not to a breakdown of the international monetary system.

In addition, there is the natural conflict which arises when the government of a highly developed industrial State is concerned to improve its international balance of payments. It is primarily interested in the transfer of profits from previous investments, whereas the developing countries would prefer further imports of capital and the uninterrupted reinvestment of profits.

(iii) Large concerns have as one of their aims the exploitation of international opportunities for the further division of labour. Most Governments, however, pursue purely national aims, at least until their countries have reached a high stage of development. For prestige reasons they would often like to have industries which can only work profitably in a large market, and they blame the international companies for disregarding national boundaries and deploying their assets where they can get the greatest local advantage either now or in the foreseeable future.

(iv) Technological progress, which has been the main spur to the development of large companies, depends today on expenditure for research and development which is mostly beyond the means available to small and medium-sized concerns. Not only nuclear energy (which often receives direct government subsidies) falls into this category; data processing, telecommunications and electronics are further examples. In this respect quite a number of the large companies can be accused of concentrating profits from many countries, as far as they serve to finance research and development, in the country of the parent company for the financing of expensive research facilities. From an economic point of view this procedure is probably the most effective. But many Governments, and not only those of small countries, wish to promote science and technology in their own countries and do not want to be deprived of an adequate contribution from the multinational companies operating in their territory. The assurance that the activities of the multinational enterprises in themselves guarantee the transmission of advanced technology is generally not considered sufficient.

(v) A settlement of these conflicting views is more difficult to achieve than agreement on such matters as the protection of the environment, the provision of social facilities including vocational training and active participation in the development of traffic and transport systems. In these fields many multinational firms have been setting the pace for modern developments, mainly because of their worldwide experience. They do not, however, escape the criticism of one-sidedly promoting their company's private interests, if necessary by relocating production plants.

(vi) The rapid growth of the multinational companies during the past two decades has not only kept some less developed countries, who are rich in raw materials, dependent on these companies and recently has given rise to severe disagreements, e.g. in the case of the nationalisation of British-American copper companies in Zambia, or the joint struggle of the OPEC countries against international oil firms. It has also led to apprehensions in the highly industrialised countries, including the United States, about the undesirable dependence on companies involved in the armament industry. Though their efficiency is high, not least owing to their worldwide commitment, they operate in permanent conflict between the aims of their organisation and those of individual Governments.[7] . . .

References

1. The directories of the largest industrial companies, published annually as supplements to *Fortune*, cover 500 firms within and 300 firms outside the USA; among the latter 75 Japanese, 64 British, and 44 German enterprises were listed in 1972.
2. Today only about 150 companies, more than half of them American, are classified in this group; the value of their industrial production outside their home countries for 1970 was estimated at more than $450,000m., compared with the total world trade figure of $300,000m. See J. N. Behrman, 'New Orientation in International Trade and Investment' in *Trade and Investment Policies for the Seventies*, Pierre Uri (ed.), Praeger, New York, 1971.
3. See Christopher Tugendhat, *The Multinationals*, Eyre & Spottiswoode, London, 1971.
4. See Dennis Thompson, *The Proposal for a European Company*, London, Chatham House/PEP European Series no. 13, December 1969.
5. Though the experience of the most advanced multinationals like the Anglo-Dutch Unilever and Shell will, no doubt, prove a useful example.
6. See Raymond Vernon, 'Problems and Policies regarding Multinational Enterprises', in *United States International Economic Policy in an Interdependent World*, Report to the President submitted by the Commission on Trade and International Investment Policy, July 1971, Washington, D.C., Supplementary Papers, pp. 1005–6.

7. See Raymond Vernon, *Multinational Enterprise and National Security*, Adelphi Papers, no. 74.

(Extracted from *The World Today*, Vol. 28, no. 11, November 1972, pp. 473 ff.)

SECTION 5

Growth and the British Economy

5.1 Introduction

Growth has become the preoccupation of politicians in the twentieth century because it is a useful shorthand by which to gauge their success.

Growth of the nation's wealth at a rapid rate suggests that everyone's standard of living is improving equally quickly, and the optimum condition exists to achieve 'the greatest happiness of the greatest number'.

Article 2 of the Treaty of Rome clearly shows that this thought was very much to the fore when the European Economic Community was eastablished. The purpose of the EEC, it said, was

> by establishing a common market and progressively approximating the economic policies of member States, to promote throughout the Community a harmonious development of economic activities, a continuous and balanced expansion, an increased stability, an accelerated raising of the standard of living and closer relations between its member States.

What all this rapid growth could mean is spelled out in the first piece, from *The Economist* (pp. 238–43). As it says, 'the common market countries are offering their people the solid prospect of improving living standards twenty-five times in a lifetime'.

The average annual rate of growth for the nine present EEC States between 1958–9 and 1969–70 (excluding Luxembourg which is tied to the Belgian economy) was as follows: Belgium, 4·8 per cent; Denmark, 5·1 per cent; France, 5·8 per cent; Germany, 5·3 per cent; Ireland, 4·1 per cent; Italy, 5·8 per cent; Netherlands, 5·4 per cent; and the United Kingdom, 3·1 per cent.

The reasons for these differing rates of growth are not perfectly understood. The Germans put their growth down to hard work, free competition and the inflow of capital and immigrant labour, and like France and Italy and the Benelux countries, *believe* (but can't prove) that being in the EEC has had a lot to do with it.

235

The Italians, on the other hand, think that their growth was aided by the exodus of Italian workers to countries like Germany and Switzerland, sending back capital to families who pumped it into the Italian economy, and then returning themselves with new skills. Cynics point to the average number of days per annum lost in Italy through strikes (1,397 per 1,000 workers for the period 1960–69) and contrast it with Britain's apparent peacefulness (about a fifth of the Italian rate, with 268 days lost per annum on average), and say that this is the way to get growth. - But U.K. had lowest growth.

The more traditional view of the reasons for growth are given in another extract from *The Economist* (pp. 243–5) which looks at the French economy prior to the 1973 election.

The high growth rate, high investment, high productivity equation is immensely appealing as the key to success—as extracts from the October 1971 Parliamentary debate on the terms of entry show (in Section 1 above)—but it needs to be said that it does not always work out that way. Despite Norway's having a high rate of investment relative to national income (28·4 per cent between 1950 and 1962) compared to Britain's much lower rate (16·1 per cent) the Norwegian rate of growth was only slightly higher than that achieved by Britain.

Equally paradoxically, as Britain was about to enter the EEC some of the Community's leading statesmen were beginning to question whether or not growth should have such an exalted status.

Sicco Mansholt, a fervent 'European' interested more in issues and policies than in institutions with fourteen years as a Commissioner of the EEC, put forward a plan in a letter to the Commission's President for a European economy in March 1972 which would be based on limited growth, environmental protection and population control (pp. 245–7).

Shortly after writing this letter Mansholt himself took over the Presidency when Malfatti returned to take part in the Italian elections. In his inaugural press conference he summarised the problem: 'In all our member States', he explained 'gross national product has been thought of as something sacred. But it is diabolical. We must think of something else—the happiness and welfare of our peoples.'

Mansholt's letter had a number of weaknesses, largely stemming from its basis in papers written by scientists interested in ecological questions. Economics Professor Wilfred Beckerman wisely suggested in his very readable inaugural lecture 'Economists, Scientists and Environmental Catastrophe'[1] that scientists ought to stick to science. Sahumakker, Brokombski.

But Mansholt knew a lot about politics. He knew that the Treaty of Rome was based on free trade principles—as Article 3 shows (pp. 248-9)—and that the functional approach of doing away with obstacles to free movement of goods and factors of production had probably contributed to the aim of maximising growth by encouraging intra-Community trade. He also knew that the farm policy he had pushed through (see Section 6 below) had tied the Six politically.

While Mansholt was pessimistically thinking ahead on European-scale approaches British politicians, academics and businessmen were largely preoccupied with growth and how to get it, and what it could mean for the average Briton. Nicholas Kaldor was a persistent critic of Britain's entry into the EEC solving Britain's problem of too little growth, as his piece on the dynamic affects of entry written before the terms of Britain's accession were known indicates (pp. 249-53).

Writing after the terms were finalised, Colin Jones summarised the views of industrialists as being marginally favourable to entry (pp. 253-5).

The British Government's White Paper attempted to spell out the advantages as the Government saw them (pp. 255-60), but Professor Kaldor remained unconvinced (pp. 260-2). Hugh Stephenson dealt with Professor Kaldor's criticisms of the White Paper (pp. 262-5), while Professor John Williamson weighed up the economic pros and cons (pp. 265-9) and got in a few digs at the fundamentals of Kaldor's analysis at the same time.

Professor Alan Day (pp. 269-71) summarised the professional economist's dilemma in reviewing a piece of research carried out by Kaldor and Johnson that showed academic economists to be split roughly down the middle in their 'guesstimates' of how Britain might be affected. Day showed the importance of the *political* factor in the calculations. The White Paper itself had said—in paragraph 59—that 'The costs of joining the Community are the price we should have to pay for the economic and political advantages.' It added that outside the EEC 'our power to influence the Communities would steadily diminish, while the Communities' power to affect our future would as steadily increase'.

The difficulties of getting good economic data by which to plan an economy were indicated by *The Economist* which reviewed (pp. 271-2) the 'pessimistic' calculations being made in the EEC countries in the 1950s.

Christopher Layton (pp. 273–8) develops the point made by both Professor Williamson and *The Economist* that a major advantage which should accrue to British industry, especially in the motor industry, would be through 'economies of scale'—Michael Shanks, Director of British Leyland's Marketing and Planning division, spelt out (pp. 278–83) what this meant for Britain's largest export earner, British Leyland.

Michael Shanks says that the picture is not as simple as one might imagine it to be. 'Europe' could not be contained within the neat boundaries of the EEC, even though the demand for new cars there was growing fast.

In the final article on the car industry D. G. Rhys puts the position and British Leyland into perspective (pp. 284–8), and shows that even a European giant like British Leyland is dwarfed in the international context of the motor industry with its handful of dominant multi-national companies.

Reference

1. *Oxford Economic Papers*, New Series, Vol. 24, no. 3, 1972, pp. 327–44.

5.2 Falling Behind Again

Defenders of the old order in both political parties complain that everyone is now obsessed with growth, or in Britain, the lack of it, as if it were something wholly materialistic and indecent. But growth translates into standard of living, which must be the ultimate goal of economic management. People may be divided as to whether they want cars or culture, houses or hospitals, anti-pollution or what you will, but all except the dropouts want betterment of one kind or another.

Where economists are to blame is in their failure to communicate what the growth debate is really about, confining it, as they mostly do, to esoteric arguments as to whether the annual target should be 3 per cent, $3\frac{1}{2}$ per cent and so on (and then, of course, how to reach it). The differences seem so small: what can you do with an extra $\frac{1}{2}$ per cent or even 1 per cent? What gets left out is the compounding effect of small differentials, which over a man's lifetime can determine whether he has enjoyed relative prosperity or relative poverty.

To some extent, the Government's White Paper on British entry into the common market makes the right point. If through membership, it says, we achieve a rate of growth in our national income even $\frac{1}{2}$ per cent higher, then by the end of five years our national income would be £1,100 million higher. But the paper might have gone further and looked at the consequences over a generation: at the end of twenty-five years the extra $\frac{1}{2}$ per cent of output, year in, year out, would provide every family with an extra £350 (at today's prices), a bonus no one would sneeze at.

One can only guess the quickening of pace which Community membership will bring to Britain, but *The Economist* believes that an acceleration in growth will result and that it is badly needed if British life is not to become unbearably shabby and increasingly resented by those who have to put up with it. The series of charts shows how far our standard of living, relative to others, has already declined, and the unpalatable prospects of a further relative decline if we remain outside Europe.

The first chart shows Britain at the bottom of the growth league in the 1960s, and remaining there in the 1970s. The projections are those of the Organisation for Economic Co-operation and Development, made at the turn of the year. The OECD assumed that the British rate would be stepped up from 2·7 per cent to 3·2 per cent; this was the British official view at the time, making no allowance for community membership. It is true that since these projections were made the British target for the coming year has been upped to 4 per cent, but it cannot be emphasised too often that even if that is achieved, it will do little more than correct the most recent shortfalls and get the economy back on to the prescribed 3·2 per cent growth tack. That would still be only half the rate expected in other industrial countries. As in the past, a Britain outside Europe will go on being a half-rater.

Our second chart shows the yawning gap between the common market's output and Britain's since the EEC was formed in 1958. Here one sees the compounded effect of a common market growth rate of 5·4 per cent a year, almost exactly twice Britain's 2·8 per cent. After allowing for increases in population, the common market's standard of living rose 74 per cent, Britain's only 31 per cent.

Of course, not all common market members have done equally well over the period (as the first chart shows), nor did they all have the same starting point. But whereas in 1960 Britain still had a better standard of living than any common market country, today it has fallen behind all except Italy (on to the third chart); and, as things are going, Italy will be ahead within the next few years. Already we are fifteenth among the big nations, behind the Finns and, yes, the Japanese, according to the OECD.

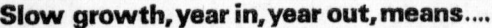

Slow growth, year in, year out, means....

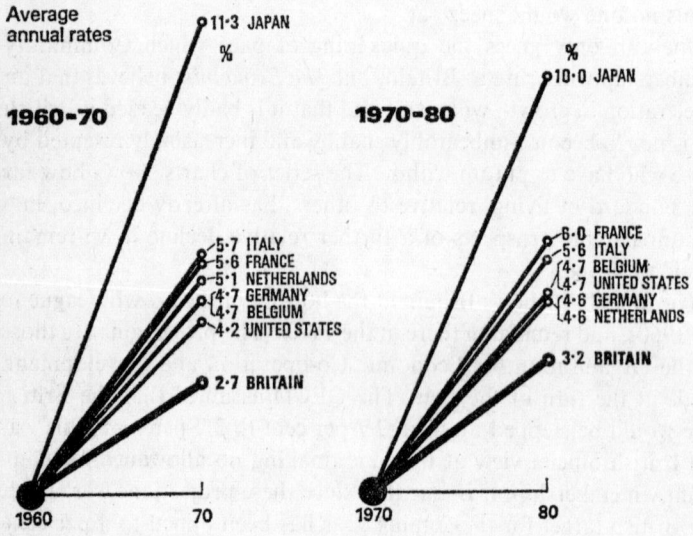

If the OECD's growth projections for the next ten years are adjusted by the demographers' anticipations, then Britain will have slipped at least two further rungs down the ladder by 1980, having let the Italians and the Austrians pass. And among those moving up swiftly, ready to be ranked above us in the 1980s, would be the Greeks and possibly even the Spaniards. . . . This astonishing picture of Britain all set to become the worst off in Europe has some simple arithmetic behind it which is illustrated in the two curves in our final chart. One of these shows how many years would be required, at a growth rate (per head of population) on the bottom scale, to double the standard of living. It was Mr. Rab Butler (now Lord Butler) who, when Chancellor in the 1950s, encouraged the British to hope that they could do this in twenty-five years: it requires, as the chart shows, an average growth in real product per head of 2·8 per cent throughout

falling still further behind richer neighbours and....

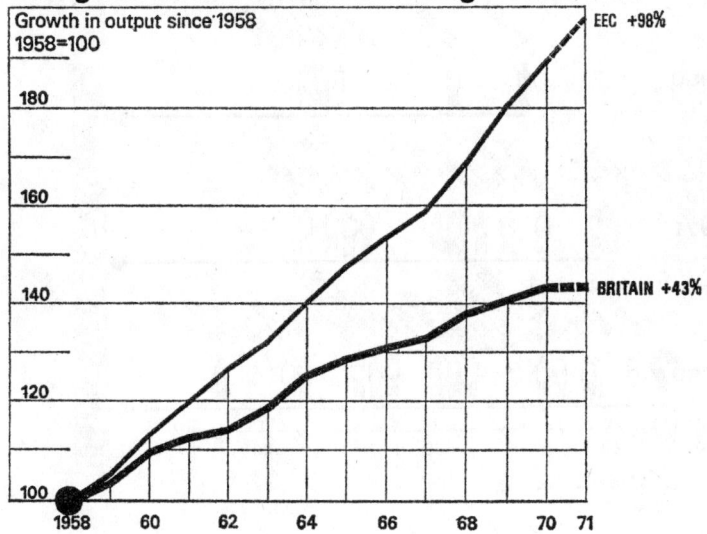

the quarter century; more than the 1960s' 2·1 per cent and more, too, than the 2·6 per cent forecast for Britain in the 1970s. On the other hand, if the EEC achieves its 4·5 per cent rate and keeps it up, it will treble its standard of living in twenty-five years and double it in fifteen and a half years.

How growth snowballs can be seen even more clearly in the second curve, which shows how many times the original standard of living will be multiplied in the course of a full lifetime. In the 2 to 2½ per cent range above which Britain seems unable to raise its eyes at present, the multiplier is around 5: that is to say, if that rate continued over his lifetime, a child could expect to spend his old age in a community five times as well off as that into which he was born. That may not seem too bad a prospect, until one considers what it is for others. . . .

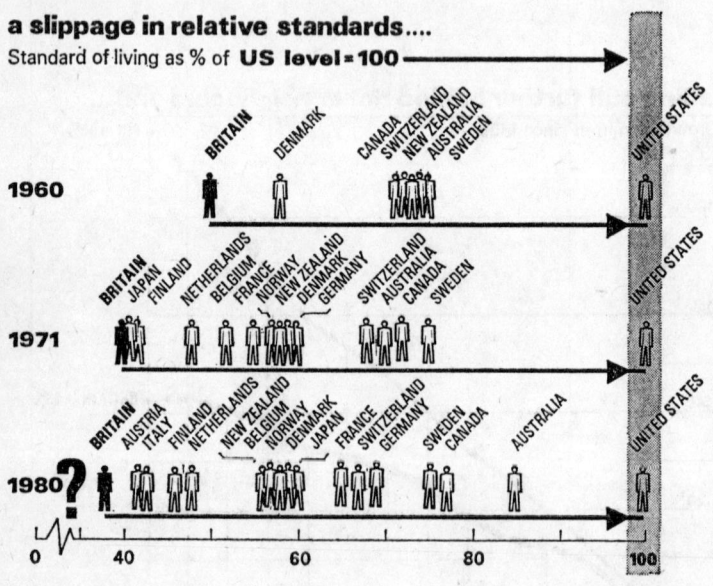

a slippage in relative standards....

Standard of living as % of **US level = 100**

The common market countries are offering their people the solid prospect of improving living standards twenty-five times in a lifetime.

So one sees how hitherto poor countries could soon be leaving Britain behind: Greece is expected to double its standard of living in this decade, Austria and Spain to increase theirs by half. Britain has got past the point of take-off which gives this sort of return. But it should not be content to think in terms of less than the EEC's 4 or 5 per cent . . . within the framework of improved efficiency and competitive power that would come from joining the common market. This should allow the British to taste the benefits of post-war technology for the first time. If we do not we will be on course to

as the multiplier takes effect

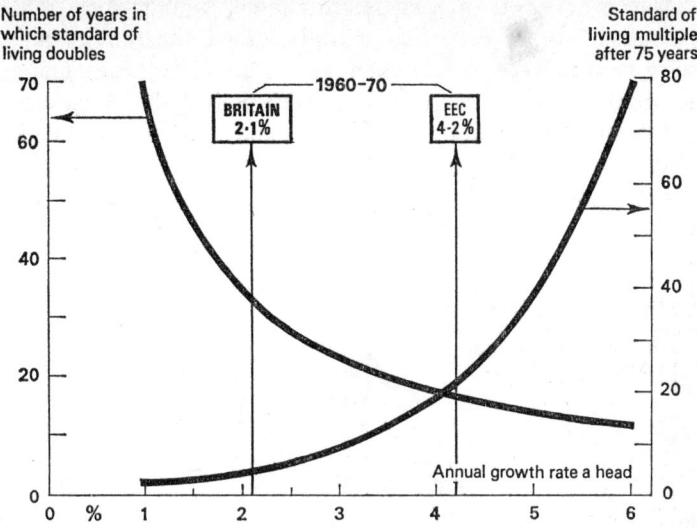

becoming the poor man of the much enlarged, multiracial industrial world of tomorrow.

(Extracted from *The Economist*, 14 August 1971.)

5.3 Politics is Bad for Growth

. . . For about eighteen years France has been in a virtuous circle of high growth, high investment and high productivity, and the Hudson Institute has stoutly defended its forecasts, which have been much criticised as a public relations exercise for the gaullists. It says it is quite reasonable to assume that the French economy will go on doing well for ten to twelve years more. But is it? France's success has been achieved partly because spending on housing, education, health, hospitals, welfare and roads has been relatively neglected. It has been achieved, too, because the relative inequality of incomes (by European standards) and the predominance of family firms have generated a high ratio of savings. France has also retained a distinctly nineteenth-century mentality about free enterprise. The divided trade unions have been weak and more concerned with politics than wages and working conditions; and the welfare state and social security system are relatively primitive—many firms still have a relatively undeveloped social consciousness.

The French lead – for now

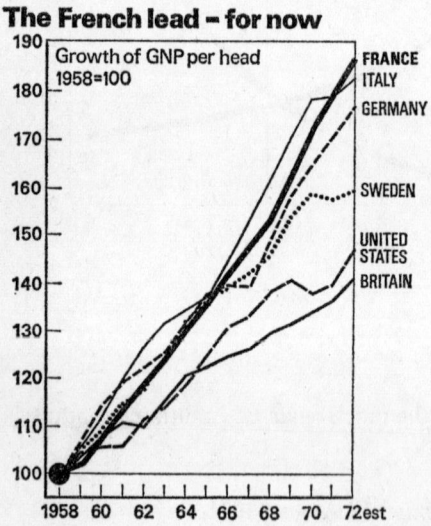

Even in this election, social issues have not been paramount in the swing to the left; the unpopularity of the Gaullist Party has a largely political origin. But the attitudes in industry are changing, and if the gaullists survive in office—and still more if they do not—the chances are that the next French Government will move towards a shorter working week and earlier retirement. There may be further increases in the minimum wage, even though this has recently been beating inflation, and also a raft of welfare improvements, all of which will represent a transfer of resources away from industry.

In the medium term, growth will be increasingly impeded by the sort of labour shortage that is hurting Germany now, as the reservoir of labour on the land dries up. This time is not far off. The Mediterranean could be the next growth region of Europe, making it less and less easy to recruit from Mediterranean countries as they grow richer: the flow of workers from booming Spain has already slackened. Portugal, Greece and the North African countries will go the same way in due course. French factories may even have to turn to black Africa or Latin America, which might not go down at all well. . . .

France's growth depends on a high, sustained level of investment. In the past two years this has not been kept up. Growth has kept rolling as investment projects approved some years back began to come on stream, but one big company now says that 'the profitability of our operations abroad is twice as high as in France'. Because falling profits brought about by the combination of price controls and wage pressures have depressed investment, France does not have the margin of spare capacity that exists in Britain and Italy with which to sustain its growth. Unless investment recovers very quickly, the French expect to waver off their 5–6 per cent growth track. . . .

(Extracted from *The Economist*, 17 February 1973.)

5.4 Letter to the President of the Commission (Franco Malfatti) from Sicco Mansholt

Dear President,

I feel that during its final year of office our Commission would do well to pay special attention to the economic policy to be followed. We will probably not be able to submit concrete proposals to the Council of Ministers, but we could draw up a number of basic ideas on the basis of which a new policy could be worked out.

I think that . . . the Commission is the only body in a position to make proposals from an entirely independent position.

May I begin by quoting some facts:

1. It is increasingly clear that the national Governments are no longer capable of ensuring stable growth in their economies . . .
2. Monetary equilibrium has not been established. . . .

These problems are connected with the following factors which will play major roles in deciding the future of mankind:

(i) Demographic trends in the world.
(ii) Food production.
(iii) Industrialisation.
(iv) Pollution.
(v) Use of natural resources.

I have mentioned only these points because they form the basis of the report by the System Dynamics Group of the Massachusetts Institute of Technology, Cambridge, Massachusetts (July 1971).

The following topics might be added:

(i) The meaning of human work.
(ii) Establishment of a genuine democracy.
(iii) Equal chances for all.
(iv) Our relations with developing countries.

. . . nothing is done, world population is going practically to double in thirty years, to increase from 3,500 million to 7,000 million inhabitants by the year 2000. . . . In the industrialised countries of the West the consumption of raw materials and energy is about twenty-five times higher per inhabitant than the average in the developing countries. . . .

Our duty is to point to economic action which can help in limiting births. Tax policy and the abolition of assistance for large families spring to mind. We should be able to make concrete proposals on this matter.

Supposing stable world population, it would seem possible, at least in theory, to bring about a certain equilibrium in the growth of various factors; this is necessary if mankind is to survive.

For this, however, all the following conditions must be met:

1. Priority must be given to food production, with investments also being made in supposedly 'unprofitable' agricultural products;

2. The consumption of material goods per inhabitant must be reduced considerably and offset by an expansion in the provision of immaterial goods (social security, possibilities for developing intellectual activities, organisation of leisure and recreation, etc.);

3. The life of all capital goods must be distinctly lengthened by avoiding wastage and by not producing non-essential goods;

4. The battle must be joined against pollution and the using up of raw materials by redirecting investments towards recycling and anti-pollution measures. This will naturally result in changes in demand and, consequently, in production. . . .

As State socialism, etc. do not provide the solution, we should perhaps seek a wide variety of forms of production implying strongly centralised planning and largely decentralised production. In theory, the problem is as follows:

To achieve a stable balance, the world population will have to fall far more sharply still. Meadows calculated that for a world population of 500 to 1,000 million (with a very low standard of living) the balance could be maintained for more or less 500 years. I do not think that we can take that as our starting point. We shall have to set our present political objective for a much closer date and consider which measures will help in attaining it, supposing a stable world population.

It is clear that tomorrow's society cannot be concentrated on growth, at least not as far as material goods are concerned.

To begin with we should stop directing our economic system to the search for maximum growth and to a constant increase in the gross national product. A suggestion would be to replace the GNP by gross national utility. (It remains to be seen whether this utility can be quantified.) In this connection Tinbergen's concept of 'gross national happiness' is relevant. We would do well to examine how we could help in establishing an economic system which is no longer based on maximum growth per inhabitant. . . .

Here I shall consider only two aspects of the problem:

1. A rigorously planned economy which would ensure that for each person the minimum requirements for existence are met.

2. A non-polluting production system and the creation of a recycling economy.

To attain the second objective there will have to be a distinct fall in the material well-being of each inhabitant and restrictions on the free use of goods. . . .

I feel that the Commission should work out a proposal for drawing up:

(a) A 'European central plan' (or European economic plan). In this plan the search for the highest possible GNP is abandoned and replaced by the GNU. . . .

(b) A five-year plan for the development of a new anti-pollution production system based on a closed circuit economy (CR production = clean and recycling).

I feel that it is highly desirable that we should devote this last year to these questions so that we can submit to the Council proposals which have received mature consideration.

Sicco Mansholt

(Secretariat Sec (72) 596. Commission of the European Communities, 14 February 1972.)

5.5 Article 3, Treaty of Rome

For the purposes set out in Article 2, the activities of the Community shall include, as provided in this Treaty, and in accordance with the timetable set out therein:

(a) the elimination, as between member States, of customs duties and of quantitative restrictions on the import and export of goods, and of all other measures having equivalent effect;

(b) the establishment of a common customs tariff and of a common commercial policy towards third countries;

(c) the abolition, as between member States, of obstacles to freedom of movement for persons, services and capital;

(d) the adoption of a common policy in the sphere of agriculture;

(e) the adoption of a common policy in the sphere of transport;

(f) the institution of a system ensuring that competition in the common market is not distorted;

(g) the application of procedures by which the economic policies of member States can be co-ordinated and disequilibria in their balances of payments remedied;

(h) the approximation of the laws of member States to the extent required for the proper functioning of the common market;

(i) the creation of a European Social Fund in order to improve employment opportunities for workers and to contribute to the raising of their standard of living;

(*j*) the establishment of a European Investment Bank to facilitate the economic expansion of the Community by opening up fresh resources;

(*k*) the association of the overseas countries and territories in order to increase trade and to promote jointly economic and social development.

(Treaty establishing The European Economic Community, Cmnd. 4864, London, HMSO, 1972.)

5.6 The Dynamic Effects of the Common Market

Written before UK. accession

NICHOLAS KALDOR

It is generally agreed that the initial effects of joining the Common Market are likely to be unfavourable to Britain, mainly owing to the heavy cost of assuming the obligations of the Common Agricultural Policy. It is argued however that these unfavourable impact effects are likely to be more than offset by the long-term advantages—the so-called 'dynamic effects' of membership. . . .

But can they be brought about by joining the EEC? In the light of our large losses of trade in overseas markets in the post-war period, the idea of a 'secure home market of 300 million people' sounds very tempting at first sight as a long-term solution to our problems. But a closer analysis of the likely magnitude of both the costs and the benefits, and the restraints on our freedom of action which would follow from membership of the Community, do not sustain the favourable first impression.

As the issue is a complex one, it is best to tackle its various aspects one by one.

(*a*) First, what are the benefits of a 'larger home market' and what precisely does a 'home market' mean in this context? The only tangible gain is free access to the markets of the other members of the Community, in exchange for giving free access to Community producers in the British market. The meaning of 'free access' in this connection is the abolition of import duties on British goods which, under the Community's new Common External Tariff, amount to only 7–7·5 per cent *ad valorem*, and the abolition of British customs duties on manufactured imports from the Community, the level of which is estimated at 10–11 per cent *ad valorem*. Since the EEC market now takes about 25 per cent of our exports, the benefit gained is the same as a 7·5 per cent reduction of British prices on one-quarter of our exports, in return for a 10–11 per cent reduction in the British prices of rather more than one-quarter of our imports of manufactures. So long as the Community's tariff remains a moderate one, the creation of a customs union cannot in itself make a great deal of difference. . . .

(*b*) On the other hand, by joining the Market we should lose the benefit of the existing preferences in favour of British goods in the Commonwealth markets, in EFTA and in the Irish Republic. Since these markets account for a much larger share of our total exports than the EEC, the net effect on our exports will be adverse: the [1970] White Paper estimates that there will be a net loss of exports of £75–£175 million in consequence. At the same time the net effect on our imports of manufactures is also likely to be adverse, since the abolition of duties on EEC goods will have a greater impact on our imports than the abolition of preferential treatment to Commonwealth goods and to goods imported from those EFTA members who remain outside. The White Paper estimates the net increase in imports of industrial goods at £50–£100 million, so that the net demand for British manufactures will be adversely affected to the tune of £125–£275 million.

(*c*) This is before taking into account the adverse effects on real income and on the balance of payments of assuming the obligations of the Community's Common Agricultural Policy. . . . The average level of effective protection accorded to agriculture—the excess of Common Market prices over world prices—is 45 per cent. By joining the Common Market we therefore face a large adverse change in the relationship of the prices of industrial goods to agricultural goods. There will be a loss on our 'external' terms of trade of at least £400 million a year—i.e., our food imports will cost that much more, in terms of our industrial exports—and there will be a similar shift in our 'internal' terms of trade, in that payments to our own farmers after allowing for the withdrawal of present subsidies will cost about £300 million more for the same output as now. The real income generated by the industrial sector at any given level of physical productivity will be reduced on both counts: each unit of manufactured goods produced in Britain will buy 20–30 per cent *less* in food-stuffs than now.

(*d*) In addition to the loss due to the unfavourable change in price relationships, we shall face the further loss on account of the net contribution to the Community's Agricultural Fund in excess of the receipts from the agricultural levy (which have already been included in the above calculation).

(*e*) This means that in terms of balance of payments cost in current account (apart from the change in the export–import balance of industrial goods referred to above) we shall start off (after the transitional period) with a debit of between £530–£820 million (£400 million a year on account of the additional cost of imported food; £230–470 million in further contributions to the agricultural fund, *less* £50–£100 million in receipts from the agricultural fund) which will have to be covered by additional net exports if a deterioration in the balance of payments of current account is to be avoided. To obtain these additional exports inside or outside the Common Market, we should have to lower our labour costs in terms of international currency in relation to our competitors (depending on the size of the cost) by 5 to 10 per cent. This would require an additional devaluation (at the present relationship of our productivity and of our industrial wages to the industrial productivity and wages of our competitors) of 10 to 15 per cent, which, in terms of the further resources that we would have to transfer from domestic consumption to the balance of payments means an additional burden of £205–£340 million. . . . Hence in terms of total resource cost, the requirement for the balance of payments adjustment is the equivalent of £735–£1,160 million. . . .

(*f*) However, this takes no account of the deterioration in our competitiveness on account of the rise in money wages that is bound to result from the rise in the cost of living. The counterpart to the deterioration in the terms of trade is a rise in food prices of 18 to 26 per cent (on the White Paper's estimates). . . . If past (and present) experience is any guide, the rise in food prices and in indirect taxes will cause a rise in wages which will call for *more* devaluation if adverse effects on our exports are to be avoided.

(*g*) But once we are inside the Common Market, it will be more difficult to regain competitiveness through adjustments in the exchange rate. One reason for this is that under the Community rules, the prices paid for both imported and home produced food are fixed in terms of 'international units' so that whenever the exchange rate is altered, domestic food prices will be raised by the full extent of the adjustment. This increases the real resource cost of achieving any given improvement in the balance of payments; and it means that the rise in the cost of living resulting from devaluation is greater than it would be now. On both these grounds it will be harder to regain competitiveness by devaluation. The second and more fundamental reason is that the possibility of offsetting adverse trends in competitiveness through exchange rate adjustments will itself become impossible as the Community proceeds with its current plans for full economic and monetary union.

The long-term benefits to Britain of joining the Common Market depend entirely on attaining a higher rate of growth of productivity. But we could only hope to achieve this if the rate of growth of our industrial production is accelerated, which in turn presupposes, as the White Paper recognises, a faster rate of growth of exports—both absolutely and in relation to industrial imports. For all the reasons listed, this would require a large *initial* cut in the level of our real wages. . . .

If we failed to reduce real wages initially (or failed to reduce them to the extent required) the 'dynamic effects' of membership would not be favourable but increasingly adverse. Industrial production and employment would fall, both on account of the deterioration of the trade balance, and on account of the restrictive policies we would be forced to adopt in order to restore the balance of payments and to finance our contribution to the Community. This would be aggravated by an increased capital outflow as domestic industrial investment became unprofitable owing to the fall in domestic demand, and full transferability of capital funds was introduced under EEC rules; and this would necessitate further restrictive fiscal and monetary measures to avoid a balance of payments crisis. In those circumstances Britain would become the 'Northern Ireland' (or the Sicily) of Europe—an increasingly depressed industrial area, with mass emigration the only escape.

The critical assumptions which lead to this gloomy prognosis are: (*a*) that we can enter the Community only by assuming the obligations of the Common Agricultural Policy and the relation of EEC agricultural prices to world prices remains much the same as now; (*b*) that we shall not be able to offset the adverse initial effects on our industrial export–import balance by devaluation.

If we could enter the EEC on the same terms as we entered EFTA, and also made sure—by repeated devaluations if necessary—that our industry benefited from entry from the beginning, we might gain considerably through greater industrial specialisation as well as through a higher rate of growth of total output.

(Extracted from D. Evans (ed.), *Destiny or Delusion: Britain and the Common Market*, Gollancz, London, 1971, pp. 59 ff.)

5.7 Weighing up the Opportunities
COLIN JONES — Written after terms for U.K. entry had been agreed.

Some companies see more loss than gain from the increase in competition at home and the loss of existing tariff preferences abroad—in Ireland, EFTA and the Commonwealth preference countries. Others can see no benefit. One such is Sir John Hunter of Swan Hunter. Shipbuilding is already a world market: so entry into the EEC would not open doors that have hitherto remained locked. It would merely, because of the EEC farm policy, mean higher food prices and thus the possibility of bigger pay claims and higher wage costs. But, at least on the management side of industry, out-and-out opponents of membership seem to be in a minority.

The reasons why, on balance, industry would expect to profit in the end from entry into the Common Market have almost become truisms through constant repetition. Basically, there are five. First, membership would provide British exporters with tariff-free access to the large and faster-growing markets of the Six.

Second, the removal of the distortions imposed by tariff barriers and exchange control restrictions would enable the more dynamic, capital-intensive industries to operate on a Continental scale, free of the limitations imposed by Britain's slower growth rate.

In a ten-nation Market, there would be more opportunities for economics of scale, and plant specialisation in industries like chemicals, plastics and motor vehicles. New investment could be planned more selectively and perhaps with less risk—by phasing capacity additions, it should be possible to work up to economic levels of operation more quickly.

Third, the Common Market is in the process of moving from the 'customs union' phase to something approaching a fuller economic union. The opportunities for a deeper form of economic integration—common standards, common specifications for technically-advanced products, a common company law and opening up public sector contracts to cross-frontier competition—are only now beginning to emerge. It is important that British industry should not be excluded from the benefits that should flow from the dismantling of these non-tariff barriers to trade.

Growth Rate

Fourth, the opportunities for a faster rate of increase in direct exports to the rest of the EEC and for the capital-intensive, technologically-advanced or mass-production industries to grow faster by planning their production and marketing on a Continental basis should eventually lead to a gradual quickening in Britain's overall growth rate.

This should benefit all industries, including those who, because of geography or differences in consumer taste would continue to find all or most of their market at home. Indeed, even those companies who have most to gain from the removal of tariffs and exchange controls consider that this could be the greatest single benefit, particularly if Britain's overall growth rate becomes more stable at the same time, as it became faster.

Finally, all these factors, together with the increased competitive environment at home, should stimulate investment, productivity and structural change and thus lead to an improvement in British exporters' competitiveness *vis-à-vis* their European, American and Japanese rivals in other world markets.

Of course, the dismantling of tariff barriers and the eventual removal of exchange controls between Britain and other EEC members provides merely the opportunity and incentive to reap these benefits. They will not flow automatically.

Privileges

The potential gains also have to be weighed against the reduced protection against imports and the loss of British exporters' existing tariff privileges abroad in Ireland, EFTA and the Commonwealth preference countries. Not only would EEC manufactures arrive duty-free after the end of the transitional period but there would be reduced protection against third-country imports in products where the EEC external tariff is lower than the British.

In many consumer products, it is thought that our more efficient retail distribution system gives us a greater built-in propensity to import than that of the Six. No Continental country, for example, offers a British consumer goods exporter the nation-wide coverage that British Home Stores, Tesco or, say, Marks and Spencer can provide for EEC manufacturers selling to the UK.

However, broadly similar anxieties expressed by French and Italian businessmen at the outset of the Common Market fourteen years ago have proved groundless.

The stimulus EEC entry would offer British industry would also be on a totally different scale to the one that British accession would provide for Continental industry. Britain and the three other applicant countries—Ireland, Norway and Denmark—would raise the EEC population by just over a third and its total purchasing power (gross national product) by just under a third.

For Britain, a European Community of ten nations would mean a 'home' market five times larger in population and nearly six times larger in purchasing power. Compared with the duty-free or preferential tariff markets at present provided by the Commonwealth, EFTA and Ireland, the EEC and its associates would be twice as large in purchasing power, much faster growing and geographically more compact.

(Extracted from the *Financial Times*, 29 June 1971.)

5.8 The United Kingdom and the European Communities (Paras 44–56) Cmnd. 4715

44. The effects of membership on British industry will stem principally from the creation of an enlarged European market by the removal of tariffs between the United Kingdom and the Community countries, and, less importantly, from other tariff changes.* The

---

* British exporters will benefit from preferential access to those markets associated, or having special trade arrangements, with the Community. On the other hand they will share with Community exporters their present preferential

response of British industry will be broadly of two different kinds. First, there will be the immediate reaction of a British exporter to each annual reduction in the tariff on his exports to the Community. This response will involve a decision whether, for example, to maintain his prices and so increase his profit margins, or reduce his prices and so expand his sales. But secondly, and in the long run far more significant than his response to relatively small annual changes in tariffs, will be industry's decisions on how to take advantage by structural changes of the opportunities opened up by the creation at the end of the transitional period of a permanent, assured and greatly enlarged market. Manufacturers will be operating in a 'domestic market' perhaps five times as large as at present, in which tariff barriers cannot be put up against them however well they do. There will in consequence be a radical change in planning, investment, production and sales effort.

45. Any calculation of the effects on the balance of trade of these tariff changes will only produce a valid estimate if it takes account of the parallel existence of both these influences operating on industry. And a simple summation of estimates of industry's immediate responses to the small annual tariff changes involved would reflect only the false assumption that no other changes were taking place. The Government do not believe that the overall response of British industry to membership can be quantified in terms of its effect upon the balance of trade. They are confident that this effect will be positive and substantial, as it has been for the Community.

46. Growth and prosperity in any country, including of course each of the six Community countries, depend first and foremost upon the size and effective use of its resources of manpower, plant, equipment and managerial skill. It is essential to deploy these resources to the maximum benefit, and this requires the pursuit of appropriate economic policies. This requirement would be mandatory upon the United Kingdom in any event. However, the general economic and commercial environment within which a country operates is also a vital element in its success in creating wealth and promoting welfare. The environment can be conducive to growth, or it can be unfavourable to growth. It is generally agreed that for advanced industrial

position in other EFTA countries and in the Irish Republic; and must expect a faster erosion of existing Commonwealth preferences, which have, however, been steadily eroded over recent years and which would probably continue to diminish in future even if we remained outside the Community.

countries the most favourable environment is one where markets are large, and are free from barriers to trade. These conditions favour specialisation, the exploitation of economies of scale, the developing and marketing of new products and a high level of investment in the most modern and up-to-date equipment. Through increased competition, they foster the more efficient use of resources over a wide area of industry and help to check the trend to monopoly positions on the part of large-scale organisations.

47. In particular, the development and exploitation of modern industrial technology, upon which so much of our employment and income increasingly depends, requires greater resources for research and development and wider markets than any one Western European nation can provide. The different national systems of corporate law and taxation in Western Europe make it difficult for European firms to combine and co-operate effectively to meet competition from the great firms whose resources are based on the much larger home markets of the United States and, more recently, of Japan. In recent years Western European markets for jet aircraft and aero engines, for computers and advanced electronic equipment, for nuclear fuel and power, for motor vehicles and for many other products have been increasingly dominated or penetrated by the much larger international corporations based outside Europe. Together, the Western European nations can organise themselves to compete with these giants, which are otherwise bound to go on increasing their share of European industrial markets.

48. If we enter the Communities we shall be able to profit from the general advantages of a larger market and, in particular, to play a full part in the development of industries based on advanced technology. If we do not join, we shall forgo these opportunities which the members of the Communities will increasingly enjoy. Their industries will have a home market of some 190 million people, with preferential markets in other European and overseas countries. Our industries would have a home market of some 55 million people, with perhaps another 45 million in EFTA, as against the home market of some 299 million people we should have if we joined the Communities.

Experience of the Six

49. The economic growth of the Six countries had already been considerable in the 1950s, as they recovered from the disruptions of war and occupation. The formation of the European Economic Community then created an environment within which they have each made further and striking progress over the past decade. In considering the likely effect upon our economy of membership of an enlarged Community we must first examine the evidence of that decade.

50. The members of the Community created a common market in industrial goods by steadily eliminating the tariffs on imports from one another over the years 1959–68. The abolition of tariffs provided a strong and growing stimulus to the mutual trade of Community countries. It is estimated that by 1969 the value of this 'intra-trade' in manufactured products was about 50 per cent higher than it would have been, had the Community not been formed; moreover it appears that the stimulus to intra-trade is continuing. The abolition of tariffs and this consequent increase in intra-trade were accompanied by important changes in the performance of manufacturing industries in the Six countries. Those industries which competed with imports faced an intensification of competitive pressure as tariffs fell, obliging them to seek ways of raising efficiency and reducing costs. By the same token, prospects for exporting dramatically improved. Import competition and export expansion were closely associated with a growth in investment. The outcome of these processes was a significant improvement in the rate of growth of manufacturing productivity, and, therefore, higher national incomes in the Community than the member countries believe they would have enjoyed otherwise. Moreover, the increase in productivity was accompanied by a low level of unemployment, even though large numbers of farm workers left the land for industry.

51. The rate of growth of manufacturing output per head in the five major Community countries had already been at a generally high level over the 1950s and early 1960s, faster than in nearly all other comparable industrial economies. In the latter half of the 1960s, however, this growth rate showed a further marked increase (with the one exception of Italy, where the very high rate achieved in the earlier period was not quite maintained).

52. The rapid growth in manufacturing productivity in the Six was a key factor in their impressive economic record in the past decade. But other indicators also show clearly the extent of the advances made by comparison with the United Kingdom. For example, in 1958 average earnings in Britain were similar to those in France, Germany,

Belgium and the Netherlands and well over half as high again as those in Italy. By 1969 average earnings in Italy had caught up with British earnings, and in the other Community countries, earnings were now between a quarter and a half higher on average than those in Britain. In real terms (i.e., after allowing for price inflation), average British earnings had increased by less than 40 per cent between 1958 and 1969, while in the Community countries average real earnings had gone up over 75 per cent. Similarly, all the Community countries enjoyed rates of growth of gross national product (GNP) per head of population, or of private consumption per head, roughly twice as great as Britain's.

53. Moreover, at the same time a high proportion of the Community's output continued to be channelled into investment, so providing the basis for further rapid growth. In the period 1959–69, the Six devoted 24 per cent of their GNP to investment, whereas the figure for Britain was 17 per cent.

54. Finally, the Community as a whole have maintained a strong balance of payments position, earning a surplus on current account of more than $25,000 million over the period 1958 to 1969; by comparison the United Kingdom had a small cumulative deficit on current account over these years.

Prospects for Our Economy

55. This, then, has been the experience of the Community. It is the conviction of the Governments, of the industries and of the trade unions in the Six countries that their economic progress has been promoted in large measure by the changes brought about by the creation of the Community. The economic structure of the United Kingdom is in many respects similar to that of the member countries of the Community. We, like they, are a highly industrialised society, without large indigenous resources of raw materials, and thus heavily dependent upon foreign trade. Like the three larger members of the Community—which in size of population are closely comparable to ourselves—we have a widely diversified industrial structure, which has great potential for development in a larger market.

56. In the light of the experience of the Six themselves, and their conviction that the creation of the Community materially contributed to their growth, and of the essential similarity of our economies, the Government are confident that membership of the enlarged Community will lead to much improved efficiency and productivity in

British industry, with a higher rate of investment and a faster growth of real wages. The studies, mentioned earlier, made by the Confederation of British Industries show that this belief is shared by a substantial majority of British industry, whose own interests are at stake, and who are in the best position to judge. A more efficient United Kingdom industry will be more competitive not only within the enlarged Community but also in world markets generally.

(Extracted from 'The United Kingdom and the European Communities', Cmnd. 4715, HMSO, London, 1971.)

5.9 The Distortions of the White Paper
NICHOLAS KALDOR

The Real Cost of Entry

The White Paper makes no attempt to estimate the total balance of payments cost, and makes no mention whatever (any more than its predecessor), of the 'resource cost' of the whole operation. . . .

If the Government persists in saying that no such estimation is possible, how can they say, in the same breath (para 56) that 'the Government are confident that membership of the enlarged Community will lead to much improved efficiency and productivity in British industry, with a higher rate of investment and a faster growth of real wages'? If nothing can be estimated or 'quantified', where does this confidence come from?

Mysterious 'Benefits'

The answer is that it springs from mystical beliefs like the basic tenets of religion which are no more susceptible to logical scrutiny or empirical verification than the doctrine of the Holy Trinity. These are set out in paragraphs 44–45, 47–48, 49–54. The term 'dynamic effects' is now dropped and there is no reference as in last year's White Paper to the growth of exports 'outpacing' the growth of imports. The direct stimulus to exports is now only one of two 'parallel . . . influences operating on industry'; the other, and far more important, one will be the 'radical change in planning, investment, production and sales effort' due to taking advantage 'by structural changes of the opportunities opened up by the creation of a permanent, assured and greatly enlarged market'. As far as I can make out from a careful and repeated perusal of paragraphs 44–45 these two 'parallel influences' are supposed to operate independently of each other.

But if so, what is the link between the political act of joining the Market and all the 'radical changes in industry' with 'positive and substantial' productivity effects if they do not stem from a higher demand, and a faster growth of demand, for the products of the firms concerned? And why should industry invest more in Britain just because we are 'in the Market' unless at the same time existing capacity is more fully utilised, and profit prospects are higher as a consequence? And whether this *would* happen or the very opposite is the main question to be examined—it cannot be taken for granted any more than belonging to the 'assured British market' ensures the prosperity of Scotland or Northern Ireland.

No Growth Miracle

Another great mystique is the importance of huge international concerns and the suggestion that they require a home market of 290 million and could not prosper with a home market base of only 90 million (as we now have with EFTA). If so millions are too few for advanced modern technology, how did Japan manage to get ahead of the US in electronics and over a large field of steel engineering? And if increasing the size of the home market has such a miraculous effect in itself, why has this not shown itself in a more modest way through the creation of EFTA? This, after all, has nearly doubled the size of our 'home market'; joining the EEC now would treble it again. A baby is still a baby, even if only a little one. Yet our growth rate was no higher after 1968 (after EFTA became fully operational) than before, and no British industrialist would now argue that the creation of EFTA made for great 'structural opportunities' generating a lot of planning, investment and sales effort.

This paean for joining the Six ends appropriately by recounting how much faster the Six have grown, how much greater their investments were and how much better their balance of payments have been. It does not occur to the authors of the White Paper that some EFTA countries (such as Sweden, Switzerland or Austria) have done even better than the Six, not to speak of Japan or Taiwan. The idea that comparative success or failure may have causes other than the size of the home market is a tenet of which the authors of the White Paper are wholly oblivious.

(Extracted from the *New Statesman*, 16 July 1971.)

5.10 Facts Behind the Omissions
HUGH STEPHENSON

The Great Debate about British membership of the Common Market is essentially the conflict of 'gut' reactions. Since, however, most of us like to pose as rational men, there is a need for the argument to be conducted with a certain minimum of what seems to be objective fact. In the current issue of the *New Statesman*, Professor Kaldor has provided anti-Common Marketeers with what will surely become their main economic source material for arguments.

The burden of his argument is simple. It is that the Government in their own White Paper have omitted parts of the economic and balance of payments calculation, where the figuring turned out to be inconvenient and that they have based much of the rest on disingenuous assumptions. For example, Professor Kaldor asserts that there must be Whitehall calculations for the contribution to the Community budget 'at least up to 1980' and that 'if these estimates have not been published it is because the Government wished to suppress them, not because they were not available'.

Perhaps it is here worth two general comments on the sort of comparison that Professor Kaldor makes between this White Paper and the previous one, published in February 1970 by Mr. Wilson's Government. On the basis of that economic assessment, the Labour Government concluded that, without entry, Britain and the European Communities would have 'lost another historic opportunity to develop (their) full economic potentialities'.

The first is that much of the 'fuller' economic analysis of the earlier White Paper, which Professor Kaldor misses in the later one, was scarcely worth the paper on which it was printed. The previous White Paper, for example on the effects on trade of items other than higher food prices, said (paragraph 60):

'. . . it has been necessary to make a whole series of assumptions about the future course of world trade over the next five years or so and to adopt highly over-simplified assumptions about the effect and timing of a complex series of tariff and cost changes on the wide range of good entering into our foreign trade. Each of these assumptions can be little more than an informed guess which may be very wide of the mark.'

Precise economic forecasts several years ahead, based on this sort of methodology, are indeed scarcely worth the paper on which they are written. The statisticians and others who worked on the earlier White Paper advised against their inclusion on these grounds. They have been left out of the present White Paper on the same grounds.

The second general observation is on the criticism which Professor Kaldor levels at the White Paper for not containing a full discussion about a likely British devaluation, as a consequence of British membership. It is a criticism that, in that case, should also have been levelled at the Labour Government White Paper, which observed an equal cathedral silence on this subject. But it would seem to be a somewhat unfair criticism, even in this day when licence to talk about parity changes has become liberal. For newspapers and others to discuss devaluation is one thing. For it to be included as part of this sort of White Paper is still another, under whatever Government. And while it is undoubtedly true that a net balance of payments drain is a net balance of payments drain in any man's language, it is equally true that a large number of more important factors than the EEC budget contribution will decide whether the present $2.40 parity for the pound can or should be held.

These are basic methodological criticisms of Professor Kaldor's attack. But there are also a number of detailed points in his argument, which appear to be errors, or at least weaknesses.

There is his contention that the post-1977 contribution to the EEC budget must be known, since it will consist of levies on agricultural imports, an increasing proportion of custom duties on all goods and up to a 1 per cent value added tax. No such calculation is included in this White Paper. The previous White Paper gave a range of from £150 to £670 million (with up to £230 million of this perhaps coming from the VAT element). It is not at once clear which presentation is more or less informative.

Even with the gross figure of our contribution, crystal balls not economic forecasting would be required. The calculation would need to include not only an estimate of food imports from outside the Community, subject to levy, in future years, plus a forecast for other imports subject to customs duty. It would also need a forecast of the same figures for all the nine members of the presumed Community. And even then this would not provide the answer to the VAT part of the sum. For the only commitment is to pay 'up to a 1 per cent VAT to the Community budget'. Whether there would be a need to call on that extra contribution requires a forecast of the total level of the future Community budget and future Community revenue from the other two sources.

And even then we are only speculating about the *gross* contribution to the Community budget. What matters, of course, in balance of payment terms is not this figure, but the *net* figure (contributions less receipts). And the future balance between revenue and expenditure to and from the Community depends on decisions about Community activity as yet untaken. There is no reason to suppose, for example if the Community budget was expanded for regional development programmes, that we should not get at least as much as we give of the extra monies.

Then Professor Kaldor makes heavy play of the figure put in the White Paper for the extra balance of payments cost of higher-priced food imports. The £50 million figure, he says, is highly suspicious, for the previous White Paper gave a range from −£85 to +£225 million. The mid-point of that very unhelpful range is in fact +£85 million for the extra cost on the balance of payments. Professor Kaldor asserts that 'the best estimate' from the previous wide range was +£200 million. It is an assertion for which no proof has yet been given and would make nonsense of the Labour White Paper 'range'.

In fact, much of the reduction to the present figure of £50 million arises from the fact that the earlier calculation assumed that there would be no special arrangements for New Zealand butter or Commonwealth sugar. The present figure includes the concessions which the Community have made on these two fronts.

Two final points on an article that will provide the basis for controversy throughout the summer. The balance of payments costs have come out lower from these calculations because any estimates about the impact effects of lower tariffs on our trade have been dropped. There is no conspiracy here.

There is also the impossibility of forecasting what will happen to Commonwealth preference arrangements, or indeed what would have

happened to them outside the Community. The major Commonwealth Governments have not yet decided what is in the best interests
of their own economic policy. In any case, Commonwealth preference
in favour of our exports has effectively been eroded.

(Extracted from *The Times*, 16 July 1971.)

5.11 The Prizes and Penalties of a Larger Market

PROFESSOR J. H. WILLIAMSON

It is clear that some of the economic effects of British entry to the
EEC, such as the requirement that we adopt the common agricultural
policy, would be disadvantageous. Other consequences, such as
participation in the attempt to construct a monetary union, could
well result in useful benefits, despite the danger that would be involved in a premature freezing of exchange rates. (Fortunately the
prospect of this danger materialising is now infinitely more remote
than it was portrayed by Professor Kaldor in his horror story in the
New Statesman a mere two months ago.) But it is generally agreed
that the major benefits of membership would stem from the creation
of a unified market in industrial products covering the whole of
Western Europe.

. . . I have endeavoured to see how far it is possible to go in analysing and quantifying the effects of industrial free trade with Europe.
My conclusion is that we are very far indeed from having a reasonably
reliable figure that could be weighed against the agricultural cost to
form an estimate of the net benefit or cost of membership.

Those of us who regard Britain as a typical advanced industrial
country, rather than a case-history in economic pathology, believe
that the natural way to answer this question is to examine the extent
to which formation of the Common Market stimulated trade between
its members. I believe we are now in a position to construct a reasonably reliable estimate of the increase in trade attributable to the
Common Market. The diagram shows my estimate, which indicates
that intra-EEC trade in manufactures was over 50 per cent higher in
1969 than it would have been if the EEC had not been formed. That

means that an extra 3 per cent of GNP was being exported and imported.

It is reasonable to suppose that membership would result in Britain participating in a parallel expansion in trade by the end of the transitional period. One needs to make allowance for the lower tariffs now prevailing, which means that the trade expansion would be rather lower than that experienced by the EEC. On the other hand, our

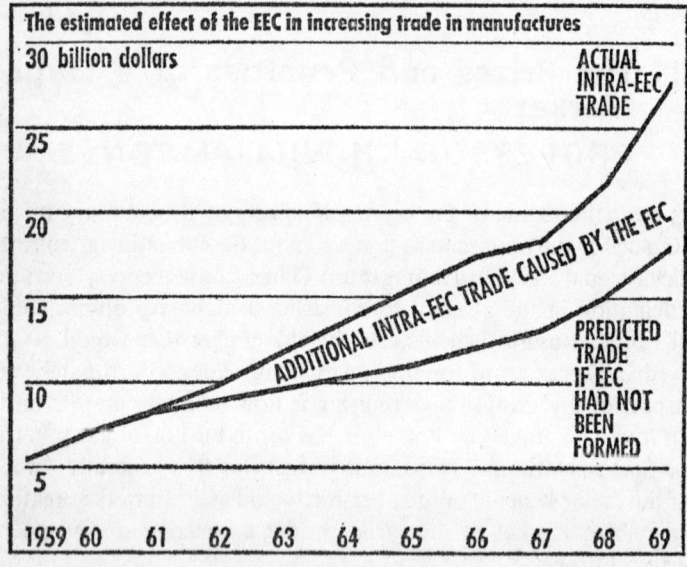

Source: J. H. Williamson and A. Bottrill, The Impact of Customs Unions on Trade in Manufactures (Warwick Economic Research Papers).

exports will get an additional boost as we recapture markets that were lost during the 1960s as a result of our suffering from EEC discrimination. In all, manufactured exports to the EEC might be expected to benefit by something like a 45 per cent increase. This would be partially offset by lower exports to EFTA and the Commonwealth as a result of the loss of discrimination in our favour. But these declines are likely to be modest. . . .

Imports from the EEC will also rise, probably by a rather higher percentage than exports. But part of this increase will represent a diversion of imports that we now buy from other sources. Taking exports and imports together, there seems little reason to expect the balance of payments to either improve or worsen significantly: the increased exports and imports will largely cancel each other out. One will be left with a significant, though not revolutionary, increase in the proportion of manufactured output that enters international trade. On the basis of the figures quoted above, an extra 1·2 per cent of GNP would be traded. This is a conservative estimate. If, instead of assuming that our trade would expand by the same percentage as in EEC experience, one had assumed that the expansion would be the same *proportion of GNP* as they experienced, the predicted expansion in the traded sector would be over 2 per cent of GNP.

But predicting the effect of entry on trade is only the first stage of the analysis. The really important steps involve analysing the way in which increased trade contributes to raising real income (or, what is the same thing, to increasing growth).

The textbooks tell one that this mechanism involves each country specialising in the production of those goods it is particularly well-equipped to produce, and then exchanging these for goods which the foreign country has particular advantages in producing. If one takes the motor industry as an example, this analysis suggests that there would be one country best suited to produce motor-cars, which would then supply cars throughout the Common Market. Since this has not happened, it is tempting to conclude that the analysis is misleading.

Even though one does not get specialisation at the industry level, however, it may well be that countries have tended to concentrate on producing particular types of car, or perhaps particular components. There is also the possibility that countries have continued to produce much the same goods as before but have exchanged a larger part of their output, so enabling consumers to enjoy a wider range of choice.

The above mechanisms are usually referred to as 'static effects', and contrasted to so called 'dynamic effects'. The term is an unfortunate one, and not only because it seems to have misled Professor Kaldor into believing that the case for entry depends on membership generating an export-led boom. This is not to deny that an export boom would help to raise investment and thereby make a useful (if marginal) contribution to raising the growth rate of productive potential. The point is that an export boom depends on the Government pursuing appropriate macro-economic policies rather than on whether we enter the EEC. The 'dynamic effects' as usually conceived are quite different.

In the first place, when trade expansion involves a reorganisation of production, it is likely to require additional investment. There is no need to rely on the psychological effects of an improved trade balance (as Kaldor does) to promote investment. A balanced increase in trade would also have this effect—and this can be expected to materialise from entry to the EEC.

Second, there is the possibility of exploiting economies of scale. While there is no reason for thinking that scale is an important factor throughout industry, evidence indicates that it is significant in three major areas. These are the high technology industries (where increased scale enables one to spread R and D costs over a larger output), much of the engineering industries (where learning results in lower costs as batch sizes increase), and a large part of the chemical and allied industries (where plant costs do not increase in proportion to throughput as the size of plant is increased). A bigger industry may also reduce costs through promoting new firms specialising in the manufacture of components.

Third, there is the benefit of greater competition. It seems to me mistaken to equate 'competition' to having firms tottering on the verge of bankruptcy. On average, I see no reason to suppose that firms would be better or worse off in a larger market. What would differ would be the responsiveness of profits to effort. The cosiness of a small market tends to ensure a tolerable minimum level of profits, while exclusion from foreign markets makes it difficult to greatly improve performance no matter how much effort is expended. A bigger market should increase both the penalties for failure and the rewards of success. To the extent that Britain's poor growth record reflects the lethargic attitudes of its businessmen, this is surely desirable.

Fourth, there is the benefit of participating in a fast growing market. At present the growth of the progressive section of British industry is probably restrained by the slow growth of demand for their products. To expand faster than the rest of the economy requires increased reliance of exports. So long as exports face a foreign tariff, this is liable to mean accepting decreased profitability. This would change if Britain were in the EEC, since the more progressive sectors could realise their potential by sharing in the growth of

Continental demand without facing lower profitability. This should increase the opportunity of the high-productivity sectors of the economy to expand at the expense of the incompetent and lazy. . . .

There is scattered evidence which suggests that market size is a more important determinant of productivity than the above analysis would indicate. The rational interpretation of this finding is that the 'static effects' are not all that matter and that factors like competition and increased flexibility are important. This is vital in assessing the magnitude of the prospective benefits, because it no longer follows that the gains are just a fraction of the trade expansion. A more competitive climate may increase the efficiency with which the whole of a firm's output is produced, rather than just the small part representing the increased exports.

My own interpretation of this fragmentary evidence is that the gains are unlikely to be so large as to transform our growth rate, but also unlikely to be so derisory as to leave us worse off by entering the EEC.

(Extracted from *The Times*, 26 May 1971.)

5.12 The Dons Who Want to Go to Market
ALAN DAY

One claim that has been assiduously put around by the anti-Marketeers was well and truly nailed last week—as it happened, by the objective investigation of two economists who have been among the most effective opponents of British entry.

The claim—which has had the backing of politicians as able and well informed as Mrs Barbara Castle—is that there is no economist of standing in Britain who now thinks that there is an economic case for joining the Six. The investigation took the form of a simple questionnaire sent to all full-time teachers of economics in British universities by Harry Johnson of LSE and Nicholas Kaldor of Cambridge.

The basic question was what each economist's judgement was about the overall economic advantage or disadvantage to the United Kingdom from joining the Common Market, taking both short-term and long-term considerations into account. The question implicitly asked the economists to disregard their views on the political or cultural advantages and disadvantages, on which they could claim no expertise. At the same time it allowed them freedom to use their judgement about those economic consequences of joining which are not easily amenable to conventional economic analysis.

As I guessed when I filled in my answer (in favour) the 504 professional economists who replied (600 were approached) were pretty evenly split in their response. A considerable number said either that they could give no answer or that they thought the balance of advantage and disadvantage would be even. At the latest count 199 were in favour of entry on economic grounds, 208 were against and 97 were unable to take either a pro or an anti position.

These results clearly show that it is nonsense to hold that the pro-Market position is believed by only a handful of reputable economists—let alone the assertion that no reputable economist takes that position. This completely false view has been getting a great deal of currency in political circles recently. Those politicians who consider that there is an economic case for joining now know that they do have substantial intellectual backing.

At the same time, the fact remains that there is an almost even split among economists about the economic case for joining. This will obviously be used as an argument to demonstrate that the opinion of economists is useless. But again, that would be quite wrong.

In the first place the wording of the question, which was deliberately broad, means that an honest answer must largely be based on judgements about political forces. For example, will the political forces within Europe lead towards a common currency (à la Werner Report) or leave us with exchange rate flexibility? Some of the most effective opponents of joining are perfectly prepared to concede, at least in private, that they would be happy to join if exchange rate flexibility could be maintained.

There is also the political question whether the current American situation will lead to a trade war between the United States and other countries in which Britain, as a non-member, could be very vulnerable? And what will be the outcome of the political bargaining over the years for the future of Europe's agricultural support prices?

Another reason why the judgement of individual economists can differ arises from the fact that the standard *corpus* of economic theory and the statistical data available give us much clearer indications of some elements in the costs and benefits of entry than they do of others.

We can much more easily estimate the size of the short-term 'static' consequences such as the cost over the next few years of the common agricultural policy than the size of the long-run 'dynamic' effects, such as economies of scale, the stimulus to competition and encouragement to investment. It is pretty clear that the short-run 'static' effects will, on balance, be unfavourable. On the other hand it is much harder to estimate the longer-run 'dynamic' effects, even though few economists appear to have any doubt that they will be something of a 'plus.'

It is here that the professional caution and self-respect of economists have done harm to the pro-Market case. It is one thing to write an article and stake part of one's professional reputation on arguments against the Market based on standard textbook theory and easily available figures. It is quite another to try to push forward the frontiers of knowledge by entering the profoundly difficult territory of the longer-run dynamic effects.

At any serious level an analysis of the economic case for or against joining is immensely complex and must largely depend on judgement. . . .

(Extracted from *The Observer*, 24 October 1971.)

5.13 Who Got It Wrong ?

As the Six moved towards their Community in the years 1955–8, the gloomy prophets in each country said that their own economies would be badly hit—using all the arguments familiar in Britain now.

It was said that **Germany** would face an impossible balance of payments burden from the common agricultural policy: a policy which required it to prop up the 25 per cent of France's population who, in 1955, were still on France's farms. Instead, Germany's balance of payments has been embarrassingly strong.

It was said in 1955 that **France's** bravely planned and expansionary economy would be curbed within the Common Market by having to keep to Community rules which would make devaluations impossible, and which would increasingly be influenced by the German Herr

Erhard's dislike of direct controls or planning. Since the signing of the Treaty of Rome, France has devalued twice without any trouble, it has imposed as many direct controls as it wanted and it has increased its rate of growth of productivity in manufacturing at the fastest pace.

It was said in 1955–8 that **Italy**, which then had the highest tariff barrier in Western Europe, would be murdered in free market competition by mighty Germany, particularly the infant Italian industries like cars and refrigerators (in 1955 supposed to be highly technological industries) which would simply have to close down. It was said that **Belgium**, which suffered from an antiquated industrial structure and which in 1953–60 had the same mingy 2·9 per cent annual average growth rate as Britain, would be crushed under German competition even more quickly than poor Italy; and that **Holland**, which outside the EEC was beginning to show some promise in high technological industries, would lose all its best workers and ideas over a free border to Germany.

In the event, Italy has done particularly well in industries like cars and refrigerators; Belgium, despite huge political problems, has pushed up from a growth rate equal to Britain's in 1953–60 to one that has been an annual average $1\frac{1}{2}$ per cent higher than Britain's since 1960 (which, if the EEC had the same effect here, would give Britain an extra £10 billion a year of resources by the mid-1980s); and Holland has been second only to France in growth of productivity in manufacturing.

Britain applied for membership in 1962–3 partly because of this experience, and partly in pursuit of 'economies of scale'.

Modern industries seemed to require a steadily bigger economic base. Even small countries could now operate old industries like textiles, but a country needed a GNP of above £15 billion a year to run an efficient motor industry—and motor cars were a development that by 1963 were already three-quarters of a century old. . . .

(Extracted from, *The Economist*, London, 1969.)

5.14 The Benefits of Scale for Industry
CHRISTOPHER LAYTON

For roughly a hundred years, or since the end of the American civil war, the long-term trend of growth in the US economy was faster than that of Western Europe as a whole. One major reason was economies of scale. For the first time in history modern industrialism developed within a continental economy. In the first half of this century the mass US market bred giant companies and new management techniques to control them. It generated mass-production technology for the first time. In the last thirty years there have been a whole new range of American economic developments that are a function of scale: a federal government market and federal government finance supporting advanced technology on a scale never known before in history. The result has been the creation of a new range of industries: computers and data processing, semi-conductors and integrated circuits, communications satellites. As a result, there is not merely a technological 'gap' between American companies and their competitors; in some areas they dominate the world.

The higher living standards and wage levels of the United States reflect in large part economies of scale, economies, not merely in the size of individual plants or factories, but in the total system. Within one enterprise the economies start with the purchase of components; they move into the production process where larger throughput makes profitable greater capital intensity using new technology and hence higher output per man; they can be found in handling, stocking and warehousing, where the provision of standard products for a larger market can cut costs; they are important in marketing and technical servicing where it can be a great deal cheaper and more efficient to market a homogeneous product over a market of two hundred million people than to launch eight versions in eight smaller markets. They are crucial in research and development, where the minimum threshold is rising rapidly in many industries, particularly those with advanced technology, and hence therefore a certain minimum-sized market is essential; market size also determines the *speed* with which a new product can become profitable and therefore whether innovation is worthwhile. It is the current fashion to recall that big firms have extra costs in bureaucracy to carry: of course they do. But it is not only big firms that achieve economies of scale in a large-scale economy like America's. Small specialist firms—producing components, capital equipment, new-technology products—can also achieve economies in production and grow profitable faster by selling into a larger market. This is one reason why the small fast-growing high-technology firm is common in America and why risk capital is readier to back them than here.

At government level large scale public purchasing of new technologies can carry products through the first difficult phase to profitability; a single programme of spending—on telecommunications or computer development—can bring far greater results and better value for money than the penny packets European Governments separately dole out.

It is because British industrialists realise the cumulative impact of all this on productivity and profitability that they almost unanimously favour membership of a European economic union. As Samuel Brittan and others have pointed out *some* of the attributes of a larger market can be obtained by a combination of a national devaluation with unilateral tariff cuts. But there are many which cannot. There is no security or assurance of permanence of access to other markets; so if the climate for world trade should worsen the barriers could go up. There is little prospect of development of the common policies and common public market in the advanced-technology industries which are necessary if non-tariff barriers are to be removed and these industries are to obtain the benefits of a single open market. There is no prospect of achieving the rationalisation of government expenditure and effort in advanced technology which is one of the largest sources of waste in Europe. The international management of money and of companies will remain burdened by extra costs so long as taxes and laws are different and capital markets divided.

In what follows we look briefly at a few industries to suggest some of the processes by which they hope to benefit from economies of scale in an enlarged Community. These observations are preliminary findings derived from a research project being carried out jointly by PEP and the Centre for European Industrial Studies at Bath University: in this project we are seeking to explore the long-term industrial consequences of entry for a number of leading British companies.

The Motor Industry: Scale in Manufacturing

The motor industry is a classic case of such economies of scale in manufacturing. Mass production came first in the 1920s in the United States and brought with it a whole range of new types of capital equipment: the automatic transfer line, the well-organised use of conveyor belts and integrated flow production. Many of these types of equipment and methods of organising them were introduced on a substantial scale in Europe only in the post-1945 years.

Today the volume of production per model, the capital per man and the output per man of the British motor industry are far behind the American level. General Motors produces all the inside door panels for its regular models from one set of dies. It assembles different models in different places, but constantly seeks to maximise economies of scale in components, so that it achieves an optimal balance between the variety the market needs and scale. By contrast the British motor industry today still produces as many different models as the United States industry. That in turn feeds back diseconomies into the component industry.

In the safety glass industry, for instance, the basic processes are identical in America and Britain, but the variety of models in Britain over a much smaller output means a lower output per man, less automation of inspection and batch feeding of certain kinds of furnace which in America would take a continuous flow.

In the tyre industry too, the variety of British and European requirements means variations in some parts of the production process which add to cost.

A company such as British Leyland still has scope to achieve important advances in rationalisation (say in engine production) whether or not Britain is in the Common Market. All the same membership of the Common Market may be crucial. Why?

The blunt reason is that Europe is the only big market in the world whose consumers all buy the type of medium and small-sized car manufactured in Britain, and which offers the prospect of being completely open to British exports of volume cars in the next 20 years.

The motor industry has been shut out of Commonwealth markets in classic style. The fall in preferential margins for British exports to the Commonwealth has been widely documented. What is less widely understood is the nature of the tariffs and other regulations designed to foster local manufacture, which make what is left of the preferences of minimal value in countries such as Australia. Australia, for instance, has a 35 per cent tariff against British car exports (the most-favoured nation duty is 45 per cent) and a 27½ per cent preferential tariff on British components. But if manufacturers (from whatever country) assemble and then manufacture in Australia under a variety of arrangements, they obtain, for an initial period, the right to import components at a mere 7½ per cent duty until they build up local manufacture. Schemes with comparable effects exist in South Africa, India and now New Zealand. In Canada the 14 per cent preference, though more useful (the preference tariff is 0), does not apply against exports from the United States. The major Commonwealth markets (like other developing countries) may be good places to build car facilities with an eye to the future. But they do little to provide export markets which can help British factories at home to achieve economies of scale.

The United States does still provide an important potential market, especially for specialist cars. But the Japanese challenge to European exporters is rapidly growing as it is throughout the Pacific area. Transport costs begin to become important here. The US import surcharge imposed in August 1971 also underlined the fears manufacturers have about the insecurity of the US market in a time of protectionist pressures. If manufacturers are to invest in plant which achieves high-volume production they must have a political commitment that the market they depend on will stay open. This they cannot get in the United States.

A large enough base for large-scale production cannot be obtained by attempting to get a dominant position in a single national market such as Britain, and not merely because Britain is now the smallest and most stagnant home national market of any first-league car producer. Consumer taste and income levels are diverse and seek variety; in the words of T. N. Beckett,[1] Vice-President of Ford Europe, 'We live in an age of mass production but only to a smaller degree of mass consumption. There is a definite upper limit to the share of market which a manufacturer can expect to get—however attractive the car, however competitive its price, because of the desire some people at least have to be different.' The rapid growth of imports of cars in every European country, which is expected to reach at least one-third of each domestic market by the mid-1970s (for Common Market members), therefore fulfils a crucial economic function. It is the only means by which the European motor industry can both supply consumers with the variety of products they want and achieve economies of scale.

In Mr. Beckett's words 'with sales distributed over a wide range of markets, it will be possible for manufacturers to have the advantage of large production runs to a much greater extent than now. Europe will become one domestic market for vehicles. Dependence on a single national market within Europe will not be possible, and the international location of each manufacturer's plants and the international coverage of the whole European market will be essential for survival.'

Mr. Beckett suggested, in the same article, that 'the special tooling, design and development by a major manufacturer of a new model to sell in Europe can cost, on average, including a share of power train expenditure, £50 million a time at current prices'. To stay in the first league a company, in his view, had to attain investment of £50 million a year on new models and £50 million in expansion and modernisation. These kinds of figures require a cheaper volume model to sell some 400,000 to 600,000 units per year to achieve viability and a company to achieve an output of some two million vehicles (a figure also suggested by Signor Agnelli).

To a high degree the British motor industry is therefore already turning towards Europe, as it seeks these scale economies. It has no choice. Ford, since 1967, has been integrating its European operations—making the Escort and the Capri standard models for all Europe, manufacturing automatic transmissions for the entire company in Bordeaux. It took the view that sooner or later European countries would have to remove the barriers between them and that those who worked on this assumption and developed a maximum division of labour between their manufacturing centres would be the first to benefit.

Nonetheless Ford's UK operations today are disadvantaged by Britain's exclusion from the Common Market in two ways. First tariffs do penalise the intra-company trading which it has developed as part of its European policy. As one Ford executive remarked, 'we moved a bit ahead of history'. Second, during the last 10 years there has been a massive shift in location of investment to Ford of Germany, partly to satisfy the growing German market, but partly to serve the Common Market as a whole. The shift happened long before Henry Ford got upset by British strikes and indeed at a time when Ford's management had, if anything, a predilection for Britain.

British Leyland now also has a five-year European strategy, designed to build up sales in Europe, outside Britain, from the present 200,000 to 500,000 cars by 1975–6. Under present plans some 270,000 of these units are expected to be from assembly plants on the Continent (in Italy, Belgium and Spain)—a big growth in Continental investment.

The major car companies that operate from Britain are thus all planning operations on the assumption that they must aim at a major share of the European market as a whole. The question is how Common Market membership or non-membership will affect the location, scale and efficiency of their investment in Britain within the framework of this strategy.

Reference

1. T. N. Beckett, 'The European Motor Industry in the Seventies', *The Business Economist*, Spring 1971.

(Extracted from J. Pinder (ed.), *The Economies of Europe*, Charles Knight, London, 1971, pp. 46 ff.)

5.15 British Leyland—European Industrial Organisation

MICHAEL SHANKS

Background Information on British Leyland

I will start by giving a few background facts about British Leyland. It was formed from the merger of the two surviving large British-owned companies in the motor industry, BMC and Leyland in 1968. The combined company had a sales potential of about £1,000 million p.a. At the time of the merger, sales were not at this level, although we currently sell annually around this figure, half coming from overseas, either being direct exports from the UK or overseas earnings through local assembly and/or manufacture. Thus, British Leyland is the biggest exporter in the British economy. There are about 75 factories in the UK alone and a large number of overseas factories.

Economies of Scale

The world motor industry is one where the economics of large scale are becoming more and more powerful each year and where the industry is in the process of concentrating itself effectively into about twelve large international companies. The reasons for this are well known. The economies of mass production are extremely important in the car industry; at the same time the customer increasingly wants a wide variety of products and the only way of meeting these marketing and production requirements is by maintaining a large, uninterrupted flow of production. Similarly, if one is to meet the needs of dealer organisations throughout the world, one must have not only a large variety of products specially tailored to particular markets, but also one must be able to finance a very heavy investment in sales and after-sales facilities. There are also very important large-scale economies of purchasing and research and development, because the design and development costs in developing a new car model are very heavy and becoming increasingly so. Something between £10 and £20 million is now normally required for a new car, simply to get it on to the market. Then the most important economy of large scale is the ability to survive disasters. The motor industry tends to be accident-prone: new models are not always as successful as companies expect them to be, and the motor industry tends to be one of the first targets for a governmental clamp down on expenditure. The market is one which is subject to fluctuations, even apart from the actions of governments. In most countries there is quite a big cyclical element in the motor market. For these reasons, it is a risky industry, and while small firms may be very successful for a period of years, at some stage they usually run out of capital through one or other of these difficulties. The motor industry is therefore increasingly becoming international, concentrated in the hands of about a dozen firms, and there is no evidence of the reversal of this trend. If you take British Leyland in the context of this constellation, in terms of size we are about middling: we are similar in size to Fiat or Toyota, slightly smaller than Renault and Peugeot, if taken as one firm, though bigger than each in isolation. Above us are the three American giants, General Motors, Ford and Chrysler, who are our direct competitors in our home market through their subsidiaries over here. Volkswagen comes fourth, substantially ahead of other European companies. Our peculiarity is that we are the one international motor company whose home base is the UK and we are also the one international motor company whose direct competition in our home markets consists of three American companies all with their manufacturing operations in the UK. The basic marketing problem of British Leyland derives from this fact.

Possible Marketing Strategies

Of all the major car markets in the world, the UK is the only one where there has been no net growth since 1963 and where sales in 1970 will still be substantially below what was achieved in 1964. We have been overtaken by France, Italy and Japan as a market for cars; we have for many years been below west Germany. There were approximately twice the number of west German domestic car registrations last year compared with UK registrations, and British Leyland do not expect domestic car registrations in the UK to reach Germany's current level until around 1980. This is a very unsatisfactory situation, because all motor companies depend very heavily on their home markets to generate the finance to mount the investment required for export. From this basic situation two possible marketing strategies can be followed.

The first would be to concentrate on the home market, because it is the most profitable even with all its defects, and we must make the best of it. We are the market leaders in the UK with between 40 per cent and 45 per cent of the home market. However this would not be satisfactory for two reasons: firstly, because with the best will in the world one cannot see the UK growing very fast in relation to other markets. Secondly, up to now the UK has had a very low proportion of imports. In any of the Common Market countries the average share of import in the total car market is between 20 per cent and 25 per cent and in the UK until very recently the share of imports was only about 10 per cent. It is now up to 15 per cent. From the long-term planning point of view one must reckon, whether or not we go into the Common Market, that imports from continental firms are going to take rather more than 20 per cent of the home market since there is no reason why the British home market should behave differently from the other European home markets. What is quite clear is that the continental car firms have been doing in reverse exactly what British Leyland are doing in Europe. What they have done is to look at Britain and say, 'Well this is a market where we are not achieving the penetration we are in other markets, therefore this is a good market to go for.'

. . . The time for them to get into the British market is believed to be now when an organisation can be built up and a name for themselves in the market developed, so that they will be in a position to take advantage of the situation when the tariffs come down. It is therefore going to be very hard for my company or for our three American competitors in the UK to increase our market share, and we must develop an alternative internationally based market strategy.

The export market in which we see the biggest growth potential is in Europe (which includes the EEC, EFTA and Spain) where we expect our sales to be a larger proportion of a much faster total growing market.

Therefore if overseas sales are to be built up it will be necessary to increase the amount of overseas assembly and manufacture in all countries and in particular the developing countries. Very often the only way of getting into the market is local assembly leading to local manufacture.

The alternative marketing strategy is to become more international. . . .

Local Manufacture

The European countries where our products are at the moment being manufactured (by which is meant that more than 50 per cent of the value of the product is local) include Italy, through our agreement with Innocenti, who manufacture our products in Italy, and Spain where we now have the widest range of vehicles on the Spanish market because we have acquired controlling interest in a company called Authi, are in partnership with a company called Pegaso which makes a whole range of trucks, 'Sava' which makes light commercial vehicles and vans, and 'MSA' which makes land-rovers. Our biggest areas of wholly-owned assembly in Europe are in Belgium where we have assembly plants at Seneffe in the Borinage and at Malines. These are being built up to provide a capacity of 120,000 cars. . . .

Growth of Sales in Europe

Last year for the first time the number of cars sold in Europe actually exceeded the number of cars sold in the USA and we believe that by 1980 Europeans will be buying two and three million more cars every year than will the Americans. Europe is a growth market in which we believe we should increase our share as a company. . . .

Reorganisation of Sales Operations in Europe

At the time of the BMC/Leyland merger we found that our sales organisation in Europe was extremely fragmented. Some dealers were selling Jaguars, for example, others selling Rovers or Triumphs or Austins. Very few were selling the whole of the British Leyland range, which meant that to very few of our dealers were we very important. There was also a bewildering range of importers into each of these countries, so the wholesale operations tended to be controlled by independent firms. We were therefore selling through two tiers: we were selling to wholesalers and they were selling to retailers. Consequently the profits tended to evaporate at each stage of the process and the degree of control that one had at each marketing stage was not as great as it could be. To overcome these problems we set up British Leyland Europe to co-ordinate all our selling and manufacturing operations in Europe. Under that organisation we are setting up a wholly-owned subsidiary in each European country to control all the wholesaling and selling operations in that country. We now have these companies in eight European countries, Switzerland, Austria, Sweden, Norway, Belgium, Netherlands, Spain and France. Underneath these national wholesaling companies we are the dealer organisation, so that wherever possible the dealer is selling either the whole or a large part of the range, which is obviously a very much more attractive prospect than if he is only selling a small part of it. We can now obtain much better dealers and require from them much higher standards in stock-carrying, after-sales service, sales promotion, advertising and premises. These criteria are what make car-selling effective rather than an amateur operation. This is the first stage of our European strategy.

The second stage is to build up our assembly and manufacture operations. Of the 450,000 cars which we plan to be selling in Europe by 1975, something like two-thirds will be assembled or manufactured on the continent. By the end of 1972 we shall have facilities to manufacture or assemble over 300,000 cars a year in Europe, 120,000 in the Belgian assembly plants, the rest in Italy, and in Spain through the firms mentioned above. What we are increasingly trying to do and will be doing throughout the 1970s is to try to make these plants as much as possible interdependent in order to derive economies of scale, so that we shall be feeding parts and components from one of these factories into one of the others and have an interlocking manufacturing complex in the Common Market to supply the European countries. Now there is no doubt that the motor industry throughout the world will become more and more international in its operations. By establishing a variety of plants for production and manufacture, we have tried to achieve economies of scale, access to the market, minimising the disadvantage of market changes of costs (exaggerated by changes of exchange rates) and also the disadvantages caused by labour relations problems. This has allowed a greater degree of flexibility and for advantage to be taken of movements of comparative costs between countries. . . .

To conclude therefore my company feels that it must become international in order to survive. We are doing this. Europe we regard as our biggest growth market, both in absolute terms and in terms of the market potential. Our market share has traditionally been small and we think we can improve it by better organisation: in this respect the record up to now is reasonably encouraging. Obviously survival would be easier in every way if we were part of the EEC rather than outside it. From the outside, planning would become rather precarious. Once inside the UK would become a better base to supply Europe, provided that relative wage and other costs remain competitive. The least important consideration is the tariff cuts. The really crucial element in not joining is the constant risk of some kind of trade war which could leave one frozen out and in a very difficult position regarding internationally interlinked operations. British Leyland's basic problem is the small size of the UK market and the legacy of stagnation on our competitiveness. We do not disguise the difficulties involved but as far as our industry and our own firm is concerned we really see no alternative in any of the other international groupings or communities which have been suggested.

(Extracted from *Industry and the Common Market*, Federal Trust, 1971, pp. 52 ff.)

5.16 An Integrated European Motor Industry Takes Shape

D. G. RHYS

The removal of tariff barriers within the Community has given manufacturing industry the opportunity to plan for and to supply a greatly increased home market. . . .

At present many European firms and industries still seem to think and plan on a national scale. They do not appreciate that their domestic market is now the Community and that they should therefore direct their marketing and production to cultivating this market.

It is now short-sighted to introduce a new product with only the firm's old national market in view; the new conditions indicate that products should be planned and produced for, and sold to, a European market. One industry that has demonstrated the soundness of this policy is the Community's motor industry. This industry, and especially certain firms within it, are in the vanguard of European integration.

During the 1960s any trade diversion stemming from the formation of the Common Market was small: few customers bought cheaper cars and commercial vehicles from abroad. Only around 5 per cent of the sales in the German and French markets in 1960 were accounted for by imported cars, whereas by 1971 the proportion was almost one quarter.

One factor leading to the integration of the European car industry and market was the merger movement between producers. In the 1960s mergers were a result of the effects of increased competition on the finances of smaller firms, and of larger firms' desire to create organisations big enough to take advantage of the opportunities presented by the creation of the Community.

The 1960s saw over twenty take-overs and amalgamations. Among the most significant were:

* Volkswagen purchased Auto Union and NSU, and joined them together in its Audi-NSU subsidiary to compete in the European luxury car market.
* Daimler Benz added to its commercial vehicle side by purchasing Krupp's and Henschel-Hanomag's sales outlets, to reinforce its

pre-eminence in the Community's heavy truck and coach market, where the company accounts for 40 per cent of production.

* In France, Peugeot, after failing to come to a satisfactory agreement with Citroën, formed close technical research and development links with state-owned Renault; one result was the jointly owned engine plant at Lille, started in 1969.

* In Italy, Fiat purchased the moribund Lancia concern, both for social reasons and to compete in the lucrative market for luxury cars. . . .

Discrimination Offset

To offset discrimination and to participate in a growing market, firms outside the Community increased their productive capacity within the Six. Scania of Sweden built an assembly plant in the Netherlands, while British Leyland expanded its investment in Belgium. In Italy British Leyland cars were built under licence by Innocenti, an agreement cemented in 1972 when Leyland purchased the plant outright. These facilities, plus Leyland's Spanish Authi subsidiary, illustrate how half of the 500,000 cars Leyland plans to sell in Europe in 1974 will be assembled outside the UK.

Manufacturers home-based in the Community have been active in expanding their productive facilities into new locations. Firms have moved to new areas not only to minimise the effects of trade discrimination, but also because it is economic even within the context of a single unified market.

The main beneficiary so far has been Belgium, where relatively abundant and cheaper supplies of labour, allied to government inducements, have meant that within the decade 1961–71, vehicle manufacture and assembly grew from almost nothing to over one million units. Over 80 per cent of output is accounted for by Ford, Opel, Renault, VW and British Leyland.

Ford in 1970 chose Bordeaux as the location of its plant to supply automatic transmissions for all its European subsidiaries' needs. Genk in Belgium is the site of Ford's highly automated plant to supply wheels to Ford's entire European operation.

However, another facet of the emergence of an integrated market appeared in 1971, when Fiat closed its German assembly plant: it had become more efficient to supply the needs of this market from Italy.

Although economies of scale in the motor industry often require the use of plants with outputs large enough to supply the entire market, the different stages in the car-making process have different least-cost output levels. So whereas the expensive and specialised plants needed to forge and machine components operate most efficiently at output levels above one million units a year, assembly plants achieve maximum efficiency at output levels as low as 200,000 a year.

Therefore a limited number of, say, engine plants can supply a larger number of assembly plants located near strategic marketing points, or where enough labour is available to man the assembly lines. The emergence of a single West European market unhindered by trade barriers clearly gives firms greater freedom of choice in determining the best location for new plants. . . .

Evolution of European Corporations

All these factors have contributed to the growth of an industry with a European outlook, but the most obvious manifestation of this has been the evolution of the European corporation. This stems from both an American and a European source.

Ford and General Motors from their American headquarters have obviously regarded Europe as a single entity, but the economic division of Western Europe into two areas (EEC and EFTA) tended to solidify the differences between the British and German controlled subsidiaries. The managements involved tended to treat each other with suspicion and the relative success of one subsidiary was seen as a threat to the continued existence of the other. . . .

Failing to persuade its European subsidiaries to work in harmony, US Ford in 1968 created Ford of Europe—as the body responsible for long-term planning for Europe as a whole and to co-ordinate the activities of its scattered European facilities. . . .

The other two American firms are following Ford's lead. GMC already concentrates commercial vehicle manufacture in the UK and from there supplies assembly plants in Belgium and elsewhere; Ford UK similarly supplies its Dutch assembly line.

General Motors in 1970 put its entire European activities under one director in order to integrate the management of their European concerns so that they could compete with European firms, whose trade was already highly integrated. Chrysler established its European activities by purchasing, in the 1960s, relatively small firms in financial difficulties. As these firms were too small to find life easy in their home markets, Chrysler attempted to overcome this problem by introducing a policy of concentrating particular activities in the separate countries. . . .

The most obvious European initiatives in creating a pan-European firm have come from Fiat, and Dunlop-Pirelli. Fiat, first by purchasing Unic as part of the deal whereby Fiat sold its shares in Simca to Chrysler, and then by its 49 per cent stake in the capital of Citroën, tried to lay the basis for a corporation organised on European lines, but its ties with Citroën have been strained recently.

Fiat had already been the first motor firm to change its corporate planning, model and marketing policy to one where the requirements of the Community market as a whole took precedence. Since the mid-1960s the cars Fiat introduced were directed at meeting European consumers' needs rather than just those of its traditional low-income Italian clientele.

The Dunlop-Pirelli merger of January 1971 was aimed at establishing a corporation tailor-made to satisfying the European market and challenging Michelin, the market leader. This link, too, has been undergoing difficulties. . . .

Similarity in Financial Fortunes

A sign of the interdependence of the car markets in the Six is shown by the similarity in the financial fortunes of the various car firms. In the 1960s the growing market allowed all firms to increase their profitability.

However, the slowdown in growth, complicated by inflationary pressures, in 1971–2 led to a downturn in the finances of all main producers. VW's German profits were little more than £1 million from a group turnover of £1,700 million, whereas Renault lost £15 million. . . .

A feature common to most of the motor industry in northern Europe in 1972 was the difficulty of finding indigenous labour willing to work on the final assembly lines, despite high wages. In France and Germany immigrant labour is being used increasingly, and even in Belgium the car industry is becoming more dependent on Greeks and Italians.

In the UK the monotony of the final assembly line may be a factor in the industry's poor strike record, a problem appearing throughout the European motor industry. . . .

The general structure of the car industry will be one where medium-sized firms will have to coexist with giants, for already by 1971 over

75 per cent of the West European market was in the hands of just seven producers. The dozen or so medium-sized firms could survive by cultivating particular markets, as long as they avoid introducing an unsuccessful model. If this occurred, such firms could hardly survive the shock to their financial position. . . .

In the larger Community countries Fiat leads the list of importers, being ahead of Opel in France and ahead of Renault in Germany. Fiat's excellent sales network and its large vehicle range have been major factors in the company's bid to establish a pan-European enterprise.

Within the enlarged Community market the three US-owned firms may find that their most vigorous competitors in the market for cars of straightforward design are each other, while the main European firms—Fiat, Renault-Peugeot, VW and British Leyland—develop and market more individualistic designs, each with its own particular appeal and growing market. As a result these firms could perhaps grow collectively in relation to their American-owned competitors.

(Extracted from *European Community*, December 1972.)

SECTION 6

The Problems of Agriculture

6. Introduction

The main problem of European agriculture has been that there have been too many farmers and farm workers. All other problems are related to that simple statement.

'Too many farmers and farm workers' means that the percentage of people working on the land has generally been higher than the proportion of the national income produced by them. In short, they have been relatively inefficient in national terms.

In France—which has a mixture of large efficient farms and many smallholdings—the farmers and farm workers represent 13 per cent of the work force, and produce only 8 per cent of the gross national product. In Denmark 11 per cent of the work force are engaged in agricultural production, and produce only 8 per cent of the annual national wealth.

But not all farmers can be termed inefficient. In Britain, 2·9 per cent of the work force produces 3 per cent of the annual wealth, and in Belgium 4·5 per cent produces 5·2 per cent. But in none of these European countries can production rival the output of countries like Canada—whose prairies are ideally suited to producing vast quantities of wheat very cheaply—or New Zealand, where the climate is just right for dairying.

The general problems facing farmers are dealt with in the first extract, from Marsh and Ritson (pp. 293–303). They define the three major causes of farmers' unhappy position: rising individual incomes unaccompanied by increases in food consumption; improved technology helping to produce more; and resource immobility which makes it difficult for farmers to switch their production easily, and more difficult for the smaller farmers than the big ones.

These problems have shown themselves in a number of ways. Marsh and Ritson describe the main 'symptoms' of the farmers' problem. These include the low incomes of many farmers relative to industrial workers, the variations in production between the inefficient and the efficient, the attendant social problems caused in certain regions, the visible political discontent of farmers at their generally unfavourable lot and the difficulties in getting an acceptable world agricultural policy. The problem for the European Community can be seen when the figures for the percentage of agricultural workers in relation to the total work force are examined.

In 1961, 18·9 per cent of the EEC's workers were on the land. Italy had as many as 28·2 per cent of its work force there, France 19·5 per cent and Germany 13·7 per cent. By 1971 the EEC figure had dropped to only 12·1 per cent of its workers in agricultural production—a fall of more than a third of those who had been farmers and farm workers.

Put another way, the farm work force totalled 20 million in the Six in 1950, 15 million in 1960 and just over 9 million in 1970. Britain did not have this problem. The reduction began with the enclosure movement of more than two centuries ago, and was hastened by the abolition of the Corn Laws in 1846 which had protected the high prices British farmers needed to charge to make a living from the cold winds of competition. It was a ruthless way to cut back the number of farmers and farm workers, but it gave the British housewife cheap food, at about the lowest world prices.

To give farmers a reasonable standard of living, the British Government gave them a subsidy to make up the difference between what it cost to produce food in Britain (plus some profit margin) and the price the food would sell at in competition with the cheap foods produced more efficiently in other parts of the world.

The EEC evolved a different policy, making the consumer pay the farmer directly instead of through taxation. To do this it was necessary to fix a price that would give the farmer a 'reasonable' income, and place a tax—or levy—on foods imported into the EEC. The system is briefly described by John Mackintosh (pp. 303–4). The definitions of different types of price at which the Community acts indicate some of the complexities of the system (pp. 304–6). The operation of how this works for the 'intervention' buying of grain is then detailed (pp. 306–10).

There has been a lot of criticism of this policy—and not only from the British who expect to be large contributors to a central fund of which they will only get back a small proportion. One such critic is Hermann Priebe, a German, who argues (pp. 310–15) that the 'key weakness is the ineffectual price policy'. It failed, he says, because you cannot use the price mechanism to do two jobs—both to get a balance between supply and demand, and to give farmers a reasonable income.

The agricultural objectives of the makers of the Treaty of Rome were five in all:

(*a*) to increase agricultural productivity;
(*b*) to ensure thereby a fair standard of living for the agricultural population;
(*c*) to stabilise markets;
(*d*) to guarantee regular supplies;
(*e*) to ensure reasonable prices in supplies to consumers.

It was left to the Commission to put flesh on these bones.

Agriculture is one of the cornerstones of the EEC, partly because the Rome Treaty can be seen as 'a bargain between German industry and French agriculture', and partly—as Nielsen points out in his work on the producers' pressure group, COPA, in Section 3 above—because 'the agricultural sector represents the most integrated sector of the Community'. The problems of the integration process, and the contrast of agriculture with the proposed transport arrangements are discussed in Section 2 in the extract from Stephen Holt and the piece by Lindberg and Scheingold.

The problem of France—which accounted for 47 per cent of the Six's agricultural area and had a ruling Gaullist Party which was very much aware of the farmers' vote—was dominant in all discussions in the Community in the early years. By 1972, Dr. Sicco Mansholt, who became the virtual European Minister of Agriculture, played a crucial part in the formation of this policy, joining the Commission after time spent in farming and as the Dutch Minister of Agriculture.

Articles 38–47 of the Treaty of Rome dealing with agriculture show that the same rules were intended to govern agriculture and industry. Internal barriers to trade were to be removed, and a common external tariff agreed. National agricultural policies which gave rise to wide differences in the competitive conditions between member States had to be unified. As article 38, paragraph 4, stated:

The functioning and development of the common market for agricultural products must be accompanied by the establishment of a common agricultural policy among the member States.

In the first decade, effort was concentrated on obtaining a common policy for pricing and marketing arrangements. The Commission then put forward the Mansholt Plan in 1968 which is outlined by Mansholt in the next extract (pp. 315–18).

The Council of Ministers agreed in principle early in 1971 to implement some of Mansholt's proposals for farm improvements and structural reform, and in 1972 directives were made dealing with farm modernisation, pensions for older farmers and improved training and retraining services for farmers.

What this means for British farmers and the effect it could have on how much of what is produced in Britain is analysed in extracts from a study by Brian Davey (pp. 319–25). He indicates the inter-relationship of the possible policies which are especially important in mixed farming where alternatives have to be weighed one against another. One result of the research, for example, is to indicate that under EEC policies it is far more profitable to produce grass-fed beef instead of by intensive farming methods. Some readers may question however, whether or not British farmers would adopt such a complex microeconomic approach to find what might be the most profitable output to produce, or how far and how fast they would then change their production.

The Common Agricultural Policy affects farmers in other ways, also, as Professor Denman indicates in his article (pp. 325–7). At the end of this piece he argues that the possible changes in land holdings could have profound social and political implications. This is a point which Dr. Tim Josling considers in the final extract (pp. 327–31) where he deals with the effects of rising food prices either inside or outside the framework of the Common Agricultural Policy. Some commentators would not agree with the rather optimistic assessment of the likely overall or average effects of harmonising agricultural policies—'virtually no drop in living standards'—which Dr. Josling states. Only if real income rises will the regressive social effects be offset; or, as John Mackintosh put it in his pamphlet 'The impact of EEC policies on British Fishing and Agriculture':

What can be asserted is that a sharp rise in food prices which was unaccompanied by increases in the wages of lower-paid workers and in the benefits of those dependent on social security payments, would clearly lead to a reduction in the standard of living.

6.2 The Economic Origins of the Farm Problem

JOHN MARSH and CHRISTOPHER RITSON

Rising Income and the Demand for Farm Products

The most important changes affecting agricultural policy are changes in the pattern of demand and changes in technology.

The central fact about the demand for food in relatively high-income countries is the limited capacity of human appetites. At low income levels extra purchasing power may be used to supplement a quantitatively inadequate diet. Once the pangs of hunger have been assuaged, further increases in income add relatively little to the amount of food demanded, although they may induce expenditure on a higher-quality, more varied and more interesting pattern of purchases. At very high income levels even this potential increase in demand for some farm products peters out. In its place people may require their food to be produced in more convenient forms and more evenly throughout the year. Such increases in convenience and out-of-season availability are likely to add more to the revenues of the distributive and processing sectors than to those of farmers.

Economists describe this phenomenon in terms of the income elasticity of demand for a product. This, in effect, expresses the percentage change in demand for a particular commodity in response to a 1 per cent increase in income. When demand for a particular product exactly keeps pace with changes in income the income elasticity coefficient is one. Coefficients larger than one indicate a larger than proportionate increase in demand for the product in question. Where the coefficient is below one, demand expands less rapidly than income. Where it is negative the community buys less of the product as its income rises.

The income elasticity figures used by FAO in making projections of demand for a variety of agricultural products up to the years 1975 and 1985 . . . make it clear that, for virtually every agricultural product except poultry-meat, demand is unlikely to keep pace with rising income levels. For some products, wheat, potatoes and fluid milk, the levels of consumption are likely to fall as people become richer. Significant contrasts exist between the expected changes in demand anticipated in different countries. . . .

A rising income level in the economy is likely to create difficulties for the agricultural sector through its effect on the demand for farm products. . . .

First, a richer community requires a higher proportion of its total enlarged resources to be employed in non-agricultural activity. This pressure, which in a free market situation is manifest through relative increases both in level of prices and in the volume of sales of the non-agricultural sectors of the economy, opens up a gap between farm revenues and those of the non-farming sector. If costs remained constant, this would mean a deterioration in the level of farm incomes in comparison with those enjoyed by other workers. . . .

Second, the nature of demand may imply (and, given insufficient inter-sectoral mobility, will imply) not just a relative but an absolute pressure on the levels of income enjoyed by farmers. The more favoured sectors of the economy (more correctly, those sectors whose products have income elasticities of demand which are greater than one) will find it profitable to increase their output. To do so, assuming that their efficiency in using resources remains the same relative to other sectors, they require proportionately more factors of production. To secure these they must outbid competitors for their use. Thus labour and capital unit costs are likely to rise and land prices show increases wherever this resource is required by an expanding industry. . . .

Third, the income elasticity coefficients vary greatly between products. In general, increases in *per capita* demand may be expected for meat products but the demand for such products as liquid milk, wheat and potatoes is likely to fall. Farmers must adapt to this shifting pattern of demand, concentrating more of their resources on the growing sector of the market. The capacity of farmers to make such shifts in their production pattern varies greatly. To succeed the farmer requires a combination of new husbandry and managerial skills and access to new forms of capital. The skills needed for adaptation are not evenly distributed through the farming community, even within particular farm-size groups, but it seems especially unlikely that small-scale traditional farms can have provided their occupants with the experience necessary to venture successfully into new activities. . . . The small unit is less likely to adapt adequately to the new pattern of demand. In Europe, the proportion of small units is very large. . . .

The inability of these units to adapt to changing demand patterns helps to explain the existence of a very real problem of agricultural poverty in Europe while, at the same time, a small number of larger farms are able to enjoy fairly high income levels.

Fourth, the table of income elasticity coefficients does not indicate fully the switch which is taking place in the pattern of consumer expenditure on food in so far as this is now directed towards more processed and more conveniently presented food items. Data for the United Kingdom show that between 1960 and 1966 expenditure on convenience foods rose by some 32 per cent. Such a change implies a shift in the bargaining position of the farmer. Increasingly farm goods have to be sold to large-scale processors and distributors with whom traditional methods of price bargaining may not be possible. . . .

Selling to a large processing firm may not be entirely to the farmer's disadvantage, particularly if there exists a fair degree of competition between processors, but it does tend to discriminate in favour of the larger and more technically advanced farmer and against the small producer. From the processor's point of view procurement through a few large producers is less costly, and may well be more reliable than buying from a multitude of small-scale farmers.

The previous paragraphs indicate some of the difficulties which arise for agriculture in a situation of rising income levels in the community as a whole. If such changes, desirable on other scores, take place, a substantial adjustment problem arises for farmers and, more especially, for the smaller types of farm business. Unless the rate of outflow of resources from the sector can keep pace with changes in its economic environment, farm incomes are likely to be depressed. Yet if such a flow does take place, a substantial secondary problem arises for rural communities in which shopkeepers, schools and service industries find their capacity under-utilised. The overall impact may be to leave some regions depopulated and derelict.

It is against the background of these long-term shifts in demand that agricultural problems can be seen to be a continuing feature of the present stage of economic development. No policy can produce a once-and-for-all solution. The ideal aim of policy must be to make a continuing process of transition acceptable by balancing, and somehow reconciling, the advantages to the community from rapid change and the dislocation which such movement implies for those engaged in agriculture.

One other feature of the demand for farm goods must be mentioned because it complicates the process of adjustment by adding an element of uncertainty. This is the small response of demand to changes in the price level of farm goods. Changes in the level of output produce more than proportionate shifts in the price level for most farm goods. Especially where output of several commodities is affected by some common factor such as weather, the resulting shifts in price level may produce unpredictable windfall gains or losses for the farmer. Such uncertainty makes it difficult to discern price movements of a longer-term nature and may mask the true position from farmers whose experience suggests that a bad year is likely to be followed by an improvement. Thus, they tend to postpone major adjustments which may be needed.

Technological Advance

Technical advance, like rising levels of *per capita* income, is a much-prized goal of modern economic policy. Improved techniques enable output to be increased without a corresponding increase in the volume of resources employed. The additional output may add directly to consumption. Alternatively, output may be held constant and resources directed to the production of more highly-valued goods. In this way improved technology is itself one of the prime sources (with an increasing stock of capital) of higher real income.

In recent years agriculture in Western Europe has maintained a relatively rapid rate of technical improvement. Advances have taken place through the application of scientific discovery and scientific method to farm production. As a result of a greater understanding of genetics, improved breeding policies for both seed and livestock have added to the production potential. The activities of the agricultural chemists have provided ample supplies of low-cost and effective fertilisers, pesticides and weedkillers. Animal health has been improved by a variety of advances in veterinary medicine. Mechanisation has enabled cultivation, seeding and harvesting to be done more quickly and more adequately, thus extending the cultivable area and diminishing the vulnerability of farming to adverse weather. Modern management techniques have enabled individual farmers to identify profitable changes in their systems of farming more quickly and more certainly. . . . Yields have risen markedly in the past fifteen years, the use of nitrogenous fertilisers and tractors has increased dramatically, and even in the shorter period from 1958 to 1967 labour productivity has risen by some 50 per cent in the countries of the Common Market. . . .

Most technical improvements on the farm tend to add directly to output rather than to displace existing resources. Especially on small farm units there exist few opportunities for reducing costs by cutting the labour force or selling obsolescent capital equipment. Instead farmers find themselves under substantial pressure to increase output in order either to increase or maintain income. Individually their contribution to total supply is so small that its effect on prices is imperceptible. Therefore each farmer sees extra units sold as adding to his receipts. In aggregate, the effect of such decisions is so to increase supply as to depress prices and thus tend to frustrate the income-raising plans of individual farmers. . . .

It is this tendency for supplies to rise more rapidly than demand which is the primary problem of technical progress for agricultural policy. If prices are allowed to fall, the incomes of farmers will be cut and those farmers who are least able to offset this by raising output may be forced into bankruptcy. If through policy decisions prices are maintained, more output will be forthcoming than the market can absorb and the cost of price support to the rest of the community will progressively increase.

A secondary problem arises from the nature of much of the technical progress made in recent years. To a considerable extent this has tended to substitute new forms of capital for labour, land and traditional capital equipment. In order to exploit fully the new possibilities, farmers need access to capital and flexibility in the use of existing resources. Those farmers who are unable to secure fresh capital or who cannot reduce their existing labour force are placed at a competitive disadvantage. In Europe this weakness is most apparent for the small family farm. Many such farms are fragmented, badly sited in relation to roads, power and water supplies, and remote from markets. The labour force, which often consists of the farmer and his wife, is highly inflexible. . . .

The Immobility of Resources in Agriculture

Rising levels of *per capita* income and improving technology together change the economic situation of the farming sector. For existing farmers they imply a cost-price squeeze in which income levels are unlikely to keep pace with those of other sectors and may well fall in absolute terms. Particularly for the smaller farmer who is unable to increase his output to compensate for smaller margins on each unit sold, the prospect is bleak. If the competitive position of the agricultural industry *vis-à-vis* other sectors of the economy is to be maintained, resources must flow out of the sector and the pattern of those remaining change very substantially. The rate at which these changes must take place if factor incomes in agriculture are to keep pace with those in other sectors is governed by the speed with which new technology is applied and incomes in general increase.

Very dramatic outflows of labour have taken place in recent years. The proportion of the population and the proportion of the labour force engaged in agriculture have declined. This change has been especially marked since 1950 when the period of post-war recovery was well under way. For the Common Market countries as a whole some six and a half million people left agriculture between 1950 and 1965, and it is estimated that a further two million departed between 1966 and 1970. Changes on this scale represent an important degree of mobility in the farm labour force and it is certain that, had they not taken place, the farm income problem would have been even more acute.

There exist, nevertheless, substantial limitations on the degree of labour mobility. Where several workers, particularly hired workers, are engaged, farmers may reduce their employment without substantially modifying the activities of the farm. Where the farmer works alone, outward mobility means giving up the farming business and often abandoning the family home. Ties of tradition and fears of insecurity in a strange environment make such movement difficult. In France, for example, between 1954 and 1962, 43 per cent of the family workers and 25 per cent of hired workers left the industry. In contrast the number of farmers fell by only 12 per cent. As more and more manpower is withdrawn from the industry, it is increasingly necessary that farmers, as distinct from family or hired workers, should form a larger proportion of those who leave.

Mobility is easiest for those who are young. For such workers the prospects of training for a better-paid job outside farming are good. Family responsibilities are small so that the problem of finding a new home in a different area is less. Again, young people probably find it easier to make the social and psychological adjustments needed to cope with a different environment. In fact, a large proportion of the agricultural working population, and especially of farmers, is relatively old. In France 48·9 per cent of farmers are aged more than fifty-six years and only 8·7 per cent are less than thirty-five. These figures suggest that it is likely to become increasingly difficult to maintain the outward flow of labour as more and more farms become one-man activities. . . . The predominance of small farm units emphasises the need to create larger farms. . . .

It is not surprising that, despite government aids given to such movement, progress has been relatively small. In the 1950s and 1960s there was a substantial net decline in the number of farms of under 10 hectares in Common Market countries and an increase in farms of between 20 and 100 hectares. Despite these changes, the average size of farms of over 1 hectare in the Community is still only some 11 hectares. While it is impossible to define any single right size of farm, due to inherent variations in soil type, location, the skill of the operator, etc., it remains true that 11 hectares is far too small for most modern agricultural activities. . . . ✳

Apart from changes in the overall size of farm units, mobility of land use requires the farmer to shift the employment of land from one kind of production to another: from potatoes and wheat to the production of coarse grains and forage, and from low-value extensive grazing to high-output pasture fed to stock in a systematic and controlled manner. Such enterprise flexibility is more difficult where farms are small. Milk production provides an important example of such inflexibility. More than 80 per cent of dairy farms in the EEC have ten or fewer cows, and of these two-thirds have less than five. Despite low profitability in milk production there is no satisfactory alternative to which most of these small producers can turn. Shortage of land prevents beef production, even at the high prices prevailing in the EEC, providing an alternative. Traditional small farm enterprises, such as pigs and poultry, are becoming progressively more capital-intensive. The small farmer has neither the resources nor the experience to switch to these activities. As a result land, which in response to economic pressures ought to shift to some other activity, remains committed to milk production.

Much farming capital is of a highly illiquid nature. In some cases, buildings in particular, it is tied to the specific holding and has no second-hand value. In others, such as machinery, a second-hand market may exist but the price which can be expected for out-of-date equipment, even if it is still capable of useful work, tends to be very low. This inability to turn existing assets into cash, except at very much reduced prices, compels the farmer to make use of equipment which may be obsolete and inefficient compared with that available to more recently-equipped farms. The longevity of much of this

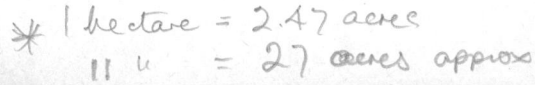

✳ 1 hectare = 2.47 acres
11 " = 27 acres approx

capital, particularly where it is under-utilised, as on most very small farms, means that it cannot be expected to pay for itself quickly and thus enable cost-reducing replacements to be bought. . . .

Symptoms of the Farm Problem

This analysis of the nature of the agricultural problem in modern economic conditions traces its origin to three basic elements: rising *per capita* income levels, improved technology and resource immobility. In practice it is not these basic elements which attract the attention of the policy-maker but the symptoms which flow from them. As a result, policy is often directed at the obvious symptoms of difficulty rather than at the underlying causes. Inevitably there is a danger that such a piecemeal approach may prove ineffective. The reason for its adoption is the very acute nature of some of the symptoms.

These symptoms fall into a variety of categories, of which five are considered here.

(a) Income Problems

. . . The size of the gap between agriculture and other sectors in the EEC seems larger than that necessary to establish appropriate incentives, and does constitute a real social problem.

This problem is complicated for the policy-maker by the very wide differences which exist between incomes on the poorer and the more prosperous farms. In part this can be related to differences in farm size. In Belgium, for example, the average incomes of the smaller size group were less than one-fifth of those in the larger in 1961/2. In the Netherlands in 1960/1 estimates of income in the larger size group were six times those of the smaller. Even within size groups, however, substantial variations occur. Variations in the suitability of land, buildings, etc. and variations in farming skill, as well as differences in the incidence of hazards which affect the outcome of farming operations, help to explain such contrasts. They mean that, so far as income problems are concerned, a solution cannot be attained through manipulation of the overall market price. A price level which is tolerable for the poorest is likely to prove over-generous to those better placed.

(b) Disparities in Technical Performance

Surveys of farming in all countries reveal sharp contrasts between the more progressive and technically advanced businesses and the more traditional farms. At one extreme farmers employ modern methods of intensive husbandry, making full use of the array of new techniques in order to increase and sustain the level of output. At the other, farming continues to be carried out in ways which differ little from those employed fifty or more years ago. Within the Common Market the range of these contrasts is extensive. Size of herd provides one example of such contrasts. Traditionally, herds have been limited by the need to provide fodder and by the exigencies of hand milking. In more modern systems, purchased feed, better pasture husbandry and machine milking have dramatically increased the numbers of cows which can be adequately managed by one man. As a result, the scale of enterprise provides some indication of the up-to-dateness of farming technique. In the Netherlands more than 40 per cent of the farms with cattle have herds of over twenty cows. In Germany, Belgium and Italy fewer than 20 per cent of the herds are in this size category, while in France only slightly more than 20 per cent of the herds are larger than twenty cows. . . .

(c) Regional Problems

Two types of regional problem arise from the present pattern of economic change affecting agriculture. In some areas the problem is one of rural disintegration. Villages become depopulated; rural services which depend on commercial activity, shops, service industries, etc., become unprofitable; those which are provided by the State tend to be under-utilised and, in proportion to their output, costly. In other cases the problem is reversed as people move to the growing urban industrial areas, creating pressure on housing, schools, hospitals, roads and other public-service supplies. The rural aspect of this problem is more acute in those areas within which agriculture is least able to apply new methods. . . .

(d) Political Discontent

The distress of many farmers has made itself apparent in demonstration in almost all the countries of the European Community. Farmers have complained about the level of prices and have taken such measures as obstructing traffic, attacking Ministers who have visited rural centres and campaigning for a more favourable deal in Brussels.

In political terms such unrest must be assessed in the context of local political situations. Parties which derive much of their support from the agricultural community fear that this may be withdrawn if they do not appear to support the farmers' interests. Especially in periods immediately preceding elections, this may make Governments reluctant to adopt measures which appear to be adverse as far as farmers are concerned.

(e) World Trade Problems

Agriculture has proved the most difficult area within which to negotiate a liberalisation of international trade. The very substantial advances made within the framework of the GATT so far as industrial goods are concerned has not extended to agricultural products. . . . This is undesirable especially in so far as it affects with severity some of the world's poorest countries. Despite a variety of attempts to improve the situation by regulating trade through international commodity agreements, very little progress has been made. The world market remains distorted and the growth of international trade constrained by the policies adopted in most countries to protect their own farmers.

Conclusion

The implication . . . is that agricultural policy has to deal with a position which is progressively changing. Solutions which appear adequate in terms of the current situation are likely to prove unsuccessful by the time they are applied. No country is prepared to forgo the prospect of rising income per head in order to evade these problems. In no country can people afford to ignore the benefits of technical advance. At the same time, the rate of mobility which can be attained in agricultural resources is limited. Taken together, these factors mean a chronic tendency for the symptoms of low incomes, technical obsolescence, regional problems, political discontent and dislocated world markets to recur.

Attempts to alleviate these symptoms by maintaining farm prices involve growing cost to the remainder of the community. In part this is evident as a transfer cost—in the form of taxes, higher consumer prices or both. More seriously it represents a loss to the community of the extra output which the resources committed to agriculture might have produced if they were used in other sectors.

A satisfactory solution requires a mechanism which will assist the process of adapting overall resource use to the needs of the market and the process of technical change. Essentially the problem is one of regulating the rate of change in agriculture in an acceptable manner; policies which attempt to prevent change are condemned to fail and to do so at heavy cost; policies which allow unrestrained freedom to the pressures for change involve social and political damage which is not tolerable in the modern world.

(Extracted from *Agricultural Policy and the Common Market*, Chatham House: PEP, London, 1971, pp. 14 ff.)

6.3 Making the CAP Fit
JOHN MACKINTOSH

The main similarity between the CAP and the British system of guaranteed prices is that both are intended to protect agriculture. The effect of guaranteed prices was to protect the industry by giving farmers a subsidy if the market price was low. The CAP (and the national systems on the Continent which preceded it) protected farming by giving a high market price which, after deductions for transport and marketing, went back to the producer. This system operates by fixing a 'target price' for various products. Market prices will fluctuate but are kept close to the target price by a variable levy on imports and by support-buying if the price falls below a fixed ('intervention price') level. Exporters of agricultural products are refunded the difference between EEC prices and the lower world prices. All the administration is in the hands of the member Governments but all the costs of support buying and export subsidies are met by the Community's Agricultural Guidance and Guarantee Fund (usually known by the initials FEOGA). From 1971 to 1975, the EEC is moving to an automatic method of financing FEOGA by paying in all customs duties and levies minus 10 per cent to cover administration costs together with the product of a 1 per cent Value Added Tax (VAT).

This general approach is applied to all products governed by Community regulations, the best example being the arrangements for cereals. In this case it is assumed that cereals are in shortest supply at Duisburg, in the Ruhr, and a target price is fixed for each product at that point, with differing target prices for other centres depending on transport costs. Then threshold prices are fixed at the ports and levies are added to the import prices to bring them up to the threshold prices. There is also an intervention price which is 5 to 7 per cent below the target price at which support-buying has to take place. Separate prices and levies operate for each type of grain and they alter, depending on world prices and the time of year, as well as on the distance of markets from the centre of the Community. Variants of this basic pattern have been devised for almost all the other main agricultural products.

(Extracted from *New Europe*, October 1972.)

6.4 Terminology of the Common Agricultural Policy

The Common Market's framework of official prices is fixed each year by the Council of Ministers on a proposal by the Commission for all the main agricultural products except mutton and lamb, potatoes and wool:

Target price (*prix indicatif*): Community policy is geared to keep market prices as close as possible to the target price. For cereals this price is seasonally stepped to allow for storage costs throughout the year and it is at its highest in areas which are most in deficit in grain.

Guide price (*prix d'orientation*): This applies to beef and veal and is designed to act both as a target price and as a trigger for import control and support buying. There is a single rate throughout the Community.

Basic price (*prix de base*): This applies to pig-meat and to fruit and vegetables. Once average market prices fall below the basic price, action may be taken to support the market by buying in surplus output.

Intervention price (*prix d'intervention*): This is the price at which national intervention agencies are obliged to buy up commodities which are offered to them. It is set at a given level—for cereals about 8 per cent below the target prices. From the basic intervention price derived intervention prices for areas are set throughout the Community to allow for differences in supply and demand. For pig-meat the intervention price is set at 85–92 per cent of the basic price. It includes transport costs and is thus a wholesale rather than an on-farm price.

Threshold price (*prix de seuil*): This is the minimum import price at which non-Community supplies of cereals, milk products and sugar can be delivered at Community ports. Once transport costs from the port are added, imports should be marketed at or above target price. Commodities shipped into the EEC below the threshold price are subject to levies to bring their cost up to the threshold level.

Sluicegate price (*prix d'écluse*): This is fixed for pig-meat, eggs and poultry and is reckoned to represent cost of production in non-member countries. A levy is payable on imports above this price and a supplementary levy on imports coming in below the sluicegate price.

Reference price (*prix de référence*): Similar to the sluicegate price, but applying to fruit and vegetable imports. Also used to describe weighted Community average prices for livestock.

Levy (*prélevement*): For cereals, the levies on non-Community imports are fixed each day according to the cheapest offers at Rotterdam. For animal products such as pig-meat, the levies are fixed quarterly and contain two elements, one allowing for the difference in cereal cost between world and Community production costs and another giving extra preference for Common Market producers.

Export refunds (*restitution*): To enable a Community exporter to sell on world markets, a refund or restitution payment can be made to bridge the gap between high Community price levels and lower world prices.

Denaturing (*dénaturation*): To encourage the use of wheat as animal feed, a denaturing premium can be granted to authorised users which makes wheat competitive with less expensive coarse grains. Sugar can also be denatured so that it must be used for animal feed.

Customs duties: These are not connected with the levies. As far as agricultural imports are concerned, they are applied at fixed rates on certain products imported from non-EEC countries—16 per cent on live cattle, 20 per cent on beef and veal, 15 per cent on live sheep and

20 per cent on mutton and lamb. Various rates apply to fruit and vegetables.

Unit of account: The monetary unit used in pricing in the Community budget. . . .

(Extracted from 'The Common Agricultural Policy', The Commission of the European Communities, Brussels.)

6.5 Cereals and the EEC Home-Grown Cereals Authority

General

The following section is a short background to the EEC cereal market arrangements to help put in context the individual Marketing Notes which follow.

When fully integrated into the EEC system, cereal growers obtain their total return from the market. . . . Market prices are maintained well above world prices by a system of levies on imports and by support buying. The main features of the support buying system are:

(i) regional intervention prices (which are delivered and not ex-farm prices) are derived from, and generally lower than, the basic intervention prices at the area of greatest deficit. These prices rise through the season by monthly increments;

(ii) *minimum* quantity and quality standards;

(iii) price paid varies according to:

(a) deviation from a standard quality;

(b) location of grain in relation to local intervention price centre;

(iv) end-of-season compensation payments to cover the fall back in price at the beginning of the new season;

(v) the designated intervention agency is obliged to purchase any grain offered to it which meets the minimum standards for quality and quantity.

For wheat the high (milling) price is also supported by subsidising the use of wheat for feed (having ensured its removal from the milling market by 'denaturing' it). To be eligible for the subsidy the wheat must be of EEC origin, conform to certain minimum standards of quality and quantity and the denaturing must be carried out under controlled conditions.

Before each cereal year the EEC Council lay down three sets of basic prices, 'intervention', 'indicative' and 'threshold', which can be regarded as support, target and minimum import prices.

Intervention Buying of Grain in the EEC

1. This note provides a more general but simple description of the intervention buying arrangements, and the background against which they operate.

2. Each member country of the EEC has an agency which is responsible for intervention buying, storage and selling of cereals. Subject to the terms and conditions laid down for intervention purchase the agency must buy any wheat, barley, rye or maize (but not oats) which is offered. . . . Having bought the grain it is the agency's responsibility to arrange for it to be stored until it can be resold.

3. A range of intervention prices is announced before the beginning of each cereals year. The basic intervention prices relate to Duisburg in West Germany which is regarded as the point of greatest cereals deficiency in the EEC. From these prices other intervention prices are derived for each of the designated intervention centres in each country. The regional patterns of intervention prices are constructed to correspond to normal price patterns so that customarily high-price deficit regions have higher intervention prices than customarily low-price surplus regions. No centre can have a higher intervention price than Duisburg.

4. In the EEC market prices are freely negotiated between buyers and sellers but tend to lie within a comparatively narrow range. This is because of the existence of a lower as well as an upper limit to market price formation. The lower limit to the market price is related to the intervention price since the possibility of selling grain into intervention provides a floor to the price a seller is willing to accept. The upper limit in EEC countries is the price at which competitive imported grains are available. Cereals imported from outside the EEC have to bear levies designed to bring their prices up to predetermined 'threshold prices' which are above the intervention prices. The rate of import levies can vary day by day according to prices at which competitive imported grains are available.

5. Intervention prices and threshold prices increase month by month through the year in a way which should enable market prices to show an equivalent rise and so provide incentives to cover the cost of holding and storing grain. The total spread of intervention prices is nearly £4 on wheat and £2·75 on barley. . . .

Intervention prices for June and July take the values of the following August (the first month of the new cereal year) to ensure that no new crop grain can benefit from the high prices at the end of the previous year.

6. The announced intervention prices for the various intervention centres relate to grain of a standard quality delivered up to, but not into a store and are thus on a delivered, not an ex-farm, basis. The actual prices paid can differ from the announced prices according to:

(i) deviations from specified standard qualities (quality being assessed in terms of moisture, specific weight, i.e. bushel or 'hectolitric' weight and admixture);

(ii) where the grain is actually taken over by the intervention agency.

7. Although the Commission specify certain minima, individual member countries of the EEC have some latitude in setting higher minimum quantity and quality standards of grain eligible for offer into intervention. For example for the 1972/3 year the maximum moisture content may be set within the range of 14 to 16 per cent and minimum tonnages higher than 80 metric tons may be adopted. Variations can also be made in admixture allowances.

8. An offer to sell grain into intervention has to be made on a prescribed form and will include details such as the type, quantity and quality of the grain, where the grain is currently stored, and the intervention price centre for which it is offered. The offerer will then be informed of the store at which he must deliver, but his grain will only be accepted for purchase if, on inspection, its weight and quality characteristics meet the minimum requirements. The offerer is responsible for arranging the delivery of his grain. The price payable to the offerer will, ignoring adjustments due to quality, depend on the respective locations of the grain at time of offer, the nearest intervention centre for which an intervention price has been announced and the intervention store where the cereals are to be taken over. Three cases can be identified:

(i) grain which is taken over at an intervention store situated in an intervention centre receives the intervention price applicable to that centre;

(ii) grain which is accepted into intervention at the store where it lies at the time of offer and not at an intervention centre receives the intervention price applicable to the nearest intervention centre as reduced by a sum representing the cost of transport between that centre and the store;

(iii) if the offerer is instructed to move his grain from where it is situated at the time of offer to a different store, but one which is not at the nominated intervention centre, he receives the price as for case (ii) above but increased by an allowance for transporting the grain to the intervention store.

9. When considering whether to sell into intervention a holder of grain will compare the price he can get on the open market with the intervention price for his nearest centre adjusted for factors such as:

(i) the transport costs—which he has to bear—to the intervention centre;

(ii) the payment terms (while the intervention agencies are expected to pay 'promptly' their practices vary greatly from country to country);

(iii) possible disadvantages arising from the more elaborate buying procedures of an intervention agency;

(iv) the hazards of failing to meet the strict quality and quantity requirements which could entail responsibility for removing grain from the intervention store.

10. Storing grain bought under intervention could present a particular problem to a UK cereals intervention agency because of the relative scarcity of purpose-built off-farm grain storage and practical difficulties connected with the use of on-farm grain stores for this purpose. . . .

11. Grain purchased by the intervention agency may be resold on the EEC market or exported to third countries with the aid of export restitutions. In both cases the sale procedure is normally by open tender. Grain may be sold on the EEC market only when the local market price has risen above the local intervention price by at least $1\frac{1}{2}$ units of account per metric ton (approximately 64p per ton). To be accepted a tender must at least equal the local market price. . . .

12. The intervention agency in each country, being responsible for purchase, storage and sale of intervention grain, both pays out and receives money. Certain of its costs are eligible for recovery from the Guarantee Section of the EEC Agricultural Fund. These are the actual difference between the purchase and sale price, intake, drying, storage and discharge costs at standard rates, and where applicable, certain approved transport costs. The administrative expenses of the agency are not eligible for refund.

13. The foregoing paragraphs have outlined the system of regular or mandatory intervention sometimes called 'intervention A'. There is another, less commonly used, method of intervention called 'intervention B'. In principle intervention B is an action which is designed to avoid large-scale intervention A. Special permission is required from the EEC Commission for each intervention B operation. The sorts of actions taken so far have involved (i) offering prices a little above the regular intervention price to halt a slumping market price in particular surplus areas and shifting the grain for storage in deficit areas; (ii) continuing the monthly increases in intervention price beyond May to extend the marketing season; (iii) offering an extra storage premium to grain owners to discourage current offerings so that an overburdened intervention storage situation has time to ease.

(Extracted from *Cereals and the EEC—Background Notes*, Home-Grown Cereals Authority, London, 1972, pp. 2 ff.)

6.6 European Agricultural Policy—a German Viewpoint
HERMANN PRIEBE

Difficulties in agricultural policy existed in each of the six member States before the Common Market was formed and were passed on as an inheritance to the European Community. In every highly industrialised country a tendency to produce agricultural surpluses can be observed.

Balanced structural adjustments, within the general framework of economic development, can hardly be said anywhere to date to have been pursued successfully. Almost everywhere a check on incipient imbalances between production and supply has been attempted by political instruments, instead of by measures that get at the root causes. Agricultural policy in the industrialised countries has accordingly been moving out of the realm of economic competition proper. It has degenerated into what may be called a policy of competing by subsidies, a kind of economic warfare with each of the countries concerned trying to shift their agricultural difficulties on to the other ones, mutually offsetting their protective measures as far as their respective financial means and political leverage permit. For some time, in the 1950s, the farm surpluses of the United States represented the greatest disturbing factor in international agricultural trade. Since then, the European Community has become another important source of distortion in international agricultural trade, representing an impediment to the agricultural earnings of many developing countries as well.

Agricultural policies in the countries of Europe had diverged considerably as far back as the end of the nineteenth century. The main differences existing at the European Community's beginning can be illustrated best by comparing Germany with the Netherlands or Denmark. The last two, being small countries, were in a position which allowed them to combine an agricultural policy oriented on international trade with model modernisation on their family farms. With corn and feedstuffs available at low prices, the emphasis was put on intensive, low-cost animal production. This made possible an expansionary export policy which, with the help of excellent marketing facilities, resulted in the capture of European markets to a very large extent.

German agricultural policy, on the other hand, was tuned much more to the interests of the larger arable farms and therefore gave preference to staple foods. The prices of corn and sugar-beet were raised far above world market levels, which meant that feedstuffs also grew more expensive. Animals and their products, therefore, could not compete abroad and, in due course, an agricultural policy protecting all home production had to be adopted.

France accounts for nearly half the arable land of the European Community and farm-land per head is three times as much there as in the Netherlands and in Germany. If these large production reserves were not to be mobilised, a very careful price policy was needed. This led to an extensive farming system ensuring a rather modest standard of living in the French farm community. . . .

Another severe problem is presented by the agglomeration of French industry, which means that people in vast rural districts cannot find alternative employment. Although great efforts are being made to bring about a less unbalanced regional structure of the economy, this cannot be done within a short time. The French Government, for a transitional period at least, simply had to give the rural population some hope of quickly improving their standard of living by supporting agriculture in various ways. It therefore needed a secure market for expanding French production and as only the Common Market offered itself as an outlet the common financing of agriculture was an important expedient. This explains why, from the very beginning, France set great store by the European Community setting up a common agricultural policy.

At the start of the Common Market, Italy had proportionately the largest farm population; that is, more than a third of all gainfully employed persons. In the north of the country a highly developed industry operates alongside an efficient way of farming. But the whole economy of southern Italy is underdeveloped and poses great difficulties for regional policy aimed at opening it up. . . .

Thus for some time in Western Europe countries with expansive and aggressive agricultural policies, like the Netherlands and Denmark, were facing others with defensive and protectionist agricultural policies, like Germany and, to a certain extent, Belgium, Switzerland, Austria and also Britain (which protects her agriculture no less than Germany, although the method has been different).

In the EEC highly divergent systems and interests had to be brought under one common denominator. Italy and France wanted to change from their previously passive and defensive agricultural policies to more aggressive strategies in order to make use of their large untapped production reserves. The Dutch hoped for unrestricted access to the larger market. . . .

Great Expectations

It was hoped that the difficulties and tensions arising from the different conditions in the farming sector of each member country could be settled in the greatly widened marketing area. From the beginning, however, the Community was confronted with more difficult problems in the agricultural sector than in any other sector. . . . In the agricultural sector abolition of trade barriers was not sufficient. Here a new uniform system of farm-support had to be developed out of differing market regulations and other special national arrangements. The Treaty of Rome indicated only general guidelines under Article 39 and left their further elaboration to the governing organs of the European Community it created. A greater degree of intervention than in the industrial sectors, as well as overcoming considerable centrifugal powers, was called for.

Looking back to the first steps towards a common agricultural policy, to the Conference at Stresa in 1958, and to the suggestions of the EEC Commission in 1960, one could almost say they amounted to a system of ingenious simplicity. The free exchange of agricultural products, and competition on the basis of a uniform level of prices, was to become possible in the new Europe by abolishing all direct subsidies, all quota regulations, all bilateral arrangements and all other obstacles to internal trade. These were the main instruments of German agricultural policy. All monopolistic regulations, too, were to be done away with, such as those used in the Netherlands in marketing arrangements, in Germany in dairy production and in France in the complex quantity controls on corn production.

All this meant that the economic functions of demand and supply were to be regulated by the price mechanism, with the important provision, though, that a minimum price level was to be maintained by import levies to be used in regard to countries outside the EEC. Inside the Common Market, on the other hand, intervention prices were fixed for the staple products, corn and sugar, as well as for dairy products, in order to prevent undesirable deterioration in prices. The price of grain had to be given a key position, cereals being both a staple food and a raw material for animal production, greatly influencing the price of pigs, poultry, eggs and, therefore, in an indirect way, the price level of all animal products.

In principle, the EEC system of market regulations, which was developed step by step after 1960, fits into a free market economy better than the earlier system of the Federal Republic . . . striking a balance between prices for staple products and animal products at the border to outside countries. Germany had not been able to achieve this. While she guaranteed high prices for corn, the markets for pigs, poultry and eggs had been fairly liberal, so that the farmers producing them had to bear higher costs for feedstuffs and therefore could not really compete with foreign suppliers.

The EEC's system of market regulations . . . is predominantly dependent on price levels which are connected with the market guarantees. Here lies the weakness of the whole system: in the establishment of levels of prices by political bodies and in the possibility of the extension of government intervention. If prices are not fixed according to sound economic criteria, imbalances must inevitably arise. This has been the experience of the last few years.

Wrong Assessment of Trends

Every member of the European Community must share the blame for the apparent shortcomings in the common agricultural policy. The rigid attitude of individual countries on the question of prices has been as detrimental as the efforts of the EEC Commission to attain wider competence by trying, as a substitute for the wider range of political activities denied to them, to perfect the agricultural system.

During the discussions on the European price of corn valuable years and energy were wasted, for, by the time the price was agreed in 1964, the guidelines for agricultural policy had already been wrongly devised and decided. German price demands enforced an average price increase of 18 per cent in the EEC, which implied a 30 per cent increase in France, the country with the largest reserves of production. In order to be able to carry their price demands through, these two countries had to accept the counter-demands of other countries, which sought compensation in many areas. Thus was started the disastrous development of more and more regulation and intervention in controlling the market for numerous products, the end result of which can only be described as an escalation of protectionist devices.

Results of the Common Agricultural Policy

One can sum up the common agricultural policy pursued by the EEC up to the time of its enlargement as having neither attained equilibrium in agricultural markets nor having fulfilled the expectations of farmers in respect of their incomes. The key weakness is the ineffectual price policy.

Considering the overall political situation the Commission, Parliament and the Council of Ministers endeavoured to proceed pragmatically; that is, they tried to solve the conflicting aims by compromise. In this process they tried to keep up the appearance of rationally founded decisions. Anything else, be it a lowering of prices in order to achieve equilibrium, or an increase of prices in the interests of income policy, would only have resulted in adding to the tensions in one way or another.

If this is recognised, it might be concluded that fault has to be found not so much with the actual prices set, but with the underlying price policy of trying to combine two goals, which from the economic angle simply was not possible at the same time. The question is really whether it makes sense to insist on having prices set so as to attain both equilibrium between demand and supply as well as having an income function, or whether in the long run a complete change of this system will be necessary.

(Extracted from *Fields of Conflict in European Farm Policy*, Trade Policy Research Centre, London, 1972, pp. 3 ff.)

6.7 The Promised Land for a Community
SICCO MANSHOLT

On 10 December 1968, I put before the European Community's Council of Ministers a memorandum on the reform of Community agriculture. Hitherto, the policy followed in the Six had led to an absurd state of affairs. Huge sums were being spent to bolster prices of surplus products, and huge sums were being spent by the member Governments on structural improvements. Yet these did nothing to remedy our real agricultural problem—farms were too small, and farmers' incomes and living standards were lagging further and further behind those of other population groups.

To try to remedy this, I drew up for the Commission a programme entitled 'Agriculture 1980', which provided for:

1. A different price policy, aimed at restoring a more normal relationship between market and price trends.
2. Radical land-reform measures to bring farms up to a viable size and enable farmers to live as comfortably as everybody else.

The plan's basic premise was that the Community's farming population of 10·6 million should be reduced by five million. This exodus was to take place in an orderly manner, accompanied by all the measures necessary to provide financial assistance and create new

If U.K is in Community, surely more intensive farming could be carried out to produce extra food : no reduction in farming — Community would be needed.

316 EUROPEAN COMMUNITY: VISION AND REALITY

jobs. The allocation of structural improvement aid among those who did not leave the land would be progressively concentrated on farms large enough to pay their way. . . . *(& employing more)*

It shocked the public and brought an avalanche of criticism from politicians. . . . This memorandum, however, was only a proposal for discussion. . . . We received many highly favourable reactions, but a great deal of criticism still persists on certain points, which need some clarification. . . .

Why didn't we present a plan earlier? Mainly because the member Governments would not hear of it. In its first memorandum, the so-called Green Bible of 1960, the Commission proposed a comprehensive policy, covering not only prices and market organisation, but also structural reform—which the Council never tackled. When the common agricultural policy took shape, it covered only prices and market organisation. The Governments had jealously kept the structural side in their own domain, thereby depriving farm policy of an essential element for its success.

The price policy, based on consensus politics rather than economics, has taken us almost to the end of the road, with structural surpluses costing astronomical amounts. Dairies churn out subsidised butter regardless of market needs; no one worries about packing the stuff, because no matter whether it is bought, stored, sold cheaply or destroyed, the producer gets the guaranteed price.

At the same time, the member States spend their own money to nobody's advantage, on farms so small as to condemn their occupants to constant want. . . . There are many examples: one country provides grants to build stalls for fifteen cows, when no farm can possibly make a profit on fewer than forty. Others offer easy terms to buy tractors or subsidise the purchase of threshing-machines, when most tractors in the Community are utilised to barely half their capacity and threshers to only a third. Eight out of ten Community farms have fewer than ten cows, and two-thirds have fewer than five, although on a fair-sized modern farm one cowman can tend a herd of forty to sixty head. At the current rate of increase in average size, it would take our structural policy a century to make the average farm big enough to provide all Community farmers with a decent livelihood. . . .

Inefficiency

Accordingly, we decided to tell the public the truth and show the member States where their duty lies. . . .

We are out to enable modern, lucrative farms to be set up, capable of providing farmers and farm workers with the same standard of living as the rest of the population. Farmers' wives should not have to toil in the fields, cowhouses or pigsties, but rather look after their families and keep the accounts. Normal working hours, weekly days off and the usual holidays should be the rule on the land, as they are everywhere else. Farms must be large enough to make the capital investments necessary for modernisation. Financing farms with five cows is tantamount to financing chronic destitution. . . .

The plan is not supposed to do away with family farms. We have no special preference for collective rather than individual ventures, though collective farming seems to be more suitable, for instance, for stock farming, while individuals often do best at crop-raising. The plan provides for the possibility of enlarging individual farms as well as for amalgamations. . . .

At the same time, anyone who wants to carry on alone with an uneconomic smallholding can remain an 'independent yeoman farmer', at the cost of living poorly. The choice will be up to the individual. . . .

The Commission's plan presupposes a halving of the current agricultural population, to five million people. . . .

In contrast to the past *laissez-faire* attitude to the flight from the land, we offer farmers and farm workers a choice, on terms. They can stay if they co-operate in a programme enabling them to run a fair-sized modern farm, live as comfortably as the rest of the population and work at a profit. Or they can leave, in which case they will receive financial compensation, occupational retraining and arrangements to have their children trained for other jobs.

Eight in ten holdings are now too small to keep one efficient man busy full-time. One new idea in the plan is that the land of farmers who pull out should be either sold or rented to those who stay on. . . .

More than half the Community's farmers are over fifty-seven, and of the estimated total departures in the next ten years, a substantial proportion (three million) will be of farmers over fifty-five. Most of these men will not be seeking other work, particularly as the plan offers them security for their old age. For younger ex-farmers the plan specifies that at least 80,000 new jobs should be created each year in the less industrialised parts of the Community.

Some critics maintain that reorganising agriculture on modern lines will aggravate the farm-surplus problem instead of solving it. . . .

Since estimated production in 1980 was higher than consumption, we concluded that about 12·5 million acres would have to be taken out of cultivation. These figures may have to be revised as the plan goes forward. . . .

Prices are a psychologically charged question to be treated with caution. Here is an example of how the different aspects of the plan dovetail: action on prices will be practicable only when modern, viable farms have replaced the million little ones now entirely dependent on the price of milk for a living. . . .

Again, the producers themselves may be called upon to part-finance the support and guarantee systems through farmers' unions. . . .

Finally, the plan would be carried out in stages, to ease the change.

The Facts

Anyone who thinks it will cost too much should look at the facts. The current policy condemns three-quarters of Europe's farmers to stagnate on unprofitable holdings while producing utterly unmarketable surpluses. It costs as much each year as the Americans were spending on reaching the moon, and if the money we are wasting on the present system keeps increasing at the current rate, it should soon be enough to put a man on Mars.

Under our plan the costs would be halved by 1980, after reaching a peak in 1973–4. We are now spending $4,000 million a year on structural improvements and price guarantees. The aim is to cut this by 1980 to $1,800 million ($670 million for price support, the rest for structural outlay). The Community and member States would share the costs.

In France and Italy particularly, farmers are beginning to realise that our programme offers them a fair deal and their only chance of prospering in the future. . . . The means of reform are open to discussion, but one can scarcely contest our account of the present state of affairs, our insistence that reform is vital and our objective of modernising the structure of agriculture. Those with whom the decisions rest—the Governments of the six countries—can no longer shirk their responsibility.

(Extracted from *The Guardian*, 14 December 1970; originally published in *European Community*, November 1970.)

6.8 Trade and the Changing Structure of Farm Production

BRIAN DAVEY

By adopting the common agricultural policy (CAP) of the European Community (EEC)—based on variable import levies, support-buying and export subsidies—and increasing British farm prices to Common Market levels, 'home agricultural output [in the United Kingdom]', according to the British Government's 1971 White Paper, 'can be expected to expand more quickly' than if Britain remained outside the Community. Thus 'the Government expect additional expansion of some 8 per cent overall on this account by 1977' (paragraph 87).

The White Paper, however, attempted little detailed analysis of the implications for British agriculture of adopting the EEC's common agricultural policy. . . . This [extract] attempts to outline the likely impact of EEC membership on agricultural production and farm incomes in the United Kingdom. It arises primarily out of the preliminary results of research currently under way in the Agricultural Adjustment Unit of the University of Newcastle upon Tyne to construct a micro-economic supply model for United Kingdom agriculture.

Shift to EEC Farm Prices

It is difficult to make direct comparisons between British and EEC prices because, while in the United Kingdom the guaranteed prices for the major commodities produced on Britain's farms at the annual farm price reviews relate to prices at the farm-gate, the official prices in the Community are fixed at the wholesale level. In general, however, producer prices for the major commodities are significantly higher in the EEC than in the United Kingdom, although the differential has been tending to narrow in recent years as British prices have been increased at successive annual reviews while EEC prices have been held constant in money terms. . . .

Most farmers can therefore anticipate sizeable increases in product prices. . . .

It is not easy to make precise estimates of the prices that British farmers might expect to receive in the Common Market. . . .

Full EEC farm prices will not apply in Britain until 1 January 1978. It seems unlikely that the present gap between British and EEC prices will be maintained over that period. . . .

With Britain a member of the EEC by 1973 and playing a full part in the determination of Community prices, it seems unlikely that farmer pressure and cost inflation will force EEC prices up in money terms by more than an average rate of 1 per cent per annum. Internally, any change which further widened the gap between EEC and world prices would stimulate farm production in the Community and increase the cost of the Common Market's farm-support programme. . . .

Along with the EEC Commission, the United Kingdom, as a major net contributor to the European Agricultural Guidance and Guarantee Fund (Fonds Européen d'Orientation et de Garantie Agricole [FEOGA]), will thus have an interest in keeping the Common Market's farm prices down. But even if the general level of relative prices remains about the same, it is probable that the relationships between the prices of different commodities in the EEC— for example, milk and beef or wheat and barley—will be changed in order to influence the pattern of production. . . .

A comparison of British prices in 1971/2 and the Newcastle estimates of British prices in the EEC in 1977/8 indicates that substantial increases in the farm-gate prices of cereals, fat cattle and fat pigs can be expected, with smaller increases in the price of sugar beet, fat sheep and milk. A marginal reduction may occur in the price of potatoes. Conversely, the price of broilers could increase from around 7½p per pound in 1971/2 to around 9p per pound in the EEC in 1977/8, mainly as a result of an increase in demand following the steep rise in beef prices, poultry-meat and beef being close substitutes.

The change in the method of price support, away from the deficiency-payment and guaranteed-price system, will mean that farmers' returns will be less assured than at present. In addition, changes in marketing methods are probable, especially with the introduction of intervention agencies to operate the support-buying arrangements.

Some brief comments on the price changes anticipated for individual commodities would seem to be appropriate at this stage. The increase in the British producer price for milk reflects a steep rise in the realisation price of milk for manufacturing into butter, cheese and other products. Even if EEC official prices rise only slightly, the price of manufacturing milk in the United Kingdom is expected to more than double after Britain joins the EEC. So far as fat cattle prices are concerned, a further stimulus to production can be expected in the EEC by 1977/8, in an effort to shift the balance between milk and beef production in favour of beef. On the other hand, when account is taken of the probable changes in the calf and beef cow subsidies, the advantage to British beef producers of being in the Common Market is less marked since it seems likely that none of these direct subsidies to production could be retained when Britain becomes an EEC member. Like the hill-farming grants, these subsidies infringe the EEC regulations regarding fair competition between member States. At the same time, it is primarily the rise in the price of beef which will lead to an increase in lamb prices, together with the introduction of a 20 per cent tariff on sheep-meat imports. The estimated British price for pig-meat, following EEC membership, assumes that the present relationship between pig-meat and barley prices (about 10:1) is maintained. The scope for the 'industrialisation' of egg production in the Community is such that little increase in egg prices over current levels can be expected. As already mentioned, poultry-meat prices may rise somewhat due to an increase in demand stemming from the increase in beef prices.

Turning to crops, on the basis of the earlier general argument on price levels, EEC grain prices will probably rise slightly during the transition period, with the price of grain for animal feedstuffs increasing relative to the price of grain for human consumption. Thus, for British grain producers in the EEC it is estimated that prices of wheat and barley will rise by 39 and 48 per cent respectively by 1977/8. . . .

Higher Prices for Inputs

As well as receiving higher prices for their output, British farmers in the EEC must also expect to pay higher prices for their inputs. In particular, the higher prices for feed-grains such as barley will result in a considerable rise in the price of animal feedstuffs, notwithstanding any recombination of ration ingredients in different proportions or the introduction of new ingredients in the interest of minimising ration costs. So far as the prices of the ingredients of compound feeds are concerned, prices of cereal ingredients can be expected to move in harmony with changes in producer grain prices, and thus to rise very substantially, while an increase in demand will push up the prices of cereal substitutes—grass meal, molasses, beans, cereal offals and the like—by some 15 per cent. On the other hand, oilcake prices are not expected to show much change. . . .

Why?

Increases in input prices will not be confined to feedstuffs. Abolition of the British fertiliser subsidy under EEC rules governing fair competition would have the effect of increasing fertiliser prices in the United Kingdom by some 30 per cent above present levels. On the other hand, there are some mitigating factors including the removal of the British fertiliser industry's protection *vis-à-vis* its European competitors and the excess capacity in the industry not only in the United Kingdom but also elsewhere in Western Europe. On balance it seems improbable that fertiliser prices in Britain would rise by much more than 20 per cent by the end of the transition period.

In general, rents and land values are likely to increase, reflecting the general improvement in the profitability of British farming under EEC conditions. Work undertaken by Graham Ross at the University of Newcastle has demonstrated that in recent years a close correlation has existed between changes in the profitability of farming and changes in land values. Rents and land values will probably increase at differential rates, as between one area of the country and another, depending on the type of farming system which is possible. Agricultural wage rates will continue to rise with inflation and economic growth. So far as machinery costs are concerned, while some machinery prices may be reduced following the removal of tariffs on equipment imported into the United Kingdom from Community sources, in general these can also be expected to increase by the end of the transition period, partly on account of inflation and partly as a result of the introduction in the Community of a value-added tax. It is hard to quantify these increases in agriculture's fixed costs—other than rent—but at current rates of inflation an annual increase of 4 per cent over the transition period is probably the least that can be expected.

Effects on Profitability and Farm Incomes

Changes in prices and costs will affect both the absolute and relative profitability of the various enterprises on British farms and, in turn, the combination of enterprises and net incomes on different types and sizes of farm. The most usual way of measuring enterprise profitability is in terms of the gross margin per unit of production. (The gross margin of an enterprise is the difference between gross output and the variable costs of production such as seed, fertiliser and feedstuffs.) . . .

The figures confirm the widely held view that the higher grain prices in the EEC should lead to a marked improvement in the profitability of cereal production. They also confirm that barley will become nearly as profitable as wheat. Of the major cash root crops, sugar beet margins seem likely to increase by over a quarter, but the profitability of potato production will show little change. On the livestock side, margins from milk and land-using beef production systems will improve substantially, particularly for those systems which rely more heavily on the use of grass and grass products in their feeding regimes. In addition, the gap in profitability between milk and beef—though still favouring milk—seems likely to narrow. Sheep, on the other hand, seem doomed to fall further behind their competitors.

The situation is rather mixed so far as intensive livestock enterprises are concerned. The margins per head for intensive (barley) beef and broiler production are expected to contract, notwithstanding any improvements in the efficiency with which livestock convert feed into meat, as the impact of higher feed prices outweighs increases in product prices. Poultry production is likely to be particularly hard hit. Little change is expected in the gross margin from egg production. On the other hand, pig producers may find their gross margins increasing with British entry to the EEC; in their case the higher pig prices and improvements in productivity seem sufficient, more than to absorb the effect of higher feed costs.

This all suggests that many British farmers face the happy prospect of a significant increase in their incomes and land values as a result of British membership of the EEC. . . .

The trend in aggregate gross margin does not necessarily correspond to the changes in net income that will occur during the transition period, since no allowance is made for labour, rent, machinery and other fixed costs. In addition, the increases in aggregate gross margins on cropping farms are probably understated as a consequence of the tight rotational constraints that were built into the farm models. These placed an upper limit on the acreage of cereals that could be grown. EEC entry seems certain, however, to give a substantial boost to incomes on cropping, livestock and mixed farms in Britain, even after allowing for fixed costs and the effect of inflation between 1972 and 1977. Incomes on dairy farms should also increase, particularly if the opportunity exists of rearing calves for beef. . . . Only pig and poultry farms seem likely to suffer a major reduction in income on account of EEC entry. . . . The deleterious effects of EEC entry on incomes in the horticultural farms sector of British agriculture has perhaps been overstated by some commentators. For while it is true that the mainland European horticulturist may have climatic advantages over his British counterpart for a range of salad crops—but not, it should be noted, for field-scale vegetables (peas, beans, carrots and brassicas)—the latter benefits from the economic protection afforded by proximity to his market and, in many cases, the perishable nature of the products. . . .

Adjustments in Agricultural Production

The expansion in domestic agricultural production expected by the British Government on Britain's incorporation into the EEC will come about as farmers respond to higher prices for their output and benefit, in particular, from further improvements in yields and livestock feed conversion rates. With the generally higher profitability of farming in the EEC, expanded production is also expected to be encouraged by the retention of resources in agriculture that might otherwise have moved out of the industry to other, more profitable, sectors of the economy. It is from these higher incomes that the resources for expansion of production must be generated. With the dual incentives of higher land values and higher product prices, farmers cannot reasonably expect to receive other inducements, such as credit facilities that discriminate in favour of agriculture. Even so, while aggregate output is growing, the production of the various commodities will be expanding—or contracting—at differential rates, reflecting changes in relative profitability under EEC conditions. . . . For many farmers the balance of advantage, in terms of profit, lies with grazing livestock. . . . Within the cattle enterprise, beef production is expected to expand more rapidly; this reflects the shift in profitability in favour of beef and a consequent diversion of resources from dairying to beef production. The estimated increase in beef production stems not so much from an expansion in the cattle herd as from a marked change in the distribution of beef production between intensive concentrate-based systems and the extensive grass-based systems in which cattle are built up to higher weights before being slaughtered. It is here that the conflict between cereals, grassland and livestock mainly arises. For while a reduction in dairy cow numbers and also the expected contraction in the national sheep flock would release land for beef production, some expansion of the grassland acreage is required to accommodate fully the shift towards land-using beef systems.

So far as pig and poultry production is concerned, EEC membership could lead to a substantial contraction in the United Kingdom in the output of poultry meat and a smaller reduction in egg production. This is the consequence of a marked fall in profitability due to the impact of higher feed costs on relatively stable product prices. A change in the relative profitability of pigs and poultry in favour of pigs could, however, stimulate intensive livestock producers to diversify out of poultry into pigs, leading to an expansion in pig-meat output.

To sum up, entry by Britain into the EEC seems likely to lead to the following changes in the pattern of British agricultural production: (1) an increase—perhaps not as large as is sometimes thought—in the output of grain; (2) within the grazing livestock sector, a contraction in the dairy herd and in sheep numbers accompanied by some increase in beef production, and a shift towards production systems relying more on grass and grass products; (3) a major cut-back in poultry production; and (4) some increase in pig output.

(Extracted from *Burdens and Benefits of Farm-Support Policies*, Trade Policy Research Centre, London, 1972, pp. 12 ff.)

6.9 The Price of the Farm in the Balance
PROFESSOR D. R. DENMAN

The little that is known about the prices of farmland in the EEC indicates that the levels are considerably higher than our own. Recent figures show land and buildings on holdings in northern Germany comparable in size with those in the United Kingdom but fetching between £500 and £1,000 per acre on the land market. Prices of farmland in Belgium have been running at six times the average price of land in the United Kingdom.

High land prices lock up needy capital for the larger farmers in the EEC today and with Britain a partner in a common agricultural policy these farmers would be tempted to compete for our relatively low-priced farmland and force up the land cost to the British farmer.

There could be other pressures. Governments are not likely to buy out farms on a grand scale but since the Mansholt Plan serious thought is being given to encouraging the return of the landlord by financial aid as the one who can shoulder the burden of land costs. The Mansholt formula would pay a lump sum of eight times the rental value of the land to an owner-occupier to encourage him to let his land to a tenant. The landlord would keep the land himself and the substantial sum given *in lieu* of vacant possession. Once so endowed he could sell out and re-invest the proceeds in the purchase of a farm in Britain and make a handsome profit in the bargain.

Rise in Prices

Already in the Netherlands the Government has set up a land bank to buy out farmers who would take back the land as tenants and retain the land price as cash. Current land prices indicate that such tenants could eventually become occupiers of freehold farms in Britain and still have liquid capital to spare to equip their holdings.

The probable price of farmland in Britain, especially in the south, is much affected by the residential market and the high cost of country housing. This influence upon the price of rural acres is likely to increase. If joining the Common Market is to prove a net advantage to the nation as a whole, success must be measured by economic growth, especially in industry.

Land prices for our farmers will rise, stimulated by the transfer of rural land to industrial expansion and the demand for residential amenities in the countryside to meet the requirements of the domestic and wider Community market.

Efficiency

The land question—who owns the land and how—is critical for the further success of the common agricultural policy of the EEC.

An obvious difference between us and the continental mainland is the pattern of our farmland and the consequential efficiency of our farms. Although the pattern of ownership and the size of farms is in the first instance a national and not a community concern, the agricultural guidance and guarantee fund carries 25 per cent of the cost of policies aimed at altering farm structures and equipping farms and estates to promote efficiency.

So far the cost has been small. Expenditure on the guidance section is only 10 per cent of the total fund. Under the Mansholt Plan, the percentage would jump to 47 per cent and with the modified plan would reach 36 per cent, and in absolute terms Mansholt would mean an increase of 464 per cent in costs and the modified version 379 per cent. With Britain in the Common Market and paramount among the importers of food, we would bear a substantial proportion of these costs of realigning and improving the structure of continental agriculture.

Land Controls

Apart from the economic consequences the land policies have political and social implications. To discuss the removal of five million hectares from an established agricultural system is one thing; to achieve it is another. The land would either have to be bought out from the private sector and held as public domain by the community or costly and intricate controls would need to be imposed on the private use of land and upon the operation of the land market.

Presumably these controls would have to be subject in some manner to the scrutiny of the EEC. In either event there could be a serious encroachment upon national sovereignty and a politically unpalatable curtailment of social liberties.

(Extracted from *The Times*, 3 June 1971.)

6.10 In or Out—an Inevitable Rise in Food Prices
DR. TIM JOSLING

The Common Agricultural Policy (CAP) of the EEC has achieved notoriety. It is widely accepted by friend and foe of British membership that this policy is a wildly expensive extravagance, which would impose a severe burden on the British economy if not drastically modified by major price reductions.

Consumers would be hard hit by having to purchase food at

'European' price levels, and only an acceleration in the rate of growth in our manufactured exports would offset the ill effects on the economy. . . .

British farm prices and the prices of several agricultural goods on the world market have recently risen sharply. Our own farm support system is being modified and in Europe the concept of aiding agricultural adjustment through structural rather than price policies is gaining legitimacy.

In addition, a study has just been completed by a team of economists from Britain, Ireland and the United States which analyses food consumption, farm output and agricultural trade in Britain for the period up to 1980. This study—co-ordinated at Michigan State University and supported by the United States Department of Agriculture—suggests that consumers will adapt rapidly to different price levels and that the burden of the CAP on the British economy will be much less than is usually realised.

It is necessary to separate the effect of the CAP levy and price system from that of the financial contribution to the Community budget. This latter aspect of the 'price of entry' has little or nothing to do with the maintenance of farm incomes or the development of farm structure in Europe.

Throughout the 1950s British farmers enjoyed relatively high prices for their output. But dependence on a deficiency payment system of support implies that the budget cost of farm policies spirals when world prices are weak, as happened in the early 'sixties. Farm prices were actually reduced for many commodities. As measures introduced to isolate the domestic market from imports began to bite so farm prices were once again raised.

A commitment to compensate farmers for a major part of their cost increases has ensured that recent high rates of inflation have been reflected in farm prices. The guaranteed prices for the major farm products have been rising at about 5 per cent per year over the past four years. By contrast, the European farm price levels set under the CAP have not increased with inflation; they have in fact been almost stable for three years, and were increased by a modest amount last month. As a result the price difference has narrowed considerably.

It may be argued that the recently announced change to a variable levy system and the sudden increases in farm prices in this country represent a shift towards the European policy in advance of any transition period. In fact it is likely that these changes would have taken place even if membership were not on the cards. The first move towards a levy system, the cereals minimum import prices, was undertaken by the Labour Government in 1964.

This system is more flexible than a deficiency payment policy. Governments can raise prices steadily to offset the effect of inflation on farm incomes without incurring additional expenditure; indeed the exchequer usually gains from additional tariff receipts. Consumers in general seem unaware of the extra cost of the policy and appear to be more concerned with the benefits to themselves as taxpayers.

In the Community a different set of pressures operates. European farmers are equally anxious to be protected against inflation. But national governments are unwilling to press for increases in the Community prices since these would then apply to all countries in the Community and would involve additional burdens through the Farm Fund. Net contributing countries such as Italy and Germany are not anxious to see farm output increase. France is concerned with the effect of food prices on inflation and on shrinking markets in the rest of Europe. . . .

In addition, the European Commission, not directly responsible to the rural electorate, has an incentive to oppose CAP price increases in order to devote its considerable energies and resources to other European projects. On this basis one would expect little in the way of price increases under the CAP for the next few years.

The likely convergence of the United Kingdom and CAP producer prices for cereals and beef under these conditions is apparent from the diagram. Prices for pigs and milk are already at or above the corresponding European level. Instead of requiring a special transition period in the event of entry, our own farm policy prices may be at the EEC levels within six years whether or not we join. . . .

But the change to a variable levy system implies that our wholesale prices will also be about the same levels as in the Community for most commodities. The exceptions would be butter and cheese, for which no levy scheme is proposed at the moment in this country. We choose to keep up returns to milk producers by maintaining a high price for liquid milk; whereas the European system supports milk prices through the prices of butter and cheese. With this exception the implementation of the price provisions of the CAP will have a negligible effect on consumers and farmers in this country.

But even assuming that our own farm and wholesale prices do not rise as fast if we remain outside the Common Market, the evidence is strong that the impact on household expenditure patterns will be small. The study referred to earlier projects future consumption trends on the basis of past behaviour for the major food items which would be affected by the CAP.

UK and EEC beef cattle and wheat prices.

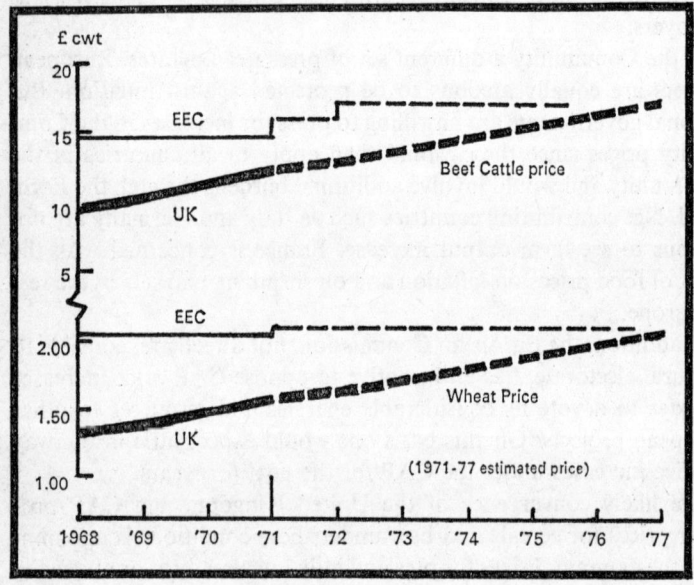

The table shows the projected food and non-food expenditure per head over the next few years under the alternative assumptions about entry. Expenditure on the food items considered would be higher per person by £2·60 in 1978 in the event of entry; from a given *per capita* income (or alternatively, for people whose income was not affected by EEC membership) the cutback in expenditure on other items to pay for the extra food bill would be 5p per week. This is not a full measure of the disadvantage to the consumer, since the necessity to change food buying habits implies that families would be less satisfied with the diets that they consumed under the higher prices even if total food expenditure were unchanged.

Ideally each consumer could evaluate individually the implied changes in food purchases. . . .

The standard economic technique for approximating this reduction in 'consumer welfare' suggests that it represents the equivalent of a further drop in income of £0·12 per year or 0·24p per person per week.

Projected expenditure on food and non-food items in 1978, United Kingdom
(figures in £ per person).

	Major food items	Non-food items
1972	75·92	541·67
1974 Out of EEC	81·29	612·29
1974 In EEC	82·00	611·54
1976 Out of EEC	86·71	692·21
In EEC	88·63	690·29
1978 Out of EEC	92·08	782·71
In EEC	94·67	780·13

This discussion of food expenditure assumes no change in income arising from entry. . . .

These conclusions should not be taken as exonerating the Common Agricultural Policy. It is very expensive in relation to its achievements, which have been primarily to disrupt trade patterns, to exacerbate income distribution problems within the farm sector, to perpetuate a farm structure which denies hope to much of rural Europe, and to impede progress in European development. . . .

Since we are committed to an almost equally cost-ineffective and trade disruptive farm policy in this country irrespective of entry, the change to harmonise with European policy will involve virtually no drop in living standards for British consumers.

(Extracted from *The Times*, 12 May 1971.)

SECTION 7

Workers of Europe

7.1 Introduction

Four freedoms were enshrined in the classical nineteenth-century economic doctrines written into the Treaty of Rome—the free movement of goods, of labour, of services and of capital. In practice there have been restrictions on all four, although the Community has moved towards the original *laissez-faire* aims in fits and starts.

Article 67 of the Treaty of Rome (p. 335) calls for all restrictions on the free movement of capital to be ended presumably so that capital might be allowed to concentrate at a place where it could be used to best advantage. The aim of providing wider markets, allowing firms to adapt to modern methods of production and hence ensuring either cheaper goods or a wider choice for the consumer, is reinforced by the EEC's rules to maximise competition.

Some men, like Charles Levinson, the General Secretary of the International Federation of Chemical and General Workers, argue that what is good for the owners of capital or the consumers of their products may not be good for those who are employed in capital-intensive industries. These arguments are set out at length in his book *International Trade Unionism* (Allen and Unwin, London, 1972). In particular he says new investment by these corporations is primarily aimed not at increasing overall production but 'to improve their profit margin and the resulting cash flow into the company by raising the rate of productivity'.

Without a European Communities' director to dictate where industry would develop—possibly in conjunction with a Regional Policy—those who wanted work needed to go to the places where it was to be found. Articles 48 and 49 of the Treaty of Rome (pp. 336–7) set out the principles governing free movement of labour and some of the measures necessary to put it into effect.

The people who have taken advantage of the opportunities offered by the regulations—workers moving from one Community country to another—have been far outnumbered by those coming to work in EEC countries from outside, as the next extract shows (pp. 337–42).

Migrant workers are in two categories depending on whether they start from member or non-member states, with Community nationals the more privileged class. The retention of social benefits while moving from one EEC state to another (see Article 51) removes a major disincentive to moving from one state to another (p. 342). The term 'worker' has a definite meaning in Community Law, referring to all wage- and salary-earners with the exception of civil servants in local or national government. Self-employed workers are governed by Articles 52–8 of the Treaty of Rome and those providing services under Articles 59–66.

The extract following the one on the benefits of being a Community migrant is a classical Marxian analysis which shows both the role of immigrants in the capitalistic economy, and how in practice those who suffer most are the workers entering the Community from outside its boundaries (pp. 344–50). Castles and Kosack end their piece with a call for workers' solidarity to end the evils of the system as they see it.

The apparent complacency of European trade unionists to the plight of the less privileged manual worker is brought out in the article by Jonathan Power that follows (pp. 350–5). Power quotes Pompidou's statement that 'Immigration is a means of creating a certain easing in the work market and of resisting social pressure', and also quotes an Italian trade union leader who says 'If we didn't have foreign workers there would be inflationary pressures. You have to remember we have to compete with the Japanese and the Americans.'

For British workers the problem has not been seen as just competing with the Americans or the Japanese, but with the rising economic power and opportunities in the European States she had fought for or against in two world wars. The emotional content of the headline placed in giant letters above the front page story by Keith Mason which is the next extract (pp. 355–6) would not have been lost on those who were old enough to remember the voice of the Briton who broadcast from Germany during the Second World War. 'Germany Calling' were the opening words of each broadcast by Lord Haw Haw (as he was popularly known), and the headline was an ironic reminder of the power of German industry.

The realities of the situation, with the opportunities seen in perspective, are analysed at slightly greater length by Peter Stephenson (pp. 356–9), and the changing patterns of employment away from the purely manual are considered in the extract from Campbell Balfour (pp. 360–1). Balfour makes the point that in addition to the economic forces of 'demand pull' and the 'push' of unemployment there are other circumstances which affect the willingness to move.

The *ability* to move is governed by additional factors such as the regulations imposed by separate national laws mentioned in the piece by David Cross (pp. 361–2), and the difficulties in arriving at agreed definitions of what are equivalent qualifications so that skilled or professionally qualified workers are able to move freely, which are shown in the next two extracts (pp. 363–9).

The final piece (pp. 369–70) is a short exchange from question time in the House of Commons in which the Scottish advocate, Ronald King Murray, drew the attention of the Education Minister, Mrs. Margaret Thatcher, to the fact that after more than three and a half centuries of union, Scotland and England did not have mutual recognition of the certificate given to school leavers.

7.2 Article 67 (Free Movement of Capital) Treaty of Rome

1. During the transitional period and to the extent necessary to ensure the proper functioning of the common market, member States shall progressively abolish between themselves all restrictions on the movement of capital belonging to persons resident in member States and any discrimination based on the nationality or on the place of residence of the parties or on the place where such capital is invested.

2. Current payments connected with the movement of capital between member States shall be freed from all restrictions by the end of the first stage at the latest.

(Treaty establishing the European Economic Community. Cmnd. 4864, HMSO, London, 1972.)

7.3 Articles 48 and 49 (Free Movement of Labour)
Treaty of Rome

Article 48

1. Freedom of movement for workers shall be secured within the Community by the end of the transitional period at the latest.

2. Such freedom of movement shall entail the abolition of any discrimination based on nationality between workers of the member States as regards employment, remuneration and other conditions of work and employment.

3. It shall entail the right, subject to limitations justified on grounds of public policy, public security or public health:

(a) to accept offers of employment actually made;

(b) to move freely within the territory of member States for this purpose;

(c) to stay in a member State for the purpose of employment in accordance with the provisions governing the employment of nationals of that State laid down by law, regulation or administrative action;

(d) to remain in the territory of a member State after having been employed in that State, subject to conditions which shall be embodied in implementing regulations to be drawn up by the Commission.

4. The provisions of this Article shall not apply to employment in the public service.

Article 49

As soon as this Treaty enters into force, the Council shall, acting on a proposal from the Commission and after consulting the Economic and Social Committee, issue directives or make regulations setting out the measures required to bring about, by progressive stages, freedom of movement for workers, as defined in Article 48, in particular:

(a) by ensuring close cooperation between national employment services;

(b) by systematically and progressively abolishing those administrative procedures and practices and those qualifying periods in respect of eligibility for available employment, whether resulting from national legislation or from agreements previously concluded between member States, the maintenance of which would form an obstacle to liberalisation of the movement of workers;

(*c*) by systematically and progressively abolishing all such qualifying periods and other restrictions provided for either under national legislation or under agreements previously concluded between member States as impose on workers of other member States conditions regarding the free choice of employment other than those imposed on workers of the State concerned;

(*d*) by setting up appropriate machinery to bring offers of employment into touch with applications for employment and to facilitate the achievement of a balance between supply and demand in the employment market in such a way as to avoid serious threats to the standard of living and level of employment in the various regions and industries.

(Treaty establishing the European Economic Community. Cmnd. 4864, HMSO, London, 1972.)

7.4 Migrant Workers in the EEC

There are two main groups of migrants: firstly those from other highly developed countries (usually within the Community) who move in search of a better job and new experience; secondly those from countries outside the Community—Southern Europe, North Africa and even further afield—who leave their own countries to escape unemployment and poverty. In many ways, workers who come from Southern Italy are more like the second group than the first. As the figures indicate the group of people from backward regions with poor educational standards and little industry is by far the largest.

Some immigrants come to Community countries permanently. Others come for a few years only, in the hope of saving enough money to go home and build a better life there. There are important differences in the cultural backgrounds of the various immigrant nationalities. On the one hand are the Italians and Spaniards whose cultures and languages are not very distant from those of France; on the other the Turks and North Africans whose languages are quite unlike those of Western Europe and who have been brought up in Muslim societies. An intermediate position is taken up by people coming from the most backward parts of Europe, like Portugal and Greece.

But once these different groups arrive, their aim is a common one: they hope to gain prosperity for themselves and their families by working in the highly developed industries of Western Europe. In recent years, the economic, social and cultural integration of immigrants has become an important problem for several Community countries as well as for the governing bodies of the Community itself.

Economic Importance

Foreign workers make a vital contribution to the labour force in all the Community countries except Italy (which is still a major source of emigrants) and the Netherlands (where foreigners were only 2·1 per cent of all employees in 1966). . . .

The economic importance of foreign workers lies not just in their numbers, but in the fact that they are willing to take jobs which nationals of the host countries reject because the wages are poor, the working conditions unpleasant or the social status low. Immigrants, usually hampered by ignorance of the language, poor basic education and lack of vocational training, enter the occupational hierarchy at the bottom. Their presence helps to make it possible for nationals of the host countries to leave the less desirable jobs and move up into skilled, supervisory and white-collar positions. Thus immigration is a factor assisting the social promotion of the national population. . . .

Immigrants from within the EEC

Community Policy

The free movement of labour within the Community was a basic part of the plan for European integration laid down in the Rome Treaty (Article 49). It has been achieved in three stages, concluding with the adoption of Regulation No. 1612/68 by the Council of Ministers of 29 July 1968—18 months ahead of the original schedule.

Citizens of EEC member States have the right to take up employment in any member State and may even go there for up to three months to seek work. Member States may no longer discriminate against citizens of other Community countries by giving their own nationals priority in employment or placement through the labour exchanges. Furthermore, all EEC citizens enjoy 'Community priority' over the nationals of outside countries. A Community worker no longer needs a work permit, but still requires a residence permit, which is issued for five years and is automatically renewable. This may be refused only for 'reasons of public order, safety or health'.

Community workers now enjoy equal treatment in virtually all matters relating to employment. This includes taxation, social security, the right to bring in family members, the right to own a house, access to public housing, and the right to be elected to workers' representative bodies at the place of work. Only a few restrictions still exist: Community workers can only bring their families if they provide evidence that they have an adequate dwelling, which can be very difficult in some countries; they do not have full civic rights, like the right to vote, in other Community countries; they cannot be elected to public office, which in France includes the post of trade union official.

Freedom of movement for workers within the Six has become a reality, yet, at the same time, the actual number of workers taking advantage of the opportunity has not increased. Indeed, migration between the Community countries has actually declined. In 1961, 292,494 first work permits were issued to citizens of member States moving within the Community. In 1967 the figure was only 129,138. Even if we discount 1967, which was a recession year in some Community countries, and take the 1966 figure we still find a slight decline—only 260,619 workers moved within the Community.

This apparently paradoxical situation is explained by the development of the Italian economy, partly as a result of the new opportunities presented by the EEC. About four-fifths of migrants within the EEC have always come from Italy, but now the large reserves of unemployment which existed there only ten years ago have been largely absorbed by rapid industrial development. Northern Italy is even beginning to experience labour shortages and some Italian firms (Alfa-Romeo for instance) have sent recruiting teams to Germany to persuade their compatriots to return to highly-paid jobs in Milan or Turin.

The pool of unemployed which still remains in Southern Italy is no longer a source of labour for the rest of the Community since, for reasons of their age, background and so on, many of these people are not readily adaptable. The solution to their problem must lie in social and regional development policies and not in emigration.

The legal barriers to migration within the Community may have disappeared, but social, linguistic and cultural barriers still exist. As wages and conditions in the Community countries level off, the economic incentive to surmount such barriers declines. The main type of labour movement which is now developing between Community countries is no longer a south to north migration of impoverished, unskilled men. It is that of highly-skilled technicians and experts, whose services are required throughout the Community. Such employees tend to take their families with them and adapt easily to their new surroundings, so that temporary migration no longer means involuntary separation and hardship.

Workers from Outside

Apart from the temporary economic setback of 1966–7, the demand for unskilled and semi-skilled workers has continued to grow. Due to losses in both World Wars and low birth-rates in the 'thirties, all the Community countries have populations with increasing proportions of old people, dependent on a relatively static labour force. Thus the additional workers needed cannot come from within these countries. Moreover, Community nationals who have been able to benefit from vocational training and promotion opportunities are less and less willing to take dirty arduous manual jobs. A situation of international competition for scarce labour has developed, and employers and labour ministries have had to look further and further afield for new workers. . . .

No Common Policy

The Community has no common policy towards immigrants from non-member countries, and the regulations and practices governing the workers' legal, economic and social position vary widely. Migrants from outside the Community are usually at a considerable disadvantage compared with Community citizens. Their freedom to change jobs is restricted, for some years at least, and this helps to ensure that they do not compete for the more desirable jobs. They are usually only allowed to bring in their families after a year or more. Their political and trade union rights are severely limited.

Although some EEC countries have bilateral agreements with non-Community countries about the social security of immigrants,

immigrants from outside the Community do not always have equality with regard to social security. If a Community national has an accident or loses his job, he is entitled to social insurance benefits in his home country, but such benefits are not generally transferred abroad in the case of non-Community citizens. Such workers are also often worse off with regard to family allowances—an important factor in countries like France, where family allowances may form a very high proportion of a family's income.

Illegal Immigration

Many problems arise from the spontaneous nature of the migratory movements. Both France and Germany have recruitment offices abroad which select workers, tell them about the working and living conditions to be expected and provide transport. Men recruited in this way find work and housing awaiting them. But an increasing proportion of the migration does not go through the official systems. In 1968, 82 per cent of immigrants to France came 'clandestinely', i.e. without work permits, or often without passports or any papers at all. This is because the official system is slow and inefficient. Many Portuguese workers come illegally in order to escape military service, which lasts three to six years and usually means being sent to fight in Angola or Mozambique.

The clandestine immigrants arrive in a completely new and strange society, with no idea of how to find work or accommodation. Such men are easily exploited and have no chance of help from the law or the unions as they are illegal immigrants: taxi-drivers overcharge them, 'agents' take large sums of money for finding them work and getting documents. Many employers (particularly in small building firms) take them on because their weak position compels them to accept low wages. . . .

Future Trends

The home countries of the immigrant workers hope that labour migration will help in their economic development. They hope to get back a core of highly-trained industrial workers and that workers' savings will provide a source of foreign currency for the purchase of capital goods abroad. At present such potential benefits are often merely wishful thinking. Most foreign workers from countries outside the Community do not obtain vocational training which would be useful to them on their return home, and their savings are usually spent on consumer goods or on unproductive small businesses in the services sector. . . .

The emergence of a new lower-class of immigrants can only be prevented by the recognition of the international unification of the labour market which is already coming about, and the granting of full social and political rights to immigrants, wherever they come from.

(Extracted from European Studies Teachers' Series no. 8, London, Centre for Contemporary European Studies, University of Sussex: European Community Information Service, 1970.)

7.5 Article 51 (Social Rights of Migrant Workers) Treaty of Rome

The Council shall, acting unanimously on a proposal from the Commission, adopt such measures in the field of social security as are necessary to provide freedom of movement for workers; to this end, it shall make arrangements to secure for migrant workers and their dependants:

(a) aggregation, for the purpose of acquiring and retaining the right to benefit and of calculating the amount of benefit, of all periods taken into account under the laws of the several countries;

(b) payment of benefits to persons resident in the territories of Member States.

(Extracted from the Treaty establishing the European Economic Community, Cmnd. 4864, HMSO, London, 1972.)

7.6 Equal Treatment of Migrant Workers
ROGER BROAD and R. J. JARRETT

One of the few cases where the Treaty does give clear powers to the Community institutions in the social field is that of ensuring equal treatment for Community nationals working in another member country under the free movement of labour arrangements. These workers now have the right to exactly the same conditions of employment, trade union rights, social security and housing entitlements as nationals of the country in which they are working. Thus for example, an Italian worker residing in Germany with his family—he has the right to bring his family with him of course—is entitled to exactly the same medical care, family allowances and other social benefits as a German worker, and must pay the same contributions too. Furthermore, if he has left his family in Italy, though he will be paying into the German social security fund, his wife can draw full benefits from the Italian scheme. And the aggregation of periods of employment and contribution means that on retirement, whether he returns to Italy or remains in Germany, he will draw a full pension based on his contributions throughout his working life, irrespective of which member countries he may have worked in. It is estimated that well over two million people—workers and their families, and pensioners—are receiving benefits under these EEC regulations. It is also illegal for a Community employer to pay lower rates to workers from another member country than to fellow nationals.

(Extracted from *Community Europe Today*, Oswald Wolff, London, 1972, pp. 182–3.)

7.7 Immigrants: West Europe's Industrial 'Reserve Army'

STEPHEN CASTLES and GODULA KOSACK

Labour immigration has become a general feature of modern western Europe. The total of over eleven million immigrants forms a significant percentage of the population, and an even larger share of the labour force, in every highly industrialised country. Considerable attention has been paid to the impact of immigration on the labour market, and even more to the social problems of immigrants. Yet few attempts have been made to examine the role of immigration in the political economy of contemporary capitalism. This is probably because immigration has—on the whole—developed spontaneously and without planning. But the general nature of the phenomenon shows that it cannot be regarded as coincidental. It is necessary to seek its origin and function in the structure of the capitalist system. To do so, however, requires the re-examination of certain traditional structural features of capitalism.

One of these features concerns the relationship between employment level, wages, profits and economic growth. Marx regarded a pool of unemployed workers (the 'surplus population' or 'industrial reserve army') as 'the lever of capitalist accumulation', and 'a condition of existence of the capitalist mode of production'. Only if employers bring more and more workers into the production process can they accumulate capital—the precondition for extending production and applying new techniques. These new techniques replace labour with capital, and make workers redundant, providing a labour reserve to be thrown into other sectors as required. The pressure of unemployment forces those workers lucky enough to have jobs to accept long hours and poor conditions. Above all, says Marx, 'the general movements of wages are exclusively regulated by the expansion and contraction of the industrial reserve army'. If unemployment falls, workers are in a better position to demand higher wages. Profits and capital accumulation then fall, investment declines and there is a new down-turn in the economy. Men are thrown out of work, and this leads to a growth in the reserve army and a fall in wages. This is the basis of the capitalist economic cycle: the boom–

slump pattern typical of the system before 1945. But if capitalism has to manage without unemployment, how can the growth of wages, and the resulting pressure on profits, be avoided?

The solution adopted by western Europe has been to recruit immigrant workers from the underdeveloped areas of southern Europe and the Third World. Just like the impoverished agricultural workers of Marx's time, the unemployed and underemployed masses of these areas today form a 'latent surplus-population', ready to move into jobs in the industrial sector of western Europe as soon as they are allowed to. The possibility of recruiting this industrial reserve army in other countries has the same economic effect—putting pressure on wages and keeping profits up—as an internal reserve of unemployed workers. But its important advantage is that it does not lead to political tension in the event of a recession: the social costs of unemployment can simply be exported to the countries of origin of the immigrants—as the United National Economic Commission for Europe aptly put it, regarding the West German recession of 1966/7.

Another traditional feature is the relationship between socio-economic differentiation within the labour force and the development of working-class consciousness. From the beginning of industrialisation, employers have given special privileges—better pay, salary instead of wages, different clothing, more security—to certain sections of the working class, such as craftsmen, foremen, non-manual workers. The aim was to make such workers regard themselves as better than other workers, and identify their interests with those of the employers. This 'labour aristocracy' weakens class consciousness and provides an opportunistic leadership for sections of the labour movement.

Employing immigrant workers creates a new form of differentiation within the working class. The immigrants form 5 to 10 per cent of the total labour force in the major industrial countries (over 30 per cent in Switzerland). But, due to their concentration in specific jobs, the percentage in certain industries and socio-economic categories is much higher. Immigrants are overwhelmingly manual workers (in Germany, for instance, only 1 per cent are non-manual) and this category contains the mainly unskilled and semi-skilled groups. They are concentrated in productive industry and in construction, and generally have jobs offering poor wages or bad working conditions or both. In Germany, for example, nearly a quarter of all construction workers are foreigners, as are 19 per cent of plastic, rubber and asbestos workers, and 16 per cent of leather, textile and clothing workers. Immigrants tend to be under-represented in the services sector, except for domestic service (29 per cent of all foreign women in France) and catering (19 per cent of all catering workers are foreign in Germany). Certain tasks, like monotonous assembly line work, are overwhelmingly carried out by immigrants. This is best seen by examining specific factories: the Ford works in Cologne employs 25,000 workers, of whom 10,000 are Turks and 5,000 other foreigners. But, on the actual assembly line, nearly all the workers are Turks. The Germans, the Italians and other nationalities who have been in Germany longer, have moved into more satisfying and better-paid jobs. The newly-arrived Turks have to take the jobs which nobody else wants.

The tendency towards segregation is also found outside work: immigrants have low-quality overcrowded housing in rundown areas, or live in special hostels near the factory. Local workers get public housing or even become owner-occupiers. Immigrant children are sent to overcrowded old schools, where little attention can be paid to their special problems. In most countries, immigrant workers are deprived of civil and political rights, so that it is difficult for them to participate actively in class organisations. In general, immigrants today form a very large proportion of the working class in the occupations and in the urban-industrial centres which have been the traditional basis of working-class militancy. But the working class has become divided into two distinct sections which have little contact with each other and little opportunity to communicate (the language problem makes matters even worse).

To many local workers, the immigrants appear inferior and discrimination against them seems justified. At the same time, they are a threat to wages and conditions and are competitors for housing and other social facilities. This impression of immigrants is far from being unrealistic: they are indeed recruited by the employers, who hope that this expansion of the labour supply will put pressure on wages. But instead of recognising this and using working-class solidarity to defeat the strategy, many local workers blame the immigrants themselves and react with hostility towards them. Such reactions often show social prejudice ('the blacks are dirty', 'the Italians come to live off the unemployment benefit').

Many indigenous workers behave as a 'labour aristocracy' in relation to the immigrants. This splits the working class and weakens the labour movement. The campaigns of Enoch Powell in Britain or of James Schwardenbach in Switzerland are often regarded as the actions of a lunatic fringe, but when Governments are hostile towards the immigrants for political purposes, the matter is more serious. In 1964, the German federal Chancellor, Erhard, reacted to a trade union campaign for shorter working hours by calling on German workers to work longer to avoid the need for more foreign workers. In May 1968, the French Government tried to persuade French workers not to join the general strike by blaming it on foreign agitators, and expelled hundreds of foreign trade unionists to prove their point.

Comparing immigrant patterns and economic trends in Britain and Germany helps to demonstrate the function that immigrant labour has come to have. Britain recruited foreign workers (the 'European voluntary workers') for specific tasks during the postwar reconstruction period up to 1950. After that there was spontaneous immigration of Commonwealth citizens, which, as Ceri Peach has shown, closely matched British labour demand. However, racialist campaigns led to the end of this movement in the early 'sixties. Britain has, in fact, had no net immigration since 1945, as British emigration overseas has cancelled out the inward movements. The stagnant labour force has been a major factor in the stop-go development of the British economy. Without a reserve army, business has been forced to raise wages early on in every wave of expansion, which has quickly led to inflation and recession.

West Germany, on the other hand, has striven to maintain a flexible labour market (another name for the industrial reserve army) ever since the currency reform of 1948. At first this was provided by the seven million expellees from the former eastern provinces and by the three million refugees from the German Democratic Republic. Throughout the 'fifties, these reserves kept wage-growth slow and provided the basis for the 'economic miracle'. By the mid-'fifties, special labour shortages appeared, first in agriculture and industry, then in unskilled industrial occupations. It was then that organised recruitment of foreign labour started. By the time the Berlin Wall stopped further labour movements from the east in 1961, German industry was beginning to recruit on a very large scale in south Europe and Turkey.

By 1966, there were 1·3 million immigrant workers in Germany. But the new source of labour was not as adaptable as the old: the foreigners did not speak the language, had little basic education and virtually no industrial training. Wages for unskilled work were held back, but labour shortages in skilled occupations led to wage increases in this sector, which were large enough to affect the average wage rate for the whole economy.

In the early 'sixties, wages rose not only absolutely, but also as a percentage of national income, resulting in a squeeze on profits. This trend was stopped by the recession of 1966/7. Real wage rates fell, but the effects of unemployment on German workers were cushioned through the reduction of the foreign labour force by 400,000. A new economic expansion and further mass labour immigration followed rapidly. Today there are about 2·3 million immigrant workers, plus about 1·5 million dependents in West Germany, indicating a rate of immigration far more rapid than Britain has ever known.

If mass immigration, like any plentiful labour supply, restrains wages at first, the long-term effect may be the opposite. By providing the capital for expansion, plentiful labour provides the basis for productivity growth. German wages were far lower than British wages in 1950; today the situation has been reversed. On the other hand, the share of wage and salary earners in the national income has increased at a far slower rate in Germany than in England. The British worker gets a bigger share of a smaller cake. The British Immigration Act, 1971, may be taken as a recognition of the need for plentiful labour supply by Britain's rulers. The law could be used as a framework for setting up a system of organised labour recruitment on the West German pattern. Workers could be admitted to carry out specific jobs on time-limited permits. The right to change jobs would be restricted and the workers would remain under strict control. The current existence of large-scale unemployment in Britain makes it impossible (or unnecessary) to put these provisions into force. In fact, at the moment, British workers are joining the German labour force in ever-increasing numbers. The engineers being made redundant in the British aircraft, shipbuilding and mechanical industries could provide a new form of latent industrial reserve army: one consisting of skilled workers, which could put pressure on the wages of the German labour aristocracy.

The economic and social effects of immigration cannot be a matter of indifference to the trade unions. Immigration is a traditional weapon of the employers against labour organisations. But opposition to labour immigration as such would be a self-defeating strategy. It would lead those immigrants already present to think of unions as their enemies, and deepen the split in the working class. This is no abstract construction—it has actually happened in Switzerland. Here the unions have campaigned for a reduction in the number of foreign workers since the mid-'fifties. At the same time, they have called on foreign workers to join the unions, but with little success. Since there are many industries where immigrants form the majority of the labour force, the unions in these sectors find themselves seriously weakened. Indeed the total membership of the Swiss Trade Union Federation is declining. The unions see the only solution in compulsory 'solidarity contributions' to be deducted from the wages of non-members by the employers.

In other countries, policies have varied considerably. The British unions opposed the recruitment of European Voluntary Workers after the war, but welcomed the Commonwealth immigrants. However, action against discrimination has rarely gone beyond moral appeals. In fact the TUC was long opposed to anti-discrimination legislation, seeing it as a dangerous precedent for State intervention in industrial relations.

The French CGT opposed immigration completely during the late 'forties and the 'fifties, condemning it as a weapon of the bosses. More recently the CGT, like the other two main trade union federations, the CFDT and the FO, have come to regard immigration as inevitable. All have special secretariats to deal with immigrant workers' problems and do everything possible to bring them into the unions. The German DGB also has offices which advise and help immigrant workers. There are foreign language bulletins and special training courses for foreign shop stewards. Union membership among immigrants is relatively high (about 25 per cent) in Germany, although this figure is still below the national average for the industries where immigrants are concentrated.

On the whole, union policies have been based on humanitarian considerations, rather than on an appreciation of the function of immigration in the political economy. The policies have therefore consisted mainly of *ad hoc* measures designed to counter specific instances of extreme exploitation, or to deal with certain social problems. No global strategies to counter the use of immigration as an industrial reserve army and to weaken class consciousness have been used.

Such strategies would have to pursue the following aims: the elimination of racialism and chauvinism within the working class, the large-scale integration of immigrant workers in the labour movement and elimination of discrimination against immigrants. This last point may be regarded as the precondition for the other two. As long as there is economic, social and legal discrimination against immigrants, local workers are bound to regard them with suspicion as potential tools of the employers. Similarly, as long as segregation between the two sections of the working class persists, immigrant participation in the labour movement is very hard to achieve. Eliminating discrimination means not only equal pay for equal work, but also equal employment, promotion and training opportunities for immigrants. In the social field, discrimination in housing allocation, as well as in education, must be fought.

Above all, the unions must seek the abolition of laws restricting the labour market freedom and the political rights of immigrant workers. The unions seem, by their silence, to acquiesce in the discriminatory legislation which exists throughout Europe.

(Extracted from *New Society*, 30 November 1972.)

7.8 The New Proles of Europe
JONATHAN POWER

'Judging from the way you British talk,' one European bureaucrat said to me over coffee, 'one would think you were the only country in the world that had ever received an immigrant. Do you realise that during the 1960s Germany alone imported ten times as many immigrants as you?' I grabbed a taxi to the nearest reference library. He was right. Germany now has two and a quarter million foreign workers plus a million dependants; France has even more. Britain has a mere 1,800,000 immigrants.

In this country, the question of immigrant labour is wrapped up in the old myths of Empire. It is still seen as some sort of reparation for the sins of our fathers. In Germany, it is a fact of business life. Germany looks at and talks about its foreign labour in a totally self-interested way. The coinage of the vocabulary reflects this. The foreign workers are called *Gastarbeiter*, guest workers, implying that they are in Germany only at the behest of the Germans and for a short period of time at that. It suggests some form of privilege—that the Germans are doing *them* a service. Until very recently the German Government talked about the concept of *Konjunkturpuffer*, that is the importation of foreign labour when it is needed during a boom and its re-export during a recession. Roger Böhning of the University of Kent, who has just completed a book on immigration in Europe says: 'In 1967 the Germans had a minor recession and everyone thought this was the time when the foreign workers would go home and the German workers would move over to take their places. But it didn't happen. Recruitment figures fell, yes, and some workers went back home earlier than they had planned. Even so more than 150,000 new workers came into Germany that year. The fact is the Germans just didn't want those kind of jobs. The more the social reality showed that Germany was a country of immigration, the louder were the official denials this was or even should be the case.'

In private conversation however German officials are quite forthcoming. Indeed officialdom all over Europe is all too ready to confide its private fears. There's no debate about it—almost everyone agrees —that unless there is a radical and unprecedented restructuring of the European economy, Europe's future growth will be dependent on large amounts of cheap, unskilled foreign labour. The native European working force is shrinking, but the European economy is expanding.

All European countries have experienced a great influx since the Second World War of foreign workers. In Germany they are nearly all white—Greeks, Turks, Yugoslavs, Spaniards and Italians. In France the principal groups are Portuguese, Spanish and North Africans. In Belgium they are mainly Italians, Turks and Greeks. In Holland, besides Indonesians (who are refugees rather than immigrant workers), there are West Indians, Turks, Greeks and Italians.

They are the new proletarians doing the menial jobs, poorly paid with little job security (unless they are Italians—fellow members of the EEC), perhaps separated from their families and living in housing that is often appalling.

Yet in the opinion of most economists, industrialists, trade union leaders and politicians, the tremendous economic growth that has been experienced in Europe ... would not have been possible without them. Chancellor Brandt succinctly summed up their contribution when he said: 'In every way, foreign workers help us to earn our daily bread. Although foreign workers are in Germany because at home they live in indigent circumstances, Germany needs them urgently. They're dependent on us. But we are even more dependent on them, for otherwise they would not be here.'

President Pompidou put it rather more crudely when he said in September 1963: 'Immigration is a means of creating a certain easing in the work market and of resisting social pressure.'

The plain fact is that Europe cannot do without its foreign labourers. Ever since the industrial revolution, the capitalist machine has been sucking in labour. First its own people, and then, when the drift from the land was not sufficient, the industrialising countries reached out to the more backward areas of Europe. . . .

The foreign labour force is now of such a size and of such a strategic importance to the European economy that it can no longer be written off as a temporary phenomenon. As Dr. Waldraff, the personnel manager of Bosch, the great German electrical company, told me, 'I wouldn't be surprised if by the end of the decade half our blue-collar staff were non-German.' . . .

It is a gigantic problem and each Common Market country has tackled its responsibility differently. If there is any common thread to these policies it is that they are haphazard, makeshift and geared primarily to meeting the narrow needs of the host country.

Nowhere is this more true than in Germany. By maintaining the public fiction that it is not a country of immigration it manages to get away with all kinds of unacceptable behaviour. A court ruling in Munich last year stated that since the *Gastarbeiter* only stay temporarily in Germany they cannot be regarded as 'part of the population'. As a result, proceedings against numerous pub owners in southern Germany who had put up notices banning *Gastarbeiter* from their premises had to be dropped. The fiction of the temporary worker also helps Germans to justify their very restrictive policy on the right of workers to bring their families to join them. At the moment, only the Italians have this automatic right. The others cannot, unless they can prove they have suitable family accommodation. And in Germany that just cannot be had.

It is almost impossible to find a major employer in Germany who will publicly back a family policy for immigrants. Bosch is considered to be one of Germany's most progressive employers. It was the first company in Germany to introduce sickness benefits and accident compensation. But Dr. Waldraff was unresponsive to my suggestion that a benign family policy would give him a more effective workforce: 'The fact that they can't get housing is partly their fault. They want to save a lot to take it home. They don't want to spend it here.'

The Germans are quick to point out that their restrictive family policy means that they do not have the French immigrants' slums. That is true. What they have are special workers' camps. Long barrack-like quarters, clean and characterless. Three men to a 12 ft. by 6 ft. room, for which they each pay 30 D-Mark a week. This gives a pretty high return per square foot to the factories that own the barracks. All the big German companies that employ foreign workers use this type of housing—Mercedes Benz, Bosch, Volkswagen. The rules differ from establishment to establishment but basically they are the same—no brothels and no politics. . . .

Paris is still a most incredibly beautiful city, yet around its outer edges are some of the worst slums in the world. They are called *bidonvilles*—literally, tin-can towns. But that is now a euphemism. Today tin cans are a luxury material. For the most part *bidonvilles* are made out of wood and cardboard—mainly cardboard. The majority of their inhabitants are Portuguese and Algerians.

Maria Martins Conde is the wife of a Portuguese worker. Her husband is a road-sweeper. She told me that she had been living in *bidonvilles* for nine years. Now she is living in one in St. Denis. I asked her why she had left Portugal. 'There is no land,' she said, 'no opportunities.' Incredulously, I asked her if anything could be worse than this. 'Here we have money. In Portugal we had nothing.' Her two-room wood and cardboard shack was the best in the *bidonville*; she had lived there longer than most. But it had no toilet and no running water. There was one tap for the sprawling community of 2,000 people. The lavatory was a mud channel that wound itself in half-circles around the shacks. Even if it rained the sewer did not get a decent douche since all the filth agglomerated on the corners. Outside Maria's shack, a mere 50 yards away, workmen were building a new tower block. It was, apparently, mainly for French workers, although 10 per cent of the places would be kept for foreign workers.

As we stood watching the foreign workers building the new flat they were most unlikely to live in, a bulldozer edged up alongside us. We were told to move. It was going to knock down some of the shacks to make way for the building operation. Quietly, without fuss, the shacks toppled over. The tenants had been warned only two days before that their homes were to be destroyed.

In the winter of 1970, there was a fire in one of these *bidonvilles* and four Africans died. The Prime Minister, M. Chaban Delmas, came out to visit the *bidonville*. It was, by all accounts, the first time he had set eyes on one. He was visibly shaken by what he saw and promised on the spot to get rid of them by 1972. But despite significant progress in some Parisian suburbs the overall *bidonville* population is only just beginning to fall. . . .

France has the slowest population increase in Europe. People are retiring earlier and working shorter weeks. Children are staying at school longer. The French Government had estimated that the potential labour supply will be, by 1980, 1,650,000 less than it is today. The working population in France is only 40 per cent of the total compared with 47 per cent in Germany. 'France has no other solution, given the present economic system,' he says, 'but to import foreign labour. That is why we have 3,500,000 and 300,000 more coming in each year.'

As in other European countries, French trade union interest in immigrant workers is slight. The unions have limited themselves to making sure that the wages paid to foreign workers do not undercut their own wage levels. Beyond that very little has been done. France's largest trade union, the Communist CGT, is so institutionalised and is so concerned to aid the Communist Party in its attempt to ingratiate itself with the French middle ground, that it almost completely ignores the foreign workers.

Brussels is the headquarters of the European Free Trade Union Movement—a gigantic TUC for the whole of Europe. It does not however embrace the Communist-backed unions. I talked with Carlo Savoini, one of EFTUM's three secretaries. His view was one I had heard echoed all over Europe wherever I talked to trade union leaders. 'No one in our union disapproves of foreign workers,' he said. 'They have helped make possible the tremendous economic growth that has taken place in Europe since the war—we live in a competitive society. Our wages have gone up a lot already. I doubt if we could increase that rate. If we didn't have foreign workers there would be inflationary pressures. You have to remember we have to compete with the Japanese and the Americans.'

This tone of complacency characterises 'official Europe'. Immigration is seen as inevitable. But there is no real desire to burrow down into its implications and responsibilities. Because the new proletarians are politically handcuffed they are seen as marginal to the real decisions that confront the new dynamic Europe. The Common Market itself has no department dealing with this question in any kind of overall way. One cannot help but feel that only in very recent times has a consciousness of the huge dimensions of the problem begun to filter through that enormous bureaucracy.

The living and working conditions of the immigrants who are already in Europe is only part of the problem. The other part is what is going on in the 'sending' countries. Godula Kosack and Stephen Castles, in their forthcoming book on labour migration in Europe, describes it as 'a form of development aid given by the poor countries to the rich countries—labour migration does nothing to alleviate the backwardness of the regions from which migrants came; indeed it's often a hindrance to development'. This opinion is echoed by Common Market Commissioner M. Coppé: 'These migrations have sometimes made the search for appropriate solutions more difficult by discouraging local investment and industrialisation.'

M. Coppé stressed that the main problem of these underdeveloped countries was the loss of their youngest, most dynamic and better-educated youths. He believes 'the time has come to export capital rather than bringing people here'. . . .

(Extracted from the *Observer* Colour Supplement, 30 July 1972.)

7.9 Germany Calling!
200,000 Jobs for Britain's Unemployed
KEITH MASON

Work in West Germany is to be offered to Britain's jobless at local employment exchanges.

Britain has 815,000 people out of work. Booming West Germany wants at least 200,000 more workers—including many skilled men.

An agreement to channel German vacancies through our 1,000 exchanges was announced last night.

It was reached at a four-day London conference between employment officials of both countries.

The agreement is a foretaste of what could happen on a still bigger scale if Britain joins the Common Market.

Under Market rules, there is a free flow of workers between all member countries when there are suitable jobs for them.

An Employment Ministry spokesman said last night: '*In Britain, for every vacancy we have on our books, there are four people out of a job.*

'*In West Germany it is the other way round—four vacancies for every person unemployed.*

'German industry is especially short of skilled men in trades like engineering, shipbuilding, metal work and construction.

'We shall pass the German vacancies to exchanges in towns where there is likely to be the right sort of labour.

'There will be no obligation on anyone to go to Germany. But we shall do nothing to stop anyone who wants to go.'

The West German Government will clamp down on 'shark' agencies, some of which have recruited British workers and tricked them out of money.

All recruitment will have to pass through a central office in Frankfurt.

West Germany now has about two million foreign workers, including 15,000 Britons.

Most of the two million are unskilled workers from countries like Turkey, Spain, Greece and Portugal.

Unemployment figures out tomorrow will show that one in twenty of all men in Britain are out of work.

(Extracted from the *Sun*, 19 May 1971.)

7.10 A Common Market for Jobs
PETER STEPHENSON

From the early days of the Common Market debate in this country there have been fantasies about the effect of the free labour market, with a descent of foreign workers on Britain. More recently, there have been suggestions of a counter-flood of British workers to Germany. What will in fact happen?

It is certainly true that the Six have always accepted the principle that a free market in jobs is an essential part of setting up a Common

Market for goods. The provisions whereby workers from a Community country are intended to have the same right to work in any other member country as that country's own citizens have gradually been made more rigorous. All Community workers now have an automatic right to work-permits, residence-permits and any other necessary prerequisites for work in any member country. They have equal rights to representation by trade unions, works committees and similar bodies. Improvements are being made in the arrangements for national employment services to circulate information about vacancies throughout the Community. . . .

There is still the safeguard position that a country may impose measures to discourage Community immigration—not prevent it, just discourage it—if there were indications that it might damage conditions for that country's own workers. But a member country cannot take such action unilaterally; it must obtain Community agreement.

. . . If we look for what effect these measures have had on the labour markets in each of the existing Community countries, it is not easy to see that they have had any real impact at all.

It is true that there are over three million foreign workers in the countries of the Six. But of these, only a million—less than a third of the total—are workers from other Community countries. The remainder are Spaniards, Portuguese, Algerians, Turks, Yugoslavs—a range of nationalities, but none of them covered by the Community arrangements. All of them work under rules laid down by their host governments, with no enforceable rights. Germany is the biggest importer of workers: 2,200,000 comprising 8·3 per cent of her working population—but only 500,000 have come from other Community countries. France has 1,200,000, or 5·8 per cent of her working population—but only 280,000 from the Community.

The fact is that throughout industrial Europe, a significant percentage of low-paid or disagreeable jobs, especially in service trades, are done by imported labour. Britain, with her Commonwealth and Irish immigrants, is no exception. The main difference is that a higher percentage of Britain's 'foreign' workers do in fact speak English than the Community's immigrants speak the language of the country they are working in. And they have taken the step of working in an alien environment with a strange language, because of the contrast between the poverty they could expect at home and the joys of having work, even under the conditions that most immigrants have to accept.

The only Community country that has been a source of such workers has been Italy, and nearly one million Italians work elsewhere in the Community. But when German and French industry is recruiting all round the Mediterranean it is clear that these Italians would have found this work regardless of any Community policies on free movement of labour. The main practical effect of the Community policies is to improve the life of the Italian workers in Germany and France because of the rights they possess that the non-Community immigrants do not. Otherwise, few Frenchmen have gone to work in Germany, or Dutchmen to work in France, or any other significant movements of workers. Even the Italians are increasingly preferring to stay in Italy. For when the choice is no longer between poverty at home and a reasonable job in a foreign country, but rather between a job (or some prospect of a job) at home and a better job abroad, fewer men think the gain is worth the drawbacks of such a move.

So how would we be affected? It must be said at once that there is little reason why Community workers should come to Britain. Wages here now do no more than compare with earnings in most parts of the Community, and are much lower than in Germany. . . .

It is clear that our unemployment is much worse than in Germany or France, though better than in Italy. So when Italians look for work abroad, it will make better sense for them to continue to go to Germany and France rather than try their luck in Britain. But might British workers move abroad? How relevant is the fact that there has been little movement between Community countries, apart from Italy, when we now have unemployment at Italian levels? Could we, too, become suppliers of labour to Continental industry?

To clear our minds about this question we should first realise that it primarily concerns German industry. Only Germany, France and Italy are large enough to be potential outlets for numbers of British workers, and of these Italy is an obvious non-starter. When we look at the demand for labour in France and Germany, a major difference emerges. In France, as in Britain, the last eight years have always shown a surplus of unemployment over job vacancies, though in recent years much less in France than in Britain—in 1971 it was a surplus of 214,000 in France compared with 614,000 in Britain.

In Germany, however, every year except their cut-back year of 1967 has shown a big labour deficit . . . If a large number of

British workers went anywhere on the Continent, it would be to Germany. And it is estimated that nearly 20,000 British workers are there already. But then we have to ask: why not more? Why has not the high unemployment in Britain and labour shortage in Germany produced more movement? For again it must be stressed that Germany has been wide open to foreign workers. When we are in the Community, British workers in Germany will have a more assured status, with more rights. This, together with the general psychological impact of membership, will certainly provide more encouragement for people to move. But, if the potential for a mass movement did exist, we should be seeing it now, while our unemployment is at its peak. In hard numbers it seems unlikely that the 20,000 British in Germany is ever likely to move above, say, 70,000 or so.

It is very clear that any unification of the labour market in the Community, and any consequential effect on British industry, is not going to be caused by large movement of workers across frontiers. That, however, is not the only way unification can take place. It can be, and to some extent already is, the factories that move across frontiers in search of workers.

The most important feature of the British labour market when we join the Community will be that we alone among the members are likely to have a significant number of skilled and experienced industrial workers looking for new jobs. The massive Italian unemployment is still largely the result of men leaving peasant agriculture in order to find industrial work, or workers from small workshops and service trades succumbing to economic changes. A high proportion are young people who have never had proper jobs.

In Britain, however, much of the unemployment is the result of economic change, making industrial workers redundant. Even here, of course, skilled workers are often in short supply: but in comparison with the Continent, especially Germany, we have a surplus. And because there is more need for change in our industrial structure than that of any of our neighbours—where 'structural economic change' still means moving workers from farming into industry—the rest of this decade will see a continual situation of skilled British workers seeking new jobs as their industries run down or their firms go out of business.

(Extracted from *New Europe*, November 1972.)

7.11 Effects of the EEC on Labour Mobility
CAMPBELL BALFOUR

It would seem that the movement of labour both inside and from outside the Common Market has been due more to the 'pull' of employment and the 'push' of unemployment than to the removal of barriers to mobility. Since 1960, the rate of unemployment in Germany has been under 1·0 per cent, and with the Berlin wall halting the flow of refugees from the east, workers migrated from Italy, which had one million unemployed, to the prosperous economy of Germany.

The Italian influx into Germany rose to its peak in 1960 with 73,000 workers, which declined to an outflow of 10,000 by 1964. The Italians arrived in the 1950s and 1960s with an employment permit or the work card of the ECSC. In 1962, for example, there were some 8,000 workers employed by the Federal Railways, of whom 6,500 were Italians. This is indicative of the harder and dirtier jobs undertaken by the migrant workers, as they were cleaning rolling stock and other unskilled work. As in other western countries with expanding economies and labour shortages, immigrant labour fills the vacancies in the mines, steelworks, construction, public transport industries, catering and textiles.

In the mid- and late-1960s the pattern of mobility inside the member countries of the EEC changed from the flow of unskilled and semi-skilled, to one of skilled technicians and experts. The sociological results of this shift in the quality of immigrant labour, accompanied by families, led to greater integration and acceptance within the host country. . . .

An illustration of the way in which high unemployment levels act as a 'push' factor towards high employment areas, even with the barriers of distance and language, can be seen from the estimate that the present number of British citizens working in Germany (17,000) will rise to 150,000 by 1980. As the British had over 900,000 unemployed in September 1971, while the Germans had some 750,000 job vacancies, it seems that this estimate is not exaggerated. In view of the language difficulties, the mobile workers are likely to be the young workers, perhaps some of those who served recently in the forces in Germany, and some of the younger professional men.

(Extracted from *Industrial Relations in the Common Market*, Routledge and Kegan Paul, London, 1972, p. 118.)

7.12 Impediments to Europe's Free Labour Market

DAVID CROSS

A cameraman working for a West German film crew sent to France on a three-year contract falls sick. Under French social security laws he is entitled to draw sickness benefits locally once he has been away from work for four days. But because his contract was drawn up under West German labour laws he can still claim his full salary from his employer for up to six weeks. He thus finds himself in the enviable position of being financially better off sick than he was when he was fit.

In Belgium a French woman executive working permanently for a French subsidiary becomes pregnant. When she leaves work to have her baby she discovers to her horror that she loses out financially.

This is because in Belgium maternity benefits for the first 30 days' absence from work are covered by the employer and not by the social security authorities. But because she has a French employer, who is not bound under French labour laws to continue to pay her salary, she receives nothing during the first month of her absence.

Another West German, working temporarily on a building site in France, is injured in a fall. It is later proved that the accident was caused by the negligence of a French fellow worker. Under a Common Market regulation, the injured worker is entitled to accident benefits paid by the West German insurance authority; under West German insurance laws he cannot in addition sue for damages in a civil court. But because he is working in France he can take advantage of a contradictory French labour law which allows him to claim damages if he suffers an accident at work.

These three cases are typical of many which come up for judgement before tribunals and courts in Common Market countries. But because of the many anomalies in the laws of the Six covering working conditions for employees, it is often very difficult for a court to know exactly which regulation should be implemented in any given case.

As things stand it is quite likely that a West German court will give an entirely different verdict from a comparable court in France, Italy, Belgium or the Netherlands in any identical case.

With more and more people moving from country to country within the Community as they take advantage of EEC laws facilitating the free movement of labour and the free right of establishment for firms and individuals the number of difficult cases is increasing yearly. The enlargement of the Community at the beginning of next year will lead to further complications. Then, not only will the number of workers wanting to move abroad increase, but a new set of different British, Irish, Danish and Norwegian laws will also have to be taken into account.

In a move to remedy this already complicated situation the European Commission, the Common Market's policy-making body, has come forward with a series of guidelines for adoption by member States so that the national courts will be able to choose more readily between conflicting laws.

The proposals which have been submitted to the Council of Ministers for discussion are based on the broad principle that employees working abroad should be subject to the laws applicable in the Common Market country where they are then working.

However, there are a number of exceptions covering specific cases, for example where an employee is posted abroad on a short-term contract initially lasting less than a year.

In support of its proposals the Commission points out that the present anomalies in national laws create a feeling of social injustice among employees wanting to work in other Common Market countries. Unless this sense of unfairness is overcome, the Commission argues, the ideal of complete free movement of labour within the Community could be jeopardised.

(Extracted from *The Times*, 13 March 1972.)

7.13 Equivalence of Qualifications and the Common Market

W. D. HALLS

The main relevant provisions of the Treaty to which attention must be directed are those contained in Articles 48–51, which provide for the free movement of workers, and Articles 52–58, which deal with the right of establishment within the Community. Here one of the central problems is that of equivalences: how far will it be possible for anyone, in any category of employment, to move from one country to another in the exercise of his occupation? The convergences already mentioned in technical education will accelerate this process, but progress towards agreement on this matter has been slow. The legal problems involved are intricate—and the approach has been up to yet largely legalistic. But what is really required—and there is as yet little sign that substantive work is being undertaken in this direction —is to establish how far *educationally* qualifications acquired in one country will be 'equivalent' (read 'acceptable') in another. The practical point is this: how far can a worker arriving from another country with a qualification actually do the job for which he is required in the foreign country?

What progress has been made in this important field up to now? First a number of 'trade descriptions' (or 'occupational profiles') have been compiled. Proposals have been put forward for equivalences for truck drivers, two metallurgical and two construction occupations, and one for skilled machine tool operators. (Incidentally, this last specification alone took three years to prepare; when one recalls that the International Labour Office distinguishes some 60,000 occupations one realises the magnitude of the task that lies ahead.) The basis for the proposals for skilled workers was a documented submitted by the Commission of EEC (i.e. the civil servants) to the Council of Ministers (the politicians). This document enunciated ten principles. The eighth principle envisaged that 'harmonisation of training' (in itself a delicate euphemism) should be achieved by drawing up:

> Occupational monographs including . . . descriptions of basic requirements for access to the various levels of training, according to needs.

Furthermore, the document laid down that 'special attention should be given to the diffusion of teaching syllabuses for occupational and vocational training' and that uniform tests and examinations should be introduced at the Community level. The sheer volume of work that requires to be done before the Treaty of Rome can be implemented fully in its educational aspects is apparent.

In addition to this, thirty-four directives are now in force for occupations relating to a number of jobs for self-employed people at the middle and lower level, in a variety of occupations, from the hotel trade to insurance and real estate.

At the higher level, proposals are now under discussion for certain non-salaried occupations: doctors, accountants, nurses, chemists, bankers, engineers and architects. These proposals for equivalence of qualifications and for mutual recognition are running into heavy weather.... Moreover, the criteria set up for evaluating qualifications seem to be minimal: they concern the total number of years of training, the total number of hours spent in study (itself a loose concept), the obligatory subjects studied, the distribution of hours per subject and the conditions of any practical training given.

Slow although progress has been, the advent of new members to the Community means that the meagre achievement to date will have to be revised. Moreover, the permanent officials of the Commission— here disclaiming the principle of 'supra-nationality' which has been so hotly debated in other fields—have no desire to intervene in the educational and training systems of individual states. Unless, however, those states are themselves willing to seek a much greater harmonisation in their educational systems than they have manifested to date, it is difficult to see how much headway can be made. It is plain that my agreement regarding equivalences for any category of employment is bound eventually to have repercussions upon the whole educational structure. This is ultimately a problem for the DES, but one to which all professional organisations must give attention so as to preserve their own interests.

(Extracted from British Association for Commercial and Industrial Education Annual Conference, 'Into Europe: UK and European Trends in Education and Training', 12–14 September 1972.)

7.14 Harmonisation of Qualifications with Special Reference to the Common 'Profile' for the Training of Qualified Machine Tool Operators

An examination of the Council's pronouncements in the field of vocational training will show that they possess two common features.

Firstly, they are formulated in exceedingly general terms. This is inevitable in view of the range of conditions they have to cover, and the limitations placed on the Council's practical intervention in national systems.

Secondly, there are a few topics which recur with unfailing regularity; and they all have 'harmonisation' as their basic theme: harmonisation of statistics, information, research, methods, terminology—and qualifications. . . .

It was against this background that we discussed the subject of harmonisation of qualifications. We ranged over a wide field, covering mobility of labour, classification of jobs, certification and recognition of qualifications, educational reform and the issue of education versus training, and ending with the training 'profile' for machine tool operators; all related to the problems which entry into the EEC might pose for Britain in these fields.

Mobility of labour is covered in Articles 48 and 52 of the Treaty of Rome. Its implementation is closely bound up with the harmonisation of qualifications.

Here, as far as the UK is concerned, we came up against a difficulty which is based on fundamental differences between the British and Continental systems.

The British approach is based on relative levels of occupations involving a distinction between 'the professions' and the rest. The Continental system is concerned only with whether a person is an employee—'qualified' or not—or whether he is self-employed. Again, the level is immaterial.

If an employee, Article 48 applies; if self-employed, Article 52.

Professional qualifications as such do not exist on the Continent although in some countries titles of qualifications are protected by law. For occupations requiring a high level of theoretical competence the training takes place in state-controlled universities or institutions of similar status.

First degree courses are longer than in the UK—usually five years —and, where appropriate, include some practical training. Graduation automatically carries with it the 'professional' qualification. There are no chartered institutions possessing a legal monopoly to license practitioners.

On the Continent, everyone who has undergone an approved course of vocational training is qualified to practise his 'profession'. This applies to chimney sweeps as it does to lawyers, without regard to class distinction.

As a result, the word 'professional' in the English sense does not exist on the Continent. 'Vocational training' in French is *formation professionelle*; and *Beruf* in German means 'calling', covering every level of gainful activity.

This caused constant confusion among the Commission's highly 'professional' interpreters, and will no doubt continue to do so for some time after British entry . . .

An approach which is common to most systems is the compilation and publication of officially approved training 'profiles' for all main occupations, both technical and commercial. These 'profiles' are nationally adopted, regardless of whether the training is industry- or training-school-based, and the tests of competence are nationally recognised. A very high proportion of the working population qualifies. These systems therefore provide at least a basis for inter-country comparisons.

The absence of a similar national system covering a wide spectrum of occupations in the UK is another point requiring attention.

It was emphasised that, while the possession of a recognised qualification was normal, and a distinct advantage when seeking work, employers were under no obligation to employ only formally qualified applicants. The presence of a large number of British workers in German shipyards was quoted as an example. This liberal approach was likely to continue as long as the present acute labour shortage persisted.

All qualifications originate from the state or from organisations appointed for this task under state supervision. Employers cannot confer qualifications; but this does not debar them from choosing job titles which confer a degree of authority on the holder within the organisation. . . .

As will be apparent from the national reports, job classifications form an important basis of vocational training in Europe. The EEC has made a start with the preparation of a list of occupations dealing with agriculture, metal-working industry and 'information technology' at the level of craftsmen. . . .

The problem of classifications is not regarded as acute by the EEC. The work being undertaken is an attempt to deal with those occupations which are expected to feature prominently in the labour migration pattern within the EEC.

The differences in levels existing for similar occupations in member countries have caused problems. Italy, for example, has only two levels of engineers above that of craftsman, Germany has three. This has led to demands for the creation of a third level in Italy, while in Germany the intermediate engineers wanted to be upgraded. A new designation—'Ing. Grad.'—has, in fact, been introduced in Federal Germany. Like the more senior 'Dipl. Ing.' its use is protected. . . .

To date the Council has issued no directive on the harmonisation of qualifications. The question of certification and recognition of qualifications has been under consideration by an EEC working party on which the candidate members are represented. It has met twice so far. . . .

There are three methods, in descending order of intervention, of bringing about harmonisation: to lay down a syllabus and training plan; to set a common examination; or to establish comparisons between existing qualifications. The Council has now opted for the last of these solutions.

This method poses practical problems. Levels of qualifications vary, even in the same country. The solution lies in discovering the reputation which individual institutions gain for their qualifications, though this is difficult, if not impossible, to put on a formal basis.

The Commission is now exploring a new avenue. It starts from the premise that a diploma is the starting point for a young person, but becomes less relevant for older people. As a result, attempts are now being made to examine the validity of qualifications according to the date of conferment. Under the modern concept of continuous training the first diploma will gradually become irrelevant. . . .

Finally, we dealt with the first and only specific example of a European training profile: that for the training of qualified machine tool operators.[1]

The evidence gained from member countries is conclusive: they support harmonisation in principle, but are not prepared to accept recommendations which require major changes in their domestic training systems. Consequently the common profile, which has the status only of a Recommendation, has failed to gain general acceptance.

Nevertheless, it can be claimed that it is not without influence when appropriate changes are contemplated in national training profiles.

As the Commission's spokesman testified, the preparation of the profile was difficult and protracted. In took two and a half years, though the Commission believes that if it were asked to produce further profiles the experience gained would considerably reduce the time required.

In the present climate of opinion the preparation of further profiles is not contemplated.

While the machine tool operator's profile is only in the form of a Recommendation, it is within the competence of the Council of Ministers to issue training regulations in mandatory form where this is felt to be in the Community's interest. One such regulation is on the point of acquiring legal force. It concerns the training of long-distance heavy goods vehicle drivers. This has already been approved by the Council of Ministers and is now awaiting ratification by the European Parliament, after which it will become legally binding on member governments.

The Times of 17 April 1972 included an article in which the proposed Community legislation is attacked as requiring 'a degree course for lorry drivers'. The Commission's spokesman said that criticisms of the Bill were not confined to Britain: the Commission had received similar complaints. One Government had just suggested curtailment of the course through the deletion of the requirement that drivers must be literate and understand the language of the country concerned. Yet the Commission was aware of serious accidents having been caused by migrant lorry drivers in charge of heavy goods vehicles without being able to read traffic signs and warning notices.

New technologies, which are being adopted on an international scale, and which require the introduction of new training schemes, are seen to offer opportunities for the development of common profiles in the future. The operating of modern steel furnaces was quoted as an example.

Likewise the spread of educational technology is tending to standardise instructional techniques. The Commission has published a number of reports on this topic.

On the question of how long harmonisation would take, the Commission's spokesman would not hazard a guess. He made the interesting observation that progress might be accelerated when migration of skilled and 'professional' labour led to questions of admissibility of qualifications which involved the right of employment or establishment. In these events, a series of legal judgements might create not only a useful body of case law, but might also act as an incentive to positive action.

Reference

1. *The Utilisation of the European Occupational Profile for the Training of Qualified Machine Tool Operators.* Recommendation of the Council of Ministers, 29 September 1970.

(Extracted from *Vocational Training in the European Economic Community*, British Association for Commercial and Industrial Education, London, 1972, pp. 19 ff.)

7.15 Replies to Parliamentary Questions 8 July 1971

Mr. Fred Evans asked the Secretary of State for Education and Science what studies her Department has made of the effect on the British educational system of entry into the Common Market; and whether she will make a statement.

Mrs. Thatcher: No changes in the British educational system will be required as a condition of entry into the Common Market. The Treaty of Rome refers only to:

'mutual recognition of diplomas, certificates and other qualifications' in the context of freedom to practise a profession or calling in another country. The implications of the proposals to implement this part of the Treaty are being studied.

Mr. King Murray: Is the Rt. Hon. Lady aware, when she talks of mutual recognition of qualifications, that there is still not mutual recognition of school certificates between Scotland and England? Should not this matter be put in order before we look at Europe?

Mrs. Thatcher: I do not think that we could wait quite so long as that to look at Europe.

(Extracted from *House of Commons Debates*, 5th Ser., Vol. 820, Col. 1509–10.)

SECTION 8

Community Welfare

8.1 Introduction

Women are unequal. That simple statement is both true and untrue, depending on who and what you are comparing, where you are comparing it and why you have chosen that particular area to compare.

In the context of the European Economic Community women and the pay they should receive is the only aspect of wages policy on which there is a specific rule. Men and women, it says in article 119, should receive equal pay for equal work (p. 373). Like much of the section on Social Policy this has not been achieved.

The French wanted an equal pay clause included when the Treaty of Rome was drawn up, as it was already a legal requirement in France. Even where there have been moves towards women getting equal pay, as with the Dutch minimum wage level, it cannot be said that it has been because of the Rome Treaty. Women's pay in the Community has increased more rapidly than men's in the last decade, but this was not confined to countries which signed the Treaty of Rome—as David Haworth points out (pp. 374–5). Readers may be a little sceptical about the report that British TUC representatives attributed the 1970 Equal Pay Act passed in Britain solely to Britain's impending entry to the EEC. The Act was passed well before there was any indication that Britain would be successful in negotiations to join the EEC.

In 1961 the Six passed a resolution to implement Article 119 and eliminate all discrimination by 1967. What actually happened, and how women in Britain and the original Six have fared is detailed in the next extract (pp. 375–83).

The statistics being compared here, as in other comparative international tables, ought to be treated warily as it is difficult to be sure that like is being compared with like. (The comment that 'only a fraction' of the under-sixes are able to go to a school of some kind is misleading, at least for the Netherlands—where it is 100 per cent—and France—where it is 70 per cent.)

371

The general point that Britain spent relatively little on the fringe benefits and social security side of industry (thus giving them an 'unfair' advantage with regard to wage costs in the eyes of many EEC businessmen) is made in an article by Peter Stephenson (pp. 383–8). Although the precise figures ought again to be taken with a pinch of salt, the overall picture is an accurate one.

The failure of the Community to reach an objective spelled out in unambiguous terms—equal pay—is worth remembering when considering the possibility of achieving an effective European social policy. The general vagueness of the other social policy Articles in the Rome Treaty are not very comforting for those who suspect that the drafters of the Treaty may have had their priorities wrong, with commerce being put before the personal interests of ordinary people (pp. 388–9).

Articles 117 and 118 are declarations of good intent, with the demand for 'harmonisation' of social policies, without a definite commitment, and a list of things where the member States would aim for close collaboration. Article 120, on trying not to reduce the amount of paid holidays, sounds positively stingy now, and article 121 is a procedural measure which emphasises that migrant workers must not be allowed to suffer. Article 122 is a vague catch-all, but is a clause potentially useful to member States which might be interested in doing anything together.

In the extracts that follow, from Mr. Laurie Pavitt and Sir Keith Joseph, the essential difference between the British system of social services—universality v. selectivity based on contribution levels—is emphasised, and put in context (pp. 389–92).

As Sir Keith says, the initiative is left with the individual countries as to what they do, and in which fields. His speech indicates why this may have worked to the advantage of certain countries where the social security element has been of some importance in bargaining for trade unionists. In Britain, talks about 'pay and conditions' have emphasised the former, while continental trade unionists consider both to be important.

Comparing the British and European systems of social security there are three (inter-related) areas which divide Britain from her Community partners across the Channel: (1) Continental European employers and employees both directly contribute more to the social services; (2) the emphasis in Britain has been on financing social services through taxation; (3) the level of payment has been much lower in Britain, but it has been universal (providing a wider net with which to catch the weak, but only giving them a subsistence payment when they fell).

Shirley Williams, in her article (pp. 393–400) deals with the widely-believed myth that Britain's welfare state is one of the most advanced in the world, and the subsequent article (pp. 400–8) fills in a few more details.

The final articles by George Teeling Smith (pp. 408–13) and Charles Hargrove (pp. 413–15) examine a feature of the social security provision which is generally regarded as a separate service in Britain—health care. The first piece lists the differences in the systems of health care, with nationalistic fads and foibles, and concludes that little seems likely to change in Britain as a result of EEC membership; the second highlights the emerging social services problem through the eyes of the French—the number of people who will need to be helped in future is likely to increase as a proportion of the population. Social security could one day be the largest part of the Community's spending, but it may have to await the redrafting of the Treaty of Rome.

8.2 Article 119 (Equal Pay for Women) Treaty of Rome

Each member State shall during the first stage ensure and subsequently maintain the application of the principle that men and women should receive equal pay for equal work.

For the purpose of this Article, 'pay' means the ordinary basic or minimum wage or salary and any other consideration, whether in cash or in kind, which the worker receives, directly or indirectly, in respect of his employment from his employer.

Equal pay without discrimination based on sex means:

(a) that pay for the same work at piece rates shall be calculated on the basis of the same unit of measurement;

(b) that pay for work at time rates shall be the same for the same job.

(Treaty establishing the European Economic Community, Cmnd. 4864, HMSO, London, 1972.)

8.3 Unequal Pay ad lib
DAVID HAWORTH

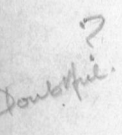

The International Confederation of Free Trade Unions held a conference here this week and pledged itself to an international campaign to secure equal pay for women. Its basis was a survey showing that women in 13 countries earned an average 20 to 30 per cent less than men for similar work.

A Treaty of Rome provision pays lip service to the equal pay principle and British TUC representatives attending the conference were in no doubt that, but for the prospect of her entry into the Common Market, Britain would not have passed an equal pay Act giving a deadline for equality to be realised three years from now. . . .

In Germany, women's average earnings in a number of industrial sectors are approximately 70 per cent of men's earnings. In only one industry, textiles, was the figure 80 per cent. In Belgium, women's earnings are around 75 per cent of men's earnings in most industries, but in a number of sectors the figure is only about 60 per cent.

Developments in the relationship between women's and men's wages in the EEC from 1964 to 1971 show great variations from one country to another and between different industries. In Germany, there were small increases in most industries, whereas in France there was a stagnation in nearly all of them. In Italy, the development has been uneven, although in the past few years the gap between men's and women's wages has been reduced in all sectors. In Belgium and Holland, there has been a definite narrowing of the gap.

It was evident from the speeches of many delegates that patience is wearing thin. Belgium, for instance, has just seen the creation of a women-only political party, and Denmark now boasts a trade union from which men are excluded.

A recent report which the EEC Commission sponsored into the question of equal pay concluded that in all the Common Market countries, in all sectors of the economy, women were less well paid than men.

Nonetheless in Belgium, Germany and Italy public service workers enjoyed equal pay. But this was far from being the case for workers in private industry. These and other States, said a conference report, had merely interpreted the obligation to 'encourage' the equal pay principle and had judged it sufficient for both sides of industry to have complete freedom to settle the issue between themselves.

In France, the principle was recognised just after the war, when laws were passed to do away with reduced wage rates for women and that is still the position. But despite this the French committee on women's employment showed that some 20 per cent of women wage-earners in private and semi-public industries receive only £38 or less a month.

The equal-pay picture throughout the Common Market is still, therefore, a discouraging one for the trade unions. So discouraging, in fact, that one diplomatic observer at the conference remarked at the end of it: 'There is still plenty of time and enough resentment to justify the calling of an equal-pay conference soon.'

At the end a bland statement was issued, but it is clear that unless the women through their unions and their Governments manage to get equal pay on the agenda of the influential EEC employment committee in the near future, progress will be slow—as usual.

Otto Kersten, the ICFTU president, promised that the subject would soon come before the committee—after the Common Market was enlarged next year. But there will be a hard struggle ahead because member-country Governments will fight hard to keep equal pay out of the committee's clutches for as long as they can. They fear that equal pay would only add to the inflationary flames which are scorching all EEC economies.

(Extracted from *The Observer*, 21 October 1972.)

8.4 Women at Work in the Common Market

Article 119 had a very limited aim, but even so its initial impact was small; it did little to reinforce the application of a principle already enshrined in the constitutions of France, Italy and Germany or to induce the Benelux countries to revise their customary practices. In 1961, therefore, its meaning was more precisely spelt out and brought into line with the International Labour Office convention 100, already ratified by four of the Six (and now ratified by all but the Netherlands); this calls for equal pay for work of equal value. At the

376 EUROPEAN COMMUNITY: VISION AND REALITY

same time it was stipulated that differentials between men's and women's pay should be reduced to 15 per cent by June 1962; to 10 per cent a year later and eliminated by December 1964. A Commission Survey, published last year and relating to end 1968, reported progress, but noted that member States were still far from having completely respected all the commitments entered upon. In all countries except the Netherlands, a woman, who feels that she is being discriminated against in respect of pay on grounds of sex alone can bring an action in the courts, and there has been a substantial reduction in instances of direct sex discrimination in collective agreements throughout the Six (it still exists, for example, in dairies and cheesemongeries in Belgium, in the German leather industry and widely in the Netherlands); but the Commission deplores the continued absence of such agreements in a number of industrial sectors and geographical regions in every country, particularly in distribution and the service industries and in small businesses. It is also fully alive to the fact that an apparently non-discriminatory collective agreement does not guarantee a woman the same treatment as a man. For example, only in Holland are the rates set in such agreements roughly the same as those actually paid; elsewhere agreed rates are minima, each firm negotiating actual pay scales. Again, the outlawing of the category 'women's work' has solved no problems: such work has been rechristened 'light' in Germany, 'simple' or 'light' in Italy, 'asexual' in Belgium; it remains ill-paid and is undertaken only by women. Yet again, in evaluating jobs male attributes such as strength are rated more highly than female ones, such as dexterity; France is criticised on this count; the Netherlands, on the other hand, is commended for having a very fair system of job evaluation.

Thus, despite the Common Market's thirteen years, it is impossible to generalise to any great extent about the position of working women in the Six, let alone to make confident comparisons between their status and that of British women workers; each country tends to maintain its traditional ideas of woman's place in society, modifying long-standing practices only slowly and reluctantly.

A Profile of Women at Work in the Community

In Germany and France, as in Britain, about 40 per cent of women of fourteen years and over are at work; in Belgium about 30 per cent; but in Italy and the Netherlands only about a quarter. If the over-65s as well as the under-14s are eliminated the proposition rises to not far short of a half in France but remains at 26 per cent in the Netherlands. Most women workers are married; the proportion ranges from 62 per cent in Belgium to 28 per cent in Holland and is something over 55 per cent in Britain and France. In all countries except Belgium there are substantial regional differences in activity rates. In Britain the highest proportions are found in a diagonal belt of industrialised country running from the South-East through the West Midlands to the North-West; the lowest, in the agricultural areas of the South-West and East Anglia. In the Community, however there is no such close correlation between industrialisation and women's activity rates; Berlin and Paris, it is true, have the highest rates in the Six—with more than half of all women in the appropriate age groups working—but in the Rome region the proportion is under a quarter and in north-west Italy between a quarter and a third. Against this the agricultural areas of west and central France boast among the highest rates. In the 14–19 age group about the same proportion of boys and girls are at work; but whereas most men between 20 and 60 work, among women the activity rate is highest in the 20 to 24 age group, falling sharply in the next quinquennium and remaining low until the forties when there is usually some recovery before a renewed decline in the fifties and sixties.

	West Germany	France	Italy	Belgium	Nether-lands	Great Britain
Working women, 1968—million of whom:	7·8	7·4	5·0	1·0	1·0	8·9
self-employed %	6	9	16	16	4	4
employees %	76	75	62	69	85	96
family helpers %	18	16	22	15	11	—
Women as a proportion of the working population %	34	37	27	28	23	35
Activity rates among women of 14 years and over %	37	39	25	29	24	40
Proportion of working women who are are married %	52	55	53	62	28	57

In West Germany, France and Great Britain women form rather more than a third of the active population, but in Italy and Belgium they represent only 27–28 per cent and in the Netherlands under a quarter. Their status within the labour force varies a good deal both within the Community and between Britain and the Community. In Britain the vast majority are employees; self-employed and family helpers account for only 4 per cent of the total. In the Community, however, family helpers play a substantial role, particularly in Italy, and self-employed women are very important in Italy and Belgium and to a lesser extent in France and West Germany. Most of these self-employed women are, in fact, small farmers—sometimes widows, sometimes wives whose husbands have left the land for more profitable work in the factories. Throughout the Community women provide a greater proportion of all workers in agriculture than they do of paid workers—in Germany they account for more than half of all agricultural workers, only about a quarter of paid agricultural workers. In Britain the opposite is the case. In other sectors the self-employed and family helpers are less important, and women account for roughly the same proportions of all workers as of paid workers. Their contribution to the work force is greater in the service industries, where in Britain, France and Germany they make up over 40 per cent of the total, in Belgium and the Netherlands more than a third; in Italy, however, their share amounts to only 30 per cent. In industry they are least well represented in the Netherlands (only 14 per cent of the work force), while in the major countries they contribute about a quarter.

The service industries, to which women make such a big contribution, in their turn provide women with the greatest employment opportunities: they employ over 70 per cent of all women workers in the Netherlands, about two-thirds of those in the United Kingdom, France and Belgium, and about half in Germany. Agriculture is an important employer in France, Germany and Italy, but negligible in the Low Countries and the UK. Industry takes the highest proportion of women employees in Italy, followed by Germany, with France and Britain next and the Netherlands well behind all the rest.

Within the manufacturing industry, women are heavily concentrated in a few sectors and in the lowest grades: they remain as they always have been, a major element in the textile and clothing industries, although in Britain the introduction of sophisticated machinery is depriving them of some of their traditional jobs, particularly in cotton textiles. For the rest, they are mainly in work that has never involved heavy physical labour, that requires little training, or that demands manual dexterity, such as electronic engineering. Within these broad groupings, custom and practice lay down that some work

Women's Part in the Labour Force: Proportion of all Workers/ Employees (per cent)

	West Germany		France		Italy		Belgium		Nether-lands		United Kingdom	
	All Workers	Employees	All Workers	Employees	All Workers	Employees	All Workers	Employees	All Workers	Employees	All Workers	Employees
Agriculture	52	26	34	15	31	26	29	—	12	7	10	19
Industry	24	28	24	24	21	21	18	19	14	14	25	26
Services	42	41	48	48	31	30	39	36	33	34	42	48
Total	34	31	37	36	27	24	28	26	23	24	35	38

is for men, other for women, often on a wholly irrational basis and varying not only between countries but quite locally within countries.

In general, a third or slightly more of all manufacturing workers in the Six are skilled and roughly another third semi-skilled, but as the enclosed chart shows women make up a near negligible fraction of the total. It is claimed that in Italy 18 per cent and in Belgium 16 per cent

Distribution of the Female Labour Force (per cent)

	West Germany		France		Italy		Belgium		Nether-lands		United Kingdom	
	All Workers	Employees	All Workers	Employees	All Workers	Employees	All Workers	Employees	All Workers	Employees	All Workers	Employees
Agriculture	14	12	14	2	27	12	6	—	4	1	1	1
Industry	35	38	26	31	32	42	29	36	24	26	36	33
Services	51	50	60	67	42	46	65	64	72	73	63	66
Total	100	100	100	100	100	100	100	100	100	100	100	100

of women in manufacturing are skilled, but in France and the Netherlands the figure is only 12 per cent and in Germany a mere 5 per cent; unskilled workers make up more than half the total female labour force in manufacturing in Belgium and Germany and nearly 70 per cent in Luxembourg. Only in Belgium and Luxembourg are more than a third of men in manufacturing classed as unskilled.

Women Employees as a Proportion of all Employees in Certain Major Manufacturing and Service Industries (per cent)

	West Germany	France	Italy	Great Britain
All manufacturing industry	29	31	28	31
Food	44	37	41	42
Textiles	60	57	66	47
Clothing	82	81	74	79
Leather	51	45	43	43
Electrical goods	42	40	33	39
Metal goods	21	16	18	18
Chemicals	26	27	23	29
All services	41	48	30	48
Distribution	54	44	31	55
Banking and insurance	44	44	15	45
Administration	26	40	31	30
Miscellaneous services	61	71	51	62

In the service sector the separation in men's and women's work is no less pronounced: in all countries domestic, personal and welfare services are overwhelmingly female preserves, though with characteristic national distinctions: for example, restaurant workers in Germany are mainly women, in Italy mainly men. In the professions, teaching is predominantly a man's job in Germany and the Netherlands, a woman's in France and Belgium, as it is in the United Kingdom. In Germany most furriers, in France most pharmacists are women. Women have done better in the legal profession in France than they have in the rest of the Six or in Britain; on the other hand there are more women doctors in the UK than there are in France, Germany or Italy. In no Western European country do women engineers approach the importance that they have in the

USSR: in France, which makes the best showing, even now fewer than 4 per cent of all engineers are women.

Although in general women probably have easier access to training in the service sector than they do in industry, they are still concentrated in the lower-paid occupations and except in women's professions hold very few top jobs. No statistical comparison of men's and women's pay is possible in this sector; but the Commission has attempted to compare the average hourly earnings of men and women in manufacturing. Although the figures are not very up-to-date and are very general they serve to illustrate the very secondary position occupied by women.

Protective—and Discriminatory?—Legislation

Some of women's difficulties in the labour market *vis-à-vis* men lie in legislation which enshrines real or supposed differences between the sexes; but some lie in the failure to acknowledge that men's and women's life patterns are different—and that women have changed very substantially and are still changing. Today's labour market is organised by men for men, and employers continue to claim that female labour is less flexible, less trainable, less reliable and more costly to organise than is male labour.

The legislation can be divided into two groups: that centering round childbearing and that which stems from the image of woman as something frailer and less than a man. All the Community countries protect the working mother, but each in its own way. In general

Average Hourly Wage of Workers in Manufacturing (per cent)

	Rate of Increase			Differential between men's and women's wages, October 1966			
	1964–1966	1966–1968	1964–1968				
	Men / Women	Men / Women	Men / Women	Skilled Workers	Semi-skilled Workers	Unskilled Workers	All Workers
Germany	13·9 17·3	9·5 8·8	24·7 27·8	−26·8	−25·6	−21·8	−30·3*
France	12·3 11·3	22·1 24·7	37·1 38·7	−25·8	−19·4	−15·6	−27·5*
Italy	10·9 12·6	9·8 10·0	21·7 23·8	−29·4	−24·0	− 9·1	−24·8
Belgium	18·9 21·8	11·5 12·1	32·6 36·5	−33·2	−28·7	−25·0	−31·9
Netherlands	18·8 24·2	17·0 20·5	38·9 49·7	−40·1	−39·9	−31·3	−39·3

* The apparent anomaly by the average being higher than the individual groups is explained by the fact that women workers are concentrated in the unskilled group while men dominate the skilled and semi-skilled groups.

work prejudicial to health (variously defined) is forbidden to pregnant women and nursing mothers; and expectant mothers may not be forced to work for a period varying from three months (in Italian industry) to four weeks (Germany) before childbirth—though in Holland there is no obligatory pre-natal holiday. The mother is usually accorded a four to six week holiday after a birth, and in Italy this can be prolonged to 6 months without any loss of seniority rights. Women may not be sacked during pregnancy in France, Germany or Italy, or for one month after a birth in Belgium, four months in Germany or until the child is a year old in Italy. In the Netherlands, on the other hand, a work contract may, without offence, specify pregnancy as a grounds for termination of appointment. In Germany sickness-insured women on maternity leave get a maternity allocation in lieu of a salary, based on average pay over the last three months; in Belgium they get approximately 60 per cent of their normal pay; in France they get 0·5 normal pay from social insurance (two-thirds if they have three or more children); in Italy they get about 80 per cent. But maternity leave over, working mothers sink to being the least privileged members of the labour force; their chances of getting a good job, of being trained or being in line for promotion are all lessened, while they run the risk of being the first to get the sack if activity slackens. It is assumed that their children's needs will have priority over their employer's. Like Britain, the Six have hardly touched the problem of the care of the pre-school-age child; crèches and kindergarten (some state-run, some private, some provided by employers) cater for only a fraction of the under-sixes. And not much has been done to align school and working hours and holidays.

Other labour legislation applying specifically to women is often antiquated—some dating back to 1914—and frankly discriminatory in barring them from ever qualifying for the highest pay scales. In Belgium a married woman must have her husband's permission to work, and women are barred from certain branches of public administration, e.g. in the ministry of finance in the Netherlands, marriage is a permissible ground for dismissal. Elsewhere, however, such illiberal legislation has been repealed; but the heavy and unhealthy work that is generally barred to women has not been redefined in terms of modern industrial techniques. Hours that may be worked—in total, at a stretch, at certain times of day—are always restricted, though not always in the same way. Overtime is variously defined and night-work (forbidden to women in industry) takes place between 6.00 p.m. and 7.00 a.m. in the Netherlands, between 10.00 p.m. and 5.00 a.m. in France, Italy and Luxembourg; Belgium more rationally forbids men or women to work between 10.00 p.m. and 6.00 a.m. except in certain listed occupations.

As in the United Kingdom, so women in the Community retire earlier than men and get lower pensions; and although taxation of single women is non-discriminatory, that of married women is not designed to encourage them to work and in many cases, particularly those of highly qualified women, inhibits them from doing so. Only in Germany can a married woman choose between a joint or a separate assessment; in France and Luxembourg husband and wife's income must be accumulated; in Italy some taxes are levied on the separate incomes, some on the joint income; in the Netherlands a wife gets a tax-free allowance of one third of her income, the rest is accumulated; in Belgium, too, a mixed system exists.

Clearly women at work in the Community, as in Britain, continue to suffer a number of disadvantages compared with men.

(Extracted from European Studies Teachers' Series No. 14, London, Centre for Contemporary European Studies, University of Sussex: European Community Information Service, 1972.)

8.5 Action Now!

PETER STEPHENSON

British firms must enter the Common Market with a very significant advantage in labour costs. But there should now—not next year, but *now*—be a major upsurge in spending by British industry on new plant and equipment.

The emphasis must be on *action*. Business men who ask: 'What will happen to my industry, and to my firm, when we join the Common Market?' have the wrong attitude to the situation. Very little will happen automatically, especially in the first years. It is much more a case of firms *doing* things, making things happen: it is a matter of seizing opportunities and this concerns firms of *all* sizes. It is quite false to assume that entry into the Common Market is mainly a matter for big firms. On the contrary, the very biggest firms are often producing on the Continent anyway. It is the small manufacturing firms, producing in this country, who have most to gain from the larger market and the opportunity it will offer for profitable specialisation in what a firm can do best.

The labour cost advantage is a substantial one. This is not widely understood, because it is more a matter of *total* labour costs than basic costs. It arises from the much higher burden of social security payments and fringe benefits in the countries of the Six.

Fringe Benefits and Social Security in 1968

Cost of benefits as % additional to wage costs		Social security	Family allowances	Holidays	Bonuses, bounties	Other benefits
Belgium	54·4	16·2	10·5	17·4	5·1	5·2
France	70·0	18·3	13·3	13·3	8·2	16·9
Germany	44·5	15·9	—	14·5	4·3	9·8
Italy	91·9	28·8	17·4	18·2	17·3	10·2
Luxembourg	40·8	14·6	4·0	10·5	6·1	5·6
Netherlands	49·9	12·0	5·5	10·6	8·2	13·6
UK	22·2	5·9	—	7·8	2·4	6·1

All the countries of the Six spend relatively more on social security than we do in this country, but less of the cost is met out of general taxation. Most is paid for by contributions—and unlike the system in this country, in the Six the employer pays the lion's share. In all the Six, except Germany, even family allowances are paid for in this way. In addition, fringe benefits tend to be more generous and therefore more costly to the employer, than in Britain. Holidays with pay are longer on the Continent, even though we have now started to catch up. The welfare benefits offered—including, for example, company-owned and subsidised housing—are on average more lavish. And such annual bonuses as the 'thirteenth month' of pay are far more common.

The most comprehensive calculation of the total effect of all these extras is the one made by the statistical office of the European Communities, and last published by them in the booklet 'The Common Market and The Common Man' in May 1971.

On this calculation, the British employer in 1968 paid an extra 22·2 per cent on top of his basic wage costs, while the German employer paid an extra 44·5 per cent and the Italian employer a whacking 91·9 per cent. And a calculation for 1972 would be unlikely to show much change in these relationships.

Naturally, if British wage *rates* were far and away the highest in Europe, the above calculation could still show British employers as having high costs. But the facts of the matter are very different from that.

Wage comparisons can never be precise, and international comparisons are very difficult. But as a very crude approximation at present, if wages and industrial salary rates in the UK are taken as 100, then the main countries of the Six compare as follows:

Germany	135
Netherlands	115
Belgium	115
France	105
Italy	90

This estimate deliberately leans towards giving a flattering comparison for Britain. Yet even so it can be seen that only Italy could be regarded as having lower basic payroll costs than British Industry.

When the extras are added, the difference becomes staggering.

Basic Pay Costs and Total Labour Costs

	Basic Pay Costs	Extras	Total Labour Costs
Germany	135	+44·5	195
Netherlands	115	+49·9	172
Belgium	115	+54·4	178
France	105	+70·0	178
UK	100	+22·2	122
Italy	90	+91·9	173

On this calculation, if a British firm's total labour costs = 122, then those of its German competitor will = 195, which is about 60 per cent higher.

All this is very approximate indeed. But no other calculation based on the facts of the case can come up with any answer other than that British industry enjoys a major advantage in labour costs over its Common Market opposite numbers.

So why don't we expect to sweep the board inside the Common Market? Come to that, why aren't we doing so already, despite the tariffs, with such an advantage? The honest answer has to be that our advantage in labour costs is offset by our disadvantage in productivity.

All the evidence suggests that overall productivity in this country, despite the recent spurt, still lags behind that of the industry of the Six. Of course, the range of variation is very great; it is as true as it ever was that the most efficient British firms can stand comparison with any on the Continent. The problem is that of the average and the worst.

The statistics show clearly how we have slipped.

Percentage Growth of Output per
Man-Hour in Manufacturing

since 1963	1971
Netherlands	+88
France	+68
Italy	+60
Germany	+55
UK	+41

Source: National Institute of Economic & Social Research.

That we have not matched Italy's productivity growth can be excused on the basis that they must have been well behind us in 1963. There can be no such comforting thought about our falling further behind Germany.

It is well known that the rate of industrial investment in Britain has lagged too much. But it is not always appreciated how far behind we are.

The mammoth Brookings Institution study of 'Britain's Economic Future' had an illuminating table of what they called 'Value of Net

Stock of Enterprise Structures and Equipment per Employed Person' in 1964. How did we rate?

On the basis that USA = 100, the ranking included:

Belgium	67
Netherlands	62
France	54
Germany	52
UK	44
Italy	36

Again, one can quibble away about the precise truth behind these calculations. But putting it at its lowest, there is no evidence that eight years ago we were better equipped than our competitors except Italy. And as it is undeniable that since then our industrial investment each year has lagged badly behind theirs, it is clear that we are now most certainly under-equipped.

Does this mean that British firms should be apprehensive about joining the Common Market? Certainly not. At present, they have a balance of labour cost advantage and productivity disadvantage. And in the first period of membership the advantage will remain, while it is possible for firms to do something about their disadvantage.

Some of the labour cost disparity must be expected to melt away. As far as basic wage rates and fringe benefits are concerned, there will be increasing pressure in this country for parity with our new partners' workers. The use of international comparisons in collective bargaining is at present little more than a gimmick, but will gradually become a reality.

The differing burdens of social costs on industry is another matter. The Treaty of Rome contains a declaration of intent to harmonise social benefits 'in an upward direction'. And one reason is that employers in the Common Market are very aware of the effect on their costs and therefore on their competitive position, of these disparities. French employers' organisations have been grumbling for some time about the unfair cost advantage that British firms will have.

But the political and social implications of such harmonisation are so significant that progress must be long drawn out. Very little is likely to happen in this decade.

Meanwhile, after this year's Budget, British firms have financial incentives to invest and expand that would be the envy of most firms in the Common Market. If they start now to invest for productivity, they will join the Common Market with an excellent competitive position. If they sit back and do nothing, then nothing very dreadful will happen to them—at first. But they will be laying up trouble for themselves in the future, as their labour cost advantage erodes away.

Now is the time for an investment boom in Britain. That is what is needed to give us a cracking start to our membership of the Common Market.

(Extracted from *New Europe*, May 1972.)

8.6 Articles 117, 118, 120, 121, 122 (Social Provisions) Treaty of Rome

Article 117

Member States agree upon the need to promote improved working conditions and an improved standard of living for workers, so as to make possible their harmonisation while the improvement is being maintained.

They believe that such a development will ensue not only from the functioning of the common market, which will favour the harmonisation of social systems, but also from the procedures provided for in this Treaty and from the approximation of provisions laid down by law, regulation or administrative action.

Article 118

Without prejudice to the other provisions of this Treaty and in conformity with its general objectives, the Commission shall have the task of promoting close co-operation between member States in the social field, particularly in matters relating to:

—employment;
—labour law and working conditions;
—basic and advanced vocational training;
—social security;
—prevention of occupational accidents and diseases;
—occupational hygiene;
—the right of association, and collective bargaining between employers and workers.

To this end, the Commission shall act in close contact with member States by making studies, delivering opinions and arranging consultations both on problems arising at national level and on those of concern to international organisations.

Before delivering the opinions provided for in this Article, the Commission shall consult the Economic and Social Committee.

Article 120

Member States shall endeavour to maintain the existing equivalence between paid holiday schemes.

Article 121

The Council may, acting unanimously and after consulting the Economic and Social Committee, assign to the Commission tasks in connection with the implementation of common measures, particularly as regards social security for the migrant workers referred to in Articles 48 to 51.

Article 122

The Commission shall include a separate chapter on social developments within the Community in its annual report to the Assembly.

The Assembly may invite the Commission to draw up reports on any particular problems concerning social conditions.

(Treaty establishing the European Economic Community, Cmnd. 4864, HMSO, London, 1972.)

8.7 Extracts from Commons Debate on the European Communities Bill, 21–22 October 1971

Mr. Laurie Pavitt (Willesden, West): . . . No hon. Member has yet dealt with the effect of the National Health Service. There has been much talk about the harmonisation of family benefits and social security. It has been said that they will be as good as or comparable with those that we have in Britain—[Hon. Members: 'Better.'].

. . . The essential point is that we are the only country in which the taxpayer carries the burden of the health services. In the other countries there is a claw-back system, and in any such system the people who are in most need do not get adequate services.

Joining will affect doctors, nurses, dentists, pharmacists and in my view, could so change our National Health Service as to be disastrous. . . .

The Secretary of State for Social Services (Sir Keith Joseph): The Treaty of Rome has very little to say in direct terms about social security and health care. There is a provision for close collaboration between member States in the social field. There is a requirement to adopt in the field of social security the measures necessary to provide freedom of movement to workers. But the treaty leaves each member State free to determine the pattern and extent of its own social security arrangements in accordance with its own national arrangements and order of priorities. That is the basic fact that the House needs to know. There is no legal requirement upon us to change in any way our social security system or health care system if we join the Common Market. . . .

It will never be requisite upon us once we are in the Community to take any decision, or to join in any decision, against our national interest. We shall have the opportunity for consultation with other members to take unanimous decisions for the harmonisation upwards of the social services. It is within the purpose and spirit of the Common Market that there should be an attempt over the years to improve the social services all round. We shall expect to join in that upward harmonisation, but there will be no obligation upon us to change. . . .

There is an area of extreme detail where we may well find obligations to change. There are areas of high strategy where we certainly cannot be required to change. There is a twilight hinterland that cannot be predicted now where something apparently very detailed may come close to making a change of substance. It is upon the definition of this twilight area that the Council of Ministers is able to decide whether a particular proposal shall be put before member Governments.

I do not want to deceive the House, but I am quite clear that there will be changes that we shall accept and want to accept and be required to accept in matters of real detail, no doubt important detail with, for instance, safety precautions for pharmaceuticals, and medicines and marking and drug detail, very important, but highly technical; and there will be great strategic issues on which no obligation to change will rest upon us. . . . It is a sober fact that most of the countries of the Six have social services which have been influenced far more than those in this country by the work of the trade unions. I say we regret that our trade unions have not seen fit to make improvement of the fringe benefits one of their main bargaining purposes. We see in some of the countries of the Six the benefits to the worker that can occur when fringe benefits are at the heart of negotiations. I state that as a fact and I much regret that it has not happened here. I point to the advantages in Europe, and hope that the trade unions will catch the idea from Europe.

. . . One common feature is that most Common Market countries have health services organised as components of social insurance systems. Health care and sickness benefit are available to contributors and their dependants from the appropriate social security institute. Their social security systems are not centralised national systems as ours are.

In most EEC countries there are scores or hundreds of insurance funds serving industries or groups of individuals and managed by employers and trade union representatives under Government supervision. There is no national safety net, but a series of local, varying provisions. . . .

The social security systems of the Six are not as universal as ours. They apply to the self-employed only to a limited extent and do not cater for the non-employed at all.

Another difference which distinguishes our present social security system from that of the Community is in the raising of the necessary money to pay for the benefits. We traditionally finance at least half our social security system from Government funds, leaving employers and employees to provide the rest in about equal proportions. In the EEC countries the situation is different. The employer has to find a much higher proportion of the total cost. In Italy his contribution may amount to over 50 per cent of his payroll, and the State in general has correspondingly less to find from taxation.

Perhaps the House would like to be reminded that despite all those differences a number of the EEC countries have provision for their elderly which either is or will be better than ours. Holland is the only country which, like us, has a flat-rate State pension system. The other countries have earnings-related pensions. They are mature in France and Germany—that is to say, they have reached their full maturity—but they are not yet mature in Belgium and Italy. Where they are mature, as in France and Germany, they provide for the better-off—for those who have had reasonably good earnings in their working life—a better standard of living in retirement than is provided for those of our people who have only the State retirement pension, or who have been in an occupational pension scheme either at a low level or for a relatively short time.

It seems to me that Europe has done relatively better than we have in dealing with the civilian disabled. That is why I have told the Disablement Income Group that I have sent a departmental study team to visit a number of countries of the Six to see exactly how they do things, and the extent to which they do things which we have always thought it would not be possible to do fairly and sensitively. We shall learn from that team when it returns.

. . . There is one quite complicated area of reciprocal extension of social security systems which accession will bring. The EEC countries recognise that movement of labour cannot be free unless social security rights are both aggregated and portable. The basis of the treaty, therefore, is that contributions paid while working in one country shall be given credit when the worker moves to work in another country, and that the contributions shall be aggregated and the benefits shall be portable, both for the worker and his family. So there are regulations which will benefit our workers going there and their workers coming here, providing that the country in which the worker is employed is made responsible for the social security provisions for both the worker and his family, taking into account previous insurance in other member States.

But those regulations will not change things much, because we already have reciprocal, bilateral agreements on social security with each of the Six countries providing much, though not quite, the same.

On the health side European workers coming here will get the benefit of the Health Service as of right instead of, as now, on a Good Samaritan basis. On the other hand, our workers going to the Common Market countries will get exactly the same health care and treatment there as do their own nationals. In some cases their own nationals have to pay what is called a patient's fraction which they do not get reimbursed. Our workers there will be treated exactly as are the local nationals.

(Extracted from *House of Commons Debates*, 5th Ser., Vol. 823, Col. 1060, 1133 ff.)

8.8 The Welfare State in Europe and the United Kingdom

SHIRLEY WILLIAMS

One of the myths that have a disturbing tendency to colour political discussions in Britain (and there are many of them) is the myth that we have the most advanced welfare state in the world, with the possible exception of the Scandinavian countries. It is as if we believed that the world froze over in 1950. Lost in admiration of Beveridge's Report, and the enshrinement of many of its conclusions in the legislation passed by the Attlee Government in 1945 to 1951, we have not noticed other countries passing us by. Yet now, by the standards of most Western European countries, we possess a primitive system of social insurance. We spend less of our national income on social services than most of them do, while complaining bitterly about the burden of public expenditure. Above all in the field of pensions we have fallen well behind the standards of provision widely available on the Continent.

There are, of course, still some social services in which Britain excels. No other country outside the Soviet *bloc* has yet embarked upon any medical service as ambitious as the National Health Service. That stands as a monument to the extraordinary vision of Nye Bevan, a high-water mark of what social democracy can achieve. In the field of education, English primary schools are much admired for their creativity and their relaxed methods; indeed the revolution of the past decade in the primary schools is beginning to be emulated in other countries. Much as we deplore, rightly, the lower proportion of boys and girls from the homes of manual workers entering higher education, a proportion that has changed very little over twenty years, it remains true that our student body more closely reflects national income and occupation patterns than does that of any other country in Western Europe. In the treatment of the mentally ill in hospital, again Britain has done important and pioneering work. But all this does not add up to a claim to leadership in social policy.

The reasons for Britain's relative failure in improving the standards of social benefits for the elderly and for large families are complex. They appear to lie partly in a stubborn reluctance to reform the structure of our social security system, and partly in our older

Puritan tradition which believes in a bare sufficiency, and no more, for those in need—what no doubt the present Government would describe as standing on one's own feet, and I could describe as standing on someone else's.

The British social security system is circumscribed by two self-imposed limitations. One is the flat rate principle, which is only minimally breached by the graduated pension scheme stuck on top of the old system. As long as the bulk of contributions and benefits are flat rate, there is a major difficulty about raising both to the level at which benefits are adequate and that is the impact of sharply increased contributions on the low-paid worker. An earnings-related scheme, as the last Labour Government realised, with or without a redistributive element, overcomes this problem. The further limitation in the present British insurance scheme is the apparently sacred principle that employers and employees must make equal contributions. Hence the scheme cannot move faster than the capacity of the poorest contributors within it to pay. Yet there is no valid reason at all for clinging to this principle. The responsibility for paying for a man's retirement, or sickness, or unemployment can as logically be regarded as one of the costs industry has to meet as, say, depreciation on machinery or buildings. Disproportionate contributions by employers have been the key to several European pensions schemes. Thus in Belgium the employer's contribution is twice the size of the employee's, and in France practically the whole contribution is borne by employers. In Germany, however, contributions are the same on both sides of industry.

Contributions, from whatever source they come, are much higher in these countries than in Britain. The total cost of financing non-wage benefits such as insurance, health, holidays, etc. amounts to between 40 per cent and 90 per cent of hourly wage rates in EEC countries, compared to 2 per cent in Britain. Yet the effect on industrial costs does not seem to have been as disastrous as might be supposed. In spite of recent improvements such as longer holidays, raised benefits, etc. costs per manhour do not appear to be rising more quickly in Europe than here.

The coverage of most European social security systems is far from universal, and in this respect our scheme is certainly better. European insurance schemes normally cover all employed persons, there is usually a separate scheme for self-employed people and for public servants, and in some countries for such special groups as miners.

Eligibility conditions may also be difficult to satisfy. In Belgium, a man has to work for his entire life—45 years—to be entitled to draw full retirement benefit. Other countries' rules are not quite as tough as this, but few are as easy to satisfy as those of Britain and the Scandinavian countries. On the other hand, most EEC countries pay old age pensioners as of right, applying neither a retirement condition nor an earnings limit like the £7·50 a week we have here.

The age at which a pension is payable varies widely from country to country. In Belgium it is 65 for men, 60 for women, as here. But more European countries have faced up to the illogicality of a later age of retirement for men (who die earlier) than for women. Indeed, once equal pay is effectively working, the argument for different ages of retirement becomes indefensible. Thus in France, the age at which persons are paid is 60 for both sexes, and in Italy, rather surprisingly, 60 for men and 55 for women. Significantly, the country whose welfare state is the most highly praised, Sweden, has one of the latest retirement ages in Europe, 67 for both sexes. (Compare Uruguay, where, worn out by the sun and the Tupamaros, you can actually get a pension at 50!) The generous level of Swedish pensions is not unrelated to this late retirement age.

It isn't at all easy to make direct comparisons of pensions and benefits. The figures can always be disputed on the grounds that official exchange rates are artificial, or that purchasing power differs between one country and another, or that the pension does not represent all the kinds of help available to old people. However, some necessarily rather crude comparisons have been made, by the OECD, the Brookings Institute and other bodies. Perhaps the crudest basis of comparison is one of straight figures. Thus, in reply to a recent Parliamentary Question, Sir Keith Joseph said that a man who had earned the average industrial wage in his own country and had paid insurance contributions for 45 years, would draw £19 a week in Italy, £11 in Portugal and £9 in Holland. If one takes flat rate schemes, where the comparison is not complicated by the effect of earnings-related benefit, then in 1967 the flat rate single pension in Holland was $67 a month, in Sweden, $81 a month, in UK $43.20 a month.

A more sophisticated approach is to consider the proportion of national income spent on pensions for the old, and what relation the pension bears to the average income per head of the country's population. Unfortunately the most complete survey is an old one, dating back to 1960, undertaken by the Brookings Institute on the basis of United Nations Statistical Office and ILO figures. There is no reason however to think the relative positions in Europe have changed much. In 1960, Britain spent 4·4 per cent of her national income on pensions for the old, compared to France's 5·8 per cent, Italy's 6·6 per cent, West Germany's 11·8 per cent. No EEC country fell below 5 per cent. Looking at average *per capita* incomes of retired people in comparison with average *per capita* incomes of the population as a whole, the same picture emerges. In Britain, the figure is 29 per cent; that is to say the old had an average income more than two-thirds below that of the population as a whole. In France, the proportion was 34 per cent, in Belgium and Italy over 40 per cent, in Holland 60 per cent and in Germany, amazingly, over 100 per cent. Since 1960, the French system has been reviewed, and the retiring industrial worker now gets about two-thirds of his average earnings as pension if he retires at 65, and well over 90 per cent if he retires at 70.

Two depressing facts emerge from these international studies. One is that Britain will go on lagging behind Europe in providing for the old so long as she has a Government stubbornly opposed to a full earnings-related system. It doesn't matter so much whether there are several schemes or only one, or whether the schemes are administered by a central Government, special approved insurance associations (as in Italy) or by trade unions and employers (as in Israel). What does matter is that coverage should be wide, compulsory and adequate. Fragmentation of the insured population into private occupational pension schemes will leave us behind the Continent for another generation. The Conservative Government are highly selective Europeans, picking out the ideologically acceptable plums like the abandonment of agricultural subsidies, and leaving social harmonisation strictly alone.

The other depressing fact emerging from these studies is that the pension, as a proportion of average *per capita* income, tends to decline as the share of the old in the population increases. This is not surprising, but it is discouraging for pensioners in a country like Britain where the proportion of over 65s in the population is rising three times faster than the population as a whole. One reason, inevitably, is that far more people now retire as soon as they can— 70 per cent of men retired at 65 in 1968, compared to only 54 per cent four years earlier.

Comparisons between other social services can be dealt with relatively quickly. In the health field, all EEC countries have widely extended compulsory medical insurance systems, under which either the insurance fund pays hospital and medical expenses direct (as in Germany, Holland or Italy) or else reimburses the patient (as in France, Belgium and Luxembourg). The insurance fund meets between 75 per cent and 80 per cent of the costs, sometimes more if the patient has a small income. In most EEC countries, pensioners receive medical treatment free. There are certain limits on the medical and hospital expenses the insurance funds will reimburse, but they are very much more generous than, say, Blue Cross in the USA. Nobody else has a true National Health Service. Whether because of this or not, most EEC countries spend a greater proportion of national income on health than Britain does.

I will say nothing about industrial injury, sickness and unemployment benefits, except to indicate that, as in Britain, sickness and unemployment benefits in EEC countries are wage-related and fairly high, and industrial injury benefits are based, as here, on assessments of loss of capacity as well as on previous earnings. These later benefits (which usually also cover benefit for permanent invalids) are, like pensions, linked to either the cost of living index or to the wages index. In all EEC countries, uprating is automatic in this sense. In Holland, there is an elaborate mechanism whereby any increase in the cost of living of more than a certain percentage involves an immediate uprating of social security benefits.

Finally, family allowances, the controversial centrepiece of many Continental social security schemes. It is important to understand why family allowances are so much larger on the Continent, and why they arouse so little controversy; after all, in Britain, family allowances are, alongside supplementary benefit for people of working age, the favourite scapegoats of the critics of welfare. I believe there are two factors which explain these widely different reactions, and that they are related to very diverse traditions. The first is the Catholic ideal of the large family, which is held to benefit the whole community and is thus deserving of support. Of course at times this approach becomes quite deliberately linked to national purposes, as when France brought in very big family allowances in an attempt to reverse the falling birth rate before the war. Second, there is the idea that wages should be related to the number of dependants a man has —the 'just wage', as Catholic theologians call it, is in some sense a family wage. Since obviously great problems arise in paying men different amounts for doing the same job, the family allowance becomes the means of discriminating between them according to their responsibilities. For this to be effective, family allowances must represent a substantial part of a man's income; and so they do. In Belgium, a man with three children will draw £26·46 a month; in France, £19·17; in Italy, £11·44. Only Germany is down at English levels with £8·58 a month for a three-child family, and nothing for the first child. Incidentally, it is an odd reflection on the age of achieving independence that family allowance is payable in Holland for children in full-time education *up to the age of 27.*

It is familiar ground to mention that statutory and negotiated holidays in EEC countries are much longer than in Britain. In France, for instance, a month is now standard for all industrial workers and, on a certain day at the end of July, French families stream like lemmings down the *Routes Nationales* to the sea. What is less well known is that Holland has a statutory minimum wage of £18·10 a week for both men and women.

So far, the EEC has not had any great impact on national social security systems, though there is a commitment by all the EEC countries to 'harmonise upwards'. That apart, countries are free to pursue their own national systems. For instance, if Britain entered, there would be no threat to the National Health Service. But where the EEC probably has had an impact is in pushing such fringe benefits as holidays and working conditions up towards the levels achieved by the most advanced members. Trade unions pressing for better holidays elsewhere in the Community have taken the French standard as the one they were trying to achieve.

The EEC has also established that all Community nationals working in a Community country other than their own, are entitled to that country's level of benefits for themselves and their dependants. Thus an Italian working in Germany would be entitled to German social benefits. But the same most emphatically does not apply to non-Community nationals, like the hundreds of thousands of Turks, Greeks, Spaniards, Portuguese, Algerians and Moroccans, simply because most of them cannot satisfy residence requirements for family allowances, pensions, etc. Indeed, hundreds of thousands of migrant workers arrive illegally, have no papers and are consequently at the mercy of whoever employs them. In France, over three-quarters of the North African migrant workers are believed to have entered illegally. They live in *bidonvilles*, shacks of tin and tarpaper, or share crowded slum rooms in the industrial cities. In Germany, employers are supposed to provide accommodation, but again there are the thousands of illegal migrants for whom no conditions can be laid down. The *Gästarbeiter* are essential in Europe's high employment economies, and now that Italy no longer provides a massive reserve of unemployed, more and more come from outside the Community. But they are unpopular, unassimilated, sadly neglected (though West Germany deserves some marks for trying, and so does Holland); they are known as 'the new underclass' or 'the new poor'. There are more migrant workers in France and Germany than there are Commonwealth immigrants in England, and they present at least equivalent problems of language barriers, cultural alienation and variations in custom. As immigrants achieve residence and then citizenship, their right to move elsewhere in the Community becomes the same as that of any other Community national. The integration of immigrants of different origins, nationalities and races will therefore become, gradually, a challenge to the whole of Western Europe and not just to Britain, France or Germany.

To sum up, the Community countries have better though less extensive social insurance systems than we do, and much less ambitious health schemes. The financial structure in most cases is one that shifts the main burden on to industry, and on to the employers' side of industry. The benefits are better proofed against inflation than ours, because they are linked to the cost of living index or, in some cases, to the wages index. Nor does there seem to be the kind of controversy about family allowances, etc. that exists in Britain. The greater financial dependence of Continental schemes on contributions rather than on taxation may have something to do with this, though in several EEC countries family allowances are in fact financed from taxes.

What is indeed the case is that in every EEC country, without exception, more is spent on the social services as a proportion of gross national product than in Britain; and with the single exception of Italy, more is spent per head as well. . . .

It is ironic that since 1967, Britain's increase in public expenditure on the social services has slowed down, and is now likely to slow down further, while in the EEC countries, the rate of increase is probably accelerating. Certainly since 1967 both France and Italy have undertaken major reforms of their social services, and these are not, of course, reflected in the figures given above.

The Labour Movement will no doubt continue to argue about the effect on prices, employment, wages and investment of joining the EEC. What is abundantly clear in the social services is that the EEC principle of 'harmonisation upwards' can only benefit Britain because she has slipped so far down the list in social service provision. There could hardly be stronger proof of Anthony Crosland's thesis that it is exceedingly difficult to get real improvements in social services without real improvements in economic growth. And growth in the Community countries, as we know, has been twice as fast as in the United Kingdom.

(Extracted from the *Contemporary Review*, Vol. 219, no. 1267, August 1971, pp. 57–63.)

8.9 Social Security in the Six

Social security developed from earlier national insurance schemes and is still very much based on insurance principles. The term means different things in different countries. For the purpose of this discussion, it has been defined as those services which provide benefits, usually in cash, to a substantial proportion of the population and without a means test. Eligibility is determined by insurance contributions or by a specified burden, such as children, rather than by a low income. Old age pensions, sickness benefit, family allowances and unemployment insurance all come into this definition and so, in the EEC countries, does medical care. Housing, education and welfare services, together with cash allowances of the supplementary benefits variety, are thus excluded from this discussion, although they form an important part of the overall protection of the citizen.

The nature of the risks covered and the post-war growth in provision are similar in both the EEC and the United Kingdom, but the services themselves show substantial differences. Perhaps the greatest of these lies in the role of the central government. In Britain, it has much direct responsibility, employing its own staff in the Department of Health and Social Security to administer the services. In the Six, the governments exert overall control but are less inclined to play a direct part in the administration. Thus in France, for example, social security is the responsibility of semi-autonomous insurance funds which pay the nationally prescribed benefits and collect the specified contributions. Membership of a particular fund depends on one's occupation: employees in industry and commerce will use the 'General' scheme, while those in agriculture will use another and the self-employed one of four others. In the Federal Republic of Germany, sickness insurance is carried out by some two thousand funds with less state control, and individuals may choose with whom they are to insure. This is very different from the British system, where there is a single national scheme covering virtually the entire population.

A further difference is that provision is less uniform in the EEC countries than in Britain. Coverage of the whole population for all benefits has not yet been achieved in any of the six countries. This is most noticeable in the Federal Republic of Germany, where higher-paid white-collar workers are not compelled by law to insure themselves for all risks: if their annual incomes exceeded £1,700 in 1970, for example, they do not take part in the sickness insurance programme. There may also be some slight variations in the benefits provided by different funds, despite the state's overall control; an example of this is the less generous family allowance provision for the self-employed in France. In general, there is a greater emphasis on the employed worker than on others, as these were the first to gain protection by social insurance; compulsory contributions are easier to exact from those earning a wage or salary. Moreover, this emphasis is not entirely deliberate, being in part due to the desires of the self-employed to remain independent.

Coverage is, therefore, by no means as it is in the United Kingdom. This is both a result and a cause of the financial arrangements for social security. In no EEC country does the contribution of the central government reach 40 per cent of the total cost and, taking the five largest countries only, the highest figure is 37 per cent. The state's financial role is very much greater in Britain, where the central government bears the entire cost of the family allowance programme and contributes approximately one-third of the cost of the other cash benefits, moreover, its contribution to medical care, the costs of which fall largely to social security in the Six is something in the region of 90 per cent of the total National Health Service budget.

The chief sources of finance for social security in the EEC countries are thus the insured person himself and the employers, and the latter are the more important. Their financial burden varies from country to country but is always higher than that of their British counterparts. In family allowances, for example, they pay a substantial contribution in five of the countries and indeed provide the entire financial resources for this service in France and the Netherlands. Employers bear the full responsibility for industrial injuries benefits in all six countries, unlike Britain where an employee must pay an insurance contribution towards this.

For the majority of citizens—those in employment—these two aspects of social security may not be very important. The emphasis on the employed worker and the consequent lack of uniform coverage will be of greater importance to others: some of the wealthier self-employed workers may be pleased not to be included in the schemes, while those with smaller incomes may be adversely affected. Of more interest to the average citizen, however, are his own contributions. These tend to be higher in the EEC countries than in Britain, except for the lowest-paid, because they are earnings-related. In the United Kingdom, there is a flat-rate contribution paid by everyone. It is largest for the self-employed and smaller for women than for men, but it does not vary with income. Above that, an earnings-related supplement is paid by all except the lowest wage-earners. In the EEC countries, contributions are a straight percentage of earnings up to a specified maximum, and there is no flat-rate element. The low-paid worker will thus pay less than his British counterpart. For others, however, contributions are generally high by British standards: even in France, where they are lower than in the other countries, an employee must contribute 6·25 per cent of his earnings below £28 per week. These figures give an indication of the size of the contributions, but they should not be taken to be strictly comparable with those in Britain, since the costs and standards of living are not the same.

Since the contributions are earnings-related, benefits usually follow the same pattern. Some of the countries guarantee a minimum retirement pension, but this—unlike the present British benefit—is not intended to be the norm. Others adhere strictly to the earnings-related principle. The only benefits to be the same for all regardless of contributions are medical care, which is not a cash benefit, and family allowances, to which the insured person does not contribute. There is thus a definite link between earnings and benefits received. A well-paid individual may find this more satisfactory than the British system but someone who is low-paid may find his benefit very inadequate. It is interesting to note here that the British system has been tending towards earnings-related benefits in social security in the past decade.

For the citizen, the greatest single difference in social security provision between the United Kingdom and the Six is concerned with medical care. In all of the EEC countries, its provision is linked, to a greater or lesser extent, with insurance. Those who have paid the required contributions may claim assistance with medical costs for themselves and their dependents. In some countries, the patient must find the full cost himself and will then be reimbursed by the insurance funds, while in others he may be entitled to free treatment, but in either case the system is very different from the National Health Service with its virtually free treatment for any citizen regardless of contributions. This will be examined in more detail later.

Thus the main features of the social security systems in the EEC which mark them out as different from that used in Britain are the lesser degree of direct state involvement and, especially, the lesser reliance on central government funds; the lack of a single national scheme and the exclusion of certain groups from some benefits; the large employer contributions; the earnings-related nature of the benefits and contributions; and the insurance basis of the medical care scheme. The risks covered by the systems in all seven countries are broadly similar. Within the EEC itself however there are many smaller differences, since each country has developed its social services in a purely national context. Some of these differences will become apparent when the services are examined in more detail.

There are four main groups of social security provision which will now be considered, old age insurance, which normally includes survivors and disability benefits; sickness and maternity insurance; family allowances; and unemployment insurance. Industrial injuries protection also forms part of social security, but it will not be examined in detail since it is less complicated. It is an employer-financed scheme paying medical costs and a pension where necessary to those suffering from an industrial injury or occupational disease. Apart from the absence of a contribution by the insured person himself, it is not very different from the British system.

Old Age and Related Benefits

Retirement pensions in the EEC are very closely related to contributions. Not only are they earnings-related but their size also depends on the number of contributions made. In France and Italy, a minimum of fifteen years contributions is required before any benefit (other than a small flat-rate one in France) may be granted, and all the countries relate at least part of the pension to the number of years of insurance. Thus a man with thirty years contributions may receive a pension twice as large as that of a man insured for only fifteen years. If his income was twice as large as the other's during his working life, the difference between the two pensioners will be even more pronounced.

The size of the pension varies very much between the countries. In the Federal Republic of Germany, it can reach two-thirds of previous earnings, although it is more usually 40 or 50 per cent; in France, the maximum is 20 per cent. However, the latter country has institution-alised occupational pensions schemes, and these now cover almost all employees outside agriculture and domestic service. In general, therefore, the pensions provided by these social security schemes are larger than those in Britain, except for persons with very low wages or few years of contributing to the scheme. Some of the countries have no guaranteed minimum pension and others provide this only on a means-tested basis, and so hardship among the elderly is no less present in the Six than it is in the United Kingdom.

All the countries include survivors insurance in their retirement pensions schemes, and three of them include disability insurance. The others administer this either separately or as part of the sickness insurance scheme. Benefits for survivors are related to the pension to which the head of the family was entitled at the time of his death and are therefore earnings-related to some extent. As in Britain, entitle-ment to benefit may depend on the age of the widow and may be forfeited on remarriage. Disability pensions are also earnings-related and may be varied according to the extent of the handicap.

Sickness and Maternity Insurance

An insured person is entitled to two types of benefit: medical care for himself and his dependants and an earnings-related sickness benefit for himself if he is unable to work. It is the first of these which is most interesting to someone accustomed to the National Health Service. In three of the countries, an individual can be treated wherever he wishes but must bear the full cost himself; the insurance fund will later reimburse some or all of the amount to him according to a fixed scale. This reimbursement may be as low as 70 or 75 per cent in France and Belgium. In the Netherlands and the Federal Republic of

Germany, treatment can be obtained only from those doctors registered with the insurance fund, but the patient does not have to pay. In these two countries, therefore, the system is nearer to that used in Britain, but it is still strictly related to insurance. Where a system of partial reimbursement operates reimbursement and means-tested assistance may be available for the poorest. This is very similar to the exemption system for prescription charges in Britain.

Maternity benefit is similar, in that the dependants of an insured person are entitled to treatment and a woman insured in her own right is also entitled to an earnings-related cash benefit during her absence from work. Treatment is available under the same conditions as that for illness, except in France, where it is free of charge. Maternity grants are also paid in four of the countries, being included in the family allowance scheme in three of these. Their level is generally higher than that of the equivalent British benefit: for example, it is approximately £58 in France.

The provision of medical care in the EEC is thus substantially different from that in the United Kingdom. Particularly in the countries operating the reimbursement system, there is greater freedom of choice in that the patient can go to whichever doctor he wishes without being registered. He can also choose his treatment to a certain extent, although anything costing more than the prescribed amount will not be reimbursed in full. However, if he cannot find the initial payment, he may be disinclined to seek treatment, and the greater independence of the doctors can lead to difficulties in planning the service. The costs in each country cause as much concern as do those of the National Health Service and contributions must be high to meet these. Even in France, with its large direct charges, the contribution of the insured individual is 3·5 per cent of earnings up to £28 per week.

Family Allowances

With the exception of the Federal Republic of Germany, the EEC countries lay greater emphasis on these benefits than does Britain. In four of the countries, an allowance is paid automatically for the first child and this also happens in France if the mother does not go out to work. Benefits tend to be larger than in Britain, for example, £9 per month for the second child in Belgium and £11 for the third and fourth child in France, although here again one must bear in mind that costs of living are not the same in each country. Additional benefits and services are provided in some of the countries, such as an extra allowance for handicapped children in Belgium and Luxembourg. France has the greatest number of these additional benefits, ranging from housing and prenatal allowances to welfare services.

The one exception to this pattern of substantial provision for the family, financed almost entirely by employers, is the Federal Republic of Germany. The system used there is very much closer to that in Britain: entirely financed out of taxation, it provides benefit from the second child only. For this child, the allowance is only £3 per month, but it is substantially larger for subsequent children. Unlike the British system, automatic entitlement to benefit comes only with the third child and only those with low incomes may receive an allowance for the second, but it may be paid for longer than the British benefit: up to age 18 normally and 25 in certain circumstances.

Unemployment Insurance

There is no great similarity between the countries of the EEC in their provision for unemployment, except that they have traditionally placed less emphasis on it than have British governments. Neither France nor Luxembourg has a statutory unemployment insurance programme, although France has occupational provision for the majority of employed workers. These two countries provided flat-rate benefits to the unemployed, with a means test in some circumstances. Belgium also grants fairly standardised benefits, but the remaining three countries pay earnings-related allowances. All six, like Britain, demand of the recipient that he be prepared to take suitable employment, and all except Belgium set a limit on the length of time during which benefit may be paid.

Social security provision in the Six thus has broad similarities, but the details of the services are varied, each country has developed its own system over a long period of time to meet its own particular needs. Although the Treaty of Rome makes provision for the countries to 'harmonise' their social services, progress has been slow in this direction. Certain agreements have been made with regard to the contributions and benefits of migrant workers, but these have been essentially administrative: they have not altered the pattern of provision. The expenditure patterns of the different countries have, however, come somewhat closer together in recent years so that some of the differences are being modified. Thus the traditional French emphasis on family allowances has been lessened in favour of old age pensions, while the reverse has happened in the Federal Republic of Germany. The overall expenditure on social security has also come closer together in recent years, but this may be for reasons unconnected with the existence of the EEC. Any substantial increases in similarity between the services of the different countries seem unlikely in the near future.

Despite the existence of these differences, it remains clear that the social security systems of the Six share certain features not found in Britain. The less direct role of government in both administration and finance is the most significant of these, but for the average citizen the contributions and benefits are more important. The relation to earnings and the frequently higher contributions provide more generous benefits than in Britain for those with average and above-average incomes, but the lowest-paid may be in an unsatisfactory position. The medical care systems are more complex, since a patient's insurance entitlement must always be investigated and there is less control over GPs and hospitals. In the countries operating a reimbursement system, treatment is more expensive for the patient, especially in the short term. In general, it may be said that social security in the EEC caters for the average citizen with a reasonable income and not for the poorer members of society. Family allowances are usually flat-rate and tax-free, other benefits reflect previous earnings, medical provision works on the assumption that the patient can afford to bear part of the cost himself. Those with exceptionally low incomes are catered for outside the social security system. Although many of Britain's means-tested benefits are also outside social security as it is here defined, she still covers lower-paid workers more fully by insurance, with the emphasis on flat-rate benefits and free medical care. However, this pattern is changing slightly and Britain is adopting certain EEC features, such as earnings-related benefits and charges in medical care.

(Extracted from European Studies Teachers' Series no. 14, London, Centre for Contemporary European Studies, University of Sussex: European Community Information Service, 1972.)

8.10 Health and the Six
GEORGE TEELING SMITH

The British National Health Service lies at one extreme in the range of extraordinarily varied health schemes of western Europe. It covers the whole population and provides very comprehensive benefits. Even with the proposed increased charges, it will still, in general, make comparatively small financial demands on patients at the time of treatment. The facilities, particularly the hospitals, are for the most part publicly owned. Finally, it is very largely financed from general taxation rather than from special contributions.

Each of the other countries of the Common Market—in fact every east and west European country—has also accepted medicine as a community responsibility. The variety and complexity of their arrangements, though, easily explain why there has so far been no harmonisation of their schemes. Their health services range from Britain's tax-financed, comprehensive and nationally organised scheme, at one end, to no more than the state co-ordination of numerous private health insurance arrangements covering the majority of the population at the other (Table 1). The schemes of the other three largest countries illustrate these differences.

TABLE 1: *Proportion of Population Covered by Health Scheme*

	%
United Kingdom	100
France	98
Germany	98
Belgium	95
Netherlands	85
Italy	83

In Italy, for example, the health schemes are administered through twenty-one organisations which each provide varying benefits. Their cost is intended to be covered by social security contributions collected mainly from employers. In practice, however, general taxation has also had to be used to subsidise health expenditure. Italy has the lowest proportionate coverage of the population—about 85 per cent. Some of the health schemes—of which the largest, INAM, covers two thirds of the total insured population—provide their own hospitals and employ full-time salaried doctors and ancillaries. Patients may, therefore, be restricted in their choice of doctor. Under these so-called 'direct' schemes, hospital and general practice treatment may be entirely free to the patients, provided that they consult a doctor who is either employed or 'approved' by their organisation. 'Approved' doctors, however, are free to charge more than the fees recommended by the health scheme, and in this case the patient must pay the whole of the difference himself. Other schemes—the so-called 'indirect schemes'—leave the patient free to choose and pay his own doctor, and he is reimbursed later for a proportion of the charge. The scales of recommended fees for medical treatment under the direct schemes have been the subject of considerable dispute, leading, in some cases, to much publicised strikes by the medical profession. In Italy, also, many of the schemes make only a limited contribution to the cost of prescribing medicines.

France, on the other hand, employs a pure insurance scheme. This covers about 98 per cent of the population and is organised through a hierarchy of local regional funds each reinsuring ultimately with the national health fund. Employees pay 2·5 per cent and employers 9·5 per cent of salaries up to a ceiling of 1,200 francs (£90) per month; these payments are part of the very heavy French social security contributions, which can total up to 40 per cent of the employee's salary. Doctors, hospitals and pharmacists remain as private contractors with the patients free to make their own arrangements with them. The patients pay directly for the medical care they receive and then apply for reimbursement of 80 per cent of approved hospital costs, 75 per cent of approved general practice fees and between 70 and 90 per cent of the cost of medicines. As in Italy, if the hospital or doctor which the patient chooses charges more than the approved scale of fees (which, again, they are entirely free to do) he must meet the difference himself.

Germany also operates a national insurance-based scheme, although this still works through nearly 2,000 different agencies. Some operate locally and some cover groups of employees in individual industries or firms. These schemes cover, in all, about 87 per cent of the population, with another 10 per cent being covered by private health insurance. Again, employees and employers contribute a percentage on earnings, up to a ceiling of 1,425 DM (£1·66) per month —in this case about 5 per cent each. The Government pays the contributions for the unemployed and the retired. Most health expenditures are covered in full by direct payments from the insurance funds to the hospitals, doctors and chemists. However, patients (except pensioners) must pay a small prescription charge for their medicines when they are dispensed.

It's clear, even from this brief account, that there has been no attempt to introduce any standardisation of contributions, organisation and benefits between countries. Indeed, there are still substantial differences, at least in countries such as Italy, between the organisation of the health services and the cover provided for different groups within a single country. This is not necessarily a criticism of the EEC. Indeed, it has often been argued that if Britain had allowed more scope for individual experiment and local variation under its National Health Service, we might have had more rapid improvements in the organisation of medical care on a national basis.

The establishment of reciprocal relations between the national schemes of the Six has seen considerable, if cumbersome, progress. Originally, workers moving between the countries were entitled to cover under the scheme of their new country of residence. Now, this applies to temporary visitors and holiday-makers as well. However, each country, while providing all the services and benefits available under its own health scheme, still charges back the cost to these services to the health scheme in the person's own country. The result is a huge mass of paperwork, which contrasts sharply with the reciprocal health service arrangements between Britain and other non-EEC countries such as Sweden, Denmark and Yugoslavia. In our case, the country providing the treatment bears the cost without attempting to recover it from the patient's own national health scheme. It works on the same principle as the 'knock-for-knock' arrangements between motor insurance companies, and saves enormous quantities of international bureaucracy.

While there may be an advantage in a variety of systems for the delivery of medical care, this is not true where there is a variety of standards of care between countries. If the doctors of one country are better trained or more skilful than those of another it would be a legitimate cause for criticism between member countries of the Common Market. It is hard to know to what extent this is true, but discussions on the subject have been protracted. . . .

It is genuinely difficult to equate medical qualifications obtained in different countries under different systems of medical education. This is particularly the case with doctors because their training still relies heavily on what is essentially an apprenticeship system and there is rarely a clear-cut point at which a specific level of ability has been achieved in a particular aspect of medical practice. If, as some people suspect, national 'qualifications' of apparent equivalence in fact mask very different standards of knowledge and ability, it would indeed be undesirable to grant them undiscerning international acceptance.

Table 2, however, suggests another possible explanation for the

TABLE 2: *Population per Doctor*

Germany	650
Italy	665*
Belgium	800
France	850
United Kingdom	870
Netherlands	950

*Includes dentists

slowness of individual countries in the Six to accept each other's medical qualifications at face value. West Germany and the Netherlands, for example, have an almost 50 per cent difference in the ratio of their doctors to population. This is largely because, over the years, West Germany accepted many medical refugees from East Germany. A similar professional drift on into the Netherlands might perhaps not be altogether welcome among Dutch doctors.

And there is still another possible explanation of why the establishment of common standards and free transfer of medical manpower may have been delayed. This is that fashions in medicine are surprisingly regional. Countries differ greatly in the sorts of diagnoses they make and particularly in the sorts of treatment they prescribe. French doctors still attribute many varied ailments to disturbances of the liver—perhaps justifiably. However, French doctors have also continued prescribing more of the old traditional remedies, being slower to adopt some of the new and more scientific treatments. It is doubtful, for example, if their *ampoules buvables*—little sealed glass vials containing a single oral dose of liquid—would gain much general acceptance elsewhere. Nor, indeed, would the German practice of prescribing analgesic suppositories as well as tablets for the relief of a sore throat or headache—'treatment from both ends' as our doctors call it. Injections are more widely used in France, Germany and Italy. And in Germany, it is common for their equivalent of our general practitioners to be equipped with their own X-ray equipment. Cynically, it can be said that some of these latter differences are perhaps more a reflection of the usual continental method of remuneration which is usually based on payment to the doctor for each item of the service that he provides, as opposed to our system based on how many patients a doctor has.

In general, as far as these differences in practice are concerned, it might benefit the people of all countries if national idiosyncrasies were exposed to the discipline of justification in a more international setting. Doctors (and Governments on whom they bring their influence to bear), however, may prefer the cosier situation which provides unchallenged continuity for their own patterns of practice within their national frontiers.

Even the pharmaceutical industry, itself highly international, has to face differing individual registration procedures for its new medicines in each of the Common Market countries. Even the Benelux countries have been unable to agree on a common procedure for the licensing of new medicines. Moreover, clinical trials performed in Britain or Germany, for example, are not accepted in France. In medical research generally, there are centres of excellence on different specialities scattered throughout Europe, such as the Instituto Superiore in Rome; but there is no co-ordinated European policy, despite the efforts of organisations such as OECD. However, even national research policies are difficult enough to co-ordinate and as medical research workers keep in close contact at international conferences anyway, the present situation may not represent any great inefficiency. In addition, the World Health Organisation already has a long-term European regional policy for the co-ordination of health research, concentrating on cardiovascular disease, the mental health of the young and the control of environmental pollution.

None of the existing EEC members, therefore, have been under any real pressure to establish a uniform 'European Health Service' and such an idea would probably be undesirable in principle as well as in practice. So there would be no reason to expect Britain to abandon or change its health service. However, the professions concerned may face some changes in training, if they are to meet the EEC directives at present under discussion, though medical training and qualifications are already under review and Common Market membership won't have much effect here either.

(Extracted from *New Society*, 18 February 1972.)

8.11 French Alarm over Health Spending
CHARLES HARGROVE

Nowhere is the average Frenchman's desire to have his cake and eat it more clearly illustrated than in his attitude to social security and national health.

As with roads and telephones, everyone complains about their shortcomings and abuse and everyone wants to benefit. Yet nobody wants to pay higher contributions, or accept restrictions on freedom of choice.

Two enduring controversies illustrate this aspect of the French character. The first is the one between the social security services (which in France include national health) and part of the medical profession over the Government's plans for a new national convention on charges and prescriptions for a period of four years.

The convention is designed to preserve the essential principles of liberal medicine, such as freedom for the patient to choose a doctor, while attempting to curb the alarming increase in expenditure on health.

'Some doctors,' the Minister of Health said recently, 'want to practise quite freely while benefiting from all the advantages of a system of social protection without accepting its constraints.'

Provision in the convention for some check on excessive charges and over-prescribing has provoked violent protests against 'nationalisation' of medicine.

The second controversy concerns the inclusion in the national social security system two years ago of the self-employed and non-employed—the independent farmers, artisans and shopkeepers, who constitute a much larger proportion of the working population than in Britain.

Until 1969 these people were insured with private organisations. After long negotiations they were included in the state system, but since in France national health is financed by contributions from both employers and employees, the benefits enjoyed by the self-employed are only about two-thirds of those enjoyed by salaried people, for there is no employer's contribution in their case.

However the self-employed insist on getting the same benefits and say that the additional burden should be financed from the contributions of the salaried, a proposal which has the unions up in arms.

To cope with the big increase in spending on health and social security, the government last year considered raising the maximum income level on which contributions are calculated, which stands now at 1,650 francs (about £124) a month.

But it has had to postpone its plans until 1973 or 1974 in the face of an outcry from white-collar workers who would have been the most directly affected. The same protest greeted suggestions for an income ceiling on those receiving family allowances.

Although they complain, the overwhelming majority of Frenchmen acknowledge that the social security system does not work too badly. Its coverage is about as wide as the British system, but in some cases the benefits are higher.

The French system is based on independent *caisses* or funds for each major type of benefit and social category.

The contributions made by employers and employees are broken down as follows: 32·20 per cent of wages and salaries up to the ceiling of 1,650 francs a month for health, pensions and family allowances; about 3 per cent for industrial injuries; and an additional 3 per cent on the whole salary if it exceeds 1,650 francs. There is also a contribution of 0·80 per cent to a separate unemployment fund financed by the state as well as from contributions.

All this adds up to total contributions of 39·20 per cent of wages and salaries. The employers' share of this is about 32 per cent, and they complain that it is a permanent burden on their competitiveness.

Prescriptions, doctors' fees, hospital charges, surgery, convalescence and health cures are reimbursed to about 80 per cent. Teeth are an exception, the front ones are regarded as an expendable luxury.

But this percentage of reimbursement applies only to doctors and hospitals which have signed a convention with the social security services. Where doctors and private hospitals have not done so, the refund is only about half of 80 per cent. In the case of serious and prolonged illness, or of proven inability to pay, health charges are reimbursed in full.

A wage-earner who has contributed 3 per cent of his wages for 30 years is entitled at 65 to a pension of about 600 francs a month. This is 'revalued' at intervals to cope with inflation. If he retires at 60, he gets only half. In fact, almost all wage-earners obtain higher pensions through contributions to supplementary funds, and the Ministry of Health estimates that a wage-earner usually obtains a pension, equal to 60 per cent of his average wages for the last ten years of his working life.

Unemployment benefits are almost equal in France and Britain, but family allowances in France are the most generous in Europe. It has been reckoned that a man with fourteen children can give up work, provided his standard of living is not too high. He can travel almost free and gets many other advantages.

The allowances amount to 96 francs a month for the second child, 257 francs for three children, and 418 francs for four with an additional 35 francs for each child over 10 and 63 francs for those over 15 to cover higher costs and schooling. Rates are a little lower in the provinces.

One feature of the French system is the allocation for a single salary. It is paid to a man whose wife does not work, to compensate for her material disadvantages in relation to those who do and to encourage her to stay at home and look after her family.

The problem of old people is acknowledged to be a tragic one. Two funds have been set up to help them, so that old wage-earners are assured of at least 3,000 francs a year if their total resources are less than 4,400 francs for a single person. It is not much, but it is something, and the government plans to raise payments to 3,400 francs a year by the end of this year. There are also rent allowances of 200 francs a month.

There are still some crying scandals and shortcomings in the over-all system, especially in the availability of doctors in some regions, the shortage of modern hospitals and institutions for the handicapped, deranged and old. Yet 98 per cent of Frenchmen are covered by social security. The problem for the government is how to continue to finance an expenditure which is now as large as the state budget and grows by 13 per cent every year.

(Extracted from *The Times*, 16 July 1971.)

Bibliography

SECTION 1

TOWARDS A NEW EUROPE

Camps, Miriam, *Britain and the European Community* (Oxford University Press, 1964)

Davidson, Ian, *Britain and the Making of Europe* (Macdonald, London, 1972)

Evans, Douglas (ed.), *Desting or Delusion. Britain and the Common Market* (Gollancz, London, 1971)

Kitzinger, Uwe, *Diplomacy and Persuasion: how Britain joined the EEC* (Thames and Hudson, London, 1973)

Mayhew, Christopher, *et al.*, *Europe: A Case for Going In* (Harrap, London, 1971)

Pickles, William, *Britain and Europe: How much has changed?* (Oxford University Press, 1967)

Spanier, David, *Europe, Our Europe* (Secker and Warburg, London, 1972)

Spinelli, Altiero, *The European Adventure* (Charles Knight, London, 1972)

Uri, Pierre (ed.), *From Commonwealth to Common Market* (Penguin, Harmondsworth, 1968)

SECTION 2

THE INSTITUTIONS AND THE POLITICAL PROCESS

Broad, Roger and Jarrett, Bob, *Community Europe Today* (Oswald Wolff, London, 1972)

Coombes, David, *Politics and Bureaucracy in the European Community—a portrait of the Commission* (Allen & Unwin, London, 1970)

Ionescu, Ghita, *The New Politics of European Integration* (Macmillan, London, 1972)

Mayne, Richard, *The Institutions of the European Community* (Chatham House/PEP, London, 1968)

Noel, E., 'The Committee of Permanent Representatives' (*Journal of Common Market Studies*, Vol. 5, No. 3, March 1967)

417

Pryce, Roy, *The Politics of the European Community* (Butterworth, London, 1973)

Spinelli, Altiero, *The Eurocrats* (Johns Hopkins Press, Baltimore, 1966)

SECTION 3

PARTICIPATION—PARLIAMENT, PARTIES AND PRESSURE GROUPS

Coombes, David, *The Power of the Purse in the European Communities* (Chatham House/PEP, London, 1972)

Forsyth, Murray, *The Parliament of the European Communities* (*PEP Broadsheet* No. 478)

Meynaud, J. and Sidjanski, Dusan, *Les Groupes de Pression dans la Communauté Européenne* (Editions de l'Institut de Sociologie, Brussels, 1971)

Tharp, P. (ed.), *Regional International Organisations* (Macmillan, London, 1971)

Vedel Report, 'Report of the Working Party examining the problem of *The Enlargement of the Powers of the European Parliament*' (*Bulletin of the European Communities*, Supplement 4/72)

SECTION 4

COMMUNITY LAW AND NATIONAL SOVEREIGNTY

VALENTINE, D., *The Court of Justice of the European Communities* (2 vols) (Stevens, London, 1965)

Mathijsen, P., *A Guide to European Community Law* (Stevens, London, 1972)

Wall, E., *Europe—Unification and Law* (Penguin, Harmondsworth, 1969)

Wortley, B. A. (ed.), *An Introduction to the Law of the EEC* (Manchester University Press, 1972)

Mitchell, John, 'British Institutions inside Europe' (*The Round Table*, January 1973)

SECTION 5

GROWTH AND THE BRITISH ECONOMY

Charnley, A. H., *The EEC: a study in Applied Economics* (Ginn, London, 1973)

C.B.I., *Britain and Europe* (3 vols) (Confederation of British Industry, London, 1966–67)

Britain in Europe: a second industrial appraisal (Confederation of British Industry)

Denton, G. R. (ed.), *Economic Integration in Europe* (Weidenfeld and Nicolson, London, 1971)

Federal Trust, *Ten years of EEC: Lessons and Prospects for Industry* (Federal Trust, London, 1968)

Han, S. S. and Liesner, H. H., *Britain and the Common Market* (Cambridge University Press, 1971)

Layton, C., *Industry and Europe* (Political and Economic Planning, 1972)

Meerhaeghe, M. A. G. van (ed.), *Economics: Britain and the EEC* (Longmans, Harlow, 1969)

Pinder, J. (ed.), *The Economics of Europe* (Charles Knight, London, 1971)

Swann, D., *The Economics of the Common Market* (Penguin, 2nd edition, Harmondsworth, 1972)

Williams, R., *European Technology* (Croom Helm, London, 1973)

SECTION 6

THE PROBLEMS OF AGRICULTURE

Atlantic Institute, *A Future for European Agriculture* The Atlantic Papers No. 4, 1970 (The Atlantic Institute, London)

Allen, G. R. (ed.), *British Agriculture in the Common Market* (School of Agriculture, Aberdeen, 1972)

Boddez, G., *The Market Economy in Western European Integration: Agricultural Policy* (Centre for Economic Studies, Louvain, 1966)

Buelens, H., *Agricultural Revolution and Structural Policy* (Centre for Political, Social and Economic Studies, Brussels, 1970)

Butterwick, M. and Rolfe, E. N., *Food, Farming and the Common Market* (Oxford University Press, 1968)

Agricultural Marketing and the EEC (Hutchinson, London, 1971)

Clout, H. D., *Agriculture: Studies in Contemporary Europe* (Macmillan, London, 1971)

Federal Trust, *Current Agricultural Proposals for Europe 1970* (Federal Trust, 1970)

A New Agricultural Policy for Europe (1970) (Federal Trust, 1970)

Franklin, S. H., *The European Peasantry; The Final Phase* (Methuen, London, 1969)

Hallett, G., 'Agricultural Policy in Western Germany' (*Journal of Agricultural Economics*, Vol. 19, No. 1, 1969)

Josling, T. E., *Benefits and Burdens of Farm-support Policies* (Trade Policy Research Centre, London, 1970)

Knox, F., *The Common Market and World Agriculture Trade Patterns in Temperate-zone foodstuffs* (Praeger, 1972)

Lane, S. H., 'A Comparison of Structural Policies in Agriculture' (*Agricultural Adjustment Unit*, Bulletin No. 11, University of Newcastle, 1970)

Muth, H. P., *French Agriculture and the Political Integration of Western Europe* (Sitjhoff, Leyden, 1970)

N.F.U., *Farmers and Growers Guide to the EEC* (National Farmers Union, London, 1972)

Ray, D., *A Guide to Agricultural Support Policies in Britain and the EEC* (East of Scotland College of Agriculture, 1971)

Rogers, S. G. and Davey, B. H. (eds.), *The Common Agricultural Policy and Britain* (Saxon House, London, 1973)

SECTION 7

WORKERS OF EUROPE

Beever, R. C., *Trade Unions and Free Movement of Labour in the EEC* (Chatham House/Political and Economic Planning, London, 1969)

Böhning, W. R., *The Migration of Workers in the United Kingdom and the European Community* (Oxford University Press/Institute of Race Relations, 1972)

and Stephen, D., *The EEC and the Migration of Workers* (Runnymede Trust, London, 1971)

Castle, S. and Kossack, G., *Immigrant Workers and Class Structure in Western Europe* (Oxford University Press/Institute of Race Relations, 1972)

C.B.I., *Working in the EEC—Rights and Obligations* (Europe Brief—Confederation of British Industry, 1972)

Dahlberg, K. A., 'The EEC Commission and the Politics of the free movement of labour' (*Journal of Common Market Studies*, Vol. 6, No. 4, 1968)

Deakin, N., 'Immigrants in Europe' (*Fabian Research Series*, No. 306, 1972)

'Plans for a common education policy' (*European Community*, January 1971)

Jarvis, F., *The Educational implications of membership of the EEC* (National Union of Teachers, London, 1972)

O'Grada, C., 'The Vocational training policy of the EEC and the free movement of skilled Labour' (*Journal of Common Market Studies*, Vol. 7, No. 2, 1969)

Patterson, S. (ed.), *New Commission—migration in Europe* (Community Relations Commission, London, 1972)

Stewart, M., *Employment Conditions in Europe* (Gower Economic Publications/Employment Conditions Abroad Ltd., London, 1972)

SECTION 8

COMMUNITY WELFARE

Commission, *Guidelines for a Social Action Programme* (Commission of the European Communities, 1973)

C.B.I., *Social Welfare Policies in the EEC* (Europe Brief—Confederation of British Industry, 1972)

Employee Benefits, *Europe—a social security survey* (Employee Benefits Ltd., London, 1972)

European Community, 'Social Policy—what the EEC has achieved' (*European Community*, June 1971)

R. Titmuss, 'Social security and the Six' (*New Society*, 11 November 1972)

W.H.O., *An international study of health expenditure* (Public Health Papers, World Health Organization, United Nations, 1967)

Vasey, M., 'New impetus for social policies' (*European Community*, January 1973)

Acknowledgements

The authors and publishers wish to thank the following for their kind permission to quote extracts:

Thames & Hudson (1.3); Routledge & Kegan Paul (1.4.1; 7.11); H.M.S.O. (1.4.2; 1.4.4; 1.4.5; 1.4.6; 1.5; 1.8; 5.3; 5.8; 7.2; 7.3; 7.5; 7.15; 8.2; 8.7); Oxford University Press (1.4.3); *The Observer* (1.6; 4.8; 5.12; 8.3); *Le Monde* (1.7); George Allen & Unwin Ltd. (2.3); Hamish Hamilton (2.4); Richard Norton-Taylor (2.5; 3.6); Prentice-Hall Inc. (2.6); *The Times* (2.7; 4.7; 4.3; 5.10; 5.11; 6.9; 6.10; 7.12; 8.11); Fontana Paperbacks (3.2); *Government and Opposition* (3.12); Macmillan (3.3; 3.10); Basil Blackwell (3.4); *The Sunday Times* (3.5); *The Round Table* (3.7; 3.8); Confederation of British Industry (3.9); Marguerite Bouvard and *European Community* (3.11); *Vision* (3.13); *Municipal Review* and British Section of the International Union of Local Authorities (3.14); G. Bebr and the *Modern Law Review* (4.2); *Daily Telegraph* (4.4); *The World Today* (4.5; 4.6); *The Economist* (5.2; 5.3; 5.13); European Communities (5.4; 6.4); Victor Gollancz Ltd. (5.6); *The Financial Times* (5.7); *New Statesman* (5.9); Charles Knight & Co. Ltd. (5.14); Federal Trust (5.15); D. G. Rhys and *European Community* (5.16); Political and Economic Planning (6.2); *New Europe* (6.4; 7.10; 8.5); Home Grown Cereals Authority (6.5); Trade Policy Research Centre (6.6; 6.8); Charles Levinson (7.2); Centre for Contemporary European Studies, University of Sussex (7.4; 8.4; 8.9); Oswald Wolff (7.6); *New Society* (7.7; 8.10); Transworld Feature Syndicate Inc. (7.8); the *Sun* (7.9); British Association for Commercial and Industrial Education and Dr. W. D. Halls (7.13); British Association for Commercial and Industrial Education (7.14); *Contemporary Review* and Mrs. Shirley Williams (8.8).

Index

Notes:

1. The terms 'EEC', 'European Community' and 'European Communities' are used interchangeably and often inconsistently throughout the text, to describe the European Economic Community, the European Coal and Steel Community, Euratom and the European Communities as a whole. This is further complicated by references to 'The Six', 'The Nine', etc. To overcome this problem, which, it is to be hoped, is peculiar to the present transition phase after enlargement, all references appear under 'European Communities', unless it is clear that a specific reference is intended to ECSC or Euratom.

2. Sub-heading under major headings are usually in alphabetical order. On the few occasions where this is not so, the reason will be evident from the text.

3. Headings such as 'Industrial Policy', 'Monetary Policy', etc., refer to policies of the European Communities. National policies in these areas are indexed under the country in question.